17/6

THE FUTURE
OF
AUSTRALIAN FEDERALISM

Published by arrangement with the Commonwealth Literary Fund

By the same author . . .

EARLY AMERICAN-AUSTRALIAN RELATIONS
Demy 8vo, pp. x, 184, *illus.*   10/6 *net.*
M.U.P., 1944

The Future of Australian Federalism

A Commentary on the
WORKING OF THE CONSTITUTION

GORDON GREENWOOD
M.A. (Syd.), Ph.D. (Lond.)

Senior Lecturer in History
University of Sydney

MELBOURNE UNIVERSITY PRESS

1946

MELBOURNE UNIVERSITY PRESS
CARLTON, N.3, VICTORIA,
in association with
OXFORD UNIVERSITY PRESS,
MELBOURNE AND LONDON

Wholly set up and printed in Australia by
WILKE & CO. PTY. LTD.,
19-47 Jeffcott Street, Melbourne.

To my Mother

PREFACE

MY APPROACH to the treatment of this subject has been historical, but I would emphasise that this book is not, in the traditional sense, a history of Australian federalism, but rather, as the sub-title indicates, a commentary on the working of the constitution. To avoid misunderstanding it is perhaps necessary to define the compass of this book more closely. Though a short summary has been included of the forces which, in my view, were responsible for federation, this section does not purport to present in any exhaustive way an analysis of how federation was achieved, for that is in itself a separate study which still requires a full treatment. Similarly, there has been no attempt at a specialist examination of either the financial or administrative aspects of federalism. A certain amount of work has been done on the financial side, but a critical study of the operation of the State and Commonwealth administrative systems is badly needed.

My general aim can be indicated in this way. An effort was made to discover just what forces led men in the Australian colonies to federate, and what expectations were excited in their minds by the prospect of federation. In the light of the answers suggested by the evidence it was possible to approach the operation of federal government in this country with a view to establishing whether or not the constitution had operated in the way anticipated by its framers—whether, in short, their expectations had been fulfilled.

This book is, in essence, a study of the operation of federal government in its Australian setting with the object of determining to what extent the federal system has proved an adequate form of government for a country passing through the successive stages of development which have marked Australia's history in the past forty-five years. The test which has been applied has been the ability or otherwise of the federal system to cope with the social, political and economic problems with which it was confronted. In Australia federalism has undoubtedly had signal successes, for within its framework it has been possible not only to advance from a parochial to a national outlook but to develop the country industrially and organise the nation in two great wars.   Yet, despite its achievements, the evidence points decisively to the conclusion that the federal system has outlived its usefulness, that the conditions which made federation a necessary stage in the evolution of Australia's nationhood have largely passed away, and that the retention of the system now operates only as an obstacle to effective government and to a further advance.   The problems which are to-day of greatest urgency are those which can best be solved either by a unified government or by a central government possessed of vastly expanded powers.   It is time to recognise that the federation should be replaced by a unified state.

My obligations to those who have proffered suggestions and constructive criticism are large.   Though not directly associated with this particular work, I would like again to acknowledge my indebtedness to Professor S. H. Roberts, for his initial training has been a source of continuing inspiration.   Much of this research was carried out during my two years at the London School of Economics, and I owe a great deal to the unfailing interest displayed by those with whom I worked, notably Professor H. J. Laski, Mr. C. H. Wilson and Dr. H. Finer.   The stimulus of Professor Laski's personality and teaching is too well known to require comment.   I can only repeat the testimony of his former students everywhere to his devastating critical ability, his acute historical sense and his genuine interest in all who work in association with him.

In Australia it was my good fortune to secure, and I trust profit from, the advice of Professor K. H. Bailey and Mr. H. Burton, both of the University of Melbourne, and Mr. J. D. Holmes, a leading Sydney barrister and lecturer in constitutional law at the University of Sydney.   All these gentlemen went to considerable trouble in writing comments upon several of the chapters in this book.   To Professor Bailey I owe an especial debt, for, despite the pressure of his own work, he generously found time to acquaint me with his views on contentious points.   Some of this information, contained in a personal memorandum, I have incorporated with acknowledgment.   References to Professor Bailey's published work are given in full—otherwise indications of the views held by Professor Bailey may be taken to refer to the comments I have mentioned.

I must also express my gratitude to Dr. G. Mackaness, the N.S.W. representative of the Commonwealth Literary Fund, for his steadfast support, and to the members of the fund itself for the assistance they have extended toward publication.   The Melbourne University Press has overcome many difficulties associated with preparation for publication during wartime.

Finally, no record of my indebtedness would be complete without a reference to the continual encouragement and help extended by my wife.

CONTENTS

Preface   vii

I.   The Nature of Federalism. The Strength and
     Weakness of Federal and Unitary Systems of
     Government   1

II. The Convention Debates and the Forces making
     for Federation   23

III. The Results produced by the Constitution. A
     Judgment on the Adequacy of the Structure of
     1900   51

IV. The Evil Effects of the Division of Powers
     between State and Federal Authorities   106

V.   The Position of the States within the Common-
     wealth, and the Work of the Commonwealth
     Grants Commission   158

VI. The Commonwealth at War   214

VII. The Future of Federalism within Australia ...   293

     Bibliography   310

     Index   317

I

THE NATURE OF FEDERALISM. THE STRENGTH AND WEAKNESS OF FEDERAL AND UNITARY SYSTEMS OF GOVERNMENT

THE half-century preceding the war of 1914-18 witnessed the growth in popularity of the federal idea of government. No clear-cut reasons could be assigned for the prestige which federalism enjoyed, though the prosperity of the United States and the military might of Germany were vaguely put forward as grounds of belief. New federations were created in both Canada and Australia, and they appeared to be functioning with reasonable efficiency. By 1914 the conviction was widely held that the federal system represented the most hopeful idea yet advanced for the solution of governmental problems. Its advocates emphasised the fact that it enabled local allegiance to be reconciled with national unity through the division of powers. They contrasted federal and unitary forms of government and reached conclusions disadvantageous to the latter.

Despite this general enthusiasm, there were critics of considerable authority who questioned the validity of the claims made on behalf of federalism. At a much earlier period, de Tocqueville, when surveying the working of government in America, had criticised the federal structure on two main grounds. It was, he claimed, an unduly complicated system, and it was one under which the central government was relatively weak.[1] Professor Dicey, in like manner, drew attention to the weakness of federal when compared with unitary government.[2] He stressed the limitations upon sovereignty necessitated by the nature of the division of powers under federalism. According to his analysis, the creation of a divided allegiance made possible a conflict between local and national loyalties. The supremacy of the constitution implied the predominance of legalism. It also implied a strengthening of the conservative forces within the nation, because, though most constitutions contained the means for their amendment, change was

---

1. A. de Tocqueville, *Democracy in America* (1864 ed.), i, 210-2.
2. A. V. Dicey, *Introduction to the Study of the Law of the Constitution* (1915 ed.), p. lxxvii.

usually difficult to effect. Constitutions, though alterable, tended to remain unaltered while their tenets took on a sanctity against which reason seemed helpless. This meant that federal structures would prove insufficiently flexible. They would be difficult of adjustment to changed conditions, and in their rigidity would contain the seeds of their own decay.

This emphasis upon the conservatism of a federal structure was a most penetrating observation on Dicey's part, especially when it is borne in mind that it was made by a Whig individualist at the commencement of a collectivist age.

The constitution of a federal state must . . . generally be not only a written but a rigid constitution . . . Now this essential rigidity of federal institutions is almost certain to impress on the minds of citizens the idea that any provision included in the constitution is immutable and, so to speak, sacred. The least observation of American politics shows how deeply the notion that the constitution is something placed beyond the reach of amendment has impressed popular imagination. The difficulty of altering the constitution produces conservative sentiment, and national conservatism doubles the difficulty of altering the constitution . . . To this we must add that a federal constitution always lays down general principles which, from being placed in the constitution, gradually come to command a superstitious reverence, and thus are, in fact, though not in theory, protected from change or criticism.[3]

Present-day conditions in almost all federal countries—though most notably in the United States, Canada and Australia—afford ample evidence of the correctness of Dicey's prediction. The federal system has been subjected to continuous strain, and if it has not broken down it has at least shown itself an ineffective instrument for dealing with the problems confronting it. The nature and extent of the division of powers between provincial and central authorities has hampered national regulation of economic and industrial conditions.

In the past it has been customary for writers upon federalism to assume that a radical difference existed between the nature of federal and the nature of unitary forms of government. From that assumption they proceeded to lay down definite characteristics for each, and to draw definite distinctions between each. Lord Bryce, Professor Dicey and Sir John Marriott all distinguished certain attributes which they regarded as characteristic of federalism. Professor Dicey, for instance, held that federal states came into being because the inhabitants of the countries which

3. *Ibid.*, pp. 169-70.

proposed to unite desired union, but did not desire unity. He laid
down three features as typical of completely developed federalism—
the supremacy of the constitution, the distribution of the different
powers of government, the authority of the courts to act as inter-
preters of the constitution.[4] But the attempt to distinguish definite
attributes of federal government was carried still further. A division of powers implied that the division might have been faulty;
several sets of machinery were required to carry out the work of
government; duplication or even conflict were possibilities; a
double citizenship was inevitable; and constant effort was required to maintain the balance between central and provincial
authority. This tendency towards the enumeration of federal
characteristics was perhaps seen in its most extreme form in a
declaration by Sir John Marriott,[5] that the following qualities were
inherent in the nature of federalism—dualism of law; duplication
of political organs, legislative, executive and judicial; precise definition of powers in written and preferably rigid constitutions;
separation of powers; a supreme court of justice competent to act
as interpreter of the constitutions and as arbiter between possibly
conflicting laws; and a bi-cameral legislature including a federal
second chamber.

The value of such attempts at classification is open to doubt.
Governmental forms exhibit varying characteristics amidst varying conditions and different periods of time. It is hardly logical
to expect a federal system to display the same distinctive qualities
in an age of unbridled individualism as in an age of state regulation. Nor is it probable that federalism in its application to divergent conditions in the United States and Canada will display
identical qualities in the detail of its operation. Certain broad
features may be noticed as inherent in the nature of federalism,
but any more detailed specification of characteristics will only be
true when applied to a specific form of federal government operating in a given period. The remarks made by Lord Bryce[6] and
his contemporaries about the attributes of federal governments
may have been significant at a moment in time, but an examination
of the qualities listed shows that they are not wholly applicable to
the federal forms existing to-day. Many of the old distinctions
are no longer valid, and accepted statements upon the nature of
federal government need to be re-examined in the light of practical
events and present-day conditions.

4. *Ibid.,* p. 140.
5. *The Nineteenth Century,* June, 1918, p. 1298.
6. e.g., in *The American Commonwealth.*

The fallacy of some at least of these distinctions is to-day apparent. Two of the characteristics which such writers emphasized may be singled out and shown to be of doubtful worth. Take first Professor Dicey's remark that federations spring from the desire for union, but not for unity.[7] Is it not true that the motive force behind federation is the attainment of unity in certain fields? What is aimed at is united action in certain matters of common concern, such as defence, and the maintenance of local independence on all other questions. But present-day conditions demand a complete reversal of the procedure adopted on federating. What is required is a single sovereign power delegating authority to local units. Next consider the issue of the division of powers. It is contended that under federalism there is always the possibility that the division of powers between central and provincial authorities may have been faulty. But that possibility is not peculiar to federalism. There is no form of government of any importance in existence to-day where some division of powers does not take place. Such division does not distinguish a federal from a unitary system. There may be division within each, with its implication that in either case the division may have been faulty. Again, the interpretation of the legal boundaries of the division of powers by the courts is hailed as a peculiar feature of federal government. No doubt it is true that in a federation provincial and central governments are constitutionally protected against an invasion of their spheres of authority, and true also that provisions of the constitution are enforced by the courts. Yet it should be remembered that under a unitary system each quarrel over a division of powers is ultimately tested in a court. If, for example, a local council in Great Britain claims that it has the right to dictate the type of building that shall be erected in its area of control, and if that right is denied, the matter is thrashed out in the courts. The distinction between the position of a province within a federation and of a local council within a unitary state is that the local council has no special status under law.[8] It is in the same position as an individual.

Nevertheless, this question of the division of powers is fundamental to an understanding of the distinction between federal and unitary forms of government. The term "division of powers" may be used in two different ways. It may denote the division of the authority exercised by the state as a whole between central and provincial governments, or it may refer to the separation of legisla-

7. Dicey, *Law of the Constitution*, p. lxxv.
8. From the strictly legal point of view the "division" which exists in a unitary system is the result of "delegation" from the body exercising sovereign powers within the state.

tive, executive and judicial powers. In the latter case it is employed to express the classical doctrine of separation of powers propounded by Montesquieu. This had three main elements which have been summarised as

the division of government into three powers or functions; the assertion of the necessary mutual independence of these three powers as the presupposition of sound government; and the desire to rest the validity of the law on a non-human, or rather supra-human, basis.[9]

All federations, and the American in particular, are subject to the double weakness of the double division of powers. It is, of course, conceivable that the separation advocated by Montesquieu could exist under a unitary system, but in contrasting a federal with a unitary state the assumption is made that a unitary state is a state with no federal attributes whatever. If it were conceived to be a democratic state it would be one in which parliamentary supremacy was a reality. As it has been pointed out, that is not to imply that the state's law-making activity must be in the hands of a single organ of government.

On the contrary, the process may be divided up among as many organs as is thought convenient. Such division, however (and this is the important point), does not correspond to a distinction between *different* powers of government, but is rather the technical organisation of a *single* power.[10]

But in a federal system the weakness of the separation of powers is apparent in the independent position occupied by the High or Supreme Court. The emphasis placed upon the authority of the court is due no doubt to the fact that, whereas in a unitary state it is possible to provide for the supremacy of parliament, in a federal state it is necessary to guarantee the supremacy of the law. The result has been, notably in America, that the curiously independent position of the court has enabled it to mould the constitution in moments of crisis. At such periods the court has obtained a virtual ascendancy over all other governmental organs. In America, also, the judiciary has hampered centralization, and it has become obvious that sovereignty may be lost as easily by division along the lines of Montesquieu as along any other.

For the moment, however, we are concerned with the division of powers between central and provincial authorities, and not with the separation of legislative, executive and judicial powers. Here the fallacy underlying most comparisons between federal and

9. C. H. Wilson, "Separation of Powers under Democracy and Fascism," *Political Science Quarterly*, viii. (Dec., 1937), 481.
10. *Ibid.*, p. 483.

unitary systems of government has been the attempt to differentiate between them on the ground that in the one case there was a division of powers and in the other there was not. Many years ago Seeley demonstrated the falsity of this distinction, pointing out that unitary states were also composite in the sense of consisting of a number of districts, each of which has its own government in a certain degree independent, but which are united together by a common central government.[11]

If the United States was a union of states, England was a union of boroughs and counties and France of departments. The unitary states possessed several bodies exercising governmental rights, and that fact necessitated some division of powers between them. No true distinction could, therefore, be drawn between the two systems on the ground of the existence of a division of powers.

The reality of such a division in a unitary country like Great Britain is everywhere apparent. To take the most obvious instance, wide powers of self-government have been conferred upon the City of London, with the result that its position in the state is very similar to that of a province in a federal structure. Here the situation is such that the machinery of parliament is simply used to alter what might be called the city's constitution. But the City of London is no isolated instance. Recent years have seen the encroachment of the central authority upon the sphere of local government. This tendency has led to a struggle for control between local and central forces. County and local councils have been fighting the government over their respective spheres of action—most notably over the question of unemployment relief, and more recently over the provision of air defence shelters.

Under unitary, then, as under federal, systems there may be a division of powers and a struggle to maintain the balance between central and local authorities. What does distinguish between them is not the existence but the degree and conditions of the division. A comparison of the two forms reveals a marked difference with regard to "the importance of local government."[12] In a federal state the power exercised by the local units is both wider in its range and subject to less control.[13] The number of matters which may be dealt with by the counties and boroughs of England is in

---

11. Sir J. R. Seeley, *Introduction to Political Science* (1901 ed.), p. 94.
12. *Ibid.*, p. 95.
13. H. J. Laski, *The Problem of Administrative Areas* (1918 ed.), p. 25. Professor Bailey has pointed out "that in a federal structure it is *supreme* powers that are divided; that the powers of the federation and its local units are co-ordinate and not hierarchical in their relations *inter se*; that the States have powers which can neither be added to nor taken away by any action of the central government alone."

no way comparable with those which fall within the jurisdiction of the state in a federal structure. There is, then, a noticeable difference in the degree of power conferred upon the local units of government. But there is also another distinction which has relation to the exercise of local government, namely, the limitation of the sovereignty of the central power. In a federal system there will be not merely a division of powers, but also an attempt to render the division rigid. The central government will neither possess the right to alter the degree of the division nor the right to encroach upon the local unit's sphere of administration. It will be seen, therefore, that the true comparison is between what the central government can do under one form and what it can do under the other.

It has been argued that there is little value in detailed lists of distinctions between the two forms, since comparative classifications of the minutiae of governmental operations tend to miss the mark. An attempt has also been made to show that some at least of the accepted notions upon the nature of federalism are no longer applicable to present-day conditions. It is pertinent, therefore, to ask what broad differences do exist between federal and unitary forms of government. The answer would seem to be threefold in its nature. The primary distinction between them is concerned with the existence of a sovereign body within the state. For it is obvious that in a unitary state there exists one body capable of exercising complete powers over the national life, whereas in a federal state there is no such one body with power to regulate every phase of the country's activity. A second line of demarcation may be seen in the extent to which the division of powers is made rigid. In other words, it is necessary to discover whether the sovereignty of the central government is limited by a rigid preservation of certain powers for local or provincial governments. The forces leading to the creation of a federal state are such that the local units are usually in a position to demand legal safeguards for their rights. The result is that the power of the central government is legally limited to the exercise of certain functions, or less frequently the powers assigned to the states are specifically defined and the residue left to the central authority. But in either case the national government is legally competent to exercise only limited powers, and is incapable of increasing its own authority at will. On the other hand, in a unitary state, though there may be a division of functions between local and central authorities, the division does not entail any limitation upon the sovereignty of the national government. However, it must be remembered that it is possible to stress overmuch the form which the division may take within a federal state. The danger lies in the fact that divisions which are constitutionally rigid tend also to become psychologically rigid, and in the public mind obtain a sanctity which makes subsequent attempts at alteration, however necessary, difficult to effect.

The third distinction is closely allied to the second and consists in the degree or the extent of the grant of power made to the local authorities. Federalism means not only that the division of powers shall be made rigid, but also that very considerable spheres of governmental activity shall fall to the local units. One has only to compare the type of subject handled by local authorities, say in England, with the type handled by state authorities in a federal structure to recognise that the degree of local government constitutes a very real distinction between federal and unitary systems. It would seem, therefore, that the broad distinctions which can be drawn between the two forms of government are distinctions which relate to three things—the existence of a single sovereign body within the state, the extent to which the division of powers is made rigid, and the relative importance of local government. In addition, it is necessary to note the nature of the powers conferred upon the respective governments under a federal system, and especially whether the reserved powers lie in the hands of the local or central authorities.

Federalism has usually proved to be a stage on the road to unification,[14] though admittedly the transformation is often a lengthy process. It is the bringing together in some kind of union of a number of groups which were previously separate. Unity is attained in certain limited fields where before there was independent action. Obviously, a measure of unity is preferable to complete disunity, and to that extent the federation of separate groups represents an advance. Federalism may well be a necessary phase in the transformation of a number of separate areas of settlement into a unified national state. In a vast, newly-settled country authority must at first be exercised through a number of independent or semi-independent local governments, as was the case with the various Australian colonies. That is, there must be government in special areas. In the next stage the various areas desire to unite in matters of common concern, and in order to do so they adopt a federal form of government. This also, as Dicey has pointed out, is a transition stage, since federalism usually gives rise to nationalism. The result is apparent in both the United States and Australia, where in each case a nation exists under the

14. See Dicey's contention, *Law of the Constitution*, p. lxxvi.

guise of a federation. This result is achieved more speedily when the central authority enforces the application of its own laws. In that case the central government comes into direct contact with the governed and rules over them in the same way as the government in a unitary state, except that its sphere of operation is more limited.

De Tocqueville long ago realised that this gave rise to a new state phenomenon. The American constitution, he argued, had introduced a new principle into federalism, since before 1789 states allied in confederations, while agreeing to obey the injunctions of a federal government, had "reserved to themselves the right of enforcing the execution of the laws of the union."

Evidently this is no longer a federal government, but an incomplete national government, which is neither exactly national nor exactly federal; but the new word which ought to express this novel thing does not yet exist.[15]

But it is not only in the political and administrative sphere that this tendency towards unification can be noticed. It is even more marked in the economic life of federal countries.[16] Australia itself affords an excellent example of economic integration. The Commonwealth Grants Commission, which was appointed in 1933 to investigate the claims of the states for financial assistance, declared in its report that Australia was tending "to develop into one large economic unit," while industry was tending "to specialise on that basis, the manufacturing industries in the south-east, the rest of the continent being devoted mainly to primary industries."[17] The trend was welcomed since it enabled Australia as a whole to enjoy the maximum available standard of living, but the difficulties which the unification of the economic life of a continent under a federal system had brought with it were appreciated by the commission. "The difficulty," said the report, "is that political control over a large proportion of the activities of the community is exercised by states whose boundaries were defined about a century ago without any consideration of the economic position which would grow up."[18] This is the fundamental difficulty confronting all federations to-day. The peoples living under them have been welded into nations. Economic unification of the country's life has taken place; but political control lags behind, remaining subject to arti-

15. de Tocqueville, *Democracy in America*, i. 201. He was really attempting to draw a distinction between the United States constitution of 1787 and the new constitution of 1789.
16. Of course the tendency towards political and administrative unification is to a large extent a result of the "economic integration."
17. Quoted, *Round Table*, March, 1936, p. 403.
18. *Ibid.*, p. 404.

ficial and regional limitations. A unified economic system exists side by side with political divisions of power which make adequate economic regulation impossible. The obvious conclusion is the need for political unification. Federalism represents a phase in the evolution of governmental structures, but a phase the limiting value of which is set by the unification of transport and thence by the unification of economic enterprise.

Conditions have changed, and in changing have borne out the contention [19] that federalism is a weak form of government. The attempt under the federal system to make the division of functions rigid has proved hampering to government in altered political and economic conditions.[20] Rigid division may not have been so important in an age in which governments seldom intervened in commercial and industrial matters. But this is an age of governmental regulation of economic affairs. Changed conditions, therefore, require a changed political philosophy and innovation in the governmental structure. A new collectivist outlook means a demand for constitutional revision.[21] The states in almost all federal countries are no longer adequate either as economic or administrative units, while attempts to obtain united action through co-operation between state and central authorities are bound to be clumsy and slow working. Consequently, control and sovereign jurisdiction is required in vital fields where it was not previously exercised. In particular, national reconstruction without sovereignty in the economic sphere seems doomed to failure. The developments in transport and communications and in banking and finance, together with the central organisation of economic control which has taken place under capitalism, make national supervision of labour and commerce a necessity. Without the establishment of unitary control there can be little hope of successful planning on a national scale, since hard and fast divisions of economic and political power result in a parochial rather than a national approach to problems.

If proof be needed of the hampering effect which the limitations of the federal system have had upon attempts at national reorganisation, ample evidence is provided by the setbacks to the efforts at national planning made by the Roosevelt administration. In this instance the federal government attempted to plan

19. Dicey, *Law of the Constitution*, p. 167.
20. See *Round Table*, Dec., 1935, pp. 106-15. The article "Federalism and Economic Control" maintains that such has been the case in Canada, the United States and Australia.
21. Stuart A. McCorkle, "Our New Line of Federalism," *Social Science Quarterly*, Sept., 1935, pp. 53-9.

on a national scale and to win the co-operation of the states in giving effect to its projects. At every turn the effectiveness of its operations has been checked by the need to pay attention to state rights. That is not to say that the states were at all times hostile to the activities of the central government. Many state planning boards admitted that the problems with which they had to deal were "beyond effective state control."[22] Transport was cited as one instance, while Pennsylvania held that pipe lines should be "part of an interstate system." Washington state said that flood control, and New York that the pollution of interstate streams, should be matters for national supervision. But despite the recognition by state planning authorities that many problems were national in scope little could be achieved, because the existence of a legally rigid division of powers enabled reactionary elements to raise the cry of state rights, and to sabotage attempts at national regulation on the ground of their unconstitutionality.

American experience has revealed other disadvantages associated with planning under a federal system. It has been found that the states are inadequate as units for planning because of constitutional, competitive and geographical defects. Moreover, this experience has been duplicated in both Canada and Australia. Problems of planning have been shown to have little relation to political boundaries, since these were laid out with scant attention to economic, social, or physical conditions.[23]

Indeed. the more important problems are almost all of national significance. For that reason the central government should be given power to govern in terms of modern needs. To achieve the requisite national standards national regulation of economic life has become essential. The futility of local regulation in such matters as crop production, transportation, commerce and labour conditions is at once apparent. Yet even when problems fall within fields where either the state or the central government is nominally supreme they may prove incapable of solution because of the conflict between federalism and adequate economic control. The inter-connection of economic life has meant that the power given to one authority to regulate trade, for example, may be rendered impotent because control over production is placed in other hands. This applies to the central government, but it is even more true of the states in a federation. They are prevented by interstate competition from exercising any satisfactory control over economic

---

22. James E. Pate, "Federal-State Relations in Planning," *Social Forces*, Dec., 1936, p. 190.
23. W. Brooke Graves, "The Future of the American States," *American Political Science Review*," Feb., 1936, pp. 25-6.

matters.   In the United States cotton and tobacco controls were ineffective for just these reasons.[24]   No state in a federation can afford to introduce legislation which would substantially raise the costs of production in that state, since its industries could no longer compete with those in neighbouring states[25] where the legislation was not in force.   Perhaps no better illustration of the ineffectiveness of local control in industrial matters could be advanced than the fate of a bill to limit the hours of work for women engaged in industry in Virginia.   The measure was defeated in the Senate because of the argument that an eight-hour working day would force Virginian industries into North Carolina, where women could be made to labour nine and ten hours a day.[26]

What emerges from the present strain upon federal constitutions is the obvious breakdown of the federal system in the economic sphere.   Economic problems are to a large extent international problems, but the unrestricted sovereignty of the nation state with its power to regulate its own tariffs, manage its own currency and engage in attempts at self-sufficiency, does give government regulation on a national scale a vital importance.   The states in a federation do not possess these rights, yet paradoxically enough they often have control over economic matters which are bound to be affected by the exercise of just such rights.   The states are frequently given exclusive or concurrent powers in such fields as the raising of capital, taxation, the provision of social services and unemployment relief, the regulation of labour conditions and the award of wages.   The consequence of this arbitrary division of closely connected subjects between central and state authorities is a partial paralysis in the control of the economic life of a federal country.   State regulation in economic matters is likely to be ineffective because the forces which dictate conditions lie outside their control.

Similarly, the central government is too often rendered impotent by constitutional limitations.   Thus when the United States government attempted to establish national jurisdiction over the economic life of the country the Supreme Court declared that it was "over-riding the authority of states to deal with domestic problems."[27]   Likewise in Canada and Australia constitutional limitations destroy the possibility of effective national regulation in many spheres where action upon a national scale can alone be effective.

24. *Social Forces*, Dec. 1936, p. 191.   Under decisions of 1937-8 the Supreme Court of the United States upheld the revised cotton and tobacco controls.
25. See *Round Table*, Dec., 1935, *loc. cit.*
26. *Social Forces*, Dec., 1936, p. 191.
27. The Schechter Case, U.S. Supreme Court *Reports*, ccxcv, 495-555.

Marketing affords an outstanding example. In Canada, by reason of the distribution of legislative powers between Dominion and provinces the Dominion government cannot draw up a marketing scheme which would embrace intra-provincial marketing.[28] Under the Natural Products Marketing Act 1934 an attempt was made to frame an act which would deal not only with foreign, but also with intra-provincial and inter-provincial marketing, but the Privy Council declared that the Dominion had exceeded its powers and that the act was to that extent invalid. Judicial decision [29] has also determined that no province has the power to regulate inter-provincial or foreign marketing. There is, therefore, no one authority capable of putting into operation a scheme of marketing sufficiently comprehensive to cover all aspects. Nor can it legitimately be inferred that an amalgamation of Dominion and provincial powers upon this subject would be equivalent to the possession of full legislative authority by the Dominion government.

Lord Atkin himself when delivering judgment upon the validity of the Natural Products Marketing Act 1934 warned of the difficulties in the way of framing a comprehensive marketing scheme even with co-operation between Dominion and provincial governments.

It was said that as the Provinces and the Dominion between them possess a totality of complete legislative authority, it must be possible to combine the Dominion and Provincial legislation so that each within its own sphere could in co-operation with the other achieve the complete power of regulation which is desired. Their Lordships appreciate the importance of the desired aim. Unless and until a change is made in the respective legislative functions of the Dominion and Provinces it may well be that satisfactory results for both can only be

28. See *Submission by the Government of the Province of Nova Scotia to the Royal Commission on Dominion-Provincial Relations*, Feb., 1938, pp. 27-31. The decision of the Judicial Committee of the Privy Council delivered by Lord Atkin in the Natural Products Marketing Act 1934 case said: "Since the Act covered transactions completed within the Province, and which have no connection with inter-provincial or export trade the Act purported to affect property and civil rights in the Provinces; that Regulation of Trade and Commerce under Section 91 (2) of the British North America Act does not permit regulation of individual forms of trade and commerce confined to the Province; that the Dominion Parliament could not acquire jurisdiction to deal in a sweeping way with such local and provincial matters by legislating at the same time re external and inter-provincial trade and committing the regulation of both intra-provincial and inter-provincial or foreign trade to the same authority" (*ibid.*, p. 29).

29. e.g., *Lawson v. Interior Tree and Vegetable Committee of Direction*, 1931 (*Supreme Court of Canada Reports*, p. 357) —an attempt at marketing legislation by British Columbia.

obtained by co-operation. But the legislation will have to be carefully framed and will not be achieved by either party leaving its own sphere and encroaching upon that of the other.[30]

Such a method of framing marketing legislation was regarded as wholly unsatisfactory by the parties to the Canadian union. Take, for example, the conclusions reached in the submission by the Province of Nova Scotia to the Royal Commission on Dominion-Provincial Relations in favour of conferring full powers upon the Dominion parliament.

(a) Under the present distribution of legislative powers between Dominion and Provinces, the Dominion cannot enact a marketing scheme effective to regulate intra-provincial marketing.

(b) No Province can enact a scheme effective to regulate inter-provincial or foreign marketing.

(c) For the reasons given power to regulate intra-provincial, inter-provincial and foreign marketing should repose in one legislative authority and it should be the Dominion parliament.[31]

Canadian experience with regard to marketing in many ways duplicates that of Australia. There also attempts at state regulation of marketing, notably by South Australia,[32] but also by other states,[33] have been held by the courts to be constitutionally invalid. The Commonwealth recently sought to obtain greater freedom of action for itself by referendum, but failed to secure the requisite majorities for the amendment.[34] The position, therefore, remains as in Canada since neither the states nor the Commonwealth are competent to deal effectively with marketing. Yet the arguments in favour of conferring jurisdiction over intra-provincial, inter-provincial and foreign marketing upon one authority seem unassailable. That authority should be the Dominion or the Commonwealth. It is obvious that under any marketing scheme uniformity in grading will be essential, but it is unlikely that this uniformity could be obtained through separate or even co-operative provincial legislation. That is one aspect of the problem. More fundamental is the fact that there can be no effective control

30. Quoted, *Submission by Nova Scotia to the Royal Commission on Dominion-Provincial Relations*, p. 31.
31. *Ibid.*
32. Marketing of dried fruits; see *James v. Cowan* (*C.L.R.*, xliii, 386-426), and Privy Council appeal (*C.L.R.*, xlvii, 386-99).
33. e.g., Queensland. *Peanut Board v. Rockhampton Harbour Board* (*C.L.R.*, xlviii, 267).
34. By inserting after section ninety-two the following section:—"92A. The provisions of the last preceding section shall not apply to laws with respect to marketing made by, or under the authority of, the Parliament in the exercise of any powers vested in the Parliament by this Constitution." See G. S. Knowles, *The Australian Constitution*, p. 272B.

of marketing without control of production and for that purpose provincial or state powers are inadequate. Marketing is but one illustration [35] of how constitutionally rigid divisions of power may operate to prevent any party to the division from exercising effective authority. The result is that federalism leads to the creation of a sphere in which control over economic matters is abdicated. The states are hampered by regional, competitive and constitutional limitations while the constitution forbids attempts at unified national control. In these circumstances, "a zone of anarchy" is created, "where exploitation of national resources and of labour can proceed free from the government's interference."[36] There seems little reasonable doubt that in all federal countries the stress which is being laid upon local rights is due in part to those who desire to maintain a zone in which they may operate free from all governmental regulation. In particular, the great industrial interests have realised that the nature of the division of powers under a federal system hampers the exercise of control over the problems associated with labour and commerce. They are, therefore, emphatic about constitutional rights and attempt to utilise the dead wood of an outworn system to prevent reform.[37]

The practical difficulties which federalism is today encountering reveal the unsatisfactory nature of the rigid division of powers. They show also the disadvantages which spring from the nature and extent of the powers exercised by local authorities. In short, they make clear that the degree and conditions of the division necessitated by federalism is inapplicable to present day conditions.

All attempts to justify federal forms of government are based ultimately on the contention that a federal system protects the local units. Yet it is just on this issue that the failure of federalism has been most apparent. That failure is especially noticeable in the United States,[38] but it is also discernible in both Canada and Australia. One manifestation of it is the extension of federal activity through the creation of new agencies[39] such as boards,

35. Other instances are social and health services and regulation of wages, hours of work and conditions of labour. See recommendations of British Columbia submitted to the Royal Commission on Dominion-Provincial Relations.
36. *Social Forces*, Dec., 1936, p. 191.
37. cf. the opinion expressed by J. E. Pate: "I feel quite strongly that the emphasis now being placed upon states' rights comes largely from those who would maintain an area free from what they describe as governmental regimentation in order that they may do to others what they would not have the government do to them" (*Social Forces*, Dec., 1936, p. 191).
38. *Amer. Pol. Sci. Rev.*, Feb., 1936, pp. 25-6.
39. *South-western Soc. Sci. Qtly.*, Sept., 1935, p. 54. See also J. P. Clark, *The Rise of a New Federalism* (1938).

bureaux and commissions. Another is the enlargement of federal powers as the result of judicial interpretation. A third is the undermining of state independence by the exercise of powers given to the central government under the constitution.

Many of these developments were essential if a greater measure of national unity was to be attained and if there was to be any attempt by the central government to deal with problems which with the efflux of time had come to transcend state boundaries and could therefore no longer be adequately handled by provincial authorities. Necessary and desirable as some of these innovations were, it yet remains true that they represented an attempt to render workable a system of government which had become largely outmoded by changes, especially economic changes, occurring within the social structure. Equally true is the fact that an expansion of federal power, however necessary, not only involved a diminution of state authority and state prestige, which aroused the resentment of the states, but also seriously upset the balance of the federal compact. Too often the states were legally left with wide powers which for financial or regional or other reasons they were unable to exercise satisfactorily, while the central government was debarred from taking efficient action by the provisions of a federally constructed constitution. The decline in state independence therefore became in time a fundamental defect mitigating against a thoroughly successful operation of existing federal systems since such structures had been erected on the assumption of the enduring virility of the states and on their adequacy to continue to perform the functions allocated to them. Moreover, such an assumption made it psychologically difficult for the framers of federal constitutions to envisage a situation which would demand not only enormously expanded powers for the central government, but also liberation from the constitutional restrictions which would hamper effective treatment of vital national problems. It was realised, of course, that from time to time some amendment of the constitution would be necessary and machinery was provided to effect it, but experience has shown that the methods of alteration provided in the various federations weight the balance heavily in a conservative direction and make much-needed changes difficult to secure.

In society as economically interconnected as that of today measures taken in one field by one authority react upon another field entrusted to some other authority. In Australia the result of this has been largely to destroy the efficacy of safeguards to state rights. Measures taken by the Commonwealth are claimed to have had an injurious effect either upon the states as a whole or upon the weaker states. The Navigation Act and the various increases which have been made in the tariff may be cited as instances of Commonwealth action affecting particular states in a manner disadvantageous to them. Both Western Australia and Tasmania assert that the Navigation Act has been harmful [40] to their development, while South Australia and Western Australia are emphatic about the detrimental effect of the tariff.[41] As states engaged principally in the production of primary products they maintain, as do the non-industrial Canadian provinces,[42] that they have to bear the costs of a high protective policy without reaping compensatory benefits. But Commonwealth policy may also affect all the states as may be judged from the ramifications of Commonwealth arbitration awards or the inroads of the Commonwealth upon the concurrent field of direct taxation. Such examples of the far-reaching effect of Commonwealth policy have brought home the realisation that constitutional guarantees of independent state control in specific fields are useless if the economic life of the community can be affected by measures of the Commonwealth taken in fields legitimately its own.

But it is in the financial sphere that the failure to protect the local units is most apparent. The extended range of central taxation has had the effect of limiting the sources upon which the states may draw to obtain revenue. Moreover, in most federations the central government has been given the most valuable sources of revenue while the states have been entrusted with the most costly functions of government. The results have been everywhere the same. State or provincial governments have not been able to meet their expenses and have either invaded the field of municipal taxation [43] or else have applied to the central government for financial aid. A series of unbalanced budgets has made the states economically dependent upon the goodwill of the central authority.

National governments have usually responded to the requests of the states for assistance, but they have not been slow to realise the valuable weapon which economic dependence has placed in their hands. In Australia, it is true, the Commonwealth has not attempted to dictate the way in which grants should be spent, but

40. But the extent of the injury done to these states is disputed by the Commonwealth Grants Commission.
41. See arguments submitted by these states to the Grants Commission.
42. e.g., *Submission by British Columbia to the Canadian Royal Commission on Dominion-Provincial Relations*, 1938.
43. Striking testimony of the parlous state of municipal finance under a federation is afforded by the submission of the Canadian Federation of Mayors and Municipalities to the Royal Commission, 1938.

it has insisted upon a detailed examination of state policy before any grant is made. After all, that is only another aspect of the same thing. If a state in its policy has to conform to certain standards regulated by an external authority before it can qualify for a grant it is left with only a shadowy independence. However, while no programme for the expenditure of grants has been laid down there has been an attempt by the Commonwealth to dictate the general financial relations existing between itself and the states. The states have demanded not merely grants in aid, but a percentage of Commonwealth customs revenue or abdication by the Commonwealth from the field of direct taxation. But these claims have not been met since the federal government has occupied a sufficiently strong financial position to impose its will in any agreement concluded on financial matters.

In the United States the tendency towards the economic dependence of the states upon the central government has been carried still further, very definite demands having been made upon the states before financial aid has been extended. An elaborate subsidy system has been built up whereby the central government has forced the states to take action along lines which it desired.[44] In Canada also the grant in aid has been accompanied by a demand on the part of the Dominion government that any province seeking assistance should submit to a measure of financial control.[45] The refusal of Mr. Aberhart's government in Alberta to subject provincial finances to the control of the Dominion Minister of Finance meant that no aid was forthcoming from the Dominion. Alberta, therefore, defaulted on a debenture maturity payment on 1 April 1936. Saskatchewan, on the other hand, having agreed to co-operate on the loan council, was given an advance by the Bank of Canada. It should be clear from these illustrations that the dependence of the states or provinces in the various federations upon subsidies from the central government has undermined both their prestige and their authority. Despite the federal structure the independence of the local units has been sapped because evident force of economic necessity has defeated and rendered anachronistic the early rigid federal divisions. To that extent federalism has failed in its principal objective.

Nor in this connection is it necessary to ask whether the local units would have been more adequately protected by a unitary system. It is no doubt true, for example, that had the Australian colonies agreed upon unification Western Australia and Tasmania

44. J. P. Clark, *The Rise of a New Federalism, passim.*
45. *Round Table,* Dec., 1935.

would probably have been affected just as much by the Navigation Act and the Commonwealth's tariff policy. But the real point at issue is that where federations have come into being almost invariably a federal form of union has been adopted because it was believed that federalism was itself a guarantee of effective protection both for the continued exercise of all powers not surrendered to the central government and for state interests within the federation. To secure such protection all the disabilities of a federal when contrasted with a unitary system—disabilities so ably revealed by Dicey—were accepted. The price which had to be paid for the retention of a large measure of state independence was the disadvantages associated with the federal system of government, but the framers of the Australian constitution along with those of other federations thought it a price worth paying. However, the outcome has been far different from what they anticipated since the disabilities of the federal form have persisted and increased while federalism has not provided the measure of protection for the local units which it was intended to confer. To a great extent, therefore, the price in terms of the weakness of the federal system was paid for a security for the local units which has proved largely illusory.

Other instances present themselves of the breakdown of the federal idea in the face of present-day problems. There have been, for example, major clashes in policy because under a federal system the nature of the division of powers is such that many subjects ordinarily considered national in character have been allotted to the provincial governments. In Australia the clash [46] between state and central developmental policies has been obvious since the Commonwealth has been mainly concerned with the fostering of secondary industries by means of the tariff whereas the states have been interested in developing primary production and aiding land settlement. Since secondary industries are concentrated mainly in the eastern states the result has been to set the interests of Victoria and New South Wales over against the less-populated states—South Australia, Western Australia and Tasmania. A further effect has been the encouragement of the growth of the large cities and the development of an antagonism between the interests of the country and the town.[47] Admittedly this antagonism is not solely the product of federalism, for the conflict is not peculiar to Australia nor confined to existing federations. At the same time it can hardly be denied that the problem is accen-

46. See *Report* of the Commonwealth Grants Commission, 1933, p. 58-62.
47. A. P. Canaway, *The Failure of Federalism in Australia* (1930), p. 11, and elsewhere.

tuated by a system which arbitrarily divides control in such a way as to hinder the emergence of a plan embracing all aspects of national development.

In addition to clashes in policy one might point to the excessive legalism which has characterized modern federations. "Because," as Professor Laski has emphasized in the case of America, "the society was governed by a written constitution, the lawyer's outlook was pivotal in the determination of its legal habits."[48] Indeed, it is not too much to say that in the case of at least one federation a decision not merely upon a constitutional issue, but upon the destiny of a nation has rested with a Supreme Court.   When that happens federalism has transformed a Supreme Court from interpreter to master of the constitution.   The responsibilities placed upon the courts undoubtedly constitute a tremendous burden, for they become in Dicey's phrase "the pivot on which the constitutional arrangements of the country turn."   Such a situation is not without its dangers since constitutional decisions in the United States and other federations show that

> the most honest judges are after all only honest men, and when set to determine matters of policy and statesmanship will necessarily be swayed by political feeling and by reasons of state. But the moment that this bias becomes obvious a court loses its moral authority. . . .[49]

Moreover, the judges are either appointed by the government, as in Australia, or nominated by the President, as in the United States, and since the decisions of the court vitally affect the process of government there is a strong inducement to appoint judges whose outlook is similar to that of the government or president concerned.

The power conferred upon judges is not, however, the sole objection to a system which sets limits to legislative authority by insisting upon the supremacy of the law.   Professor Bailey has argued that an even more fundamental objection is

> the fact that it involves the control of the present by the wisdom of the past.   The task of judges under such a system is to maintain that control, applying the criteria formulated in the past chiefly to circumstances then unforeseen or even unimaginable. They also, within the limits of the judicial technique, mould the criteria of the past, so as to make the ancient formulae responsive in some measure to the deepest trends of their day.[50]

48. *Political Science Quarterly*, Oct.-Dec., 1937, p. 509.
49. Dicey, *Law of the Constitution*, p. 173.
50. Professor Bailey believes the courts perform a difficult task with distinction.   "It is a peculiarly difficult and thankless task, and on the whole the Courts in federal systems discharge it with both ability and courage."

Excessive legalism then, has characterized most federations. Other evils in the shape of duplication and conflict in matters of major importance have been no less prevalent, while grave mechanical defects have appeared in the machinery of government.

The difficulty of adapting federalism to changed conditions and its obvious failure in the face of specific governmental problems only serves to emphasize the superiority of a unitary system.[51] That superiority lies largely in the fact that under a unitary form of government there is one body exercising sovereign powers over the whole range of the national life. It has therefore full legal competence to attempt national reorganisation at any period of crisis. Sovereignty is the power within the state which knows no limitation in the sense that it is checked by or subordinate to no other authority. Of necessity, power must be concentrated at some point within the state. Under a unitary system there is usually no great difficulty in discovering the person or body by whom sovereignty is exercised. For example, in Great Britain one can point to the King in Parliament. But under a federal organisation it is by no means easy to determine the person or body exercising sovereign powers. It has been customary to say that in federalism there is a division of sovereignty, but divided sovereignty is a contradiction in terms. That is not to imply that sovereignty cannot be unified among several people or bodies of people. If, however, one admits the expression it should be pointed out that a federally divided sovereignty is in no sense the equivalent of sovereignty. The United States affords an excellent example of the difficulty of discovering where the sovereign power resides under a federal system. It is not possessed by any agency of the central government, by Congress, by the President or by the courts. Nor is it exercised by any agency within the states. If, as one authority asserts,[52] it finds its "legal expression in the acts of two-thirds of both Houses of Congress, which, according to the Constitution, the legislatures in at least three-quarters of the several states concur" one can only say that this verbal expression is at best an unsatisfactory agent for the exercise of sovereign power. In short, the clear way in which the body exercising sovereignty in a unitary state may be distinguished is a peculiar mark of the superiority of that system over federalism.

---

51. It is not denied that there have been some instances of successful adaptation. In Australia, for example, one might point to the use of S.96 to regulate wheat marketing, the control of broadcasting and the judicial interpretation of the defence power.

52. Raymond Uhl, "Sovereignty and the Fifth Article," *Southwestern Soc. Sci. Quarterly*, March, 1936, p. 15.

The existence of a single body which is legally omnicompetent and, therefore, capable of meeting changed conditions, is a first essential in a state. That condition is satisfied by a unitary government such as that which operates in Great Britain. It is not adequately satisfied by conditions in federal states. Here authority is divided and the divisions are rendered constitutionally rigid. The result is that federal structures prove inelastic, difficult to amend and a bulwark behind which reactionary forces may find shelter. Federalism has proved unable to orientate itself satisfactorily to changed conditions, and the measure of that failure is the measure of its unsuitability to present-day requirements.

What is required, especially if there is to be anything in the nature of a planned economy, is a government exercising sovereign powers over the nation as a whole. There would still be a distribution of functions and a considerable delegation of powers to local authorities. But the central government would retain final control, which would mean that any division which proved disadvantageous under changed circumstances would be easily remediable. Long ago de Tocqueville pointed out that centralized government and centralized administration are not the same thing. There may be a very considerable measure of decentralisation under a unitary system. Power could be conferred upon local authorities to deal with matters suitably local in character. There would be local administration within local areas. But over all, giving co-ordinated effort to national life, would be a single sovereign parliament.

II

THE CONVENTION DEBATES AND THE FORCES MAKING FOR FEDERATION

NO one influence can be said to have brought about the federation of the Australian colonies. The causes which led to the establishment of the Commonwealth were numerous, though the force of their operation was unequal and varied considerably in different periods. Undoubtedly, the desire for "fiscal union"[1] was an impelling motive throughout. It was responsible for the first suggestion for some kind of super state structure and remained "to the last the central fact upon which the federal movement depended, at once the most formidable obstacle—'the lion in the path'—and the great impelling force."[2] It led also, between the years 1855 and 1873, to a series of intercolonial conferences whose object was the adoption of a uniform tariff. But in this direction little success was achieved. In 1873, by act of the Imperial Parliament, the restrictions upon establishing preferential or differential duties were removed from the Australian colonies. The hope had been that this measure would facilitate a customs agreement, but the result was rather the opposite. Victoria, in particular, had embarked upon a policy of protection—and protection aimed as much at her colonial neighbours as at foreign countries. New South Wales remained staunchly free trade and the other colonies, for the most part, established tariffs whose primary object was to raise revenue. Almost all, however, imposed duties designed to protect particular industries.[3] Victoria's policy was responsible for an increasing tension in intercolonial relations, while the existence of varying tariffs created difficult problems along the land boundaries of the colonies.

The advantages of intercolonial free trade were obvious and several attempts were made to negotiate an agreement. But the obstacles in the path were insuperable. The vested interests which had grown up under protection did not relish free competition in their markets. Protectionists were afraid that some form of union

1. The phrase used most frequently in the Convention debates for the creation of a single tariff.
2. W. Harrison Moore, *The Constitution of the Commonwealth of Australia* (1902), p. 18.
3. E. Shann, *An Economic History of Australia* (1930), pp. 270-3.

would bring about the triumph of free trade principles while free traders were even more fearful of the introduction of a high federal tariff.[4] Indeed it was the irreconcilable nature of the tariff policies of New South Wales and Victoria that was largely responsible for delaying federation.

While means of communication remained scanty no great irritation was felt at the existence of border customs duties. But with the extension of the railway systems and the consequent drawing together, an awareness of estrangement and a feeling of annoyance became apparent.[5] The necessity for intercolonial free trade likewise became more obvious. At the same time, it was realised that there was little possibility of achieving fiscal union without some form of federation. In consequence, the demand for a uniform tariff was one of the strongest forces operating in favour of federal union.

Sir Henry Parkes laid four resolutions before the 1891 Convention, which was responsible for the draft bill of that year. It was significant that two of these dealt with the question of fiscal union. Trade between the federated colonies was to be absolutely free, and the power to impose customs duties was to be exclusively lodged in the federal government. Throughout the debates at this and subsequent conventions fiscal unity was freely put forward as one of the great advantages which would ensue from federation. Again and again delegates referred to the question and pointed to the advantages to be obtained. Thus Mr. Kingston (South Australia) declared that the chief objects of federation were "defence and intercolonial free trade accompanied by a federal tariff."[6] Mr. Bird (Tasmania) spoke of "the certain large increase in commercial transactions which would follow,"[7] while Dr. Cockburn (South Australia) maintained that quite enough incentive towards federation could be found in "the consideration of the enormous advantages that we shall enjoy from a free interchange of products and manufactures."[8] The difficulties, springing from rival trade theories, which had earlier appeared so formidable, were largely overcome by the decision to leave tariff policy in the hands of the new federal government.

There would seem to be no doubt that commerce was a vital

4. See E. M. Hunt, *American Precedents in Australian Federation* (1930), p. 13.
5. Sir John A. Cockburn, *Australian Federation*, p. 14.
6. *Victorian Parliamentary Papers*, 1891 (4), Proceedings of the National Australasian Convention, Sydney, March-April, 1891, p. 76.
7. *Ibid.*, 1890 (2), Official Record of the Proceedings and Debates of the Australasian Federation Conference, Melbourne, 1890.
8. *Ibid.*, 1891 (4), p. 100.

factor in the consummation of Australian union. Such, at least, is the testimony of those who helped to bring federation about. "It is chiefly," said Mr. Gordon (South Australia), "in the commercial interests of these colonies that we desire to federate."[9] His opinion was echoed at a later date by Sir John Cockburn:

> Absolute freedom of trade is the goal towards which federal efforts of the past ten years have been chiefly directed. Strong as have been the enticements of the sentiments of union, the dominant motive has been the promptings of utility towards removal of the border customs houses, and the desire to attain that commercial and industrial expansion which must ensue from the removal of artificial limitations.[10] ·

Defence was a factor which played a subsidiary, but by no means negligible part in the creation of the Commonwealth. In the early stages of the movement it had no great significance, but from 1878 onwards defence loomed large in any discussion of the advantages to be derived from federation. It made possible the summoning of the 1890 Convention and was thus directly responsible for the ultimate attainment of federation.

At the same time there is the danger of attaching too great significance to defence as a primary cause of federation. It was found to be an excellent political catchcry, not least because it was an issue upon which there was no real divergence of opinion. It was agreed that defence was a matter which could best be dealt with by a single central authority, but there was little sense of urgency, and in the absence of obvious peril other motives undoubtedly operated more powerfully. After more than forty years it is probable that opinions about the importance of defence in consummating the union may well be coloured by later events, notably by the tremendous significance which has come to be attached to the defence power. A corrective is supplied by recalling that defence was placed only sixth in the list of legislative powers assigned to the Commonwealth parliament under Sec. 51 and was to be read "subject to this Constitution."

Between the years 1878 and 1889 the various colonies were re-organising their defence forces in consultation with the Imperial authorities, largely because of apprehension at the increasing activity displayed by France and Germany in the Pacific. A measure of federal action had been secured with regard to naval defence since all the colonies had agreed to contribute towards the upkeep of the Australian squadron. But military defence remained disorganised. Each colony had its own force. There was neither

9. *Ibid.*, 1891 (4), p. 171.
10. Sir John A. Cockburn, *Australian Federation*, p. 14.

uniform regulation nor co-operation between the separate units. In order to suggest improvements Major General Edwards was despatched in 1889 to report on the defence of the Australian colonies. His reports, issued in the same year, stressed the neces- sity of reorganisation upon a federal basis and, by so doing, sup- plied the advocates of federation with a powerful argument. In particular, he urged the federation of the forces of all the Aus- tralian colonies, a uniform system of organisation and armament, a common Defence Act, a federal military college, a federal small arms manufactory, and a uniform gauge for railways.[11] These were all recommendations which required the establishment of some central authority to render them effective. It is true that a Federal Council was in existence, but it represented a sorry approach to union. New South Wales had never joined; the Council lacked an executive, and its powers were inadequate to deal effectively with the expansion of national defence. Under these circum- stances Sir Henry Parkes appealed for a more solid union on the grounds that the defence report showed the urgency of arriving at an effective federation. After one or two rebuffs he was suc- cessful in calling together the 1890 Convention.

The Convention debates revealed that upon the defence issue at least there was almost unanimous agreement. Sir Samuel Griffith (Queensland) emphasised the stupidity of separate armies gov- erned by separate laws and instanced the possibility of six armies, operating under six different laws, concentrated in one state. "For purposes of defence, at any rate, there must be a central govern- ment in Australia."[12] And with that contention all delegates agreed. Indeed, the very unanimity of their agreement meant that there was little discussion of defence at the conventions. It was acknow- ledged [13] that defence, especially Major General Edwards' report, was the immediate cause of the summoning of the 1890 and 1891 conventions. No objection was raised to handing over defence to the central authorities. In that respect the attitude voiced by Mr. Munro (Victoria) seemed to sum up the feeling of the delegates:

> With regard to the military and naval defence of Australia being
> entrusted to federal forces, of course no one can object to that;
> in fact, one of the reasons why this Convention has been called
> into existence, and why it is necessary to have the Dominion
> at all, is to have the defences put on a proper footing.[14]

11. In 1889 there were three different gauges in existence.
12. *Victorian Parliamentary Papers*, 1890 (2), p. 10.
13. e.g., Col. Smith (Victoria), *Ibid.*, 1891 (4), p. 63.
14. *Ibid.*, 1891 (4), p. 25.

Associated with the question of defence was the interest of the Australian colonies in the Pacific Ocean. It has been frequently remarked that in the case of Australia an external stimulus to federation was lacking. It would be more correct to say that that stimulus was not of an imperative character. It did, however, exist, and in the years immediately before federation became of increasing importance.[15] The Australian colonies which hitherto had been concerned almost solely with domestic issues were awakening to the significance of their geographical position. They were rapidly becoming aware that what took place in the islands of the Pacific might have a very definite effect upon their future. This was the period of increased European activity in the Pacific, when both France and Germany were busy establishing territorial claims. Several specific issues aroused Australian apprehension. There was, for example, the despatch of French criminals to the island of New Caledonia. Transportation had become distasteful to the colonies and they had no wish to see a penal settlement established close to their shores. The possibility of escaped convicts finding refuge on the Australian coast was magnified into a danger threatening all the colonies. Indeed, Mr. Service's outburst against possible contamination from ' the outpouring of the moral filth of Europe into these seas"[16] must, in view of Australia's past, have sounded strangely in French ears. Other causes of alarm were the extension of French activity in the New Hebrides and the belief that Germany intended to annex a portion of New Guinea.

Faced with these possibilities, the various colonies gave expression to an extreme nationalistic and even imperialist attitude. They petitioned the British government to take action in order to forestall the French and the Germans, but showed no willingness to bear any of the cost of annexation.[17] Finally, the Queensland government took it upon itself to annex New Guinea. Its action, however, was repudiated by the home authorities despite the fact that the other Australian colonies strongly supported the move. This rebuff made it plain that if Australian opinion was to carry

15. H. L. Hall in *Victoria's Part in the Australian Federation Movement,* 1849-1900 (1931), attempts to show that the periods when distinct efforts were made towards union, e.g., 1856-1870 and 1881-3, coincided with the Crimean war, the Franco-Prussion war and French activity in the New Hebrides.
16. Quoted by W. Harrison Moore in *The Constitution of the Commonwealth of Australia,* p. 31.
17. e.g., Argument advanced by South Australia at the Colonial Conference, 1887 (*Proceedings,* ii. 172). Also New Guinea Correspondence in *Sydney Morning Herald,* 1 March, 1876, p. 2, and 2 March, 1876, pp. 3-4.

weight in questions relating to the Pacific it must be given unified expression. That lesson was emphasized by Lord Derby, then Secretary of State, who declared:

If the Australian people desire an extension beyond their present limits, the most practical step that they can take, and one that would most facilitate any operation of the kind and diminish in the greatest degree the responsibility of the mother country, would be the federation of the Colonies into one united whole which would be powerful enough to undertake and carry through tasks for which no one Colony is at present sufficient.[18]

The close relationship which existed between projects for federation and the interest of the colonies in the Pacific was made even more evident by the first Australasian Convention which met in Sydney in November-December 1883 to consider "The Annexation of Neighbouring Islands, and the Federation of Australasia." This Convention adopted an attitude which amounted to the formulation of a policy of hands off the Pacific by resolving that

the further acquisition of dominion in the Pacific south of the equator by any foreign power would be highly detrimental to the safety and well-being of the British possessions in Australasia and injurious to the interests of the Empire.[18]

The arguments in favour of federation voiced in the Federal Convention debates reflect the experience and the temper of the preceding years. They were best expressed in two speeches, one by Mr. Deakin, the other by Sir Henry Parkes. Outlining the reasons for federation, Mr. Deakin referred to "the storehouse of confirmed criminals" in neighbouring Pacific islands and to the unstable political equilibrium in the New Hebrides and Samoan groups. But the emphasis of his argument was placed upon the fact that experience had shown the necessity of speaking with a single voice.

It may be highly desirable, when the hour arrives for finally settling their affairs, that the voice of Australia should be a strong and a united voice—a voice which will be listened to in London, echoed in the other capitals of Europe.[19]

Sir Henry Parkes, on the other hand, gave expression to that imperialism which had sprung out of a new sense of nationalism and which was to display an increasing strength in the years immediately following. If Australia could have spoken with a single voice in 1883 New Guinea would not have been lost. Australia ought to be "mistress of the Southern Seas." Trade with the island groups should centre in Australian ports. That was her destiny

18. Quoted W. Harrison Moore, op. cit., p. 30.
19. Victorian Parliamentary Papers, 1890 (2), p. 23.

and it would come. Yet every effort should be made to bring it
about with the least delay and loss of opportunity. These, he concluded, were the great objects, but they were objects which could
"only be properly attained, properly promoted by a Federal Government."[20]

Another unifying factor of the utmost importance in Australian
life was to be found in the efforts to control alien immigration.
Attempts to check the entry of aliens, especially Chinese, were of
long standing. Large numbers of Chinese[21] had entered the
country after 1850, while in the 1870's there was a new influx,
particularly to Queensland. Several of the colonies made efforts
to exclude them, but it was apparent that control of immigration
could be far better regulated by some federal body. In this regard
the 1896 conference on Chinese immigration summed up the experience gained from other attempts at winning uniformity by co-
operative methods. "The deliberations of this conference," read
the resolution, "have made the urgent necessity for a federation
of the colonies more than ever apparent."[22] Similarly, throughout
the Convention debates mention was made of the "questions arising with the Chinese Government"[23] and of the necessity of prohibiting "the multitude of Asiatics."[24] But perhaps the strongest
testimony to the unifying force of the immigration motive was
given by Deakin when introducing the Immigration Restriction
Bill of 1901.

No motive power operated more universally in this continent
or in . . Tasmania, and certainly no motive operated more powerfully in dissolving the technical and arbitrary political divisions
which previously separated us than the desire that we should
be one people and remain one people without the admixture of
other races.

There were also certain sentimental forces working in favour of
federation. No reason existed for disunity since there was neither
racial nor religious nor serious geographical division. Both interest
and honour combined to favour union, and the greater weight and
the greater prestige which would attach to national policy was no
small incentive toward federation. The desire for union was based
upon the maxim which found expression in the recommendations
of Mr. Gavan Duffy's Victorian Committee: "Neighbouring states

20. *Ibid.,* p. 85.
21. See *Australia and the Far East,* edited I. Clunies Ross (1935), chapter by
    S. H. Roberts.
22. Quoted H. L. Hall, *op. cit.,* p. 38.
23. Mr. Deakin, *Victorian Parliamentary Papers,* 1890 (2), p. 23.
24. Sir Henry Parkes, *Ibid.,* p. 85.

of the second order inevitably become confederates or enemies."[25] Very much the same attitude was adopted by Sir Henry Parkes at the 1890 Convention when he argued that sources of irritation, examples of bad neighbourhood, had appeared and that if they were to go on increasing they

> must make these conterminous communities instead of being a people of one blood, one faith, one jurisprudence—one in the very principles of civilisation themselves—instead of that must make us as cavilling, hostile disputatious foreign countries.[26]

In addition to the forces operating in favour of union there was the expectation that certain mechanical advantages would follow from federation. A unified control could be established over matters of national concern. Improvements in the organisation of such government services as posts and telegraphs could be anticipated. There could be uniformity of legislation on such important questions as the control of the rivers for navigation and irrigation purposes and the regulation of the railways especially with regard to the fixing of rates of carriage.[27] Credit facilities would prob ably be increased [28] and arrangements entered into for the taking over of the public debts.

In fact, certain unities had become essential and some machinery for united action had to be discovered. What finally forced federation was the failure of the alternative method of co-operative action through conferences. The conference system had been given fair trial and had been found wanting. It was difficult to assemble a meeting at a time or place suitable to a number of governments. Moreover, delegates considered the furthering of the interests of their own colonies their first concern. Yet what really rendered both the conferences and later the Federal Council inadequate was their powerlessness to take executive action. There was no guarantee that resolutions passed by the conferences would be put into effect by individual governments. Indeed, the testimony of Mr. Service makes plain that the co-operative method had broken down. In 1883 he declared that only three out of twenty-three subjects discussed at the conferences had been dealt with adequately and that "of those agreements which required uniform

25. Quoted, W. Harrison Moore, *op. cit.*, p. 23.
26. *Victorian Parliamentary Papers*, 1891 (4), p. 14.
27. Discussion on whether to place the railways under federal control was one of the most important subjects of debate. Some control over rates of carriage was regarded as a minimum requirement, since certain states were employing differential rates to attract trade to their own railway system.
28. e.g., See Speech by Mr. Bird (Tasmania), *Victorian Parliamentary Papers*, 1890 (2), p. 61.

legislation not one had been carried out."[29] Co-operation had failed and the loose confederation of the Federal Council with its lack of executive power and with opposition from New South Wales, proved almost equally unsatisfactory. In view of the breakdown of alternative methods of securing united action some form of federation seemed the logical answer.

Broadly speaking, then, it can be said that the motive forces operating in the direction of federation were the necessity of fiscal union, a more adequate organisation of the defence forces, the desire to speak with authority on questions concerning the Pacific Ocean, the determination to restrict the entry of aliens and the need for uniform legislation on social, industrial and transport questions. Their individual importance varied at different stages of the movement toward federation, but most weight should be attached to the need for intercolonial free trade, immigration restriction and defence organisation.

In discussing the causes which led to federation, H. L. Hall attacks Professor Laski on the ground that he over-emphasizes the force of the economic motive in bringing about union. Hall declares that by stressing the economic aspect Professor Laski is ignoring "the importance of the factors of immigration, industrial and social matters, and defence."[30] Surely such a view is based upon a complete misapprehension of the nature of economic forces. It is difficult to understand how industrial and social matters can be divorced from the narrowly economic. They interpenetrate one another and cannot be isolated as purely independent factors. The attempt to distinguish between the "industrial" and the "economic" is fallacious and would not be upheld even by the modern school of economists, who severely restrict their field. Again, with regard to immigration, work by Willard[31] and, more recently, by Hentze[32] has shown that the vital motive underlying attempts at immigration restriction was economic—a fear of the lowering of the standard of living. It is even a moot point whether defence can be separated from the economic motive since the question which has to be asked is "defence of what?" And one at least of the answers would be "important economic interests."

In any survey of Australian federation the influence of America must be regarded as vital. The Australians saw a successful United

29. Quoted, W. Harrison Moore, *op. cit.*, p. 36.
30. H. L. Hall, *Victoria's Part in the Australian Federation Movement* (1931), p. 143.
31. M. Willard, *History of the White Australia Policy* (Melbourne University Press, 1923).
32. In *Australia and the Far East* (1935).

States and perhaps to a less degree a successful Canada and Switzerland and were content to attempt to follow in their footsteps. American history and American precedent were repeatedly referred to by members of the conventions who wished to support their particular view of the question. The experience of the United States, says E. M. Hunt,

> recorded in the constitution, in statutes, in judicial decisions, and in the writings of authorities such as Story and Bryce, provided suggestions and guidance in solving problems in interstate commerce and the control of railroads and rivers.[33]

It should be noted that it was the model of the United States rather than that of Canada which found favour in Australian eyes because the Canadian constitution was thought to be too unified. In the United States, said Edmund Barton,

> we know the States insisted on union but objected to unity, that they wished a federation of independent states, but not an amalgamation into one empire.[34]

That was the foundation upon which members desired to rear an Australian federation.

The majority of delegates to the conventions had a profound admiration for the framers of the constitution of the United States. They were, therefore, influenced by the line of policy which their American predecessors had adopted. They followed the American constitution closely but not slavishly.[35] American phraseology influenced Australian drafting, while when words in the American constitution proved suitable they were inserted without alteration. In general, it can be said that American experience acted as both an incentive and a warning. One instance may be noted. Australian delegates were not slow to realise the significance of the failure of the first attempt at American union under the Articles of Confederation and insisted that American experience afforded a warning against an incomplete form of union.[36] The main lines of the United States model were adhered to in the sense that this was to be a union based on protection of the units, but at the same time the framers of the Australian constitution did not hesitate to depart from the example of the United States. That departure was sometimes of a radical nature as, for instance, when it was decided to attempt to graft responsible government on to a federal

33. E. M. Hunt, *American Precedents in Australian Federation* (1930), p. 15.
34. *Victorian Parliamentary Papers*, 1890 (2), p. 49.
35. E. M. Hunt, *op. cit.*, pp. 255-6.
36. Mr. Munro (Victoria): "Be warned by the form of government established in the United States prior to the present constitution" (*Victorian Parliamentary Papers*, 1891 (4), p. 24).
     See also Sir Henry Parkes (New South Wales). *Ibid.*, 1890 (2), p. 6.

system rather than to follow the practice of separating the executive from the legislature. There were also numerous other distinctions, some significant, others less so, between the two constitutions. Thus the power of amendment was made somewhat easier, the list of subjects given to the central authority was extended and a state had the right to refer matters to the Commonwealth parliament for legislation. In spite of these divergences the influence of the United States was a vital one. It was responsible not only for determining that in Australia union should be upon a federal basis, but also for indicating the type of federation which should be adopted. It was an all-important if not an exclusive influence.

Certain causes had combined to make federation possible. American success had exercised a powerful attraction in the same direction. It is, therefore, pertinent to ask what was expected from federation in the light of the attitude which brought men to federate. It is clear that what men had in mind was the surrender of certain limited powers to a central government in order that unified action might be taken on matters of common concern. The nature of the resolutions placed before the convention of 1891 shows plainly the basis upon which federation was to be founded. The resolution which is placed first reads:

> That the powers and privileges and territorial rights of the several existing Colonies shall remain intact, except in respect to such surrenders as may be agreed upon as necessary and incidental to the power and authority of the National Federal Government.[37]

Federation was to be consummated upon a guarantee of state rights and member after member of the conventions insisted that the only possible foundation upon which any sort of union could be built was that of a large measure of state autonomy.[38]

Since the forces making for localism were so strong it might be asked why it was necessary to federate at all. The answer is simply that the colonial governments had been found inadequate to deal with certain classes of business. There were some things which they could not effectively do. What those things were was indicated by Sir Henry Parkes in 1891.[39] They were concerned with the questions in which the Australian people as a whole had an interest. Defence was one issue, the construction of a single

37. *Ibid.*, 1891 (4), p. 11.
38. Geographical factors of area and isolation, as in the case of Tasmania and Western Australia, were partly responsible, but the sentiment was strong in all colonies.
39. *Victorian Parliamentary Papers*, 1891 (4), p. 153.

tariff not subject to state interference was another. There was
the regulation of the railways and the control of communication
between the colonies, there was intercourse with other parts of
the world and the execution of a policy with regard to Australian
interests in the Pacific; and there was the protection of one colony
against another. The implication from the inadequacy of the
separate governments was the necessity of erecting a central authority competent to deal with questions which had become of national
consequence. That was the attitude which members of the convention brought to the framing of a federal constitution. It was
expressed very well in an excellent speech which Mr. Deakin made
to the 1891 convention. He claimed that the meaning of the
mandate given to members was that the Australian colonies realised
that though they had not yet reached a point at which they desired
amalgamation they had reached a point at which they desired
closer union. The colonies refused to part with their powers on
all questions where local self-government could operate efficiently,
but they were willing to surrender authority on certain matters
of common concern. Deakin continued:

> They believed that on certain specific subjects there were no
> longer two interests—that there were no longer state interests,
> but only national interests. They believed that on those special
> subjects it would be possible to safeguard all state interests, and
> to commit to a new parliament . . . the power of dealing with
> particular subjects within certain lines, as the people were in
> reality on those subjects one people with one destiny and one
> interest.[40]

Certain unities had become essential and the compact of federation was very largely the result of an attempt to secure them with
a minimum sacrifice of local powers. The representatives of
the various colonies had therefore to decide what price they were
willing to pay to secure a measure of unified action. The price
could only be stated in terms of the exercise of diminished control
by each of the self-governing states. That federation would have
to be bought was clearly realised by the representatives of the
states. As Sir Samuel Griffith (Queensland) said:

> The advantages of federation, like everything else, will have
> to be paid for; we cannot get them without giving something
> in return, and every power which may be exercised by the
> Federal Government with greater advantage than the separate
> governments involves a corresponding diminution in the powers
> of the separate Governments and Legislatures.[41]

40. *Ibid.*, p. 185.
41. *Ibid.*, 1890 (2), p. 10.

The sacrifice the colonies were called upon to make was not limited to prestige. Not only were the subjects upon which they could legislate curtailed, but their influence was also threatened by a serious decrease in revenue. Customs duties were to be handed over to the central authority and customs was the source from which most of the states drew their revenue. In addition to the financial sacrifices from fiscal union there was the question of policy. New South Wales espoused free trade principles, whereas Victoria was strongly protectionist. Neither wished to see a policy with which it disagreed forced upon it by a federal government. Yet union had been demonstrated to be essential for certain definite purposes. State representatives, therefore, sought to impair state authority as little as possible by surrendering only limited fields of action to a federal body.

An examination of the convention debates shows that two things were regarded as fundamental to union. In the first place, it was taken for granted that the union should be along federal lines. Unification was rarely proposed and certainly would not have been countenanced by the states.

We are not here to advocate the question of federation, that being looked upon already as a settled subject. We are sent here simply to draft a constitution with the desirableness of federation as our major premise.[42]

Federation, then, was undisputed as the method by which union was to be obtained. The adoption of such a position was not without disadvantages, since it meant that there was little discussion of the dangers which might lie in federalism as such. This untroubled acceptance of the federal form was the result of the impact on the latter half of the nineteenth century of the idea that the federal state provided a method of solving governmental problems which no previous system had made possible. In such circumstances the principles underlying federalism were accepted without question. All that had to be discussed was what measure of unity was desirable and to what measure the people within the various colonies could be induced to agree.[43]

In the second place it was insisted that the federation to be brought about be limited in character. There was an insistent demand by almost all members of the conventions that the only

---

42. Dr. Cockburn, a representative of South Australia (*Ibid.*, 1891 (4), p. 95).
43. *Ibid.*, 1891 (4), p. 29. Sir Thomas McIlwraith (Queensland) argued that federation could only be achieved if each colony could be shown that it gained some substantial advantage (*Ibid.*, 1897 (2), p. 140). Mr. Reid (N.S.W.) emphasized that delegates must frame a bill which could "command the approval of the constituencies."

basis for union was that of a large amount of state autonomy. No union was possible in Australia, said Mr. Deakin (Victoria), "which did not preserve in the fullest form the power and dignity of the several communities which comprise it."[44]   Other speakers were equally emphatic. For instance, Mr. Barton (N.S.W.) declared that federation was "well nigh impossible" unless territorial rights and privileges were reserved to the states,[45] while Mr. Fitzgerald (Victoria) expressed the "settled conviction . . . that not one iota" should be taken from the states "beyond that which is absolutely necessary for the formation of a national government."[46]   Indeed, the unanimity of expression upon this point showed the solidarity of the interests pressing for the preservation of state rights.   The federation which members were attempting to bring into being was not viewed by them as a necessary historical step in the direction of unification.

There were, of course, some dissentients who not only favoured an immediate conferring of wider powers upon the central government, notably in the direction of greater control over railways and industrial matters, but who also believed that in the future it would be necessary to unite more closely by strengthening the authority of the federal parliament.   The majority, however, regarded federation not as a stage, but as something permanent.   They could favour so much unity, but not more.   More would mean the destruction of the states as independent entities and that possibility they would not tolerate.   Accordingly, state rights had to be safeguarded and a certain element of rigidity imported into the constitution in order to prevent undue encroachment by the central government upon the arena of state authority.

At the same time it was realised that if the federation was to function effectively the central government must not be unduly weak.   It must act directly upon the citizens of the union and not require the mediation of the several state governments.[47]   It must be "a government of power" with adequate strength to carry out the functions for which it was created.[48]   Emphasis had, therefore, been placed by delegates upon two semi-contradictory ideas —the retention of powerful states and the creation of a strong central government.   Clearly there had to be some division of powers between state and central authority.   The broad basis of that division was obvious enough—questions which were national in scope should go to the federal government, whereas questions

44. *Ibid.*, 1891 (4), p. 35.   45. *Ibid.*, p. 44.   46. *Ibid.*, p. 80.
47. e.g., Deakin at the 1890 Convention.
48. See the speech delivered by Sir Henry Parkes to the 1890 Convention, *Victorian Parliamentary Papers*, 1890 (2), p. 7.

which were local in character should remain with the states. But the division was not always clear cut, and the difficulty of deciding just what was national and what was local remained. It was further clouded by the jealousy of the states and by their desire to retain the widest possible powers. The issue of just where and how to make the division was among the vital subjects of dispute.

Throughout the debates there was inadequate discussion of the dangers inherent in federalism itself. Enquiries tended to be made rather into the expectations, the promise which federalism held out for the future. What discussion there was referred to the dangers to particular interests which might be involved in federation and was couched in terms of the immediate present. Nevertheless, there was a measure of enquiry into the nature of federalism and spasmodic reference to possible dangers arising out of its character. For instance, Mr. Baker (South Australia), in attempting a definition of federalism, declared that federation consisted of a compact between states which left the legislatures of the states supreme concerning the powers delegated to them and which also gave them a voice as states in the powers entrusted to the federal government.[49] That is, in so far as the Council of States or Senate was concerned the states were not to become unified, but were to preserve their individuality. Such an attitude was attacked as the frustration of a true federal union, and Mr. Higgins (Victoria) pointed out that federation really meant "unification for certain purposes."[50] In this regard, he quoted Chief Justice Marshall, of the United States, with approval: "We are one people for war; we are one people for peace; we are one people for the purpose of commercial regulation." The same attitude to federation was displayed by Mr. Deakin, who stressed the fact that "a host of questions, like the question of patents," had no relevancy as state issues and had been included in the bill because they were of national concern.[51] Upon these defined points there should be unification. But discussions such as these arose out of debate upon other specific problems, and were in the nature of passing references to the characteristics of federalism. There was no attempt at a general survey of the nature of federal government and of the implications in its principles.

Of those issues which were raised relating to the structure of a federal organisation perhaps the most important was concerned with the relations between the two houses and the executive. This

49. *Ibid.*, 1891 (4), p. 54.
50. *Ibid.*, p. 956.
51. Deakin at the 1897 Conference (*Ibid.*, 1897 (2)', p. 588)'.

brought to the front the whole problem of whether or not the system of responsible government was to be retained under federation. Sir Samuel Griffith early pointed out that it was proposed to create two houses, in one of which the states should be represented equally, and in the other the people of Australia in proportion to population. That meant that every measure submitted to the federal parliament had to receive "the assent of the majority of the people and also the assent of the majority of the states."[52] It signified the introduction of a new principle into Australian governmental practice and a principle which was bound to affect the relationship between the executive and parliament.   The American Constitutional Convention, following the arguments of Montesquieu, had separated the executive from the legislature, but in Australia it was proposed that the executive should sit in parliament and be responsible to one house. There lay the difficulty. Responsibility was to be to one house, but in order to safeguard state rights the houses were to exercise roughly co-ordinate powers. Such a position implied the possibility of very serious deadlock. The dilemma which faced the convention members was clearly stated by Mr. Playford (South Australia) :

> You cannot graft responsible government on to the American system . . . and make it work, because directly you graft on to it responsible government you take away at one stroke some of the powers the Senate possesses.[53]

The same warning was given an epigrammatic flavour by Sir Richard Baker (South Australia) : "If we adopt this Cabinet System of Executive it will either kill federation or federation will kill it."[54]

The debate which ensued revealed considerable difference of opinion.   Some held that responsible government was unworkable under a federal system, that it was not feasible to make the executive responsible to one house alone and still retain a states house exercising roughly co-ordinate powers.   Others maintained that there was no reason why a combination of two systems should not work, while others again held that the ministry could be responsible to both houses.   The outcome was a decision to adhere to responsible government and an attempt to combine it with the federal principle of a states house.   The dangers were realised, but the conviction remained that an experiment of this sort was less hazardous than a departure from the established practice of mak-

52. Sir Samuel Griffith (Q.) at the 1891 Convention.
53. *Victorian Parliamentary Papers*, 1891 (4), p. 28.
54. *Ibid.*, 1897 (2), p. 617.

ing the executive responsible to parliament. The fact that financial power had been vested in the House of Representatives had
exalted it above the Senate.   Additional importance was now given
to its position by the conception that the ministry would have to
command the confidence of the lower house.

A further instance of enquiry into dangers associated with the
federal form of government can be found in the discussion which
centred about the rigidity of the constitution.   There seems to have
been an uneasy awareness of the disadvantages of an over-rigid
constitution, and, in particular. a demand by a number of representatives that the process of amendment be made easier than in
the case of the United States.

The plea for a more elastic constitution was made upon several
grounds.   First stood the needs of the future.   It was impossible
to foresee all future developments and requirements.   Common
sense, therefore, dictated that the constitution be made elastic and
capable of expanding to meet future needs.   Otherwise, the future
threatened dissension and the possible destruction of the whole
edifice.   The second argument was allied to the first, and dealt
with the question of secession.   If it was agreed, as it generally
was, that secession was not permissible, then it became necessary
to make the constitution capable of easy alteration, so that a point
was never reached at which the strain upon it became unendurable.
Some remedial machinery must be provided if a state with grievances was to be left with any alternative other than revolution.
The danger of too rigid a constitution was, as Sir George Turner
(Victoria) pointed out, that it would not bend, but would break.[55]
One more line of argument was advanced, and again members
were faced with the old difficulty of how to safeguard state rights.
In order to give the states some basis of confidence a measure of
rigidity seemed essential, yet as against this there were all the
dangers associated with rigidity.   Dr. Cockburn maintained that a
rigid constitution was inescapable under federation, but he went
on to outline the very real disadvantages which it introduced.   Not
least among these was the fact that constitutions were prone to
become psychologically rigid because an attitude of "superstitious
reverence" on the part of the people tended to make the original
division sacrosanct.   Instead of being regarded as utilitarian devices to carry out the object of union, which was good national
government, the clauses of the constitution were liable to be looked
upon as sacred in themselves.   That represented a formidable dan-

55. *Ibid.,* 1897 (2), p. 625.

ger because under such circumstances a rigid constitution became "one of the strongest engines of conservatism."[56]

Enquiries into the threat to particular interests were much more thorough than those carried out into possible dangers inherent in federalism. Indeed, it was a consideration of the effect which union might have upon various groups of interests which occupied the major part of each convention's time and which certainly aroused the most heated debate. As a result, the immediate difficulties were stressed rather than those of a long-term nature or those which might become of importance in the future. Foremost among the interests affected were the governments and legislatures of the several colonies.[57] They were, not unnaturally, jealous of their powers and privileges, and viewed the encroachment of a federal authority with suspicion and hostility.[58] Not only would their prestige be diminished, but the area of their control would also be seriously curtailed. In consequence, almost every speaker was emphatic that it should be made plain to the state governmental authorities that their powers would not be trespassed upon except in those matters which could best be dealt with by a central government. But more than this was required. Inducements had to be offered to those who exercised power in the states before they would be willing to countenance any loss of prestige. In return for the surrender of definite powers it was necessary to show that there would be definite gains. Both the citizens and the governments of the individual states would ask certain questions. They would say, "We are giving up a number of powers and we want to know what we are getting in return." That was an attitude which implied not only bargaining,[59] but also a limited unification at best. It was summed up in a slightly different way by Mr. J. Forrest, a Western Australian representative, who declared: "I venture to think we shall have to show that the scheme is practically not disadvantageous to the different states, or I feel sure it will be almost impossible to obtain their acquiescence."[60]. Those who favoured federation had the onus upon them of proving that the states as states were going to gain more than they gave up.

The debate upon the control of the railways furnished an excel-

56. *Ibid.*, 1891 (4), p. 96.
57. See Sir Samuel Griffith's speech to the 1890 Convention (*Ibid.*, 1890 (2), p. 10).
58. Mr. Bird (Tasmania), *Ibid.*, 1890 (2), p. 61.
59. See Sir Thomas McIlwraith's speech to the 1891 Convention upon the inducements which must be offered to the weaker colonies in order to secure federation (*Ibid.*, 1891 (4), p. 29).
60. *Ibid.*, 1891 (4), p. 107. He attempted to argue that Western Australia occupied a special position, and, therefore, deserved special treatment,

lent example of the strength of local feeling. The railways were state-owned, and delegates emphasized that neither the governments nor the people of the various states were willing to see the railways handed over to federal control. "The feeling," declared Mr. Barton, "against amalgamating the railways is so strong in every one of the colonies that the people would not consent to its being placed in the constitution."[61] Those who favoured state retention argued that railway construction was closely allied to land policy, and land settlement was to remain in the hands of the states. Many railways were built for settlement purposes and for the development of localities. These lines were designed to meet local requirements, and it was only in the exceptional case—such as inter-colonial trunk lines—that any question of federal interest arose.

Nevertheless, it was clear from statements made by several speakers that there were cases in which the railways could assume a federal significance. For instance, it was evident that competition had existed between the rival state railways to secure trade from areas which could be tapped by both systems. Competition had usually taken the form of differential rates. This "filching away of trade by rebates on railways," as Mr. Donaldson (Queensland) called it,[62] had caused jealousy between the colonies, especially between New South Wales and Victoria over the Riverina trade. If the future union was to operate efficiently it was essential that such causes of friction be eliminated. Moreover, one of the principal gains anticipated from federation was inter-colonial free trade, but the maintenance of differential railway rates would partially destroy the benefits of free trade. Finally, there was the experience of the evils which had resulted from divided control in the past—evils which might be carried on into the future. These considerations led a number of members to urge the institution of federal control of railways. Thus Mr. Glynn (South Australia) argued that federal administration would promote economy, do away with differential tariffs and destroy secret rebates.[63] Other advantages might also accrue, such as uniformity of gauge and a reduction in the mileage of lines built for purely political purposes. Notwithstanding these arguments, the weight of opinion was against the surrender of local control. However, the necessity of taking some action remained, for it had been demonstrated that railways did affect interstate relations. Indeed, it was obvious. They were the links in inter-colonial communication; they were

61. *Ibid.*, 1897 (2), p. 615.   62. *Ibid.*, 1891 (4), p. 148.
63. *Ibid.*, 1897 (2), p. 642.

vital to the carrying on of interstate trade; and they were equally essential from a defence point of view. There seemed much common sense in the statement of Mr. Carruthers (New South Wales) : "If you federate without federating the railways it is like a man marrying a girl and leaving her at the church door"![64]

Some action was clearly necessary, since a means of preventing unfair discrimination had to be provided. Opinion was against a complete handing over of the railways, so that the task which confronted the conventions was how to reconcile state management with as large a measure of trade equality as possible.[65] The main difficulty lay in the mutual suspicion of New South Wales and Victoria, since every proposal made upon railway rates was criticised as being too beneficial to one side or the other. The outcome was an agreement to leave the decision upon whether a rate was prejudicial to another state to the Inter-State Commission. The Commonwealth was forbidden to give preference to one state, and it had the authority to prohibit discrimination by any state, provided the Inter-State Commission adjudged it unreasonable. At the same time there was to be no interference with any railway rate so long as the Inter-State Commission thought it "necessary for the development of the territory of the state" and so long as the rate "applied equally to goods within the state and to goods passing into the state from other states."[66] In this manner jealousy between the states over possible loss of trade through railway regulation was largely overcome.

Certain concessions were also made to the demand for federal regulation. Members felt the logic of centralised control of a nation's means of communication, but they were unable to escape from local tradition and interests. In consequence, federal control became a vague possibility rather than an accomplished fact. The Commonwealth was given the power to acquire the railways of a state, with the state's consent and on terms to be arranged between State and Commonwealth. In addition, the Commonwealth could control transport for naval and military purposes and construct railways in any state with that state's consent. This was at best but a halting measure of control and fell far short of a federation of the railway communications of the country.

Perhaps the clearest instance of inquiry into the danger to parti-

64. *Ibid.*, 1897 (2), p. 651.
65. Quick and Garran, *The Annotated Constitution of the Australian Constitution* (1901), p. 202.
66. *Ibid.*

cular interests came from the discussion upon fiscal union. Victoria had for many years been fostering her industries behind a protective tariff. By the time federation became possible they were well established and should have been able to compete advantageously under free trade conditions with those in other colonies. Yet, peculiarly enough, Victorian representatives claimed that their industries were entitled to special consideration. They declared that certain vested interests had been fostered under protection and that they could not be expected to tell those interests that in future they would be left to the mercy of free competition.[67] Such an attitude was roundly condemned by the members from other states. "To my surprise," said Mr. Dibbs (New South Wales), "I have gathered that Victoria, in discussing the fiscal question in this convention is seeking for guarantees to secure the protection of her vested interests—despite twenty-five years' start on the whole of Australasia!"[68]

But while Victoria's attitude was condemned on the ground that she was in a better position than anyone, some of the lesser states felt that the introduction of free trade would ruin their less well-established industries. Speaking on behalf of South Australia, Dr. Cockburn maintained that his state's industries were in their infancy and could not face direct competition "with the long-established industries of their powerful neighbours."[69] He, therefore, wanted a breathing space before the introduction of free trade. The same attitude was voiced for Queensland by Sir Thomas McIlwraith when he asked, "Who would get the trade?" and answered, "Those who had the start and would now be given an increased area of trade."[70] He, too, asked for special consideration for colonies with weakly-established industries. Such concessions were found to be impossible, since they would have meant the continuance of the very conditions which federation aimed at abolishing. But the fact that such demands were made—and strongly made—shows that the manufacturing interests were vocal on their own behalf.

Throughout the debates there was much evidence of an attitude of deep-seated particularism. Local feelings were strong, and though often displayed over petty considerations, they had a wider significance, since they underlay the demand for the preservation

---

67. e.g., at the 1891 Convention, Col. Smith (Victoria) required "a guarantee of interests" established under protection.
68. *Victorian Parliamentary Papers*, 1891 (4), p. 87.
69. *Ibid.*, 1890 (2), p. 44.
70. *Ibid.*, 1891 (4), p. 29.

of state rights. Sir Henry Parkes, in his speech to the 1890 conference upon federation, had remarked:

> We cannot become a nation and still cling to conditions and to desires which are antagonistic to nationality. We cannot become one united people and cherish some provincial object which is inconsistent with that nationality.[71]

Yet the very attitude which he urged should be abandoned continued to find expression in subsequent meetings. Numerous speakers felt obliged to protest against an attitude which Mr. McMillan (New South Wales) summarised by saying: "From the debates it would seem the delegates have come here with more or less suspicion of one another's colonies."[72] At least, many continued to regard the benefit which would or would not accrue to their individual colony as the primary consideration.

The state rights question in its various forms was by far the most important problem with which the conventions had to deal. It has been emphasised that the only basis upon which the states would agree to union was the retention of a large measure of state autonomy. That signified not only a limited federation, but a demand for adequate protection of state interests. Safeguards were asked for in order to ensure that there should be no encroachment, beyond what was specifically surrendered, upon state authority by the central government. The attempt to safeguard state independence had two aspects. It was a demand for protection, first against the Commonwealth, and then against a combination of other states. The twofold nature of the state rights problem was illustrated by the debates upon revenue and upon the Senate.

The financial debate turned largely upon the fact that it had been agreed to hand over the tariff to the federal government. That surrender meant that several colonies were robbed of their largest source of revenue. Such a weakening of state finances was liable to undermine the independence of the states—the very thing which delegates wished to avoid. "We cannot," said Mr. Barton (New South Wales), "do away with the solvency of the several states. If we do that those states die, and we have no longer a federation but a legislative union."[73] Perhaps the chief difficulty was the wide range in tariffs in the different colonies, and as a result the varying degree to which they were dependent upon customs revenue. New South Wales had a practically free-trade tariff, obtaining a large percentage of its revenue from land, while West-

71. *Ibid.*, 1890 (2), p. 5.   72. *Ibid.*, 1891 (4), p. 128.
73. *Ibid.*, 1897 (2), p. 203.

ern Australia, with its mining population, was dependent upon customs and excise. But every state was dependent upon customs revenue to a greater or lesser extent, and was unwilling to resort to alternative means of taxation. Besides, it was considered unnecessary to do so, because it was thought that the federal government would have a very handsome surplus which could be returned to the several states.

The redistribution of the anticipated surplus proved one of the most troublesome issues. Several alternative methods were proposed, but none really met with approval. Mr. McMillan and some others urged that it was best to leave the whole matter to the federal parliament. Another group favoured distribution on a population basis,[74] while still another supported a return in proportion to contribution.[75] Wrangling ensued between the parties until Mr. Bird (Tasmania) was led to exclaim:

Has it really come to this: that such a pettifogging, parochial spirit of selfishness is to be embodied in a clause of this bill . . . as to take into consideration whether Queensland drinks a little more whisky than South Australia. . . . Surely if we are going to federate at all we must learn to lose sight of all these trifling difficulties and feel that we are all one.[76]

No solution of the financial problem was reached until the concluding session of the 1897 convention. Victoria and Tasmania in particular wanted some guarantee that revenue would be returned to the states inserted in the constitution. They were ultimately successful in securing the Braddon clause, which assured the return over a ten-year period of three-fourths of the customs revenue to the states.

If the revenue issue had shown the determination of delegates to safeguard state finances against the Commonwealth, the struggle which took place over the Senate reflected the desires of the smaller states to be protected against the more populous. The principle of equality of representation for each state was early conceded, and it was about the question of the powers to be conferred upon the Senate that the struggle revolved. The representatives of the smaller states were emphatic that the upper house should have co-ordinate powers with the lower house. But those from New South Wales and Victoria were unwilling to concede the right of veto upon financial measures. This was the vital point, because control of finance implied ultimately control of government. To give the right of veto meant that the minority would rule the

74. See speech by Sir J. Bray (S.A.) to the 1891 Convention.
75. See speech by Sir S. Griffith (Q.) to the 1891 Convention.
76. *Victorian Parliamentary Papers*, 1891 (4), p. 399.

majority. It was essential that the house elected upon a population basis should have the power of the purse. "You cannot," said Mr. Munro (Victoria), "allow a small section to govern the majority on a question of finance; you cannot give 250,000 persons the power to tax 2,500,000 against their will."[77]

The debate concerning the powers to be conferred upon the Senate was of such heat that it nearly prevented federation. The smaller states were loath to surrender the right to veto on financial measures, declaring that to do so made the Senate a mockery and turned federation into unification.[78] Ultimately, the right of veto was rejected, because certain members of the smaller states had come to the conclusion that its surrender did not involve any real threat to state interests. Underlying the whole issue had been the belief that the large states might unite, and through their numerical strength in the House of Representatives push through measures disadvantageous to other states.[79] Many delegates believed that the possibility of such action could only be prevented by a strong Senate. But such an argument was founded upon the idea that representatives would vote along state lines. However, as both Mr. Gillies and Mr. Macrossan pointed out, the likelihood of such a happening was remote, because of the operation of party government. "We have been arguing all through," said Mr. Macrossan (Queensland), "as if party government were to cease immediately we adopt the new constitution."[80] The division upon party lines would prevent either a combination of small states against large in the Senate or large states against small in the House of Representatives.

Evidence of particularism may also be found in the debate which centred about the possibility of a deadlock[81] between the two houses. In the first place the fight for state rights had been concerned with equal representation on the Senate. Next it had become a question of the powers to be entrusted to the Senate—especially the right to veto money bills. The state rights party were successful in securing equal representation in the Senate, but were unable to carry this demand that the upper house be given equal

77. *Ibid.*, 1891 (4), p. 26.
78. See speeches by Sir T. McIlwraith (Q.) at the 1891 Convention and by Dr. Cockburn (S.A.) at the 1897 Convention. "We do not," said Dr. Cockburn, "want a House that has the appearance of having equal representation, but we do want a House that will not suffer in comparison with the House of Representatives" (*Ibid.*, 1897 (2), p. 786).
79. e.g., Mr. Playford (S.A.) wanted safeguards against united action by N.S.W. and Victoria.
80. *Victorian Parliamentary Papers*, 1891 (4), p. 210.
81. See Sir S. Griffith's warning to the 1891 Convention.

powers with the lower. Later the same issues were raised again, because those who were most insistent upon safeguarding state rights believed that the settlement of possible deadlocks by means of the referendum implied a further whittling down of the power of the Senate to defend the smaller states, since in the final outcome an appeal to a referendum resulted in the rule of the majority. "Of what value," asked Mr. Gordon (South Australia), "are checks and delays, if in the last reference, which is not very far off, the will of the majority is to prevail?"[82] It was this insistence upon the necessity of protecting state interests that was responsible for the insertion of a provision whereby the passage of a measure under the referendum could only be secured if a majority of the states, as well as a majority of the people, was obtained

Finally, it may be asked to what extent did the members of the various conventions which met to frame a federal constitution foresee the future. Was the constitution which they produced capable of effective adaptation to the needs of succeeding generations? The debates reveal that their vision of future developments and of the demands which those developments would make upon the constitution was strictly limited. They had, of course, appreciated that conditions had altered since the framing of the constitution of the United States and that changed conditions necessitated the conferring of wider powers upon the central authority. That realisation was responsible for the addition of certain subjects to the list of federal enumerated powers, but it did not bring about any vital change in the balance of the federal structure. The Australian delegates were as determined as the American that union was not to impair state authority.

There was also some awareness of the fact that the state of the future would have to display an increasing social activity, but there was an almost complete failure to realise that the action required would be on a national and not on a local basis. The more extreme advocates of state rights feared the encroachment of the federal government on the ground that centralization was incompatible with the free exercise of local government. Dr. Cockburn, who was one of the chief proponents of this view, was aware of the forces working towards the creation of a social service state.

If we know anything, we know that the advance in the future will be in the direction of the state taking upon itself many functions which are at present performed by private individuals.[83]

---

82. *Victorian Parliamentary Papers*, 1897 (2), p. 572.
83. *Ibid.*, 1891 (4), p. 97.

But he was convinced that such development should be provincial rather than federal. He, therefore, insisted that there must be no attempt to define the powers not surrendered by the individual states, because to define meant to limit. Fear of encroachment had prevented adequate powers being conferred upon the central government. Strength of local feeling was likewise responsible for the decision to enumerate federal and leave reserved powers to the states. To-day national and not provincial action is required for the regulation of industrial and social questions, yet action is hampered because it is the national powers which have been defined and hence limited.

The struggle which took place over the incorporation of a clause in the constitution giving the federal government power to deal with "conciliation and arbitration" illustrates the limitation of the outlook of members by the period in which they lived. The majority showed an immediate, rather than a far-sighted, view of the issues involved. At the same time, between 1891 and 1898, opinion developed sufficiently to ensure the passage of a clause which when first put forward in 1891 had been easily defeated. It was Mr. Kingston who at the 1891 convention proposed that the federal authorities should have the right to establish "courts of conciliation and arbitration for the settlement of industrial disputes."[84] His argument was based upon two facts. Industrial disputes had ramifications throughout the whole of Australia, and could not be adequately dealt with by any one state. The failure to confer such a necessary power meant that it could only be obtained at a later date by the difficult process of amending the constitution. The proposal was at once strongly attacked, largely on the grounds that it involved interference with private property and civil rights—subjects which had been left to the states.[85] It was defeated only to be revived at the Adelaide sitting of the 1898 convention, where Mr. Higgins proposed a sub-clause, "Industrial disputes extending beyond the limits of a state." On this occasion the proposal was again rejected by 22 votes to 10, and it was not until the Melbourne session that it was carried by the narrow margin of three votes. Ultimately, then, while the central government received a measure of power to deal with industrial disputes, it remained partial and had been haltingly given. In view of the force of the argument in favour of federal regulation, the extent of the opposition gives a good indication of the great strength of local

84. *Ibid.*, 1891 (4), p. 377.
85. Such were the objections voiced by Sir S. Griffith (Q.) at the 1891 Convention.

feeling. Labour had federated and capital had federated. That seemed, as Mr. Playford argued, an unanswerable reason for giving the central government power to deal with industrial disputes. Shipping strikes in Sydney had their repercussions in Melbourne. A coal dispute in one state affected the industry in another.[86] Yet, despite obvious nation-wide ramifications, delegates could argue strongly that industrial matters were purely local matters, Mr. Wise (New South Wales) condemned the proposal as dangerous, and insisted that local control was essential for the development of varying industrial conditions.[87] Mr. Symon (South Australia) maintained that every dispute was "local to the state in which it originated,"[88] while Sir John Downer (South Australia) attempted to prove that each dispute was "complete in itself in each state," and that the existence of the same dispute in other colonies did not create "a dispute extending beyond the limits of the state"![89]

The insistence with which these arguments were reiterated indicates that general unwillingness to hand over powers which were vital to the federal authority. There was a failure to realise the growing inter-connection between industrial life in the various colonies. Certain unities, such as customs and defence, had become essential. Members of the conventions gave all their attention to paying the price necessary to attain those unities without considering whether the form adopted would make other unities, equally necessary at a later stage, unrealisable. In many ways the very things which it now has become imperative for a national government to control were left in the hands of the individual states. The states were to continue to exercise powers in such fields as the raising of capital, taxation, the regulation of labour conditions and the award of wages. It is true that a liberal interpretation of the constitution has added to the scope of the federal government's activity, but that does not touch the heart of the problem. The retention of the states, and the important nature of the governmental powers entrusted to them under the constitution, have prevented unification in matters where it has become essential.

In all, it can be said that the convention debates show a pre-occupation with immediate problems rather than concern for those of the future. The considerations which weigh are often short-term ones, such as the solution of the difficulty occasioned by the redistribution of surplus customs revenue. The fears of members

86. See speech by Mr. Higgins (V.) at the 1897 Convention, Adelaide.
87. *Victorian Parliamentary Papers*, 1897 (2), p. 1038.
88. *Ibid*.   89. *Ibid*., p. 1037.

upon certain issues have been largely falsified by events. In particular, responsible government has proved compatible with a federal organisation, and there has been little sign of combinations between large states on the one hand and small states on the other. For this the credit must be given to the operation of party government. Many things stressed at the conventions have proved of less importance than others which were neglected or lightly regarded. What members did not understand was that federation is only a stage, the value of which is set by the growth of communications and the inter-connection of economic life. By their emphasis upon state autonomy they were in some measure at least, responsible for what Mr. McMillan (New South Wales) called a crystallization of difficulties, when he urged delegates to abandon state nationalities, lest future generations should say:

> Patriotic and able as these men were, anxious as they were to take action in these great affairs, they did not see with sufficient clearness the great future destinies of Australasia. They stopped short in the very essential element of national union, and by a wretched travesty of a constitution they actually crystallized those differences which are now the great bane of these communities.[90]

90.   *Ibid.*, 1891 (4), p. 132.

III

THE RESULTS PRODUCED BY THE CONSTITUTION

A JUDGMENT ON THE ADEQUACY OF THE STRUCTURE OF 1900

THE history of Commonwealth legislative activity affords proof that the men who framed the constitution did establish a system capable of realising many of the objects for which the colonies had consented to unite in a federal union. From a limited point of view they did, indeed, achieve a considerable success.[1] The central government which they erected took unified action with regard to a number of specific subjects upon which the several colonial governments had found themselves incapable of legislating effectively. A single tariff system was established, immigration restriction in accordance with the idea of a White Australia introduced, provisions for defence made, and a common attitude adopted toward questions relating to the Pacific and to foreign affairs in general. It might, therefore, be assumed that the results produced by the constitution were ample evidence of its substantial success. But the federal nature of the constitution was itself responsible for creating new and increasingly serious problems. In consequence, any judgment based upon a review of the whole period since federation will stress not the adequacy but rather the inadequacy of the structure erected in 1900.

Two conclusions were reached as the result of an analysis of the convention debates. In the first place, it was clear that federation was to be consummated only upon the basis of the retention of as much state power as possible. The aim of those who set up the Commonwealth was to allow the states to maintain their powers to the full, except upon a limited number of enumerated subjects which were surrendered to the central government. Secondly, the implication to be drawn from the type of federal structure adopted was that the price paid to secure certain unities, at that time considered essential, would make difficult of attainment other unities equally necessary at a later

1. See the conclusions of Professor K. H. Bailey, *Studies in the Australian Constitution* (ed. G. V. Portus, 1933), pp. 24-5, 54.

date.   The emphasis was thus placed by the framers upon the maintenance of state rights and upon the federal nature of the union, because a federal system was thought capable of protecting state interests.   Yet it is on this very question of the ability of the federal structure to protect state rights that failure has been most apparent.   For the history of the past forty-six years has shown that the constitution has failed signally to safeguard the independence of the states, and that at the same time, by the maintenance of the federal form, it has prevented or hampered the attainment of unity in directions where changing social and economic conditions have made unified action imperative.

The decline in state power has been both visible and substantial.[2]   It is now of sufficient magnitude to threaten the status of federalism within Australia.   The significance of this decline can only be judged when it is realised that a federal system, if it is to function effectively, must be capable of preserving the independence of the states or provinces within the limits assigned to them.   Or, as the Jones Commission in its report of 1934 stated:

> A federation defeats its primary purpose if, through its constitutional arrangements or by policies instituted by the national government, it accomplishes the debilitation of one or more of the political communities of which it is composed.[3]

Yet in Australia federation has been unable to prevent the at least partial destruction of the autonomy of the states.   In only one important instance, namely, the insertion of Section 105A in the constitution, has this been brought about by the granting of wider powers to the Commonwealth as the result of amendment by referendum.   The destruction of state autonomy has been due not only to Section 105A, though this has played an important part, but also to a combination of other factors, some lying almost outside the terms of the constitution, others being factors foreshadowed in the constitution which, however, have completely changed in importance with the passage of time.   In effect, the constitution in so far at it attempts to guarantee the continued independence of state action has become largely a sham.

Federalism, then, has not given that protection to the states which was expected of it.   Indeed, during the war period 1914-18 the extension of Commonwealth activity through a

2. See R. W. G. Mackay's article in *Studies in the Australian Constitution.*
3. Quoted in the Nova Scotian brief submitted to the Royal Commission on Dominion-Provincial Relations, Feb., 1938, p. 2.

liberal interpretation of the defence power was so far-reaching
that the 1929 Royal Commission on the constitution could declare in its report that the Commonwealth had functioned as a
unitary state.[4] It seemed as though the construction placed upon
the defence power meant that in war time the Commonwealth
might

pass any law or give executive authority to make any regulation which it considers necessary for the safety of the country.[5]

The validity of this wide assumption of power under Section 51
(vi) did not go unchallenged, but in a number of cases, both
during and after the Great War, the High Court pronounced in
favour of the Commonwealth. The most important case[6] was that
in 1919 of *Farey v. Burvett*,[7] known as the bread case, where it
was held that a regulation fixing the highest price at which bread
might be sold within certain localities was a valid exercise of
the defence power. Other cases determined that the Commonwealth had the power to lay down the conditions on which a
person should be deemed to be trading with the enemy. (*Wels-
bach Light Co. of Australasia Ltd. v. The Commonwealth*[8]), to
provide for the deportation of aliens (*Ferrando v. Pearce*[9]), to
authorise the expropriation of property (*Burkard v. Oakley*[10]),
and to make it a crime under the defence power to encourage the
destruction of property (*Pankhurst v. Kiernan*[11]). It should
also be noticed that regulations were made covering transactions
for the disposal and acquisition of a number of commodities,
notably wool and sheep skins.[12]

A war period may well be regarded as exceptional, and for
that reason unsuitable for drawing any inferences about the destruction of the powers of the states. It is, therefore, necessary
to examine whether encroachment by the Commonwealth has
taken place at times when the federal governmental machinery
has been functioning normally. There can be little doubt that
it has; little doubt either that Commonwealth policy even when
it has sprung from a power exclusively vested in the Common-

4. *Report*, p. 120. See also "The Working of Federation in Australia,"
   Round Table, March, 1935, p. 348.
5. *Report of the Royal Commission on the Constitution*, 1929, p. 120. For
   the interpretation of the defence power since the outbreak of war in
   1939 see Chapter VI.
6. For cases relating to the defence power, see W. Anstey Wynes *Legislative and Executive Powers in Australia*, pp. 178-182; G. S. Knowles,
   The Australian Constitution (1936), pp. 27-8.
7. 21 *C.L.R.*, 433.   8. 22 *C.L.R.*, 268.   9. 25 *C.L.R.*, 241.
10. 25 *C.L.R.* 422.   11. 24 *C.L.R.* 120.
12. *Report Commission on the Constitution*, 1929, p. 120.

wealth has affected the states not only in ways which they strongly disliked, but also in ways which were not anticipated by the framers of the constitution.

It is doubtful whether most representatives at the Conventions fully understood the inter-relation which would exist between the powers of the federation and the states or the effects which action taken by one member of the union might have upon another. Nor was it realised that by bestowing a preponderance of financial power upon the Commonwealth the structure which embodied the particular type of federalism in which they believed would be jeopardised. Often, no doubt, there were excellent reasons for the attitude adopted by the Commonwealth, and, indeed, for an expanded conception of Commonwealth functions. Often, too, the sincerity of the protests made on behalf of state rights was open to question. State politicians, in an attempt to win popularity by a policy of militant local nationalism, naturally championed state 'interests' against what they were pleased to call Commonwealth aggression. In addition, various organised groups within the states repeatedly raised the cry of state rights in an endeavour to prevent regulation of their activities by the Commonwealth. Even though the expansion of Commonwealth activity was desirable, and the sincerity of some of the protests against Commonwealth encroachment open to doubt, it yet remains true that the Commonwealth was steadily enlarging its authority, that the power and prestige of the states was diminishing, and that resentment was felt by both state governments and officials. Moreover, until very recently the protests made by the representatives of the states had a very considerable measure of public support, particularly from the inhabitants of the less populous primary producing states.

All the states have complained of the expansion of federal powers, and have voiced their indignation more especially against Commonwealth interference with state employees through the Federal Arbitration Court, against Commonwealth invasion of the field of direct taxation and against the methods employed by the Commonwealth to ensure the non-existence of any surplus revenue for distribution to the states. They have also pointed out that the federal parliament, through the exercise of certain of its powers, has legislated upon subjects not expressly assigned to it, and not generally thought of as being matters of Commonwealth concern.[13] Thus through control of posts, telegrams and telephones the federal parliament has sought to regulate lottery

13. *Ibid.*, p. 86, for a list of such subjects.

activities; through taxation the subdivision of large estates; through control over elections the signing of articles on election issues; through trade and commerce with other countries the prohibition of export of goods not manufactured in accordance with certain conditions; through the customs the admission of goods with conditions attaching to their use; through arbitration the overriding of state industrial laws; through loans and grants the imposition of conditions which are destructive of state freedom of action. All the states have been indignant about this tendency on the part of the Commonwealth to usurp many of what had always been regarded as their functions. But the weaker states, the present 'claimant'[14] states, have also bitterly protested about the adverse effects which they maintain Commonwealth policy has had upon their economic welfare. They quote the Navigation Act as one instance and federal industrial awards as another. However, it is upon the results produced by a high tariff policy that their case substantially rests. As primary-producing states they feel they bear the burden and receive but scanty rewards.

The extension of Commonwealth powers and the hostility of the states towards that extension are alike evidence of the impotence of federalism in Australia to protect state interests. The Senate, in its function of states' house, was specifically charged with the duty of defending the rights of the states. Actually, it was intended to perform a double task. It had to defend the rights of the states as such against subordination to the Commonwealth, and also to see to it that the interests of the weaker states were not submerged by their more powerful associates. In neither case can the Senate be said to have fulfilled the hopes which were placed in it.[15] The reason is principally to be found in the fact that under the Australian federal system the Senate is incontestably the weaker House. Since the government is dependent for its existence upon a majority in the House of Representatives the Senate can hope to exercise but slight influence over it. Moreover, the powers of the Senate in relation to money bills are severely restricted. Proposed laws for the appropriation of moneys or the imposition of taxation may not originate in the Senate, nor may such laws be amended by the Senate if they appropriate revenue 'for the ordinary annual services of the

14. The term used by the Grants Commission for those states seeking special assistance from the Commonwealth—i.e., South Australia, Western Australia and Tasmania. Its use enables the avoidance of the lengthy phrase "the three less populous primary-producing states."

15. *Ibid.*, p. 46.

government.' Neither may the Senate amend any law so as to increase any charge upon the people.[16]   The inferior powers of the Senate are not, however, the only cause of its ineffectiveness as a guardian of state interests.   The tendency has been for senators to group themselves along party, rather than state, lines. This was prophesied by many who took part in the convention debates.   They saw that the struggle over industrial questions would lead to a strengthening of party organisation and render it unlikely that the divisions within the Senate would be along geographical lines.   That is precisely what has happened.   In effect, a candidate, if he is to have any prospect of success, must obtain the endorsement of one or other of the political parties.   This has meant that there was little likelihood of all the senators from any one state adopting a united front, except when they all belonged to the same party, and still less of a coalition representing any group of states for the defence of purely state interests.

The failure of the Senate to function as a states' house, together with its subordination to the House of Representatives, has left the interests of the states and, more particularly, the interests of the weaker states insufficiently protected, if the federal union as originally conceived by those who drew up the constitution was to be preserved.   Western Australia, for instance, complains of the complete inadequacy of her representation in the lower house.   She does not imply by this that on a population basis the state has been unfairly treated, but simply that her five members do not possess enough political power to prevent legislation which has an adverse effect upon Western Australia.   At least, it is clear that the machinery designed for the protection of the interests of individual states has been largely ineffective in its operation, since deep-rooted and long-continued antagonism on the part of a state towards federal legislation, or the more general lines of federal policy, has rarely sufficed to secure the repeal of the legislation or the alteration of the policy.[17]   That

16.   The Senate may reject a money bill altogether, but the consequences, both political and constitutional, of such an action make the power less important than it would appear to be.   See the argument in *The Case of the People of Western Australia* (1934), p. 42.

17.   However, the primary-producing states have had considerable success in securing protection for primary industries, often through the exercise of federal powers.   They have also obtained substantial financial support from the rest of Australia by grants under sec. 96, though mainly because of their inability to maintain standards comparable with those in the other states without financial assistance.

is, after all, the final test of the effectiveness of a state's opposition to a Commonwealth measure. It is a test which in the history of Australian federalism has seldom returned a verdict in favour of the state. This failure to protect the states is in many ways the most striking feature of post-federation development, primarily because it was upon the federal structure as an instrument for the protection of state interests that such reliance was placed. The extent of that failure is made plain by the considered conclusion of Western Australia that the Commonwealth constitution, 'instead of assuring unto the states their corporate life and separate existence, contains the machinery with which the Commonwealth can destroy the states.'[18] In all, it is fair to conclude that the aim of the founders has been frustrated. The states are no longer independent entities exercising a significant measure of power. They retain only the husks of an authority which has passed from them.

This decline in the power of the states was not obvious for some time, though actually the forces which would bring it about were inherent in the constitution itself through the distribution of financial control. As early as 1902 Mr. Deakin in a letter to the *Morning Post* had indicated the probability of Commonwealth domination over the states, and, with acute insight, had prophesied the course of development which would lead to the undermining of state independence. His declaration is so apposite to the present situation that it reads more like an analysis after the event than a prediction of things to come.

The rights of self-government of the States have been fondly supposed to be safeguarded by the Constitution. It has left them legally free but financially bound to the chariot wheels of the Central Government. Their need will be its opportunity. The less populous will first succumb; those smitten by drought or similar misfortunes will follow; and finally even the greatest and most prosperous will, however reluctantly, be brought to. heel. Our Constitution may remain the same, but a vital change will have taken place in the relations between the States and the Commonwealth. The Commonwealth will have acquired a general control over the states, while every extension of political power will be made by its means and go to increase its relative superiority.[19]

18. *The Case of the People of Western Australia*, pp. 37-8. The case was prepared to justify the Western Australian move for secession. In view of its anti-federal bias it should be read critically. The Commonwealth prepared a reply, entitled *The Case for Union*.
19. Quoted, *ibid.*, p. 81.

The accuracy of Deakin's contention will be apparent from a consideration of the several ways in which the decline of state authority has been brought about.

Judicial Interpretation

In Australia, under the existing federal system, there is not only a division of powers between the Commonwealth and the states, but also a separation of the judicial from the legislative and executive power.[20]. The High Court is a co-ordinate branch of the government of the Commonwealth, and does not derive its authority from the will of parliament. The court, however, because of the federal nature of the constitution, exercises a singularly important influence. Its function was conceived to be to hold the balance between the Commonwealth and the states by seeing to it that neither party violated the terms of the constitution. From a strictly legal point of view the court was not assigned the task of passing judgment upon the acts of the legislatures with the object of determining whether they were or were not a valid exercise of authority. Constitutional issues concerning the limits of Commonwealth and state jurisdiction have only been considered when relevant to a particular case in litigation before the court. Nevertheless, the effect has been to make the court the arbiter of the destiny of the component parts of the federation. When a constitutional point is raised in a case before it, the court must perform the duty of deciding whether the statute challenged is valid or not. Moreover, in Australia every effort has been made to ensure that the High Court shall be the sole interpreter of the constitution. Thus by Section 74 of the constitution no appeal is allowed to the Privy Council

> upon any decision howsoever arising as to the limits *inter se* of the constitutional powers of the Commonwealth and those of any State or States, or as to the limits *inter se* of the constitutional powers of any two or more States, unless the High Court shall certify that the question is one which ought to be determined by His Majesty in Council.[21]

And when, through the right of appeal from a state court to the Privy Council, it was discovered that the latter body was after all concerning itself with constitutional questions, the Commonwealth parliament, by Section 40A of the Judiciary Act,

20. See W. Anstey Wynes, *Legislative and Executive Powers in Australia.*
21. Section 74 of the constitution of the Commonwealth of Australia. For notes of cases see G. S. Knowles, *The Australian Constitution*, pp. 66, 74.

provided that cases 'involving questions as to the limits *inter se* of the constitutional powers of the Commonwealth and one or more states, or as to the limits *inter se* of the constitutional powers of any two or more states,'[21] must be removed from the state courts to the High Court. It should also be noted that, quite early in its career, the High Court had no hesitation in refusing to be bound by a decision of the Privy Council upon a constitutional question as to the limits *inter se.*[22]

The significance of the position occupied by the High Court in the Australian federal system is difficult to over-estimate. At all times, by placing a liberal or a narrow construction upon the sections of the constitution, it is in a position to determine whether the weight of its influence shall be thrown into the scale on the side of the Commonwealth or of the states. At a time of crisis, by force of its decisions, the High Court may well become the paramount authority in the land for determining not only legal but also indirectly political and social questions of major importance. It is somewhat perturbing to reflect that whether the court will construe the constitution in a progressive or reactionary way will depend upon the composition of the court at any given time. This breeds a sense of instability. It is also mantained by critics of the present position of the High Court that the 'authority of the Commonwealth Parliament as a law-making body has been impaired by the paramount and incalculable power of the High Court.'[23] At least, it is certain that federalism has led not only to legalism, but to a tangled legalism.

'Major shifts of interpretation' have taken place in connection with the Canadian and American, as well as the Australian, constitution. Such shifts are inevitable and occur because of the necessity of keeping pace with the outstanding changes in the society itself. Thus within the first thirty years of its existence the Australian Commonwealth had to adjust itself to the impact of a world war and a world depression. If no such attempts at adaptation were made the constitution would be subjected to an intolerable strain which might well end in disaster. Under a federal system a High Court in its capacity of interpreter of

22. 4 *C.L.R.* 1087. In *Commissioners of Taxation (N.S.W.) v. Baxter* the court held that it was not bound to follow the decision of the Privy Council in *Webb v. Outrim*, in which the Privy Council had rejected principles of interpretation adopted by the High Court (Knowles, *Australian Constitution*, pp. 66 *et seq.*).

23. *Minority Report, Commission on the Constitution* (1929), p. 245.

the constitution will of necessity be forced to modify previous decisions, and, on occasions, to overrule them altogether if it is to render the constitution compatible with the requirements of the times. Frequently these changes have been at least contemplated over a considerable period before they actually occur, and the trend is often discernible in the judgments of a dissenting minority of justices. But since a court proceeds on the basis of precedent, and since its work is done in public with a full statement of reasons, the shifts in interpretation appear to be made in jerks. However, the necessity of making such changes breeds its own difficulties. First and most important is the fact that there is always a marked lag between the methods of interpretation actually in force and the new demands brought about by changes within the social structure. New principles of interpretation may ultimately ease the strain and prevent the disruption of the constitution, but they usually occur only after a period in which the imperfections of the constitution as expounded have become obvious to all. Moreover, manoeuvres of this sort are at best palliatives, and suffer from the additional disadvantage that the adjustment frequently lags far behind the need for change. Secondly, there is the inevitable confusion caused in making the adjustment, since previous decisions have to be overruled and previous principles of interpretation abandoned. In Australia this has led to the impression that an 'erratic' course of interpretation has been pursued by the High Court bench.

No one body of principles has been consistently followed since the inception of federation. For twenty years, with inconsistencies and with a minority of the court dissenting, a particular conception of federalism held sway. After that period it was challenged and overthrown, and another substituted for it. The inconsistency displayed by the High Court has deprived both the Commonwealth and the states of any sense of certainty as to the scope of their powers. The result has been duplication, collision, doubt as to whether a subject was within the competence of the state or the Commonwealth or neither. Of course, much of the difficulty is inherent in federalism itself, but changed principles of interpretation have added to the problem.

For instance, in *D'Emden v. Pedder*[24] it was decided that when a state attempted to utilize its authority in such a way as to

24. 1 *C.L.R.* 91; Knowles, *op. cit.*, p. 107.

interfere with the free exercise of the legislative or executive power of the Commonwealth the attempt, unless expressly authorized by the constitution, was to that extent invalid. But in later cases decisions were given which asserted that the rule in *D'Emden v. Pedder* had to be interpreted reciprocally, which meant the triumph of the principle of mutual non-interference. In the *Railway Servants' Case*[25] this reciprocal doctrine was applied rather than the true doctrine of the supremacy of Commonwealth law. The result was confusion, because the decisions given in different cases were at variance with one another. Thus the decision in the *Railway Servants' Case* was in direct conflict with that reached in the *Steel Rails Case* (*Attorney-General for N.S.W. v. Collector of Customs for N.S.W.*)[26], where it was decided that nothing prohibited the Commonwealth Customs Act from being applied to the importation of steel rails by a state. To add to the confusion brought about by conflicting High Court judgments was the fact that different principles of interpretation were being employed by the High Court and the Privy Council in coming to their decisions. Actually, the most devastating criticism of the position has been made by members of the High Court itself. Isaacs J., in delivering judgment in the *Engineers' Case*, analysed the state of affairs which at that time existed:

> The more the decisions are examined, and compared with each other and with the constitution itself, the more evident it becomes that no clear principle can account for them. They are sometimes at variance with the natural meaning of the text of the constitution; some are irreconcilable with others, and some are individually rested on reasons not founded on the words of the constitution or on any recognised principle of the common law underlying the expressed terms of the constitution, but on implication drawn from what is called the principle of 'necessity,' that being itself referable to no more definite standard than the personal opinion of the Judge who declares it. The attempt to deduce any consistent rule from them has not only failed, but has disclosed an increasing entanglement and uncertainty, and a conflict both with the text of the constitution and with distinct and clear declarations of law by the Privy Council.[27]

The first High Court supported the viewpoint adopted by the majority of those who had framed the constitution. The justices, in Professor Bailey's phrase, 'began with the states,' and

25. 4 *C.L.R.* (1906), 488.   26 5. *C.L.R.* (1908), 818.
27. 28 *C.L.R.* (1920), p. 142. Isaacs, J., delivering judgment in the *Amalgamated Society of Engineers v. The Adelaide Steamship Co. Ltd. and Others.*

held that the intention had been for the states to keep all powers except those enumerated ones which were surrendered to the Commonwealth.   That meant that Commonwealth powers must be exercised 'subject to an implied prohibition against interfering with the powers reserved to the States.'[28]   It was probably the desire to preserve state autonomy, which was responsible for the ascendancy of the doctrines of 'implied prohibitions' and 'the immunity of instrumentalities,' though actually they were reciprocal and first employed in a case in the Commonwealth interest. American constitutional practice was the chief influence leading to the acceptance of the doctrine of 'immunity of instrumentalities.'[29]   Considerable emphasis was set by the justices of the first High Court upon the guidance afforded by American cases.   For instance, Griffith, C.J., in *D'Emden v. Pedder*, dealt exhaustively with the question of how much weight should be attached to American constitutional practice in deciding cases before the Australian High Court.   After declaring that any judge would require courage not to accept a well-established interpretation of the United States constitution, he concluded:

> So far, therefore, as the United States constitution and the constitution of the Commonwealth are similar, the construction put upon the former by the Supreme Court of the United States may well be regarded by us in construing the constitution of the Commonwealth, not as an infallible guide, but as a most welcome aid and assistance.[30]

As a consequence, rules of construction based upon a supposed obligation to maintain intact the independence of both states and Commonwealth within the federation were endorsed by the High Court.   The opinion, therefore, prevailed that neither the Commonwealth nor a state could in any way control or interfere with the free exercise of the legislative or executive power of the other, unless expressly authorized by the constitution.

The first case before the High Court, in which the doctrine of the immunity of instrumentalities[31] found expression was that of *D'Emden v. Pedder*.   An attempt had been made by the government of Tasmania to collect stamp duty on the salary of a federal public servant.   The Attorney-General for the Common-

---

28. K. H. Bailey, in *Studies in the Australian Constitution*, p. 42.
29. For the history of inter-governmental immunity in the United States see Walter Pond, "Inter-governmental Immunity: A Comparative Study of the Federal System." *Iowa Law Review*, xxvi. (1941).
30. 1 *C.L.R.* 112 (1904).
31. For a tabulation of the Australian cases concerned with the doctrine of the immunity of instrumentalities and implied prohibition see Knowles, *op. cit.*, pp. 107-110.

wealth successfully appealed for the application of the principle enunciated by Marshall, C.J., in *McCulloch v. Maryland,* that one government was by implication forbidden to interfere with the action taken by another provided such action was within its constitutional powers. Marshall, C.J., said:

> There is a plain repugnance, in conferring on one government a power to control the constitutional measures of another, which other, with respect to those very measures, is declared to be supreme over that which exerts the control.[32]

It was held, therefore, by following this line of reasoning, that the stamp duty constituted an interference with a federal agency or instrumentality, and was on that ground invalid. 'A right of sovereignty,' said Griffith, C.J., 'subject to extrinsic control is a contradiction in terms.'[33] It followed consequentially that the Commonwealth, within the limits of the authority conferred upon it by the constitution, was entitled to exercise its powers 'in absolute freedom.'

In the first place, then, the doctrine had been invoked for the protection of the Commonwealth power, but its real significance was only realized when, in the *Railway Servants' Case,*[34] the High Court declared that the rule was to be regarded as reciprocal. Attempted interference by the Commonwealth with state instrumentalities was equally invalid. It was just as necessary, it was argued, for a state to preserve its agencies unimpaired as for the Commonwealth. In both cases the claim to immunity was based upon 'necessary implication,' and that claim was, in turn, 'upheld by the great law of self-preservation.'[35] But to come within the ambit of the doctrine it had to be shown that an instrumentality was 'governmental.' The significance of the *Railway Servants' Case* lay not only in the reciprocal application of the rule of implied prohibition, but also in the decision that state railways were covered by the term 'governmental.' In that way they were excluded from the jurisdiction of the Commonwealth Arbitration Court.

Although the effect of these decisions was far-reaching, definite limits were set to the doctrine. It was decided[36] that it had no

32. Quoted by Griffith, C.J., in *D'Emden v. Pedder* (1. *C.L.R.* 111).
33. 1. *C.L.R.*, 110.
34. 4 (1) *C.L.R.* (1906), 488. *The Federated Amalgamated Government Railway and Tramway Service Association v. The N.S.W. Rail Traffic Employees' Association.*
35. 4 (1) *C.L.R.*, Nelson, J., of the Supreme Court of the United States, quoted by Griffith, C.J., p. 538.
36. 5 *C.L.R.* 818 (1908), *Attorney-General of N.S.W. v. Collector of Customs for N.S.W.*, Knowles, *op. cit.*, p. 25.

application to the levying of customs duties on goods imported by
a state government, even when the goods were steel rails for use
upon what was admitted to be a government instrumentality. The
decision sprang from the realisation that at some stage there must
inevitably be interference with state liberty of action if the enumerated powers of the Commonwealth were to be utilised effectively.
The principle to be applied was succinctly phrased by Mr. Justice
Barton when he said 'If the grant is exclusive, the control is absolute.'[37]

However, broadly speaking, the interpretation which held sway
until 1920 was that based upon mutual non-interference. It had
been challenged before, but not successfully, until the *Engineers'
Case* in 1920.[38] That case saw the triumph of a new method of
interpretation. The counsel for the various intervening states
maintained that the reciprocal effect of the rule laid down in
D'Emden v. Pedder was a well-established constitutional principle
and a right one. That is, they stood for the accepted position.
But the Commonwealth challenged the whole foundation of past
construction and asked that the constitution be interpreted according to the ordinary rules applicable to a statute. The new argument
was favourably received by a bench whose personnel had recently
been altered. The High Court, therefore, proceeded to over-rule
past cases which had been decided according to the doctrine of
mutual non-interference. The idea of an implied prohibition was
no longer accepted, and those who relied upon some limitation for
the protection of state power had to point to an actual restriction
within the constitution. It was also emphasized that the Privy
Council had rejected the principle of non-interference, and that
though it had been reaffirmed by the High Court a minority had
not viewed it with favour.

The argument which now found acceptance in the eyes of the
High Court began with the powers of the Commonwealth rather
than with those of the states. Full meaning had first to be given to
the Commonwealth powers, and only after that had been done
could the residue left to the states be determined. During the
Engineers' Case the court dealt also with the principles upon which
the constitution was to be construed. It rejected the methods previously employed on the grounds that they were based upon 'necessity,' and that 'necessity' as a standard by which to interpret the
constitution meant

37.   5 *C.L.R.* 836.
38.   28 *C.L.R.* 129 (1920). *The Amalgamated Society of Engineers v. The
Adelaide Steamship Co. Ltd. and Others.* Knowles, *op. cit.*, pp. 109-112.

depending on an implication which is formed on a vague, individual conception of the spirit of the compact, which is not the result of interpreting any specific language to be quoted, nor referable to any recognised principle of the common law of the constitution . . . but arrived at by the court on the opinions of judges as to hopes and expectations respecting vague external conditions.[39]

In place of the principle of 'necessity' the court proposed that the constitution should be expounded 'according to its own terms, finding the intention from the words of the compact and upholding it throughout precisely as framed.'[39]   Interpretation was to be modelled upon the attitude adopted by the Privy Council, that is, it was to proceed according to the 'ordinary rules of construction applicable to a statute.'[40]   In short, the language used in the constitution was to be the basis for interpretation, and no attention was to be paid to such extra-legal considerations as the consequences which might follow a decision.   This complete change of front on the part of the High Court in 1920 has had a very vital effect upon the relations between the states and Commonwealth within the federation.   It has led to an expansion of Commonwealth powers which, though desirable enough in itself, would nevertheless have astonished those responsible for the phraseology in which the Commonwealth grant of power was drafted.   It has helped to place the Commonwealth in a position of very great relative superiority in its relations with the states.   Indeed, there can be little doubt that judicial interpretation, particularly after the *Engineers' Case,* has been one of the most powerful centripetal forces at work within the federation.

In the *Engineers' Case* the actual decision proved important, as well as the laying down of new lines of constitutional interpretation.   By a majority the court over-ruled the *Railway Servants' Case,* in which it had been decided that employees upon a state government railway did not come within the jurisdiction of the federal Arbitration Court.   In future, however, no differentiation was to be made between industrial employees of a state and those of a private employer.   If a dispute could be shown to exist within the meaning of the section the Commonwealth arbitration machinery would come into operation.   Thus, as the result of a single decision, the Commonwealth was enabled to expand greatly its authority over industrial disputes, though its control of industrial matters generally was still severely restricted and far from adequate. From the point of view of the states the decision was a severe blow,

39.   28. *C.L.R.* 145, Isaacs, J., delivering judgment.
40.   28 *C.L.R.* 139, Leverrier, K.C., for the Commonwealth

since state governments in large measure lost control over the mechanism by which the working conditions of employees on government-owned industrial enterprises were prescribed. The states have protested repeatedly and vociferously against what they regard as an unwarranted invasion of their sphere of activity, but have so far been unable to procure a return to the old position.[41] Indeed, the trend has been all the other way. The expansion of the Commonwealth arbitration power was carried still further in a direction which the states did not like by decisions based upon the *Engineers' Case*. In that case the court had laid it down that the true doctrine was the 'supremacy of Commonwealth law over state law where they meet on any field.'[42] It was but a natural extension of this ruling to determine, as was done in *Clyde Engineering Co. Ltd. v. Cowburn (Forty-four Hours Case)*,[43] that once a Commonwealth award had been made a state parliament could not alter its terms or impose rights or obligations inconsistent with those terms By judicial decision, therefore, an award of the Commonwealth Arbitration Court had been rendered superior to a state statute, and in the field over which it arbitrated the court had been made immeasurably more powerful.

The principles adopted in the *Engineers' Case* had consequences also in the field of taxation, for in the *Commonwealth v. State of Queensland*[44] it was decided that interest on Commonwealth bonds could be exempted from state taxation. The High Court agreed that section 52B of the *Commonwealth Inscribed Stock Act* 1911-18, which provided that

> the interest derived from stock or Treasury bonds shall not be liable to income tax under any law of the Commonwealth or a state unless the interest is declared to be so liable by that prospectus relating to the loan on which the interest is payable,[45]

was a valid exercise of the power conferred on the Commonwealth by section 51 (iv) (i.e., borrowing money on the public credit of the Commonwealth). Since the doctrine of implied prohibition had been rejected, there was no exemption of state bonds from Commonwealth taxation. The Commonwealth, however, decided to deal with the matter by legislation providing that interest on state

---

41. It is at least doubtful whether in recent years the states have been sincere in demanding a return to their own control. In any event the case of the states is undeniably weak. It has been pointed out that not even in the United States are state industrial undertakings immune from control by valid United States law.
42. 28 *C.L.R.* 158.
43. 37 *C.L.R.* 466 (1926). For cases dealing with control of state undertakings under section 51 (xxxv) see Knowles, *op. cit.*, pp. 34-6.
44. 29. *C.L.R.* 1 (1920).   45. See Knowles, *op. cit.*, p. 26.

bonds should be subject to Commonwealth taxation. At the same time the Commonwealth made a concession to the states by subjecting its own bonds to state taxation. But this concession proved to be an empty one, since state taxation was not to operate until a date fixed by proclamation. This was never done, so that Commonwealth bonds, in fact, remained free from state taxation. In 1931, however, the Commonwealth abandoned any intention of subjecting Commonwealth bonds to state taxation by announcing that new Commonwealth securities would be exempt.[46]

It is not, however, only in relation to arbitration and industrial issues that the powers of the states have been affected by judicial decision. The judgments given in *The King v. Sutton*,[47] and in *A.G. for N.S.W. v. Collector of Customs*,[48] where in each case it was held that the Commonwealth had the right to levy customs duty on goods imported by a state, were a bitter blow to the states. The claimant states, in particular, have argued that these decisions imposed a severe handicap upon the developmental policies which they have attempted to carry out. At the same time it is difficult to see how any other decision was possible. The Commonwealth had been given an exclusive power over customs, and if the states had been permitted to import without payment of duty whatever they liked (and subsequently sell within the respective state boundaries) the grant of power to the Commonwealth would have become a farce. Even those judges who held most firmly to the doctrine of immunity of instrumentalities did not believe that it was possible to read into the constitution an implication which would run so obviously counter to the clear intention of the wording.[49] A more unexpected and even less pleasant surprise awaited the states when the Commonwealth action of appropriating what would have been surplus revenue and paying it into a trust fund was held to be within its legal competence.[50] Despite the legal decision, all the states regarded the action taken by the Commonwealth upon this point as a moral infringement of the constitution. Again the interpretation given to section 92, which declares that trade among the states shall be absolutely free, has seriously af-

46. For a discussion of this matter see Walter Pond, "Inter-governmental Immunity," *Iowa Law Review*, xxvi (1941).
47. 5. *C.L.R.* 789 (1908). Wire netting had been imported by the N.S.W. government. The High Court held that the customs act 1901 applied to goods imported by the government of a state.
48. 5 *C.L.R.* 818 (1908). A state had to pay duty even when importing rails for use in connection with a state-owned railway.
49. This is the view of Professor K. H. Bailey.
50. *N.S.W. v. The Commonwealth*, 7. *C.L.R.* 179 (1908).

fected the powers of the states, since many attempts at the regulation of commerce and the marketing of goods have been either hampered or altogether prevented by judicial decision.[51]

In a number of cases decided in the years immediately before the outbreak of war in 1939, there was, as Walter Pond has demonstrated,[52] a tendency on the part of the High Court to modify the application of the doctrine which was laid down so emphatically in the *Engineers' Case*. The High Court to some extent departed from the exclusive emphasis on the supremacy of the Commonwealth and began to take into consideration 'the existence of the states as an integral part of the federal structure.' The trend in this direction may be instanced by three cases: *Victoria v. Commonwealth* (1937), *Tasmanian Steamers Proprietary v. Lang* (1938), and, most important, *West v. Commissioner of Taxation* (1937). In *Victoria v. Commonwealth*[53] the question arose of inconsistency between Commonwealth and state law. By the *Marine Act* the Victorian Parliament had legislated for the removal, at the instance of a state authority, of any ship sunk in a Victorian port. But the *Commonwealth Navigation Act* also provided for the removal, at the instance of a Commonwealth authority, of any ship sunk on the Australian coast. In spite of the fact that the Commonwealth and state legislation dealt with the same situation the High Court held that the provisions of the state *Marine Act* were not invalid on the ground of inconsistency with the Commonwealth law.

The second case (*Tasmanian Steamers Proprietary v. Lang*)[54] was the result of an apparent conflict between state legislation and an award of the Commonwealth Arbitration Court. Acting under a provision of the New South Wales *Special Income and Wages Tax (Management) Act, 1936*, an employer deducted from the wages of an employee the state wages tax and then paid the balance of the wages owed to him. Trouble, however, arose from the fact that the balance was less than 'the minimum rate of cash wage' laid down by the award of the Commonwealth Court of Conciliation and Arbitration. In view of the decision in the *Forty-Four Hours Case* it was anticipated that the state legislation would be invalidated, but the High Court ruled that the provision of the state act was not inconsistent with the award of the Commonwealth court.

The third case (*West v. Commissioner of Taxation*)[55] was even more important because it revealed the changes that were taking

51. e.g., *James v. S.A.*, 40 *C.L.R.* 1 (1927). *Peanut Board v. Rockhampton Harbour Board*, 48 *C.L.R.* 266 (1933).
52. *Op. cit.*   53. 58 *C.L.R.* 618 (1937).   54. 60 *C.L.R.* 111 (1938).
55. 56 *C.L.R.* 657 (1937).

place in the application of the doctrine of the *Engineers' Case.*
West, a retired Commonwealth official, 'challenged the right of the
State of New South Wales to subject his pension to a non-
discriminatory income tax.' West appeared to be in an unassailable position, for previous judgments had been based on the principle of the immunity of federal instrumentalities unless the Commonwealth waived the immunity.[56] This had been done with regard to federal salaries by the *Commonwealth Salaries Act, 1907,*
but pensions were not included, and were therefore thought to be
exempt from state taxation. The High Court, however, took a
different view, and in doing so clearly indicated that a departure
had been made from the doctrine accepted in a number of previous
cases. Latham, C.J., declared:

> The *Engineers' Case* involves the proposition that the *Com-*
> *monwealth Salaries Act, 1907,* is the source of the power of the
> states to tax federal salaries by way of income tax. . . . This
> proposition, however, depends upon the doctrine that a general
> income tax act passed by one parliament is inconsistent with an
> act passed by another parliament fixing rates of salaries. It will
> be seen that this proposition cannot now be maintained. . . .
> Thus, in so far as *Deakin v. Webb* and *Baxter v. Commissioners*
> *of Taxation* decide, in so far as *Chaplin's Case* assumes, and
> in so far as the *Engineers' Case* may by implication support the
> view that there is inconsistency in such case, these cases can no
> longer be regarded as good law.[57]

The High Court decided that unless Commonwealth legislation
existed prohibiting, in whole or in part, the taxation by the states of
the pensions of retired Commonwealth officials, the pensions could
be taxed by a state law provided that the tax was imposed 'generally upon the income of each citizen of the state, and to the same
extent.' By this decision the High Court both sustained a state
law and introduced a change in the application of section 109 'as
the basis of federal supremacy.' The judgment had, moreover,
this important result. Hitherto silence on the part of the Commonwealth parliament had been interpreted as implying that the Commonwealth wished to exclude its instrumentality from the application of state legislation, whereas now the implication to be drawn
from Commonwealth silence was that the Commonwealth wished
state law to apply to its instrumentalities. Pond points out that

> In spite of this, however, the doctrine of the West case is still
> predominantly based on federal supremacy. For a state law to

---

56. e.g., *Chaplin v. Commissioner of Taxes for South Australia,* 12 *C.L.R.* 375
(1911), upheld in the *Engineers' Case.* See Knowles, *op. cit.,* p. 108.
57. 56 *C.L.R.,* pp. 667, 670. Quoted Pond, *Iowa Law Review,* xxvi (1941),
295.

apply to a federal instrumentality two conditions must be fulfilled: (1) the Commonwealth must not have expressly excluded the state law's application; (2) the state law must not discriminate against the Commonwealth. According to the majority of the High Court, the Commonwealth has power to exclude by legislation the application of state law in relation to a matter entrusted by the constitution to the control of the Commonwealth.[58]

Pond goes on to remark that though some of the judges in the West case, for instance, Dixon, J., adhered to the doctrine that the invalidity of a discriminatory state law was due to section 109, others enunciated a point of view very different from that espoused in the *Engineers' Case.* Thus Latham, C.J., declared:

A state act, imposing a discriminatory tax upon Commonwealth officers or pensioners might well be regarded as not being within the power of a state parliament to make laws for the peace, welfare and good government of the state. It would be legislation specifically dealing with matters relating to the government of the Commonwealth, with which the state parliament has no concern, and not relating to the government of the state. A corresponding objection would apply in the case of Commonwealth legislation specifically singling out state servants for discriminatory taxation.[59]

Pond's conclusion is that the position adopted by Latham, C.J., leans in the direction of

a new doctrine of mutual non-interference, based upon the dual system of government in a federal state, and therefore necessarily reciprocal, but distinguishable from the old rule in *D'Emden v. Pedder* in two ways: (1) Its application is much more limited, non-discriminatory taxation not being any longer regarded as an infringement of the rule in *D'Emden v. Pedder;* and (2) the Commonwealth can limit the area of the applicability of state law by declaring the intention to exempt its instrumentalities.[60]

The recent decisions of the High Court in the cases referred to above have indicated that there has been some swing away from the doctrine of the *Engineers' Case,* though whether that doctrine can be said to have been undermined 'to such a degree that the remaining structure seems hollow and ready to collapse'[61] is open to very grave doubt. Moreover, doubt as to whether judicial in-

58. *Iowa Law Review,* xxvi. 296.
59. *Ibid.,* p. 297, quoting 56 *C.L.R.,* p. 668.
60. *Ibid.,* p. 298.
61. Pond's judgment. On the subject of the invalidity of discriminatory legislation see the important views of Evatt, J., in *West v. Commissioner of Taxation,* 56 *C.L.R.* 657.

terpretation is now operating strongly to protect the state units would only be strengthened by an analysis of the decisions given by the High Court since war began in 1939. Though limits have been set to the defence power, a wide and liberal construction has still been placed upon it, while the decision in favour of the Commonwealth in the *Uniform Tax Case*[62] enormously strengthened the position of the Commonwealth in its dealings with the states. That position was made all the stronger because the Tax Act and the priority clause (and probably also the Grants Act) were not held to depend for their validity upon the defence power. The justices also rejected the contention of the states that since the constitution was federal in character the Commonwealth could not exercise any of its powers 'in such a way as to impede the essential activities of the states' and adhered to the principles governing earlier decisions, notably the *Engineers' Case* of 1920. In this instance, therefore, a High Court judgment favoured the legality of Commonwealth legislation which, by still further strengthening Commonwealth domination of state finances, rendered state independence ever more precarious.

In all, it would seem fair to conclude that judicial interpretation has been one of the factors responsible for undermining the autonomy of the states. Commonwealth powers have proved more expansive than was anticipated, while, since the *Engineers' Case,* a system of interpretation has been in force which has progressively favoured the Commonwealth at the expense of the states. There are, necessarily, definite limits within which judicial decision is effective as a means of altering the balance of the constitution, but within those limits it cannot be doubted that the interpretation given to the constitution by the High Court has led to the aggrandizement of the Commonwealth and the decline of the states.

Financial Relations of the Commonwealth and the States

A factor of even greater importance than judicial interpretation in bringing about the decline in state independence has been the financial relations between the Commonwealth and the states. The political success of a federation depends very largely upon whether the financial resources of the federation are distributed in such a way as to enable each of the component parts to carry out the functions entrusted to them without serious dislocation of their economic life. It is the distribution of financial power which gives shape to the character of the federation by determining where the preponderating influence shall lie. Financial and fiscal relations are likely, therefore, to decide where actual power shall reside, and

62. 65 *C.L.R.* 373 (1942)'.

that decision may in practice considerably modify the nominal constitutional position.

From the first the Commonwealth was in a dominant financial position. It was given the exclusive right of imposing duties of customs and excise and the power to tax in all other fields. Apart from customs and excise, the states retained their powers of taxation.[63] But by the surrender of the tariff the states had relinquished their most important source of revenue, and since over all other sources of taxation the Commonwealth possessed concurrent powers, the states were at the mercy of the Commonwealth whenever it chose to invade any field of state taxation. Whether the financial division of power within a federation is satisfactory can only be judged in relation to the functions which the various units have to carry out. It is upon the application of this test that the inadequacy of the financial structure becomes apparent for, while the Commonwealth was given superior revenue resources, the states retained the more expensive responsibilities, such as land settlement and the provision of a majority of the social services.[64]

Financial relations were discussed as often as any other subject at the convention debates, and the solution reached was not due to any failure to explore possible alternatives. However, the outlook of the framers was bounded by limitations of time and by the necessities of the immediate situation. They had to allot certain functions to the Commonwealth quite irrespective of their cost or of the revenue which might be derived from their exercise, simply because they were national in character. Moreover, they believed that government, particularly by the Commonwealth, but also by the states, was going to be a comparatively inexpensive business. They did not foresee the rapid development of the social service state and the vast increase in expenditure that it would involve. At the same time, there was a demand that the states, having surrendered their customs revenue, should receive some guarantee of financial stability. That could only be done by a redistribution of a percentage of Commonwealth revenue, and it is probable that without some such return federation could not have been achieved.[65] None of the proposals put forward for redistribution were really considered satisfactory, but that made by Braddon was finally accepted at the Melbourne conference of premiers in January, 1899.

63. See *Report*, Commonwealth Grants Commission, 1933, Ch. II., Federation and Financial Adjustments, for a summary of the financial provisions of the constitution.
64. See "The Working of Federalism in Australia," *Round Table*, March, 1935.
65. *The Case of the People of Western Australia*, p. 67.

It was one of several clauses inserted to safeguard, at least temporarily, the financial interests of the states. Four provisions were laid down.[66] For the first ten years, and thereafter till parliament otherwise provided, three-quarters of the customs and excise revenue was to be paid to the states. Western Australia was specially permitted to retain its customs revenue for five years on a diminishing yearly scale. All surplus revenue was to be paid to the states. The Commonwealth was given power to make financial grants to the states.

Ironically enough, the emphatic insistence upon the maintenance of state rights at the conventions was to a large extent offset by the financial provisions of the constitution. The Braddon clause was at most a temporary safeguard to the financial stability of the states. Once the ten-year period covered by the clause had expired the financial relations between the Commonwealth and the states was a matter to be determined solely by the Commonwealth parliament itself. By the insertion of sections 87 and 96 the framers of the constitution had not only placed the Commonwealth in an unassailable financial position, but had also failed to secure for the states the only guarantee which would have ensured the stability of the federal form and the maintenance of the independence of the states within the limits assigned to them, namely, financial security for all units of the federation.

As already indicated, one reason why the Commonwealth was placed in a superior financial position was simply that such a situation was difficult to avoid. Customs receipts played a large part in state revenues, yet if the union was to have any meaning at all obviously the control over customs had to be an exclusive Commonwealth power. The main outcome of the financial provisions of the constitution has been that the financial history of the federation has largely consisted of an attempt by the states to secure from the Commonwealth some recognition that the states must receive a guarantee of adequate financial assistance, if they were to perform effectively the functions allotted to them. It might be argued that, in view of the non-existence of provisions within the constitution guaranteeing continued payments to the states, the states have met with considerable success in their endeavours to secure assistance. But over against the receipt of Commonwealth payments, whether regular or special, must be set the fact that without them the union would have broken down completely. The Commonwealth possessed the requisite financial power to govern, but lacked the legal authority in many of the most important fields of government,

66. *Report*, Grants Commission, 1933, p. 19.

whereas the states possessing legal power over many important subject matters would have been, without financial assistance from the Commonwealth, incapable of taking action. Perhaps the best proof of the contention that the assistance of the Commonwealth was due to recognition of the financial plight of the states, of their incapacity to govern effectively without aid, is the adoption of the principle of needs by the Grants Commission as the basis of grants of assistance to the weaker states. Without financial independence constitutional guarantees of state autonomy become a mockery, yet under Australian conditions the states have been financially dependent on the Commonwealth. The measure of that dependence affords an indication of the decline in their autonomy.

In effect, the financial provisions of the constitution established what has been called the bookkeeping period in Australian federal history.[67]   Under this system the states were credited with revenues raised in the states and debited with the cost of transferred departments and with a percentage of Commonwealth expenditure. The bookkeeping system was maintained until the expiration of the ten-year Braddon clause, though by the *Surplus Revenue Act,* 1908, the population of the states was adopted as a basis for revenue distribution. Throughout this first period the states received back three-quarters of the customs and excise revenue and an additional five million pounds. Both Commonwealth and states seem to have been able to preserve 'a reasonably sound financial position.'[68]

Nevertheless, even in this first period, signs were not wanting that financial relations were liable to alter in a manner disadvantageous to the states. Until 1906-7 the Commonwealth paid out its surplus revenue to the states, but in the following year it proceeded to appropriate money for trust accounts which meant that, although all Commonwealth moneys might not have been expended in any one year, technically there would be no surplus.[69]

67. *Report,* Commission on the Constitution, 1929, p. 187.
68. *Report,* Grants Commission, 1933, p. 29.
69. Section 81 of the constitution reads: "All revenues or moneys raised or received by the Executive Government of the Commonwealth shall form one Consolidated Revenue Fund, to be appropriated for the purposes of the Commonwealth in the manner and subject to the charges and liabilities imposed by this Constitution." The section has been interpreted by the Commonwealth as conferring a right of appropriation not limited to subjects specifically covered by a Commonwealth grant of power. Instances of acts which depend for their validity upon this interpretation of Section 81 are: *Maternity Allowance Act,* 1912-26; *Science and Industry Endowment Act,* 1926; *Australian War Memorial Act,* 1925; *Wheat Pool Advances Act,* 1923; *Belgian Grant Act,* 1914; *Westralian Farmers Agricultural Act,* 1921; and numerous others. See *The Case of the People of Western Australia,* p. 77, and Knowles, *op. cit.,* pp. 76-7.

Instances of this procedure were the *Coast Defence Appropriation Act* and the *Old Age Pensions Appropriation Act,* both of 1908. The validity of such legislation was not allowed to go unchallenged, but in *N.S.W. v. The Commonwealth* the High Court declared the practice constitutional. Despite the decision, the States have continued to feel that they have a legitimate grievance.

Mr. Butler, Premier of South Australia in 1933, declared: The history of the surplus revenue provisions is an example of the way in which provisions of the Constitution originally inserted for the protection of the states, and to secure their financial position, have completely failed to attain their object.[70]

It had always been understood that the financial relations established at the commencement of federation were of a temporary character. When, therefore, the ten-year period, during which the states received back three-quarters of the customs revenue, was coming to a close anxiety was felt concerning the future stability of state finances. Numerous conferences were held between the states, and at some of these the Commonwealth was represented. In 1909 an agreement was reached whereby the Commonwealth was to submit proposals to the people for the alteration of the constitution.[71] These dealt principally with the transference of state debts and with the payment to the states of 'a sum calculated at the rate of twenty-five shillings per annum per head of population.' But the proposal to incorporate a fixed payment to the states in the constitution was defeated at the referendum, largely on the ground that it would unduly fetter the Commonwealth. In spite of this defeat the scheme, as agreed upon, was adopted and put into effect by the Commonwealth government. There was, however, this significant difference. Since no constitutional amendment had been carried, the Commonwealth might terminate the payments whenever it desired. Actually, they were continued until their abolition by the *States Grants Act* in 1927. But proposals to suspend them were made several years earlier, and it can be said that the states experienced a feeling of continual insecurity. Nor should it be imagined that the states were content with the sum of twenty-five shillings a head of population. They repeatedly sought to obtain a larger share of Commonwealth revenue, and particularly urged that they had a right to a percentage of customs receipts.

The financial consequence of the substitution of the *per capita* agreement for the redistribution of surplus customs revenue was

70. Statement by the Hon. R. L. Butler at the Premiers' Conference, 1933. Support for this opinion may be found in the *Report*, Grants Commission, 1933, p. 20.
71. For the terms of this agreement see *Report*, Commission on the Constitution, 1929, p. 189.

that the states fared badly. An analysis of the effects of the change-over has been made by the Grants Commission.[72] It reveals that three-quarters of the net customs and excise revenue for the first two years of the new period beginning 1 July 1910 would have yielded about twenty million pounds, whereas the states actually received only eleven and a half million pounds, or fifty-seven per cent. of that amount. Throughout the whole period from federation to 1926-7, three-quarters of the customs revenue would have equalled about three hundred and sixty-three million pounds, instead of which the states received some one hundred and ninety-two millions or fifty-three per cent. The Commonwealth, therefore, retained a vastly increased proportion of its revenue, with the result that there were Commonwealth surpluses and state deficits. Despite the fact that the states received far less than they would have done if the Braddon system had remained in operation, yet it is doubtful whether this affords any proof of the unfairness of the *per capita* scheme since the limitation of the Braddon clause to a ten-year period shows that it was realised from the start that the Braddon system would become unworkable once the Commonwealth really commenced to utilize its powers. Some such increase in the amount of money retained by the Commonwealth was undoubtedly necessary, because the Central Government was attempting to carry out national and social policies such as defence and old-age pensions.

An integral part of the new system of redistribution adopted in 1910 was that of special grants to the weaker states. For instance, by virtue of the 1909 agreement, Western Australia was to receive an additional sum of £250,000, which was to diminish at the rate of £10,000 a year. It should be noticed, however, that half this sum was to be found by deducting it from the amounts due to the other states. Western Australia was thus specially favoured, because of the large *per capita* contribution which she made to the customs revenue. Tasmania, likewise, received aid from the Commonwealth in the form of special grants. In 1912, she was given a sum of £95,000, which was to be continued over a ten-year period at a diminishing rate of £10,000, and when this grant terminated arrangements were made for further annual payments in the following years. It can, therefore, be seen that a redistribution of Commonwealth revenue, both in the form of the *per capita* payments and as special grants, was a regular feature of financial relations after 1910.[73]

72. *Report*, 1933, p. 22.
73. A table of special grants made to Western Australia, Tasmania and South Australia will be found in the *Report*, Grants Commission, 1933, p. 26.

The war next upset the balance of the financial system and raised new and acute problems, such as that of double taxation.[74] Hitherto the states had been able to finance themselves more or less satisfactorily because the Commonwealth had, with the exception of the Land Tax of 1910, left the field of direct taxation to the states.[75] During the war, however, the Commonwealth undertook large commitments, and to pay its way began to impose direct taxation. The years 1914 and 1915 saw the imposition of the *Estate Duties Act* and of the *Income Tax Act*. What this has meant to the states in the way of restricting their sphere of taxation can be judged from the direct taxation collections made between July 1, 1909, and June 30, 1933.[76] During that period the Commonwealth received two hundred and eighty-seven million pounds, or more than half the four hundred and thirty-eight million pounds which went to the states. In view of these figures it can hardly be denied that the entry of the Commonwealth into the field of direct taxation had important repercussions on the finances of the states. At the same time recent events have cast serious doubt upon the validity of the contention, reputedly advanced by the states, that the scale of direct taxation imposed by the Commonwealth, even in earlier years, did in a real sense restrict the field of taxation open to the states. The doubt would remain, even if the qualification were made that the possibilities of increasing taxation depend to a considerable extent upon the political situation at the time.

The position of the states was also made very much worse by another factor which had scarcely been contemplated. In 1909 the *per capita* grant had been fixed at twenty-five shillings, but by 1920 the real value of the £ had depreciated by almost half. The states should, therefore, have been receiving roughly double the amounts which they did if they were to derive the same benefit from the redistribution of Commonwealth revenue as in 1909. Had they done so, it is possible that the states might have been able to retain their position in relation to the Commonwealth. As it was, depreciation, restriction of the taxation field and heavy borrowing for developmental purposes combined to depress the states and prevent recovery.

In 1920, the ten-year period laid down in the *Surplus Revenue Act,* by which the Commonwealth had given effect to the *per capita* agreement, came to a close. Thereafter, the Commonwealth

74. See "The Financial Problems of the Commonwealth and the States," by R. C. Mills in *Studies in the Australian Constitution.*
75. *Ibid.,* p. 77.
76. *The Case of the People of Western Australia,* p. 70.

was free to adopt whatever course it chose.[77]   It was early
apparent that the Commonwealth was bent upon either modifying
or abolishing the *per capita* system.   In 1919, the acting Prime
Minister gave an indication of Commonwealth designs when he
suggested that payments be reduced by 2s. 6d. a year in view of
the increased obligations of the central government.   Nothing was
done at the time, but from 1923 onwards until the acceptance of
the financial agreement in 1927, a series of proposals and counter-
proposals were propounded by both sides.   The basis of the Commonwealth suggestions was that the states should no longer receive *per capita* payments and should be compensated for their
loss by the Commonwealth abandoning a part of the direct taxation field.   The states, however, invariably felt that they would
be giving more than they would be receiving, and refused to forego
their claims to a percentage of Commonwealth revenue unless the
Commonwealth ceased completely to impose direct taxation.   No
agreement could be reached, despite conferences, with the result
that in 1926 Mr. Bruce decided to force the issue.   In June of
that year the *States Grants Act* was introduced with the object of
abolishing *per capita* payments.[78]   The state governments interpreted Commonwealth action as an ultimatum, and were bitterly
resentful of the coercive way in which the Commonwealth was
using its superior power.   A Premiers' Conference was hurriedly
convened in Melbourne in June, 1926, to consider the financial
position arising out of the action taken by the Commonwealth.   In
view of the charge[79] later levelled against the Commonwealth that
the states were forced into the Financial Agreement of 1927 because
of Commonwealth pressure and the inherent weakness of their
own financial position, it is as well to examine the attitude adopted
by state representatives towards the Commonwealth proposals.
This was clearly expressed in the speeches and resolutions of the
Premiers' Conference of June, 1926.

The premiers had invited Mr. Bruce, as prime minister, to
attend.   He, however, replied that 'no good purpose could be
served' by his attendance, since the matter had already been re-

77. Within the limits of the constitution, e.g., Section 81 governing appro-
    priation and Section 94 imposing a distribution of surplus revenue might
    be regarded as prescribing certain limitations.
78. The arguments advanced by Mr. Bruce in support of this change were:—
    (1) The financial insecurity of the states under the existing system.
    (2) The principle of one authority spending money raised by another
    authority was vicious.   (3) The injustice of payments based upon a
    population basis.   Reasons enumerated and discussed by R. C. Mills in
    Studies in the Australian Constitution, pp. 85-9.
79. e.g., by Western Australia and South Australia.

peatedly discussed and the states had neither accepted the principle of the Commonwealth proposals nor put forward any feasible alternative plan. The decision of Mr. Bruce not to attend aroused considerable resentment among the premiers. They regarded his attitude as cavalier and inspired by the dominant position in which the Commonwealth found itself. Mr. Lyons, who at that time represented the state of Tasmania, summed up the feeling of the conference when he said: ·

> The Commonwealth Government propose to depart from that principle upon which federation came into existence. The Commonwealth Government says to the states, 'We have got the power to make certain vital changes and trust you are prepared to submit to them, because we are going to use that power and we are not even prepared to come along and discuss the matter with you.'[80]

He was echoed by every other speaker. All showed not merely a dislike for the methods of the Commonwealth, but also a profound suspicion of its designs. For instance, the Victorian premier attacked the proposals on the ground that they could mean only one thing—financial unification.

> You can plainly see that this policy of the Federal Government in taking away the *per capita* payments, and in putting forward the referendum proposals . . . is going to mean direct unification; it cannot mean anything else.[81]

The Attorney-General for Queensland was in complete agreement. He cited as evidence of Commonwealth intentions a speech by Dr. Earle Page, in which he had described a system whereby the states were given money without any check upon how it should be spent as 'absolutely absurd.' 'Why,' asked the Queensland representative, 'should we consult the Commonwealth as to how we spend our money?' Loss of financial independence by the states would, he predicted, speedily be followed by the loss of all independence.

> It is apparent . . . that the Federal authorities would seek to dictate the financial policy of the states, and if they are once in a position to dictate our financial policy to us it is a very small step to the dictation of the whole of our policy.[82]

The events which formed the sequel to the adoption of the financial agreement afford no little justification for the fears here expressed.

In the face of the Commonwealth threat to suspend the *per*

---

80. *Report* of the Proceedings of the Premiers' Conference, Melbourne, June, 1926, p. 13.
81. Mr. Allan. *Ibid.*, p. 7.   82. Mr. Mullan, *Ibid.*, p. 9.

capita payments the conference reiterated its belief that the states were 'entitled as a basis of federation to a share in the Customs and Excise duties of the Commonwealth.'[83] It declared that no financial scheme could be accepted by the states which did not provide them with 'a fixed annual payment of not less than 25/- per head of population,' and contested the federal government's assertion that losses from *per capita* revenue could be made good from the fields of taxation to be abandoned by the Commonwealth.[84]

Notwithstanding protests, the *States Grants Act* was passed and *per capita* payments repealed, though amounts equivalent to what the states would have received were continued for the year 1927-8.[85] Faced with the loss of the *per capita* payments, the states had no choice but to accept the proposals of the Commonwealth. After two conferences, the scheme put forward by the Commonwealth, and later known as the Financial Agreement, was, with modifications, accepted by the states. There can be little doubt that they did so reluctantly. The Commonwealth throughout occupied a position of superiority, as can readily be seen from the attitude which it adopted towards the states in the years preceding the agreement. After the passage of the *States Grants Act* the states had to take what they could get or financially starve. Not unnaturally, they preferred to take what they could get, and the fact that they did so is no answer to the contention that the agreement was in large measure forced upon them.

The Financial Agreement of 1927 had two main objects in view.[86] It represented first an attempt to place the financial relations between the Commonwealth and the states on a permanent basis by stipulating an amount which was to be a fixed annual charge on Commonwealth revenue. Secondly, it was intended to secure co-ordination in the sphere of governmental borrowing. In this way it was hoped to end competition between members of the federation on the loan markets, to secure some control over the amounts to be borrowed, and to increase confidence among investors by making the whole of Australia the guarantor of all governmental borrowing and by seeing to it that adequate sinking funds were provided for each loan raised. Such, broadly, were the objects of the agreement as it was originally conceived. The results which were to spring from it were, however, of a very dif-

---

83. Mr. Lang. *Ibid.*, p. 7.
84. Resolutions passed by the Conference. *Ibid.*, p. 19.
85. *Report*, Commission on the Constitution, 1929, p. 194.
86. The full text of the agreement along with copies of all agreements made with the states under Section 105A may be found in Knowles, *op. cit.*, appendix C, pp. 167-94. For comment upon the agreement see Norman Cowper's article in *Studies in the Australian Constitution*.

ferent character, for by this seeming innocuous agreement the states surrendered a good deal of their financial independence and with it a measure of control over their own policy,[87] while the Commonwealth government discovered that it had in part abdicated its authority in favour of an extra-parliamentary body.

Although agreement had been reached in 1927, the Commonwealth lacked constitutional authority to give it effect without an amendment of the constitution. This was secured by the *Commonwealth Constitution Alteration (State Debts) Act* 1928,[88] and by the requisite majorities at the referendum. That such majorities were obtained was almost certainly due to the fact that the full implications of the proposed changes were not realised, partly because of the assurances made by Commonwealth ministers that no threat to state autonomy was involved. Nothing could have been more explicit or more in conflict with later developments than the assurances given by the federal Attorney-General on October 26, 1928. He declared:

The amendment is limited to subject matter of debts and borrowing, and gives no general power to over-ride constitutions. It operates only when there is unanimous agreement, and accordingly no state can be compelled to do or accept anything against its will. This limitation does not apply to other Commonwealth powers, and is designed for complete protection of state sovereignty.[89]

Following on the referendum, the constitution was altered by the insertion of section 105A. under which the Commonwealth was given power to make agreements with the states with respect to their public debts and to make laws 'for the carrying out by the parties thereto of any such agreement.[90] Under this section, the first Financial Agreement was enacted in the form of the *Financial Agreement Validation Act* of 1929. It was extremely involved, but its main features were these. A Loan Council was to be established with one representative from each of the states and from the Commonwealth, but the federal government's representative was to receive two votes and a casting vote, instead of the normal one. The Commonwealth and the states were to submit their proposed loan programmes for the financial year to the council, which was entrusted with the duty of determining what percentage of the total amount could be borrowed at favourable

87. R. W. G. Mackay, "The Distribution of Powers between the Commonwealth and the States" in *Studies in the Australian Constitution.*
88. *Report*, Commission on the Constitution, *op. cit.*, p. 194. For text see Knowles, *op. cit.*, p. 268.
89. Quoted, *The Case of the People of Western Australia*, p. 89.
90. Part IV, 2 (3) Financial Agreement Act 1928.

rates. If the council could not agree the loan money available was to be apportioned according to a set formula. Borrowings were to be arranged by the Commonwealth acting upon instructions given by the council. Other sections of the act provided for the Commonwealth taking over the debts of the states, for the payment to the states of an amount equivalent to the *per capita* allowances of 1927, for Commonwealth contributions to sinking funds and for payment by the states of interest and sinking fund charges. Certain clauses were also introduced with the object of allowing greater elasticity with regard to borrowing.[91]   Of these, the most important was that a state might borrow within Australia in its own name beyond the sum fixed by the Loan Council if the loan was 'solely for temporary purposes.'[92] The meaning to be given to this phrase was left indefinite, but the states probably thought it bestowed on them the right to borrow to finance their deficits. During the depression, however, the phrase lost its significance, since the banks were able to insist that all governmental borrowing should be subject to the regulation of the Loan Council.

The changes effected by section 105A were of singular and in many ways of unexpected importance, and not least because an agreement made under the section can only be changed with the consent of all the parties concerned. Since there can be no unilateral withdrawal, a state remains bound for the full period of the agreement.[93] Variation is, of course, possible if the parliaments of the six states and of the Commonwealth can be induced to take concerted action. It has, indeed, been achieved on one occasion when, under the stimulus of crisis conditions, the parties agreed to a reduction of the interest rate on internal loans. But, despite this instance, what strikes one most forcibly about section 105A is its rigidity. Under that section, declared a writer in the *Round Table,* 'the amount which the Commonwealth has to pay the states has . . . been fixed with something more than the permanence of a section of the constitution.'[94] Yet another commentator summed up the position in even more drastic language.

In effect, that is to say, Section 105A writes any such financial agreement into the Commonwealth constitution and sets its provisions not only beyond the reach of the Commonwealth Par-

91. For these exceptions from the ordinary rule see N. Cowper, "The Financial Agreement," in *Studies in the Australian Constitution,* pp. 122-3.
92. Financial Agreement Act, Part I, Section 5.
93. Financial Agreement Act, Part IV—2 (4-5-6).
94. *The Round Table,* March, 1935, p. 351.

liament, but beyond the reach even of the processes provided for by Section 128.[95]

From the point of view of elasticity, then, section 105A is open to serious criticism. From that of the effect upon the finances of the states of the actual agreement, concluded under the section, judgment is somewhat more difficult. Various attempts have been made to estimate the financial results of the agreement, and the balance of the evidence inclines to the view that, while in the early stages the states may obtain more than they would have received from *per capita* payments, their position 'will grow progressively less favourable.'[96] The commission on the constitution based its estimates on the assumption that there would be an annual increase of two per cent. in the population of Australia, and reached the conclusion, indicated above, that for a portion of the time covered by the agreement the states would obtain more, and thereafter less.[97] The length of the period during which they would receive more would be determined, in part, by the amount of the future borrowings of the states, since the Commonwealth had agreed to contribute five shillings per annum for each £100 to a sinking fund. But that period could not be extended many years, and once it had passed the states would find it increasingly difficult to finance their activities. The agreement, therefore, is of vital importance in any consideration of the future stability of the states, since what measure of independence they possess will ultimately depend upon their ability to finance themselves.

It was recognition of that fact which led Mr. Menzies (when addressing the Premiers' Conference on constitutional matters in February, 1934) to stress the danger to the maintenance of what he called the federal balance which was inherent in the Financial Agreement.

> The Financial Agreement seems to me to proceed on the assumption that the responsibilities of the States will be reduced from year to year, and that the states' need for financial assistance will be correspondingly reduced. That proposition will not stand examination for a moment. . . . I believe that it is demonstrably true that the obligations of the States, failing some constitutional amendment, will keep growing from year to year, and that the financial resources of the States will keep falling from year to year. From the once-proud resources assigned to them by the Constitution, the States have now been left with

95. K. H. Bailey in *Studies in the Australian Constitution*, p. 48.
96. *Report*, Grants Commission, 1933, p. 28.
97. *Report*, Commission on the Constitution, 1929, p. 197.

quite inadequate resources, which will become more and more insufficient as the population increases, until the period of the Agreement has expired altogether.[98]

The sense of grievance which the states nourish against the Commonwealth over the financial issue has undoubtedly been due to their belief that the position of financial inferiority in which they find themselves is largely the result of the policy pursued by the federal government. South Australia in its case to the Grants Commission said:

Whatever merits that agreement may possess, an outstanding feature is that at last the Commonwealth imposed its will upon the States and fixed the annual sum returnable to each State at a definite figure per annum, which will not increase with an increasing population, trade or Commonwealth revenue.[99]

It is essential to grasp the significance of section 105A, and of the financial agreement concluded thereunder, if any right understanding is to be obtained of the stage of development reached by federalism under the Australian constitution. It has been pointed out that the agreement came about largely as the result of Commonwealth pressure, and that in the long run the financial results produced by it would be disadvantageous to the states. Yet the Commonwealth, as well as the states, was party to an encroachment upon its liberty of action by the Loan Council. The power to borrow when and upon what conditions they liked had been surrendered by all the governments concerned.[100] The Loan Council had been endowed with the right to regulate governmental borrowing, and had in effect become 'a new unit of government' since, by the exercise of that right, it possessed the power to control the rate of development within the Commonwealth.[1] Whatever may have been the economic benefits accruing from the work of the Loan Council, from the constitutional point of view the influential position occupied by the council in the government of Australia has been the subject of much criticism. The grounds of objection were laid before the Premiers' Conferences of June, 1933, and February, 1934, by the Queensland premier, Mr. Forgan Smith. He declared that the Loan Council was 'an extra-consti-

---

98. Hon. R. G. Menzies at the Premiers' Conference on Constitutional Matters, Feb., 1934. See *Cross Currents in Australian Finance*, p. 72. Mr. Menzies was at the time Attorney-General and Acting Premier of Victoria.

99. *Report*, 1933, Grants Commission, 1933, p. 35.
100. R. C. Mills in *Studies in the Australian Constitution*, p. 92.
1. Norman Cowper in *Studies in the Australian Constitution*, p. 126.

tutional authority not responsible to any one parliament.'[2]   Financial control was the basis upon which parliamentary government rested, yet the Loan Council was rapidly undermining that control.

A parliament which ceases to exercise control over its own financial policy ceases to be a parliament in reality, and becomes a mere shadow of what it formerly was.   The operation of the Financial Agreement is rapidly tending to have that effect. Treasurers representing the various governments may arrive at a uniform agreement, which is binding on all governments in Australia.   The Parliaments cannot alter that agreement.   If they are aggrieved at it, or opposed to it, the utmost they can do is to pass something in the nature of a vote of censure on the Treasurer who signed it.   For the time being at least the agreement itself would stand.[3]

In view of such criticisms the position of the Loan Council in the Australian governmental structure is deserving of special consideration.   The strength of its position is due to the conclusion of the Financial Agreement under the authority of the newly inserted section 105A of the constitution.   The Loan Council was part of the Financial Agreement, whose terms are binding upon the Commonwealth and the states, and may only 'be varied or rescinded by the parties thereto.'[4]   The membership of the council is composed of one minister of the Commonwealth and one minister of each state.   The Commonwealth member is appointed by the prime minister, and each state member by the premier of his state.   It is possible, if thought desirable, to appoint a person not a minister as a representative on the council.   No fixed period of membership is specified, for members hold office 'during the pleasure of the Prime Minister or the Premier, as the case may be.'[5]   This may lead to important changes in the personnel of the council as political fortunes fluctuate, a case in point being the substitution of Mr. Theodore for Mr. Lyons as chairman of the Loan Council in 1931.   On almost all matters except that of the total amount to be borrowed for any one year—which in the event of disagreement is to be decided by a set formula—a decision is to be reached by a majority of votes of the members.   The Commonwealth represen-

2. Premier of Queensland (Hon. W. Forgan Smith) at the Premiers' Conference, June, 1933. D. B. Copland and C. V. Janes, *Cross Currents in Australian Finance* (1936), p. 9.
3. Hon. W. Forgan Smith at Premiers' Conference on Constitutional Matters, Feb., 1934, *Ibid.*, p. 11.
4. Section 105A (4) of the constitution.
5. Financial Agreement, Part 1, clause 3 (Australian Loan Council) (b).

tative, however, possesses two votes and a casting vote, whereas each state representative has only one.

The party structure of the Loan Council will necessarily reflect the political complexion of the various governments in existence at any one time. If, however, the government of the Commonwealth differs in its party character from the majority of the state governments a majority vote in the council may not be representative of the greater number of governments of any one party complexion because of the possession by the Commonwealth of two votes and a casting vote.

There is much justification for the view that the Loan Council has come to represent 'a new unit of government,' since it is not politically responsible to any one parliament. Political responsibility could be brought about either by a correspondence between the majority in the Loan Council and the federal government, or by treating the decisions of the council as recommendations for acceptance or rejection by the parliaments of the states and Commonwealth. But under existing conditions neither of these guarantees of responsibility necessarily exist. It is quite possible that the federal government will differ in its party character from the majority of governments represented upon the council, while the decisions reached by the council may not be treated as recommendations, but are binding upon the various governments represented. No parliament can alter these decisions. At most, a parliament could encompass the downfall of the prime minister or premier, as the case might be, through a vote of censure. The decision of the council would not be affected, and the fall of the minister would only produce an alteration in the policy of the council if the appointment of his successor meant that the viewpoint formerly espoused by a minority now had the support of a majority.

The constitutional alteration effected by the insertion in the constitution of section 105A involved a far greater sacrifice of independence on the part of both state and Commonwealth governments than had been foreseen. The full implications of the change only became apparent under the pressure of events produced by a period of crisis. It was then clearly seen that in a time of depression the machinery of the Loan Council and the Financial Agreement could be used to compel obedience to a definite policy.[6] In this instance that policy was dictated by the banking interests and involved a surrender by the states, and to a less degree by the

6. N. Cowper, "The Financial Agreement," p. 127, and R. W. G. Mackay, "The Distribution of Powers between the Commonwealth and the states," pp. 156-7, in *Studies in the Australian Constitution.*

Commonwealth, of the right to shape the details of their internal administration. The Premiers' Plan for recovery within the Commonwealth largely embodied principles of reconstruction of which the heads of the banking institutions approved. The principles upon which the plan was said to be based were balanced budgets, reduced costs and equality of sacrifice.[7] These involved a reduction of twenty per cent. in adjustable government expenditure, additional Commonwealth and state taxation, a reduction of interest upon bank deposits, a moratorium with regard to mortgages and the conversion of government internal loans. This was not the sort of programme which was likely to commend itself to a Labour government, and yet the Commonwealth Labour government finally, though reluctantly, gave adherence to the plan. Its decision to do so was condemned by the Central Executive of the Australian Labour Party on 29 August, 1930. That body expressed its opinion that the Loan Council was an instrument which could be manipulated against a Labour government, whether federal or state, and that it was 'desirable . . . that steps be taken immediately to amend the Financial Agreement and dissolve the Loan Council.'[8]

It is pertinent to ask why the federal government acquiesced in a policy involving stringent economies of which it disapproved. The answer would seem to be that it was forced to do so because a hostile majority in the Senate blocked the currency legislation, which might have rendered the government free from the dictation of the Loan Council. Such is the conclusion reached by Mr. Norman Cowper in his study of the Financial Agreement.

The Commonwealth government would not have been corralled into support of the Premiers' Plan or any other scheme of reconstruction involving drastic economies if it had not found its escape blocked by a hostile majority in the Senate.[9]

At the same time, Mr. Cowper declares that those in control of the banks, happily finding a conservative majority in the Senate, were using the provisions of the Financial Agreement to enforce the carrying out of a policy of reconstruction in which they believed. A perusal of the correspondence which passed between the banking interests, the Loan Council and the Commonwealth Treasurer can leave small doubt of the correctness of his assertion. As early as 13 December, 1930, Sir Robert Gibson, as chairman

---

7. See S. H. Roberts, "The Crisis in Australia," *Pacific Affairs*, April, 1932. Also W. R. Maclaurin, *Economic Planning in Australia*, 1929-36 (1937).
8. Resolutions of the Australian Labour Party, Central Executive, N.S.W., 29 Aug., 1930. See E. O. G. Shann and D. B. Copland, *The Crisis in Australian Finance*, 1929-31, p. 32.
9. N. Cowper in *Studies in the Australian Constitution*, p. 132.

of a bankers' conference, had written to Mr. Lyons, chairman of the Loan Council, and stressed 'the necessity of a closer control of the position as between the Loan Council and the banks.'[10] The same letter made plain that governmental borrowing 'solely for temporary purposes' would also come within the jurisdiction of the Loan Council, since financial assistance to any government had to be covered by Treasury bills issued under the authority of the Loan Council. Sir Robert concluded his letter with a remark which gave the first hint of what later became the Premiers' Plan.

> The banks throw out the suggestion that . . . a sound constructive scheme covering a period should be evolved, spreading the load of readjustment in such a manner as will enable all the component parts of the Commonwealth to cope with the situation and so eventually enable the country to return to an era of competence and prosperity.[10]

Only two months later, Sir Robert Gibson wrote to the federal Treasurer and stated in explicit terms the policy which the Commonwealth Bank Board believed the governments of Australia should pursue. Actually, the resolution of the Bank Board went further, for it intimated that the board had made the pursuance of a certain policy a necessary condition of its co-operation in recovery. This amounted to an attempt by the board to dictate the nature of the recovery programme in Australia, since the resolution was not confined to any one government, but plainly embraced all. It read:

> Subject to adequate and equitable reductions in all wages, salaries, and allowances, pensions, social benefits of all kinds, interest, and other factors which affect the cost of living, the Commonwealth Bank Board will actively co-operate with the trading banks and the governments of Australia in sustaining industry and restoring employment.[11]

Meanwhile, the premiers in conference at Canberra had passed a number of resolutions embodying a three years' plan of reconstruction. The bankers, however, were dissatisfied with certain sections of the programme, and intimated to the Commonwealth Treasurer that they would only support methods which they believed to be 'on sound banking or economic lines,' and which did not impair the existing monetary system.'[12] They particularly

10. Sir R. Gibson, Chairman of the Bankers' Conference, to the Hon. J. Lyons, Chairman of the Loan Council, 13 December 1930, *The Crisis in Australian Finance*, pp. 83-7.
11. Sir R. Gibson, Chairman of the Commonwealth Bank Board, to the Hon. E. G. Theodore, Federal Treasurer, 13 February, 1931 (*ibid.*, p. 182).
12. Letter from the Bankers to the Hon. E. G. Theodore, Federal Treasurer, 24 February, 1931 (*ibid.*, p. 185).

objected to a tax of 3s. 6d. in the £1 on government securities, and were in favour of much more stringent economies.

In face of the opposition of the banking interests to the three years' plan drawn up by the premiers, Mr. Theodore attempted to carry out his government's policy by other methods, and introduced in turn the *Fiduciary Notes Bill* and the *Commonwealth Bank Amendment Bill*. Both were defeated in the Senate, which left the government with the alternative of risking a double dissolution or of agreeing to a recovery programme of which it did not approve.

On 2 April, 1931, Sir Robert Gibson wrote to Mr. Theodore, who was chairman of the Loan Council, and announced the limitation of short-term lending to governments by the bank. The decision of the Board of Directors was couched in terms which amounted to an ultimatum.

> It now becomes the unpleasant duty of the board to advise the Loan Council that a point is being reached beyond which it would be impossible for the bank to provide further assistance for the governments in the future.[13]

Mr. Theodore realised the implications to be drawn from the bank's attitude, and in his reply charged the board with attempting to usurp the functions of the government. He pointed out that the co-operation of the bank had been sought by the government in order to give effect to the resolutions contained in the three years' plan, but it had been refused by the bank. The attitude adopted by the board throughout could

> only be regarded by the Commonwealth Government as an attempt on the part of the bank to arrogate to itself a supremacy over the Government in the determination of the financial policy of the Commonwealth, a supremacy which . . . was never contemplated by the framers of the Australian Constitution, and has never been sanctioned by the Australian people.[14]

In financial matters the government was responsible to the electorate and not to the banks, since control of the public purse was a prerogative to be exercised by the people's representatives in parliament. 'The government,' said Mr. Theodore, 'will not be a party to any attempt by the bank board, or any other authority, to subvert this principle.' The government did not infer that the

---

13. Sir R. Gibson, Chairman of the Board of Directors of the Commonwealth Bank, to the Hon. E. G. Theodore, Chairman of the Loan Council, 2 April, 1931. See E. O. G. Shann and D. B. Copland, *The Battle of the Plans* (1931), p. 44.
14. The Hon. E. G. Theodore, Chairman of the Loan Council, in reply to Sir R. Gibson, Chairman of the Board of Directors of the Commonwealth Bank, 15 April, 1931 (*ibid.*, pp. 48-49).

bank board should not offer criticism, but it did 'challenge the right of the bank to cut off money supplies to the Commonwealth government, and to do this without consultation or prior discussion.'[14]

In view of the evidence furnished by the correspondence between representatives of the banking interests and those of the Commonwealth government and the Loan Council, there can be little doubt that the banks attempted to utilise the provisions of section 105A to force upon the governments of Australia a policy which they considered best suited to a period of depression. The conclusion reached by Mr. Cowper is that

> The banks, especially the Commonwealth Bank, can by no means escape Mr. Theodore's soft impeachment that they attempted to dictate the financial policy of the Australian governments. The Premiers' Plan was largely a policy forced by the banks upon the governments through the Loan Council and by means of the provisions of the Financial Agreement.[15]

Despite Mr. Theodore's defiant reply to the Bank Board, a majority of the Loan Council bowed to the ultimatum, and appointed a sub-committee to inquire into methods by which balanced budgets might be ensured. A number of economists were co-opted by the sub-committee, and they were largely responsible for the recommendations later incorporated in the Premiers' Plan. It is important to note that the methods by which the plan was carried out involved a very considerable encroachment upon the liberty of action of all the governments. A periodical auditing of governmental accounts was insisted upon, and no funds were forthcoming from the Commonwealth Bank unless it was agreed that the plan had been observed. It is obvious that such a system transformed the Loan Council into a body determining the limits of governmental policy, and that autonomous action by any state, at least while the depression lasted, was rendered largely illusory.

During the depression, however, a much greater invasion of state independence was to take place through authority conferred upon the Commonwealth by section 105A and the Financial Agreement. The New South Wales Labour government, led by Mr. Lang, had even less chance than the Commonwealth of evading adherence to the Premiers' Plan, for it had no power under the constitution to legislate on currency questions. It was the Financial Agreement which was chiefly responsible for compelling Mr. Lang to agree to the plan, and which later brought about his downfall,

15.   N. Cowper in *Studies in the Australian Constitution*, p. 143.

because it enabled action to be taken against his government once it had defaulted.[16] New South Wales neglected to carry out the provisions of the plan, and reported to the Loan Council its inability to make full payment of overseas interest, due in February, 1932, without an advance from the Commonwealth Bank. The Council refused to sanction any such advance, and the matter was placed in the hands of the newly-elected Commonwealth government. It proceeded to pay the bondholders, and then resorted to drastic measures to recover the amount from the state of New South Wales. Acting under sub-section 3 of section 105A, which conferred upon parliament the authority 'to make laws for the carrying out of the Financial Agreement,' the Commonwealth passed the *Financial Agreements Enforcement Act*, 1932, and followed this with other acts of a similar character.[17] This legislation authorised the Commonwealth government to attach money credited to a state, and to order the payment into its own treasury of certain classes of state revenue when once the Commonwealth Auditor-General had certified that a state owed money to the Commonwealth under the terms of the Financial Agreement.[18] New South Wales at once issued a writ against the Commonwealth and claimed a declaration from the High Court that the 'whole of the *Financial Agreements (Commonwealth Liability) Act* 1932 and the whole of the *Financial Agreements Enforcement Act* 1932 were *ultra vires* the Parliament of the Commonwealth.'[19] But a majority of the court, Rich, Starke, Dixon and McTiernan, J.J. (Gavan Duffy, C.J., and Evatt, J., dissenting) held the legislation to be within the powers of the federal parliament. Similarly, when New South Wales brought a further action to restrain the Commonwealth from attaching certain trust funds, the court found in favour of the Commonwealth.[20] No appeal to the Privy Council was allowed from the decision in the first instance.

The actual case of *New South Wales v. Commonwealth* warrants some attention, since the arguments advanced by New South Wales and the other states which intervened show clearly that at the time of the conclusion of the Financial Agreement the states had no inkling that the agreement could be subjected to the inter-

16. Mr. Cowper suggests four possible reasons for Mr. Lang's adherence to the Plan. (1) He had to borrow to carry on. (2) The Conversion Loan afforded some justification. (3) The futility of defying the rest of the Loan Council. (4) The threat of Commonwealth action against N.S.W. in the High Court.
17. *The Financial Agreements Enforcement Acts*, Nos. 2, 3 and 4, 1932.
18. A declaration by both houses of parliament was also necessary.
19. 46 *C.L.R.* 155 (1932), *N.S.W. v. the Commonwealth, No.* 1.
20. 46 *C.L.R.* 246 (1932), *N.S.W. v. the Commonwealth, No.* 3.

pretation later placed upon it by the Commonwealth. They neither knew nor intended that the agreement should authorize action by the Commonwealth involving further inroads upon their own autonomy. The case has additional importance because it makes plain what was implicit in the terms of the Financial Agreement, namely, the partial destruction both of state independence and of the federal system, as originally conceived by those who framed the constitution.

Counsel for New South Wales based their argument largely on the ground that the interpretation adopted by the Commonwealth was unreasonable, in view of what was known of the intentions of the parties to the agreement.[21]   Section 105A was the only section which might authorize the action taken by the federal government, and in that section the term 'carrying out' meant 'performing' and not 'enforcing.'   Had the intention been to confer powers of enforcement it was obvious that the language would have been made explicit.   The ordinary methods of judicial procedure, it was argued, were available for the enforcement of the agreement, and 'all the parties would assume that if there were to be any question of enforcement it would be by judicial process' and not dependent merely upon the certificate of the Commonwealth Auditor-General, who did not represent the states and to whose 'arbitrament the states had never assented.'[22]   Gavan Duffy, for the states of Victoria and Tasmania intervening, urged that the harsh results flowing from the interpretation proposed by the Commonwealth implied that no such intention could be read into the language. The parties had never agreed to the means of enforcement now adopted, and 'very plain words should be found' before such action could be justified.[23]   Yet, despite the arguments of the states, the majority of the High Court were agreed that, whether unwittingly or not, the Commonwealth had been given power to take action against any state not observing the agreement.   Rich and Dixon, J.J., though finding in favour of the Commonwealth, in their summing up paid eloquent tribute to the fundamental altera-

21.   Browne (and Berne) for N.S.W., 46 *C.L.R.*, p. 157.
22.   46 *C.L.R.*, p. 158. Only section 6 of the Financial Agreement Enforcement Act depended on the Auditor-General's certificate. This was an emergency procedure, and provision was made for obtaining at a later date the judgment of the High Court. It should be noted, too, as Professor Bailey has pointed out, that "the ordinary methods of judicial procedure" did not, as the Judiciary Act stood, include anything whatever in the nature of execution against a recalcitrant government, whether of Commonwealth or of state.
23.   C. Gavan Duffy, 46 *C.L.R.*, p. 161.

tion brought about in the constitution by the introduction of section 105A. The judgment read:

> In our opinion the effect of this provision is to make any agreement of the required description obligatory upon the Commonwealth and the states, to place its operation and efficacy beyond the control of any law of any of the seven parliaments, and to prevent any constitutional principle or provision operating to defeat or diminish or condition the obligatory force of the agreement.[24]

Evatt, J., dissented from the opinion of the majority in a lengthy and masterly judgment, in which he discussed all the implications of the case. He agreed with those who argued that no 'plain words' could be found to justify Commonwealth intervention in state affairs.

> If the enforcement as against the States of their contractual obligations is the idea behind Section 105A (3) the language is singularly ill adapted to hint at, much less express, such a thought. The word 'enforcement' would have been the obvious word to use.[25]

An analysis of the nature of financial agreements concluded under section 105A only served to confirm his opinion. Such agreements conferred rights and imposed duties upon all parties 'with precisely the same force and effect.' But the *Enforcement Act* attempted to bestow upon one of the parties, namely, the Commonwealth, the right to take certain remedial action against any other party which had committed a supposed breach of the agreement.[26] No such action was permitted to any or all of the states should the Commonwealth fail to fulfil its obligations, while for the federal parliament to be clothed with authority to 'enforce' agreements against the Commonwealth was simply 'a contradiction in terms.'[27] It was apparent that the incorporation of disciplinary measures which were applicable only to a breach by some of the parties to the agreement meant 'a substantial alteration in the contractual relationship between the seven parties.'[28] Just how drastic that disciplinary action might be was made plain by the learned judge when he showed the extensive invasion of state fields of activity contemplated by the Commonwealth.

> A Commonwealth proclamation (is issued) making all specified revenues of the States payable to the Treasurer of the Commonwealth. . . . The individual citizen must pay to the Com-

---

24. 46 *C.L.R.*, p. 177.
26. Evatt, J., 46 *C.L.R.*, p. 222.
28. *Ibid.*

25. 46 *C.L.R.*, p. 204.
27. Evatt, J., 46 *C.L.R.*, p. 224.

monwealth any moneys which he owes to the State and which would have formed part of the . . . revenues of the state if received by it. He must pay not only debts existing at the date of the proclamation but those coming into existence during its currency. If he pays the Commonwealth, his liability to the State is discharged. If he does not pay the Commonwealth, the moneys may be recovered at its suit. If he pays the State, he commits an offence, heavy penalties are imposed upon him, and he is still liable to pay the Commonwealth. Any State Ministers of the Crown or State officers who receive or permit the receipt of such debts are guilty of an offence.

In respect of this taking of State revenues in advance of the High Court's decision, the Commonwealth, through its various non-judicial organs, combines the roles of plaintiff, judge and executioner.[29]

The decision by the High Court that the *Enforcement Act* was a valid[30] exercise of authority by the Commonwealth revealed the extent of the departure in Australia from the conception of federation which had prevailed among the founders of the constitution. The basis of federation had been the retention by the states of as much independence as was compatible with the surrender of limited powers to the Commonwealth. Now, however, it had been demonstrated that under certain conditions the federal government could attach the revenues of a state and paralyse its whole machinery of government. It was, therefore, no longer possible to pretend that the states were sovereign bodies, exercising untrammelled independence in the spheres of activity allocated to them. The fact that Mr. Lang's government in New South Wales was pursuing a policy which was, broadly speaking, unpopular in Australia, has tended to obscure and mitigate the extensive invasion of state autonomy committed by the Commonwealth. Yet the implications of the Commonwealth's action were not altogether lost, and it is noteworthy that other states intervened in the case of *New South Wales v. The Commonwealth* in defence of state rights. All states protested in one form or another. The Western Australian government, for instance, made it plain that while it did not

---

29. Evatt, J., 46 *C.L.R.*, pp. 194-5.
30. It should be noted that in the view of the majority section 5 of the Financial Agreement Enforcement Act 1932, though not section 6, could be sustained without reference to section 105A (3) on the ground of the Commonwealth Parliament's authority "to make laws incidental to the execution of the High Court's power to hear and determine all matters in which the Commonwealth is a party." See Knowles, *op. cit.*, pp. 47, 73.

approve of the policy pursued by the New South Wales government, yet it

resented very keenly that unforeseen and unexpected effect and operation of Section 105A of the constitution as interpreted by the High Court, which gives to the Commonwealth still another power, the exercise of which may well take away completely from the State its sovereign rights as a self-governing community.[31]

This loss of independence, it was pointed out, could come about simply because a state had defaulted in its payments to the Commonwealth. There was no consideration of whether or not the state acknowledged its debt, and while the enforcement measures of the Commonwealth were drastic enough when exercised against a state which 'was able but unwilling to pay its debt,' they were altogether unreasonable when put into operation against a state which was willing but unable to pay.[32] Perhaps even stronger disapproval was voiced by the Lieutenant-Governor and Chief Justice of Tasmania, whose conception of federalism was that which had been current at the inception of the Commonwealth.

Unless this act is repealed or allowed to expire or declared illegal by the High Court, the Federation of Australia will exist or cease at the choice of the Commonwealth Parliament, and the Ministry of the day, which will have power to destroy the States as political entities, one by one.[33]

No doubt this is an extreme view, which, like many of the other statements made at the time, reflects the heat of the moment. Indeed, a good deal of the writing about the agreement and the High Court decision has an emotional tinge which is responsible for the somewhat exaggerated terms in which the discussion has been conducted. It is true, also, that the obligations assumed by the states under the agreement were limited in number and character and that the powers of control conferred on the Commonwealth by section 105A (3) are confined to the enforcement of these obligations. Nevertheless, when all such allowances are made, it is difficult to escape the conclusion that section 105A and the agreements which may be concluded thereunder are of the utmost importance in any assessment of the nature of the developments taking place within the Australian federal structure.

Throughout the depression the Financial Agreement enabled

31. *The Case of the People of Western Australia*, p. 89.
32. *Ibid.*, p. 91.
33. Sir Herbert Nicholls. Quoted, *Studies in the Australian Constitution*, p 139.

a greater measure of co-operative action[34] to be achieved than would otherwise have been possible, since the parties were bound to abide by the decisions of the Loan Council.   This extra-parliamentary body was utilized as a means whereby a policy finding favour with the banks could be imposed upon all governments. The carrying out of the policy involved a considerable loss of independence to both Commonwealth and states.   Moreover, under the Financial Agreement, a state might suffer even more serious inroads upon its independence.   If it failed to observe the terms of the agreement it could be compelled to do so by Commonwealth legislation, which authorized the seizure of state revenues and the control of state servants.[35]   The agreement has also been used to ensure that all governments carry out their public debt obligations. Difficulties in the way of enforcing the agreement might, however, arise if the Commonwealth government were to default, or if that government were unwilling to enact enforcement legislation against a defaulting state.

Important as section 105A undoubtedly is, it should nevertheless be remembered that what occurred during the depression was made possible by the federal nature of the Australian constitution.   The disadvantages inherent in federalism—the division of powers, the rigidity of the constitution, the clumsiness of attempts at co-operation—were utilized to bring about at least a partial abdication of authority by both state and federal governments.   It was federalism which paved the way for the creation of the Loan Council and its influence over governmental policy.   Ironically enough, federalism, which had been adopted largely as a method of preserving state independence, also proved valueless during the depression as a safeguard to the states.

Financially, the Commonwealth had always occupied a superior position, and that superiority was enhanced during the depression.[36] It is true that Commonwealth revenue at first suffered severely from the decline in imports, but much of this loss could be recovered through the federal government's imposition of new taxes such as the ten per cent. tax on income from property, the primage

34. See W. R. Maclaurin, *Economic Planning in Australia.*   No doubt the constitutional disabilities of the agreement have been offset by the financial advantages with regard to the regulation of governmental borrowing.   For testimony to the success of the Agreement see *Cross Currents in Australian Finance*, introduction, p. xxvi.

35. Had Mr. Lang won the July 1932 election and defied the Commonwealth enforcement legislation, the federation might have come perilously close to disruption or civil war.   See N. Cowper in *Studies in the Australian Constitution.* p. 141.

36. See *Cross Currents in Australian Finance*, p. 53.   Report by D. B. Copland and W. E. Johnson.

duty on imports and the sales tax. In addition, the Commonwealth was helped by the suspension of war debt payments to Britain. The states also found their revenue rapidly declining during the depression, but, unlike the Commonwealth, they possessed only restricted avenues of taxation. They were constitutionally debarred from imposing a sales tax or a primage duty, while increases in existing taxation or service rates were open to 'political opposition' or 'economic objection.'[37] Moreover, the burden of state expenditure had been very heavily increased by the growth of unemployment and by the adverse exchange rate.[38] In consequence, the Commonwealth emerged from the depression with a financial superiority over the states even greater than that which it had enjoyed before. Nor had the conclusion of the Financial Agreement brought the states economic security. It had led rather to a rapid extension of Commonwealth power at the expense of the states. When, in the exercise of its right to enforce the terms of the Financial Agreement, the Commonwealth can take the control of the servants and revenue of a state out of the state government's hands, then it becomes difficult to see how any real measure of state independence remains.

Since the outbreak of war in 1939 the trend in the direction of Commonwealth financial supremacy has been accelerated. The Commonwealth, confronted with gigantically increased expenditure, felt the need to exploit the taxable capacity of the nation to the full. It found, however, that this could not easily be achieved because of the divergence between the income tax rates in the states and because of the provision in the constitution preventing the Commonwealth from imposing taxation which discriminated between the states. The Commonwealth government, after putting forward various proposals to which the states would not agree, in 1942 introduced legislation which was designed by the use of a combination of its powers to make the Commonwealth the sole taxing authority for the duration of the war, in so far as income tax was concerned. Almost all state governments were bitterly resentful of this attempt by the Commonwealth to exclude them from the field of income taxation and peg the amounts which they were to receive, in the form of Commonwealth grants, for refraining from exercising their power to impose a tax upon incomes. Four states tested the legality of the legislation, pointing out that if the Commonwealth could validly enact

37. *Ibid.*
38. Especially in N.S.W. and Queensland, where overseas interest bears a high proportion to total interest. The exchange payable by N.S.W. in 1933 was £2,430,000, compared with £2,000,000 for the Commonwealth, though the total interest burden for N.S.W. was less than for the Commonwealth.

legislation of this character, then not only was the financial independence of the states at an end, but state autonomy itself, since states which had in fact lost the power to tax had lost the power to govern.   The decision of the High Court in favour of the validity of the legislation further consolidated the financial supremacy of the Commonwealth which Deakin had visualized at the inception of federation.   Moreover, apart from the *War-Time Arrangements Act,* the legislation was upheld without resort to the defence power which implied that there was no constitutional barrier to the continuance of a uniform tax plan in peace.   The Commonwealth, therefore, forty-two years after the formation of the federation, found itself not merely able to exercise great pressure upon the states, but in a position where a Commonwealth government could virtually control the more important taxing functions of the states.

Financially, as in other ways, the decline in state power, and with it in state independence, cannot be denied.   What is clear is that the claim which federalism makes to give protection to the local units within the federation has not been substantiated by Australian experience over the past forty odd years.   All defences of federalism stress the necessity of maintaining the federal form in order to safeguard state independence, yet all recent inquiries into the working of federalism, whether in the United States, Canada, or Australia, show that federalism has failed signally to protect the interests and independence of the states.   This would not be of so great importance if the requisite constitutional adjustments in favour of increased Commonwealth powers had been made to meet the new situation created by the decline of the states and the increasing importance of the national government.   But it does matter enormously when the federal system is not only maintained but maintained with much the same rigid division of powers as at the time when the federation was formed.

The preservation of state independence does not imply that the units of the federation will operate within water-tight compartments or that the states will never be affected in the exercise of their residuary powers by any exercise of the enumerated powers of the Commonwealth.   Such a conception of federalism, while theoretically tenable, does not accord with experience of the working of actual federations anywhere.   What must be recognized is that in addition to the division of powers there is another side of federal organisation, namely, the interlocking of responsibilities. While in a federation there cannot be complete immunity for the states from federal influence, it yet remains true that the framers of the Australian constitution did believe that the states would be far less affected in the exercise of their residuary powers than has proved the case, and certainly not affected to the point where their autonomy was threatened. The destruction of state independence, both in this country and elsewhere, is not, of course, absolute. There are still considerable areas of activity within which the states may function, though whether efficiently is another matter. In Australia, one might instance the administration of justice, the legislation of professions, the control of road traffic, housing, education, railway policy, and to a large extent of production and land settlement. Despite the retention of state control in such matters, the process of decline has gone so far that the vital organs of the states have been seriously, if not as yet mortally, wounded. The area of state control has been whittled away by judicial interpretation, state boundaries have conflicted with successful regional planning; and the states, in contrast with the Commonwealth, have suffered a marked diminution of prestige in the eyes of the community. More important, powers guaranteed to the states by the constitution have been to a large extent nullified by financial instability and dependence and by changes within the society which have converted problems previously capable of solution within state boundaries into national or international problems with which the states were powerless to deal. The constitution is to-day ineffective for the needs of an industrialised society. The gap between the legal authority possessed by the states and their actual capacity to utilize their powers is an ever-increasing one. It is clear that the constitution leaves to the states too substantial powers, while the Commonwealth, though it has increased enormously in stature, has not made a corresponding advance in legal authority, and is consequently debarred from attempting national action in matters where it has become imperative.

In Australia, then, it would seem that the disadvantages of incomplete union have had to be endured without securing for the states that lasting and virile independence which was desired. It might conceivably be argued that the undermining of state independence simply meant that unification had come about under the guise of a federal form. Unfortunately, that is not the case. The federal government cannot operate with the same freedom as the government of a unitary state, since the defects of the federal form persist to hamper its activity. The limitations of a written constitution confine the boundaries of its action, while the division of powers between state and Commonwealth impedes unified effort. No doubt co-operation represents a possible means of securing united action, but the record of co-operation both in Australia and elsewhere does not support the contention that it is an adequate alternative to unification.

The price paid to secure what has proved an illusory independence for the states has prevented other unities from coming into being. In many respects the history of the past forty-five years represents an almost continual attempt to escape from the evil effects of the division of powers, and from the dilemma created by the failure to grant adequate authority to the Commonwealth, especially in matters relating to industrial control. The founders of the Commonwealth, though loath to weaken the states by bestowing wider powers upon the central government, had recognised that changed conditions might require changes in the constitution. They had, therefore, inserted machinery for amendment, notably the referendum, which was thought to be a most progressive feature, and was praised by no less an authority than Dicey as a means of introducing flexibility into the constitution.[39]   But, in practice, the referendum has proved an unsatisfactory agency for effecting constitutional change, since it has been almost impossible to obtain the requisite majorities. Twenty amendments to the constitution have been proposed, yet only three have been carried, and of these only one was of any importance. Even with regard to that amendment—the ratification of the Financial Agreement of 1928—it was not realised at the time what far-reaching changes were implied in the measure.[40]

The great issue has been the extension of Commonwealth powers, particularly in such fields as industrial regulation and trade and commerce. Here was evident need for reform, and the Labour Party, especially, recognized the necessity of conferring wider powers upon the central government.   Indeed, the Australian Labour movement can claim that it was aware, about a generation before labour movements in other federations, that without removing certain problems to the plane of central government, they could not be dealt with adequately. Actually, the first two referendums were concerned with other questions.[41]   That of 1906 secured an alteration in the dates of periodical Senate elections, while in 1910 one proposal to permit the Commonwealth to take over 'all state debts, irrespective of the date on which contracted,'

39. A. V. Dicey, *Introduction to the Study of the Law of the Constitution*, p. 533.
40. This opinion is expressed in *The Case of the People of Western Australia* and in the *Round Table*, article upon the Marketing and Aviation Amendments.
41. See *Report*, Commission on the Constitution, 1929, p. 231. For a list of Bills to alter the Constitution introduced into the Commonwealth Parliament, see Knowles, *op. cit.*, pp. 197-272B.

was approved, and another to substitute *per capita* payments to the states in place of a percentage of the customs revenue was rejected.[42] In 1911, the Fisher government brought forward a series of proposals to grant the Commonwealth increased powers in relation to commerce and industry and monopolies. The exact nature of these proposals should be noted. They were far-reaching, and would have given the Commonwealth almost complete control over the economic and industrial life of the country. Had they been carried much of the later confusion occasioned by divided and inadequate control would have been obviated. The proposals were embodied in two referendums. The first sought to empower the Commonwealth to deal with four subjects : trade and commerce generally, control of corporations, employment including wages, conditions of labour and the settlement of disputes, and monopolies in production. The second proposed the insertion of a new paragraph in section 51 whereby the Commonwealth parliament could acquire and conduct any business which each house had declared to be 'the subject of a monopoly.' In both cases the proposals were rejected by heavy majorities.[43]

Two years later very similar amendments were again the subject of a referendum. On this occasion also they were rejected, but the voting was much closer, and the states were evenly divided. The actual figures were:

Amendment	For		Against
Trade and Commerce	958,419	. .	982,615
Corporations	960,711	. .	986,824
Industrial Matters	961,601	. .	987,611
Railway Disputes	956,358	. .	990,046
Trusts	967,331	. .	975,943
Nationalization of Monopolies	917,165	. .	941,947

Queensland, South Australia and Western Australia voted in favour, and New South Wales, Victoria and Tasmania against the amendments.[44]

Once more, in 1915, proposals upon similar lines were considered, but were never submitted to referendum. After the war, however, the Hughes government put forward amendments giving the Commonwealth authority to legislate upon industrial

42. Queensland, Western Australia and Tasmania favourable; New South Wales, Victoria and South Australia against.
43. 1st proposal—483,356 in favour, 742,704 against.
    2nd proposal—488,668 in favour; 736,392 against.
    Western Australia was the only State in favour of either proposal. For details of voting see Knowles, *op. cit.*, pp. 215, 217.
44. Figures from *Report*, Commission on the Constitution, 1929, p. 233.

disputes and the nationalization of monopolies. The electorate
once more refused to increase Commonwealth powers, though,
as in 1913, the voting was close, and the states were evenly
divided.[45] No further attempt was made until 1926, when two
proposals were voted upon and rejected. The first embodied
several amendments, whose aim was to give the Commonwealth
power to legislate with regard to corporations, trusts and conciliation and arbitration generally. The second proposed to
confer power upon the Commonwealth parliament to protect the
public against the 'interruption of any essential service.' Both
amendments were rejected, and in each case only New South
Wales and 'Queensland favoured the change. The actual figures
were :[46]

	For	Against
First proposal	1,247,088	1,619,655
Second proposal	1,195,502	1,597,793

In 1928 the requisite majorities were secured for the alteration of the constitution by the insertion of section 105A.[47] This,
however, was considered simply as a necessary mechanical alteration to implement the Financial Agreement between the Commonwealth and the states, and not as a step involving any radical
change in the constitution.

The referendum in March 1937 was the result of an endeavour by the Commonwealth to secure increased powers with
regard to marketing and aviation. A hostile vote was recorded against both amendments, but the marketing proposals
were defeated by far heavier majorities.[48] In fact, it seems
probable that had the aviation amendment not been coupled with
that upon marketing it would have been accepted. The actual
figures were :

	Aviation		Marketing
Yes	1,924,946		1,259,808
No	1,669,062		2,214,388
Informal . ..	150,355		270,167
Majority for	255,884	Majority against	954,580

---

45. Industrial Disputes—911,357 in favour, 924,160 against.
     Monopolies—813,880 in favour, 859,451 against.
     Queensland, Victoria and Western Australia in favour, and New South
     Wales, South Australia and Tasmania against. (Knowles, *op. cit.*, pp. 257,
     261).
46. Knowles, *op. cit.*, pp. 264, 265.
47. 2.237,391 in favour, 773,852 against—carried in all six states (Knowles,
     op. cit., p. 268).
48. See *Round Table*, xxvii, 651.

The marketing amendment was defeated in every state, and the aviation amendment, though it received many more affirmative votes, secured a majority in only two states[49] and was, therefore, rejected. The defeat of these proposals provided a significant illustration of the defects inherent in a popular referendum. Since the leaders of all federal parties had declared in favour of increased Commonwealth powers, and since the premiers of the three most populous states had given their support to the proposals it would have been natural to suppose that both amendments would secure a majority. Such a conclusion would have been strengthened by a consideration of the urgent need for increased powers over marketing, which had been revealed through judicial decision. A favourable vote might, therefore, have been expected, yet the proposals were defeated and the reasons for their defeat were apparent. Anti-federal feeling in Australia was strong, particularly in the less populous states, whose citizens believed that many of their financial disabilities might be ascribed to Commonwealth policy. In this respect, it is noteworthy that the premiers of South Australia, Western Australia and Tasmania wholeheartedly opposed the marketing amendment. There was also considerable discontent with the Commonwealth government, a number of whose recent actions had been unpopular. There seems little doubt that many who disliked the government's trade diversion policy, or its book censorship or the exclusion of Mrs. Freer, took the opportunity to express their disapproval by voting against the amendments.[50]

One other reason of the utmost importance for the defeat of the marketing proposals was that for once the consumers were being organized against the pressure-groups of the producers. In Australia most marketing schemes have been designed in the interests of the producers who have been able to exert tremendous pressure, because of the astonishingly strong position enjoyed by primary industries in the Australian political set-up. In addition, therefore, to the reasons previously advanced which may have prompted a negative vote it is highly probable that the long-felt resentment of the consumer against the home consumption price for foodstuffs was decisive in securing the rejection of the amendment

49. Victoria and Queensland.
50. *Round Table*, xxvii, 656. The opposition of the Lang Labour Party in N.S.W. was another factor in the defeat of the proposals. Some votes may have been cast against the marketing proposals because previous marketing schemes had been used to "dump" primary products.

Finally the difficulty of securing an affirmative vote was much increased by the fact that the marketing proposal involved highly complicated legal considerations.   It proposed to limit in favour of the Commonwealth the application of section 92 which imposed absolute freedom of trade among the states.   Since it was impossible to know what interpretation the court would place on the word 'marketing' the limits to be set to the proposed extension of Commonwealth powers were difficult to determine.   In these circumstances many voters apparently decided not to venture upon any constitutional experiment and recorded a negative vote.

The experience of Australia, therefore, provides additional evidence of the unsatisfactory character of the referendum.   The almost unbroken sequence of negative votes upon amendments, many of which were essential for the efficient conduct of government in Australia, has demonstrated that the bias of the referendum has been almost wholly against any alteration of the constitution, partly, no doubt, because of the necessity of securing the approval of a majority of states as well as a majority of all the electors voting.[51]   The Australian evidence supports the contention that there are many questions which are unsuitable for submission by referendum, more especially in a federation where excessive legalism often renders the proposed amendments unduly complicated.   As Professor Laski has pointed out,[52] if proposals are limited to broad principles then the absence of details may render a verdict upon them meaningless, while if they are amplified to include detailed provisions they become too complex to be judged by a mass vote.   Moreover, an amendment is rarely accepted or rejected upon its merits, because of the impossibility of considering it apart from the record of the government by whom it is proposed.   As in the case of the marketing referendum especially, the electors too often take the opportunity afforded by the vote of expressing their discontent with some aspect of the government's policy quite unconnected with the proposals for amendment.   Finally, it is necessary to emphasize that the referendum is not always democratic in its operation, as both France and Germany have proved, and that in Australia the balance of its influence has been inclined in a reactionary, rather than a progressive, direction by compulsory voting.

51. Inserted with the intention of securing state rights.
52. H. J. Laski, *Parliamentary Government in England* (1938), pp. 131-3.

The repeated failure to secure a majority for proposed amendments has been especially disappointing, because in Australia the need for more extensive Commonwealth powers is admitted by political leaders of all parties to be urgent. In Australia economic life as a whole is being integrated, yet constitutional divisions persist, which tend to nullify the action taken by any one government. The difficulties of a system which allocates control over customs and banking to the Commonwealth and control over commerce and industrial regulation to the states are obvious In short, it may be said that the divisions which the constitution set up have been found hampering to effective government, while the methods of change which it supplied have proved unsatisfactory. New social forces and new demands have shown the federal machinery to be antiquated.

IV

THE EVIL EFFECTS OF THE DIVISION OF POWERS BETWEEN STATE AND FEDERAL AUTHORITIES

BECAUSE the Australian constitution was federal in character, there had to be a distribution of the subject matters of government among the states and the Commonwealth. The division of powers was embodied in a written constitution, and reliance was placed upon the vigilance of the High Court to prevent infringement of its terms. Provision was made for amendment of the constitution, but the machinery by which change was to be brought about proved largely ineffective, possibly because the original divisions had developed an unnatural sanctity, which made them psychologically rigid. In consequence, the constitutional division of subject matters between state and central authorities, though capable of change, has, in fact, remained almost unaltered. This inelasticity, so characteristic[1] of federations, has prevented the transference of additional subject matters to the Commonwealth, even in spheres where a stage of development had been reached which clearly necessitated legislative action by the national parliament.

In view of the long survival of the distribution of powers effected at federation, the basis upon which division was made becomes highly significant, and, more particularly, the nature of the subject matters entrusted to the states. As with the United States, the functions of the federal government were enumerated and the residue left to the states, a procedure which penalized the Commonwealth, since new subjects of legislation which might arise with the passage of time would, unless covered by the wording of one of the enumerated powers, automatically fall to the states. But, while the federal government had the enumerated functions and the states the residue, there were also certain subjects upon which their powers were concurrent. Indeed, one of the most striking things about the constitution as it has operated has been the vast area of concurrent legislative power. Legislation, therefore, fell within three categories.[2] First, there were subjects on which the Commonwealth possessed exclusive

1. See the remarks by Dicey, *Law of the Constitution*, p. 145.
2. K. R. Cramp, *State and Federal Constitutions of Australia* (1914), p. 172.

powers. Next came those on which Commonwealth and state powers were concurrent, and, thirdly, those subjects on which the states alone could exercise authority. The principal powers entrusted to the Commonwealth consisted of the imposition of customs and excise duties and the right to legislate with respect to defence, external affairs, taxation, immigration, posts and telegraphs, banking and currency, foreign and interstate trade and commerce and industrial arbitration in cases where the dispute extended beyond the limits of one state. These were almost all matters which were obviously national in character and which could not, therefore, be withheld from the Commonwealth if any worthwhile measure of federation was to be achieved. However, what is most striking about the division is not the importance of the powers assumed by the Commonwealth, though admittedly in the two major crises before the present war Commonwealth powers proved surprisingly comprehensive, but, rather, the importance of those retained by the states. The major problems of development and social experiment rested with the states, since they possessed authority to legislate with respect to land settlement, transport, wages, hours and conditions of employment, education, health, administration of justice, poor and unemployment relief and taxation in certain fields.[3] The fundamental disadvantage of this division was in its rigidity. When changed conditions within Australia made the time ripe for legislation upon a national rather than a state basis the Commonwealth lacked constitutional power to take action while the machinery designed to bring about amendment of the constitution proved ineffective.

The distribution of the subject matters of government among numerous authorities has had other serious disadvantages. The fact that both federal and state governments had to act within constitutionally defined limits led, necessarily, to what Mr. Canaway has called a 'restriction of their fields of vision.'[4] Not unnaturally, each government regarded the subjects allocated to it as of primary importance to the nation, with the result that each emphasised the particular policy with which it was concerned and excluded from its survey other equally important factors. Little attention, therefore, was paid to viewing the scene of governmental operations as a whole, and little effort

3. On some of these subjects the Commonwealth and states possessed concurrent powers, e.g., taxation. The Commonwealth also found that it could have some say with regard to wages, hours and conditions of employment.
4. A. P. Canaway, *The Failure of Federalism in Australia* (1930), p. 24.

was made to reconcile divergent aims or to avoid conflict between policies pursued by different governments. Instead, each authority acted independently, and the price for the failure to achieve a unified national effort was too often paid in duplication and collision.[5]   Instances of duplication, with its consequent complexity and its waste of time, effort and money, are everywhere apparent in the ramifications of state and federal legislation and governmental machinery.   Thus, both the states and the Commonwealth have imposed death duties, taxed land and incomes, erected Courts of Industrial Arbitration, founded Savings Banks and established departments which perform such functions as the collection of statistics.   Nor are examples of collision wanting.   An illustration is afforded by the way in which awards made by the Commonwealth Court of Industrial Arbitration have affected enterprises owned by the states.   The railways are a case in point, especially as the state governments were bitterly opposed to railway employees being made subject to federal awards.[6]   Increases in the rates of wages as the result of Commonwealth awards conflicted with the attempts of the states to make railways pay, and were criticized as a threat to state control.   Another instance can be seen in the imposition of Commonwealth customs duties upon goods imported by state governments for use on developmental projects or state-owned services and industries.   Yet, perhaps the most significant example of conflict is to be found in the divergent policies of development pursued by state and federal governments.   No doubt collision would still exist to some extent, even if the states were simply provinces in a unitary system, but where a federal organisation operates the clash may be far more serious, since it may occur as the result of action taken by different authorities in fields in which each is supreme.   A solution can then only be attained by reconciliation and co-operation, and experience in all federations has shown that it will not be easily achieved.

The Commonwealth, through its exclusive power to impose tariffs, has pursued a policy of protection with the object of fostering secondary industries.   The states, on the other hand, because of the retention of their powers over land settlement

---

5. *Ibid.*, pp. 43-4.   The mere fact of duplication is not in itself necessarily objectionable.
6. e.g., *The Railway Servants' Case*, 4 *C.L.R.* 488 (1906), where the court agreed with the contention of Victoria that state railway employees were not subject to Commonwealth awards.   The case was later overruled. See also speeches by some of the Premiers, e.g., Mr. Bavin, at the Premiers' Conference, May, 1929.

and development have been chiefly concerned with increasing primary production.   This division of interconnected subjects of legislation was carried still further since immigration was placed in Commonwealth hands, despite the fact that no successful migration policy could be carried out unless the states, with their control over land settlement, were willing to co-operate extensively.[7]   Though a measure of co-operation[8] has been achieved with regard to immigration, over the field of development as a whole there has been little attempt to reconcile divergent aims.   The failure to do so becomes obvious when those states which are principally engaged in primary production claim that the greatest disability under which they labour is the protective policy pursued by the Commonwealth.[9]   Protection was itself intended as a developmental policy, and, in the opinion of the Tariff Committee of 1929, it had been at least partially successful in its object, since it had 'enabled an increase of population to take place . . . greater than could have been absorbed on marginal land, with a diminishing scale of returns.'[10]

If protection made possible an increase in population it also raised costs of production.   An analysis of the effects of protection in a report, entitled *The Australian Tariff*, revealed that higher costs were passed on by sheltered industry, with the result that the main burden of protection fell upon unsheltered industry, which in Australia largely consisted of rural exports.   Many primary products, however, were sheltered, either naturally or artificially, so that the higher costs imposed by protection were 'passed on to unsheltered industry, which has to sell its products at home and abroad at world prices.'[11]   Wool and wheat were estimated to bear roughly 75 per cent. of the costs placed upon export industry, while metals, meat and fresh fruit carried the other 25 per cent.   In 1929 the Tariff Committee was of the opinion that although wheat and wool had hitherto been able to carry the load there were signs that it was becoming 'oppressive.'   Four years later the Grants Commission declared that a number of factors had brought about a decrease in the burden of protection, but this may well have been more apparent than real, for the commission went on to say, 'Thus the general average

7. K. O. Warner, "Australian Federalism at the Crossroads" (*Pacific Affairs*, Feb., 1931, p. 127).
8. For agreements between the Commonwealth and the states relating to immigration see *Report*, Commission on the Constitution, 1929, p. 179.
9. First *Report* by the Commonwealth Grants Commission (1934), p. 58.
10. *Ibid.*, p. 58, quoting conclusions reached in The Australian Tariff report.
11. *Ibid.*, p. 66.

of the excess tariff costs has been reduced, though, on account of the low export prices the export industries may be less able to meet them.'[12]

It would seem, then, that the adoption of protection by the Commonwealth as a means whereby secondary industries might be fostered and the country enabled to support a larger population has had the effect of imposing a handicap upon the efforts made by the states to stimulate primary production. 'In so far,' reads the report of the Grants Commission, 'as the establishment of secondary industry involves a subsidy from the community which falls with especial severity on export industry, there is a clash of interest between secondary industry and the interests which depend upon primary industry.'[13]   The conflict between the two developmental policies became also, to some extent, a conflict between the eastern states and South Australia, Western Australia and Tasmania, since the secondary industries fostered by the tariff were mostly established in New South Wales and Victoria, which possessed the larger populations and the advantages of an early start and of proximity to the coalfields. As all the States were engaged in large-scale primary production, all were to some extent affected by the policy of protection. Certain states were, however, more dependent upon unsheltered exports, and these, notably the present 'claimant' states, suffered considerably from the excess costs imposed by the tariff. South Australia and, more particularly, Western Australia have repeatedly asserted that the Commonwealth protective policy imposes an intolerable burden upon them, since they receive comparatively few benefits and almost all the disadvantages.

For example, the Western Australian case, after referring to the burden placed upon the state's export industries, instances a number of disabilities which result from the protective policy.[14] It points out that few of the primary products which have been protected are of importance in the state's economy, that secondary industries receive no benefit from the tariff, since they are incapable of withstanding the competition from manufacturers in the eastern states, and that in numerous instances Western Australian exports have suffered because foreign countries have adopted retaliatory measures when increased Australian duties have been placed upon their imports. Nevertheless, it is probable that the burden attributed to the tariff by the 'claimant' states has been exaggerated, since all states within the Commonwealth

12. *Ibid.*, p. 63.   13. *Ibid.*, p. 58.
14. *The Case of the People of Western Australia*, pp. 278-303.

show a similarity in their economic structure, particularly in the ratio between the population of the capital city and the state as a whole.[15]   Although the adverse effect of protection upon any one state is extremely difficult to estimate, especially as the indirect effects are always considerable, yet it would seem that Western Australia suffers most, South Australia a good deal, but Tasmania is not greatly injured.[16]   On the positive side, Victoria and Queensland benefit most from a protective policy, with New South Wales occupying a midway position.

While the Commonwealth was attempting to foster the growth of secondary industries through the tariff, the states were promoting schemes for land settlement and development, which are said to have amounted to 'a policy of protection for primary industry.'[17]   The methods employed were direct subsidy and heavy capital expenditure upon railways, irrigation and other works, and upon the purchase of land for subdivision into small-scale holdings.   Such projects were not only costly, but also unremunerative, and, on occasions, financially disastrous.   Indeed, in the opinion of the Grants Commission, the losses sustained through attempts at land settlement were, at least in the case of the 'claimant' states, the chief cause of budgetary difficulties. The developmental policies carried out by the state governments had two complementary aspects.   They aimed at intensification of production in areas already occupied by means of closer settlement, and at the occupation of marginal lands possessing any prospect of profitable exploitation.   In many instances settlement of marginal lands was undoubtedly carried too far, since areas were opened up which it was uneconomic to exploit at prevailing world prices.[18]   State governments were by no means always ready to learn the lessons of failure, but were prone rather to maintain settlers on land which did not warrant cultivation.   Mistakes were made both in planning and administration, but in attempting marginal settlement peculiar difficulties had to be faced.   Since it was pioneer work experimentation

15. First *Report*, Grants Commission, p. 71.
16. Third *Report*, Grants Commission (1936), p. 68.   *The Case of the People of Western Australia*, p. 237.
17. See "Problems of Developing Primary and Secondary Industries and the Interaction of Developmental Policies," First *Report*, Grants Commission, Ch. iv.
18. This was the opinion of the Grants Commission.   It is supported by other recent investigations, e.g., by John Andrews, "The Present Situation in the Wheat Growing Industry in South-Eastern Australia" (*Economic Geography*, April, 1936).   On p. 130 the author says: "Farms in risky areas are bottomless pits into which taxpayers' and investors' money is thrown." The same article details the expenses associated with marginal settlement.

was necessary to discover the limits of settlement.   Moreover, it must be admitted that in the occupation of large sections of the Mallee country, not only in Western and South Australia, but also in Victoria and New South Wales, considerable success was achieved.

The difficulties which have faced state governments in their efforts to promote land settlement and development and the huge losses which they have incurred are not solely attributable to a conflict of policies arising out of the existence of the federal form.   Many of the handicaps were imposed by climatic and geological conditions.[19]   Others resulted from the onset of the depression and the collapse in world prices for primary products. Others, again, sprang from an ill-conceived approach to the problem, and were of the state governments' own making.   Yet, even when all these factors are recognized and due weight attached to each it can hardly be denied that political divisions have not only prevented a single-minded approach to the problems associated with the development of Australia, but have also enabled policies which were in conflict with each other to be enforced by a number of different authorities.   Proof of the lack of any real attempt to harmonize the developmental policies pursued by state and federal governments may be found in the length of time during which those policies have been in conflict, as well as in the increasingly intense nature of the clash.   Such, at least, was the conclusion reached by the *Grants Commission* after a careful sifting of the evidence:

> There is almost a competition between the two factors of development; each frustrates the effect of the other; the burdens created by the one make the protection required for the other the greater, so that the clash . . . becomes more intense as each protective effort grows.   There is an increasing amount of protection to primary industry in the Commonwealth tariff, but the broad distinction set out above still remains.[20]

The evil effects of the division of powers have by no means been limited to the field of developmental policies, but have been equally apparent in the sphere of industrial legislation and arbitration.   By a sub-section of the constitution the Commonwealth was empowered to make laws with respect to 'conciliation and arbitration for the prevention and settlement of industrial disputes

19. See Griffith Taylor, "The Frontiers of Settlement in Australia" (*Geographical Review*, Jan., 1926), and "Australia as a Field for Settlement" (*Foreign Affairs*, July, 1927).
20. First *Report*, Grants Commission, p. 62.

extending beyond the limits of any one state.[21]   This power, limited though it was in scope, had been bitterly attacked when first put forward during the convention debates, and the decision in favour of its incorporation in the constitution was only reached —and then by a narrow majority—after the proposal had been twice rejected. The strength of the opposition is sufficient to account for the restricted terms in which the grant of industrial power was made to the Commonwealth. Just how narrow were the limits of Commonwealth authority may be judged from the fact that legislation with regard to industrial disputes had to be confined to conciliation and arbitration and to disputes which extended beyond the limits of one state. In reality, therefore, the federal parliament possessed no power to legislate upon conditions of employment or rates of wages, for any industry within any part of the continent.[22] Moreover, when the parliament did attempt to authorize the Commonwealth Court of Arbitration to declare a common rule in a particular industry the High Court held that parliament had exceeded its powers.[23]

If the Commonwealth grant of authority was meagre and couched in specific terms the states, on the other hand, as residuary legatees, possessed very considerable industrial powers. They could and did legislate for the prevention and settlement of industrial disputes which were confined within their own boundaries, with the result that in Australia there came to be six sets of arbitral machinery established under State authority in addition to the Arbitration Court set up by the Commonwealth. The six state tribunals were not uniform in character, though they performed very similar functions. In New South Wales there was an Industrial Commission and a number of conciliation committees; in Western Australia an Industrial Court; in Queensland a Board of Trade and Arbitration; while in South Australia, Victoria and Tasmania Wages Boards were in existence.[24] The status of these tribunals was different from that of the federal court, because within the limits of the constitution the various state parliaments could bestow authority upon them to make awards binding on all persons engaged in an industry

21. Subsection xxxv of section 51, Knowles, *The Australian Constitution*, pp. 34 *et seq.*
22. See *Report*, Commission on the Constitution, 1929, p. 162.
    K. O. Warner in *Pacific Affairs*, Feb., 1931, p. 135.
23. 11 *C.L.R.* 311 (1910), *Australian Boot Trade Employees' Federation v. Whybrow and Co.* (Knowles, *op. cit.*, p. 38).
24. In South Australia there was also a court presided over by a president, and in Victoria there was an appeal to a court.

functioning within the state. The establishment of dual control
by the erection of both state and federal machinery for the settlement of industrial disputes has led to a confusion of jurisdiction
which has rendered control over industrial matters complicated
in the extreme.

By process of judicial interpretation the field over which the
Commonwealth arbitration power operates has been much enlarged, and that over which the states exercise jurisdiction has
been correspondingly reduced. Litigation has chiefly centred
about the meaning to be given to the words 'industrial,' 'disputes'
and 'extending beyond one state.' The interpretation to be given
to these terms is now much wider than that which was at first
adopted. The word 'industrial' does not confine a dispute solely
to manufacturing. Mining,[25] for example, was early included
within its scope, and later it was held to cover not only banking
and insurance,[26] but also non-profit making industries carried
on by municipalities.[27] Teachers and strictly governmental employees were, however, excluded.[28] The term 'disputes' has
acquired a technical meaning. It, in common with the interpretation to be given to 'extending beyond one state,' was defined
by the Commission on the Constitution of 1929:

> Disputes means disputes which may be created by the service
> of a log containing a demand for changes in industrial con-
> ditions and a refusal of that demand. There need not neces-
> sarily have been any disputes existing between employers and
> employees apart from the service of the log, nor any dispute
> threatening the industrial peace of more than one State. The
> dispute becomes inter-State if persons engaged in the same
> industry employed in different States join in the service of the
> same log.[29]

The definitions of the commission, however, require serious
modification in the light of the judgments of the High Court
since the issue of the 1929 report. Of these, the most important
were the decisions in the two coal cases, *Caledonian Colleries
Ltd. v. Australasian Coal and Shale Employees' Federation No. 1
and No. 2.*[30] The coal cases arose out of an industrial dispute

25. 6 *C.L.R.* 309 (1908), *Jumbunna Coal Mine No Liability v. Victorian Coal
    Miners' Association.*
26. 33 *C.L.R.*, 517 (1923), *Australian Insurance Staffs' Federation v. Acci-
    dent Underwriters' Association; Bank Officials' Association v. Bank of
    Australasia.*
27. 26 *C.L.R.* 508 (1919), *Municipalities Case.*
28. 41 *C.L.R.* 569 (1929), *Federated State School Teachers' Association of
    Australia v. State of Victoria.*
29. *Report,* Commission on the Constitution, 1929, p. 162.
30. 42 *C.L.R.* 527 (1930) and 42 *C.L.R.* 558 (1930).

which commenced on the northern coalfields of New South Wales. The proprietors of the northern collieries demanded a reduction of wages, but the miners resolutely refused to consent. The dispute inevitably had interstate repercussions, since the coal mined in northern New South Wales was so superior in quality that its selling price played an important part in determining the maximum price for coal produced in Queensland or Victoria. It was highly probable, therefore, that a lowering of wages on the northern coalfields of New South Wales would ultimately lead to an attempt to reduce wages in Queensland and Victorian mines.

On 16 December 1929, the general secretary of the Coal and Shale Employees' Federation sent a telegram to the secretary of the branch at Wonthaggi in Victoria appealing for a stoppage there. Next day the men at Wonthaggi ceased work, but were ready to resume on 20 December, the day after Judge Beeby had made an interim award. In Queensland one mine was idle on 17 December, and two others on the 19th.

The validity of the award made by Judge Beeby was challenged before the High Court in a case which was notable both for the re-examination of the meaning to be given to the words expressing the Commonwealth grant of power with regard to conciliation and arbitration, and for the restriction of Commonwealth control resulting from the application of the court's definition of an industrial dispute. The court held that 'The words "extending beyond the limits of any one state" as applied to a dispute mean that the dispute is one "existing in two or more states," or, in other words, "covering Australian territory comprised within two or more states." '[31]

An industrial dispute was defined by the court in the following terms:

There must be disagreement between people or groups of people who stand in some industrial relation upon some matter which affects or arises out of the relationship. Such a disagreement may cause a strike, a lock-out, and disturbance and dislocation of industry: but these are the consequences of the industrial dispute, and not the industrial dispute itself, which lies in the disagreement. . . . But upon this conception of an industrial dispute, it cannot extend beyond the limits of any one State unless in each of two or more States, at one time, the disagreement exists between people or groups who stand in some industrial relation.[32]

Applying these tests to the case before it the High Court, with Isaacs, J., dissenting, reached the conclusion that upon the facts

31. 42 *C.L.R.*, p. 552.   32. 42 C.L.R., pp. 552-3.

the dispute did not extend into Victoria or Queensland. The reasoning upon which this conclusion was based was in itself indicative of the attitude which the court proposed to adopt in determining the limits of Commonwealth jurisdiction. It was admitted that miners in Queensland and Victoria were antagonistic to any lowering of wages in New South Wales, both on principle and because of the likelihood that their own wages would be affected adversely by such a reduction, and it was further conceded that they were ready to cease work in order to support the resistance of the miners in New South Wales. But it was argued that these circumstances did not create a dispute between miners and owners in Queensland or Victoria, since the closing of the mines in New South Wales had raised the selling price of coal elsewhere, which meant that until New South Wales mines 'resumed production at lower costs' there would be no thought of reducing wages in the other states. Such an argument led to the conclusion that the dispute in New South Wales did not extend to Victoria or Queensland. Nor would the High Court agree that an extension was threatened or probable.

Against such a viewpoint Isaacs, J., issued an impassioned (but logical) protest:

> In my opinion, the circumstances not only justified, but loudly demanded, the intervention of the Arbitration Court. That intervention was the interposition of the national law to save the community from the loss and suffering of a national calamity, and it has been rightfully and properly exercised.[33]

In the second case, a blow was struck against the procedure of filing a log of demands upon the employers in an industry throughout the Commonwealth, with the object of creating an inter-state dispute, and thus securing a hearing before the Commonwealth Arbitration Court. This procedure had been followed by the council of the Australasian Coal and Shale Employees' Federation in the dispute under consideration. It was agreed by the High Court that the Commonwealth Arbitration Court only possessed jurisdiction when an alleged dispute was 'real and genuine.' 'Whether it be real and genuine is always a question of fact, and upon proceedings in prohibition the fact must be determined by this Court on its own independent view of the evidence.'[34] The court, with Isaacs, J., dissenting, went on to deny that in the present instance the dispute could be described as 'real and

---

33. 42 *C.L.R.*, p. 540.
34. 42 *C.L.R.*, pp. 577-8. Quoting from the judgment in *The King v. Hibble; Ex parte Broken Hill Pty. Co.*

genuine.' Without examining the arguments which led the
majority of the High Court to their decision, it may be said
that they took the view that the demands put forward by the
Federation were simply a subterfuge to secure a hearing before
the Commonwealth tribunal. 'We think that the truth is that
all parties regarded the formulation of these demands as nothing
but a step towards enabling the Arbitration Court to deal with
the trouble in New South Wales.'[35]

It was agreed that frequently the desire to secure an award
from the Commonwealth court had led to the creation and extension of industrial disputes, but it was argued that in such cases,
where the court had jurisdiction, that jurisdiction depended not
upon the motives behind the dispute but upon the existence of a
two-state dispute. In the present instance, however, the justices
refused to agree that this was the position.

Indeed, the argument may well be said to conceal but to contain the reality of this case, namely, that paper demands were
conceived as part of a proceeding requisite to enable the Arbitration Court to regulate an industry in which a serious dispute
confined to one State was in progress. In our opinion the log
of demands was not effective to create a new dispute with the
proprietors nor to extend the existing dispute beyond New
South Wales.[36]

As a result of the decisions in these cases the practice whereby
matters could be taken away from the state jurisdiction and put
into the federal jurisdiction by what was, in effect, the filing of
a collusive log is no longer so prevalent. What is more, the
judgments of members of the High Court, notably those of Mr.
Justice Dixon, indicate that the High Court has become somewhat more exacting in its consideration of what are disputes extending beyond the limits of one state. In some ways this more
narrow scrutiny has only served to make the question of jurisdiction even more confusing than it was before, while the very
limited and inadequate, yet wholly necessary, Commonwealth control of industrial disputes has been curtailed.

The espousal by the first High Court of the doctrines of immunity of instrumentalities and mutual non-interference had the
effect of circumscribing the scope of the Commonwealth arbitration power. Awards made by state tribunals were to be affected
as little as possible, and were only to be set aside when obedience
to them was clearly incompatible with obedience to the award of
the Commonwealth court. But the real importance of the High

---

35.   42 *C.L.R.*, p. 579.   36.   42 *C.L.R.*, p. 580.

Court's attitude lay in its exclusion of state employees from the jurisdiction of the federal court. Despite the specific inclusion within the *Conciliation and Arbitration Act,* 1904, of employees upon state railways, the High Court held in the *Railway Servants' Case*[37] that state railways were a state instrumentality, and, therefore, exempt from the operation of the Commonwealth Arbitration Court. This interpretation, which was followed until 1920, when it was overthrown in the *Engineers' Case,* divided industry artificially into two camps according to whether it could be classified as private or governmental. The unfortunate effects of this division were made plain by Mr. Justice Higgins in the *Wheat Lumpers' Case.*[38] A dispute had broken out between an association of employees engaged in wheat lumping and stacking and their employers, of whom two were the states of Victoria and New South Wales, acting through their respective Ministers for Agriculture. Following the principles laid down in the *Railway Servants' Case,* a majority of the High Court held that

so far as the two States were concerned their operations were governmental and not trading, and that, therefore, the Commonwealth Court of Conciliation and Arbitration had no power . . . to hear . . . the dispute.[39]

Higgins, J., dissenting from the judgment on the grounds that operations, such as wheat marketing, were industrial, and that industries carried on by a state were not excluded from the jurisdiction of the Commonwealth court, went on to urge the expediency of a liberal interpretation of the Commonwealth power in view of the chaotic conditions produced by unreal distinctions within industry. He argued that in Australia, because of the extensive nature of state activities, the removal of state industries from the jurisdiction of the Commonwealth court would paralyse attempts at national industrial regulation. Moreover, as the state extended 'its octopus grasp' to other industries those industries also would be removed from the ambit of Commonwealth control. The difficulties encountered under the system prevailing were sufficient evidence of its unsatisfactory nature. Mr. Justice Higgins instanced the coal industry in Victoria, where in the course of negotiations it was found that the state coal mine was the dominant factor, and that 'the other mine owners in competition

---

37. 4 *C.L.R.* 488 (1906), *The Federated Amalgamated Government Railway and Tramway Service Association v. The N.S.W. Railway Traffic Employees' Association.*
38. 26 *C.L.R.* 460 (1919), *Australian Workers' Union v. Adelaide Milling Co. Ltd.*
39. 26 *C.L.R.,* p. 460.

could not come to an arrangement with the men unless the state mine became a party to it.'[40]   It was ridiculous, he argued, to assert that the character of the industrial operations performed in one mine was different from that performed in another because the one was state owned and the other in private hands. Even more important from the point of view of preserving industrial peace was the fact that the workmen concerned were themselves conscious of no such distinction.   The dispute in the *Wheat Lumpers' Case* provided additional proof both of the impossibility of distinguishing between the nature of the work performed by state and private employees engaged in the same industry and of the illogicality of permitting dual jurisdiction over any one industry. Mr. Justice Higgins in his account of the case, said:

> Some men, employed by the State, were carrying or moving bags of wheat to a stack, and other men, employed by shipowners and others, were carrying or moving the same bags to the ships.   Under the doctrine hitherto adopted, the Court of Conciliation was able to conciliate or arbitrate as to the one set of men and unable to do so as to the other set.   Contrasts as to the conditions of the respective sets of men were sure to arise and did arise, but the courts could not prevent the unrest which the contrasts caused.[41]

In 1920, partly as the result of a change in the personnel of the High Court, long-established principles of constitutional interpretation were overthrown and others substituted for them.   The judges no longer took as their starting point the powers reserved to the states, but began rather with those entrusted to the Commonwealth.   They held that full scope must be given to the terms of the Commonwealth grant of power before it could be established what residue remained to the states.   One effect of this revolution in the principles of judicial interpretation, as enunciated in the *Engineers' Case*, was the enlargement of the Commonwealth power of conciliation and arbitration to include employees engaged in state industries.   Isaacs, J., in delivering judgment, declared that section 51 (xxxv) is expressed

> in terms so general that it extends to all industrial disputes, in fact, extending beyond the limits of any one State, no exception being expressed as to industrial disputes in which States are concerned.[42]

The implications of the interpretation of Commonwealth powers adopted in the *Engineers' Case* were worked out in subsequent

40.   26 *C.L.R.*, p. 471.
41.   Higgins, J., referring to the *Wheat Lumpers' Case* during the *Engineers' Case* (28 *C.L.R.*, p. 163).
42.   28 *C.L.R.*, p. 150.

cases, notably in *Clyde Engineering Co. v. Cowburn*[43], which was responsible for a radical extension of the sphere of Commonwealth industrial jurisdiction.   It had previously been decided in *Whybrow's Case*[44] that if a federal award was inconsistent with a state law the award was invalid, the test of inconsistency being whether both could be obeyed.   This decision was now overruled, and the contrary view adopted that a federal award should prevail over any state law conflicting with it.   Isaacs, J., summing up the changes effected by the judgment, declared that the settlement of an inter-state industrial dispute by a federal award could no longer be impeded by any state law, that an award once validly made would prevail over any conflicting state law, and that the test of inconsistency would be whether the enforcement of a state law would infringe or alter the terms of the federal award.[45]

In an analysis of the position shortly after the decision in *Cowburn's Case* W. A. Holman declared:

The Commonwealth Parliament could apparently only put an end to the operation of an Award of the Arbitration Court by the heroic step of abolishing the court in toto. . . . There is now, therefore, in Australia, no general legislative power on industrial topics at all.   The State has a permitted power—so long as the Arbitration Court does not move—but there is no absolute power anywhere.

The spectacle of a community of 6,000,000 people finding their ultimate authority on industrial matters not in any Parliament, but in a Court, is a striking one.   So far as my knowledge goes no similar state of things can be found in any part of the civilised world.   It is a somewhat bewildering thought, that the return to British methods of interpretation and to British authorities, should have resulted in so singularly un-British a situation.[46]

It is obvious that these conditions would seriously undermine the position of the state tribunals and the prestige of state industrial legislation, but they did not imply an untrammelled exercise of Commonwealth jurisdiction throughout the whole field of industrial arbitration.   Commonwealth authority was still subject to severe limitations, such as that imposed by the restriction to inter-state disputes, while the possibility of overlapping and dual control remained.

Grave difficulty has been experienced in deciding just what

43. 37 *C.L.R.* 466 (1926).   See *Report*, Commission on Constitution, 1929, p. 165.
44. 10 *C.L.R.* 266 (1910).   For interpretation see *Report*, Commission on Constitution, 1929, p. 165; Knowles, *op. cit.*, pp. 37, 98.
45. 37 *C.L.R.*, p. 467, *Clyde Engineering Co. v. Cowburn*.
46. W. A. Holman, *The Australian Constitution: Its Interpretation and Amendment* (1928), p. 58.

tests should be applied in determining inconsistency between Commonwealth and state laws under section 109. Dixon, J., summing up the principles of interpretation adopted by the High Court, declared that section 109 invalidates a law of a state in so far as it would vary, detract from, or impair the operation of a law of the Commonwealth,'[47] yet even this wide-embracing rule is not capable of automatic application.   In one sense the test has always been the same, namely, whether the state law would infringe or vary the obligation imposed by the Commonwealth law, but it was a test which was applied by the High Court in rather different ways at different stages in the court's history.   During the early period it was held in *Whybrow's Case* that 'there was no inconsistency between a state law fixing a minimum wage and a Commonwealth industrial award fixing a higher minimum.'[48]   The criterion was whether both laws could be obeyed—in this instance, whether the employer would be involved in a conflict of duties if both laws were enforced.   It was argued that he would not, that the Commonwealth award could be 'obeyed' without 'disobeying' the state law, since no maximum had been laid down in the state legislation.   Subsequently, however, it was pointed out that such an approach to the question would not be decisive in all cases.   It might be satisfactory 'where the essence of the two statutes was in the imposition of duties,' but as Knox, C.J., and Gavan Duffy, J., remarked in *Cowburn's Case*, statutes may not only impose duties, but also confer rights:

> Statutes may do more than impose duties.   They may, for instance, confer rights, and one statute is inconsistent with another when it takes away a right conferred by that other, even though the right be one which might be waived or abandoned without disobeying the statute which conferred it.[49]

Cowburn's Case afforded an excellent illustration of the conferring of just such a right—the right of the employer under the Commonwealth award to work his employees, without overtime, for forty-eight hours per week. On the other hand, the state Act, the *Forty-four Hours Week Act,* 1925 (N.S.W.), declared that the ordinary working hours should not exceed forty-four, and that the employee was entitled to overtime after forty-four hours.

47. Dixon, J., in *Stock Motor Ploughs Ltd. v. Forsyth*, 48 *C.L.R.* (1932), p. 136, quoted K. H. Bailey, "Inconsistency with Paramount Law" (*Res Judicatae*, Oct., 1939, ii, 12).
48. *Ibid.,* p. 11.
49. 37 *C.L.R.* 466 (1926), p. 478.   Quoted Bailey, *ibid.,* p. 11.   It is exceedingly doubtful whether Cowburn's case should be regarded as one in which a state law was declared inconsistent with a Federal law, and therefore invalid, "by its mere existence and entirely without regard to its terms." See Bailey, *ibid.,* pp. 17-18.

It was true, as Higgins, J., pointed out, that an employer who paid his men overtime after forty-four hours, as required by the state law, could not be said to have 'disobeyed' the award. But the majority of the court nevertheless held that the Act was inconsistent with the award since the right of the employer to work his employees for forty-eight hours without overtime, was abolished by the state Act. The intention of the state law was clearly in contradiction with the Commonwealth award.

The later cases reveal a trend in the direction of regarding a Commonwealth industrial award as 'expressing an intention to operate as the sole and exclusive regulation of the matters contained therein,' the implication here being that the intention is to prevent any endeavour by a state to intervene in industrial relations dealt with by the award. Such a tendency is partly due to the altered emphasis since the *Engineers' Case,* but it has also been due to actual amendments of the Commonwealth Arbitration Act. In such a case the paramount legislature has expressly stated its intention of 'covering the field' to the exclusion of state legislation. 'When a valid federal Act evinces such an intention, a state Act purporting to govern the same matter is, by its mere existence as a law and irrespective of its content, inconsistent with the federal Act.[50] Section 30 of the *Commonwealth Conciliation and Arbitration Act* provides an example of the Commonwealth Parliament's intention to 'cover the field' to the exclusion of state law:

> When a State law or an award, order or determination of a State industrial authority is inconsistent with, or deals with any matter dealt with in, an award or order lawfully made by the (Commonwealth Arbitration) Court or by a Conciliation Commissioner, the latter shall prevail, and the former shall to the extent of the inconsistency, or in relation to the matter dealt with, be invalid.[51]

50. Bailey, *ibid.,* p. 14.
51. Quoted Bailey, *ibid.,* pp. 14-15. The outstanding case is *Ex parte McLean.* McLean, a shearer, had been convicted under section 4 of the *Masters and Servants Act* 1902 (N.S.W.) of failing to carry out a contract of employment. But the *Commonwealth Arbitration Act* provided penalties for breach of awards, and by section 30 expressly excluded any state law from dealing with matters covered in an award. The High Court upheld the view that the state law could not operate in the field covered by the award, and quashed the conviction of McLean under the state act (see Bailey, *ibid.,* p. 15). Section 30 of the Commonwealth Arbitration Act, upon which the paramountcy of Federal awards rests, has been interpreted in such a way as to limit their exclusive authority "to the regulation of industrial relations, and, moreover, to the regulation of industrial relations which are in dispute." For a discussion of more recent cases in this connection see Bailey, *ibid.,* p. 21.

The Arbitration Act is not the only case in which the Commonwealth Parliament has expressly indicated its intention of covering the field. A similar result was achieved, for example, in the *Bills of Exchange Act* and the *Bankruptcy Act*. In cases of this kind in which the intention is clearly expressed there is no real problem, but in a number of others, where the intention is grounded upon implication questions of the utmost complexity have arisen. It is sufficient to point out here that since the authority of the Commonwealth Parliament is limited Commonwealth legislation must be based upon one of the enumerated powers. Inconsistency can, therefore, only occur where a Commonwealth law is a valid exercise of one or more of the Commonwealth's powers, and, as Evatt, J., warned, 'attempts by the Commonwealth Parliament to manufacture inconsistency between its own legislation and that of the States will often be essayed only at the price of making the Commonwealth legislation *ultra vires*.'[52]

Perhaps the chief evil associated with the system of arbitration operating in Australia has been its complexity. The confinement of Commonwealth authority to inter-state disputes necessitated a division of arbitration powers which has led to a confusion justly described as chaotic. Ample evidence of the extreme intricacy of arbitration machinery is provided by Mr. Menzies in the following passage:

> The question arises as to whether the Commonwealth, as a political organisation, can deal with the trouble. We consult the oracle, and he, after profound meditations upon sub-section xxxv, and the judicial opinions evoked by it, tells us that before the question can be answered we may (according to the character of the dispute) have to consider the nature of the work normally done (to see if it is industrial), the nature of the relationship between parties (to see if there is employment as distinct from independent contract), the identity of the employer (because he may be 'state,' and the competence of a federal law to deal directly with a state government can even yet be fruitful of complicated controversy), the geographical extent of the dispute (to see that it extends beyond the limits of one state), the history and anatomy of the dispute (to see whether it is a dispute 'extending' from one state to another, and not, in fact, two separate disputes merely existing contemporaneously in more than one state), the state of mind of the disputants (to see whether they are promulgating genuine claims proceeding from real grievance, or merely going through formalities to invoke the jurisdiction of a supposedly

52. 56 *C.L.R.* 657 (1937), 707, *West v. Commissioner of Taxation* (*N.S.W.*); quoted, Bailey, *ibid.*, p. 20.

benign federal tribunal), the nature of the claims made (to see whether they are legally capable of being made the subject matter of an industrial dispute *inter partes*) and a score of other matters *ejusdem generis.*[53]

The constitutional limitations upon the Commonwealth arbitration power have produced numerous anomalies.   Those who favoured conferring a power of arbitration upon the Commonwealth had as their object the preservation of industrial peace by the provision of national machinery for the speedy settlement of disputes.   Their efforts, however, were largely frustrated by the narrow terms of the Commonwealth grant of power.   Since the federal court could only exercise jurisdiction over disputes extending beyond one state the tendency on the part of those who wished to apply for a federal award was to render any dispute which arose inter-state in character.   In this way the nature of the constitutional power directly contributed not to a diminution, but to an extension of disputes.   Overlapping has been another powerful cause of dissatisfaction.   It is still possible, though it was more prevalent before the adoption of new principles of interpretation by the High Court.[54]   Disputants were accustomed to appeal to whichever tribunal they believed would treat their case most sympathetically.   Although that particular species of overlapping has been largely eliminated, it may happen that certain employees are working under a federal award while others are subject to conditions prescribed by a state tribunal.   In addition, employees and especially non-unionists may be bound by general industrial legislation enacted by a state in cases where their conditions of employment are not regulated by a federal award.   The difficulties occasioned by this confusion of jurisdiction were the subject of adverse comment by the Royal Commission on the Constitution in 1929.

In this way there have been two awards in the same craft and in the same industry, operating in the same States, at the same time, and imposing different wages and conditions of labour.   From this cause has arisen great uncertainty and difficulty in the management of industries, owing to diversity in the details prescribed by Federal and State awards.[55]

Actually, some attempt was made to avoid the evils of a dual system of arbitration by defining relations between state and federal courts.   Under the Commonwealth Conciliation and Arbitration

53.   R. G. Menzies, "The Distribution of the Industrial and Trade and Commerce Powers" in *Studies in the Australian Constitution*, p. 61.
54.   R. G. Menzies in *Studies in the Australian Constitution*, p. 67.
55.   1929 *Report* Commission on the Constitution, p. 163.

Act, the federal court was empowered to prohibit any state organisation from handling any matter which had come or was about to come before the federal court. Moreover, when a dispute was under consideration by the Commonwealth court that court had to determine whether there was anything in the nature of the industry which made it preferable for the dispute to be heard by a Commonwealth rather than a state tribunal.[56] If no such justification for Commonwealth intervention could be discovered the dispute was to be dealt with by the state industrial authorities. In 1928 Chief Judge Dethridge enunciated a number of principles whereby it could be determined whether a dispute should or should not be heard by the Commonwealth court. In his opinion the Commonwealth should only deal with a dispute when any of the following factors were present: competition between establishments in one state and those in another, the employment of migratory labour, the management of branches in at least two states, the employment of labour in connection with imports or exports and the existence of other circumstances rendering action by the Commonwealth court desirable.[57]

That these attempts to delimit the spheres within which each industrial tribunal should operate were not wholly successful may be judged from the dissatisfaction which continued to be felt with regard to the operations of the arbitration system. Admittedly, that dissatisfaction was due not merely to the persistence of overlapping, but rather to the belief that the arbitration power should not be thus artificially divided, but should rest in its entirety either with the states or with the Commonwealth. Upon the question of which it should be there was a sharp division of opinion, though the case for the states was considerably weakened by the admission that there were certain types of industry which, because of their inter-state character, could only be regulated by Commonwealth control.

What chiefly concerned those who favoured state control over industrial arbitration was that employees upon state-owned industrial undertakings should not be subject to awards made by a federal tribunal. They, therefore, attempted to secure an amendment either of the Commonwealth Conciliation and Arbitration Act or of the constitution, with the double object of excluding state industrial employees from the jurisdiction of the Common-

56. By the amending act of 1928.
57. *Federated Hotel, Club, Rest, and Caterers' Employees' Union of Australia v. Abbott and Others* 1928. See 1929 *Report*, Commission on the Constitution, pp. 163-4.

wealth court and of curtailing as far as possible the activity of the Commonwealth in the field of industrial arbitration.   In May, 1923, a conference of the Attorneys-General of the states submitted a number of suggestions to the Commonwealth government.[58]   These proposals were largely concerned with the exclusion of state-owned industries from the jurisdiction of the Commonwealth court, and with the limitation of disputes before the court to industries employing labour which migrated from one state to another.   The Commonwealth did not find itself in full agreement with the proposals, and suggested instead the creation of a composite tribunal, consisting of federal and state representatives, whose duty would be to name those industries which were to be considered 'federal' in character.   The Commonwealth counter-proposals were discussed by a Premiers' Conference which met in May of 1923, and for the most part rejected.   The idea of a composite tribunal created no enthusiasm among the premiers, who adhered to the point of view previously adopted by the Attorneys-General.   They therefore resolved (Queensland dissenting) :

(a) That direct employees of States and employees of authorities created by States for carrying out public functions, e.g., Railway Commissioners, Harbour Boards, etc., should not be subject to Commonwealth jurisdiction.

(b) That employees of public or local authorities constituted under laws of States should not be subject to that jurisdiction.

(c) That industries which are subject to Commonwealth jurisdiction should be defined or enumerated in the requisite amending legislation and the determination should not be left to any tribunal.[59]

Discussions followed with the Commonwealth, and it was announced that once the list of industries which were to be regarded as 'federal' had been agreed upon, together with arrangements for their periodical revision, the Commonwealth government would introduce legislation incorporating almost all the amendments desired by the premiers.   The Attorney-General for the Commonwealth undertook to draw up a list of industries to be classified as 'federal,' but this was never done and nothing further eventuated until 1926, when proposals were submitted by referendum for the amendment of the constitution.   These, however, did not embody the resolutions approved by the Premiers' Conference of 1923, but ran in the contrary direction of conferring extended industrial powers upon the Commonwealth.[60]

58.   See Appendix A, *Proceedings*, the Premiers' Conference, May, 1929.
59.   *Ibid.*, p. 17.
60.   The proposals were rejected.

The struggle to prevent state employees from having access
to the federal tribunal was not abandoned because of this setback.
In 1929 a Nationalist government held office in New South Wales,
and the premier, Mr. Bavin, was strongly in favour of exemption.
He, therefore, communicated with other state governments and
asked them whether they would support the submission of his
proposals to the Commonwealth. At the same time, he secured
a promise from the prime minister, Mr. Bruce, to consider any
suggestions the states might put forward. In May, 1929, a conference of premiers met in Sydney, and it at once became apparent
that opinion upon the merits of the proposal for the exemption
of state employees would be divided according to the political
complexion of the governments represented. Victoria and
Queensland, where Labour governments were in power, opposed
exclusion, while South Australia and New South Wales, with
non-Labour governments, favoured the motion.[61] Mr. Bavin,
in a vehement speech, put forward the arguments in support of
state jurisdiction.[62] He declared that state autonomy was
threatened since the effect of Commonwealth awards was to rob
state governments of control over their own expenditure. For
twenty years, he pointed out, state employees had ben considered
exempt from the operation of Commonwealth awards. State tribunals had been established, and these by reason of their understanding of local conditions had operated very satisfactorily. Yet,
despite their success, the Commonwealth court had trespassed
upon the state preserve, 'upset a system that had grown up as the
result of twenty years' experience, and granted a number of
claims that had been persistently refused by the local tribunal,
although the men were represented on it.'[63] Commonwealth decisions had added enormously to the cost of running both tramway
and railway systems, and had largely removed control over these
services out of the hands of the state government. Intervention
by the federal court had greatly increased the complexity of the
arbitration system. Dual control had been established without
effective guarantees of co-operation between state and federal
tribunals. Mr. Bavin stated:

> The Commonwealth Court acts on its own principles and
> does not care very much how its decisions, based on those prin-
> ciples, affect State tribunals and State awards. It takes care
> to say that it will not take action where such action interferes

61. Tasmania and Western Australia were not represented.
62. *Proceedings*, the Premiers' Conference, May, 1929, p. 28.
63. *Ibid.*, p. 28.

with the jurisdiction of the States. It says that, but it does not do that.[64]

Mr. Bavin believed he had produced good and sufficient reasons why control over state employees should be abdicated by the Commonwealth, but the Queensland and Victorian representatives were unable to agree with him, and answered his arguments with others telling in favour of Commonwealth regulation. The Attorney-General[65] for Victoria declared in no uncertain terms that his government favoured state industrial employees having the right of access to the federal court. He claimed that no logical distinction could be made between the employee of a state and the employee of a private individual or corporation:

> I do not see how you can legitimately distinguish between private corporations, employers or organisations, and the respective States—if private employees have the right of access to the court so should employees of State instrumentalities.[66]

Mr. McCormack, on behalf of Queensland, argued that the arbitration power should be in the hands of the national authority in order to secure some measure of uniformity in industrial conditions. Otherwise, there was a distinct possibility that individual state regulation might lead to competition in conditions of employment and rates of wages. Mr. McCormack declared:

> I can quite conceive a State having a railway system, which is the most imporant factor in industrial development, running on wages and conditions that would destroy industry in every other State that would not adopt the lower conditions and longer hours. . . . I think the right of appeal to the Federal Arbitration Court is a safeguard in those instrumentalities which have to deal with production.[67]

The state governments had shown that they were by no means united in support of the proposal to exempt state employees from the operations of the federal court. Nevertheless, Mr. Bruce decided to restore control to the states, and in 1929 fought an election upon the issue of the repeal of the Commonwealth arbitration power, only to suffer an overwhelming defeat. The result of the election was significant for the future, for by their rejection of the proposal the electors had made subsequent attempts to increase state industrial arbitration powers at the expense of the Commonwealth so politically hazardous as to be unlikely. It is, however, interesting to note that a majority of the Royal Commission on the Constitution, which issued its

64. *Ibid.*, p. 29.　　　　　　　65. Mr. Slater.
66. *Proceedings*, the Premiers' Conference, May, 1929, p. 30.
67. *Ibid.*, p. 31.

report on 21 November 1929, were in favour of the deletion from the constitution of the paragraph conferring a limited con-ciliation and arbitration power upon the Commonwealth. They, likewise, opposed giving the federal parliament the right to legis-late upon industrial matters generally. The arguments advanced in support of their decision were those customarily employed in defence of federalism, namely, that industrial legislation is experi-mental and 'peculiarly requires local supervision.'[68] While pos-sessing an undoubted validity at a stage of development marked by backward communications, and the organisation of economic enterprise upon a local rather than a national basis, these are argu-ments which no longer carry the same weight in the face of the unification of the Australian financial and economic system. But what is of greater significance than the actual arguments used is the belief upon which they were based.[69] The majority of the commission, no less than the minority who favoured the extension of the Commonwealth's control, were convinced that industrial powers could not be exercised in isolation, but were dependent upon and interconnected with other subject matters of legislation. Since the majority had reached the conclusion that these allied topics—health, trade and commerce, mines, public works, land settlement and development—should remain in the hands of the states they, therefore, felt that the power over industry should be entrusted to the same authority.

The minority, in its recommendations, opposed the findings of the majority, though they were at least as emphatic that the exercise of industrial powers was intimately connected with con-trol over closely related subjects. However, what the minority did and the majority did not realise was that many functions of a national character were vested in the states, although the states from geographical, competitive and many other causes were incapable of performing the task of national regulation. It was only logical that national functions should be performed by the national parliament. The Commonwealth already controlled customs; it should now be given control over industry and mat-ters pertaining to industry. In the words of the minority report:

> Customs duties trading conditions and conditions of employ-ment are all so interdependent—reacting so powerfully each upon the other—that they should be placed under the same governmental control.[70]

68. 1929 *Report*, Commission on the Constitution, p. 248.
69. K. H. Bailey, "Reform of the Commonwealth Constitution" (*The Austra-lian Quarterly*, March, 1939).
70. 1929 *Report*, Commission on the Constitution, p. 244. Minority Report.

By making the control that of the central government certain definite advantages would accrue in the shape of uniform impositions upon industry and the prevention of competitive wage rates and conditions of employment.

In opposition to those who desired the deletion of the Commonwealth arbitration power and its transfer to the states was a body of opinion which favoured greater federal control over industry. A policy of extended Commonwealth powers generally commanded the support of Labour, but was also not infrequently backed by the non-Labour parties. Its objects were not confined to removing the limitations upon the Commonwealth arbitration power, for it aimed rather at bestowing complete control over all matters relating to industry upon the federal parliament. Numerous proposals along these lines were submitted to the electors by referendum on several distinct occasions, but always with the same disheartening result.[71]   At no time has the electorate been willing to countenance any extension of Commonwealth control over industry, even in matters where the need was only too obvious. These defeats seriously retarded the movement for greater Commonwealth powers, but they did not kill it. Within recent years the anomalies produced by a system of constitutionally rigid divisions of power between state and central authorities, together with the inability of the Commonwealth to take legislative action on many matters of national concern, has given new emphasis to the recommendations contained in the minority report of the Royal Commission on the Constitution. Constitutional reform is in the air once more, and amongst the proposals for expanded Commonwealth powers sponsored by the federal government are several to confer increased authority over industry.[72]

To-day there is almost unanimous agreement that the existing system of industrial control is unsatisfactory, and that change in some form or other is essential. Various alternatives present themselves.   It would be possible, by deleting from the constitution the sub-section conferring power of arbitration in interstate disputes upon the Commonwealth, to place the whole field

71. A discussion of the proposals submitted by referendum will be found in the Chapter entitled, "The Results produced by the Constitution."
72. Mr. Menzies, then Attorney-General, in the House of Representatives on 22 November 1938, instanced eight subjects upon which Commonwealth powers were inadequate.   For more recent proposals see H. V. Evatt, *Post-War Reconstruction, A Case for Greater Commonwealth Powers* (prepared for the Constitutional Convention, 1942), and *Record of Proceedings of 1942 Convention on Proposed Alteration of the Commonwealth Constitution.*

of industrial legislation in the hands of the states. This, for the reasons previously advanced against state control of industrial arbitration, may be safely rejected. It would be not only politically inexpedient, but would also pave the way for 'an intolerable condition of unfair competition between manufacturers in different states, owing to the varying rates of pay and conditions of employment . . . created.'[73] But the fundamental objection to state control is that industry is no longer organised upon a local basis. Economic unification has taken place, and only national regulation can prove effective. Another possibility would be to continue some kind of division of industrial powers between the Commonwealth and the states.[74] One suggestion is that certain industries, such as shipping and shearing, should be classified as 'federal,' and the remainder be considered suitably local to permit of state regulation. A second, slightly different in character, proposes that the Commonwealth should determine rates of pay and hours of work, but should leave more detailed specifications of industrial life to the states. Neither of these proposals seems in any way feasible, since they are both based on the misconception that the economic life of the community, and even of industry itself, is capable of division into separate hard and fast compartments. The connection between one industry and another is too intimate to permit the segregation and separate treatment of individual industries, while attempts to determine such questions as hours and wages without control over the other factors in industrial enterprise would be impracticable. Hence the one alternative remaining is to amend the constitution in such a way as to confer full powers over industry upon the Commonwealth. That is the only logical course to pursue, because it is the only one which meets all the difficulties. The ramifications of industry extend throughout the Commonwealth; both employers and employees are organized upon a national basis; while through the awards of the Commonwealth court the habit has been engendered in a large section of the population of looking toward the Commonwealth for protection and fair dealing in matters relating to conditions of work. Since there is no reason to suppose that the Commonwealth parliament is less solicitous of the welfare of its citizens than are the parliaments of the several states, complete control over industry should be placed in its hands. Such a procedure could, in the words

---

73. 1929 *Report*, Commission on the Constitution, p. 245. Minority Report.
74. See *Studies in the Australian Constitution*, p. 70 *et. seq.*, for the possible reforms outlined by Mr. Menzies.

of Mr. Menzies, 'bring about what can never be produced under our present divided system—the two great essentials of industrial regulation, simplicity and flexibility.'[75]

The failure to grant the Commonwealth exclusive powers over trade and commerce, and the attempt by the fathers of the constitution to prevent state economic nationalism by the insertion of the declaration that 'trade, commerce and intercourse among the states shall be absolutely free' have together proved almost as fruitful of evils as divided control of industrial relations. The division of power and the existence of section 92 have produced not only a similar confusion, but have also led to a sphere in which control by any authority is non-existent. This has been especialy noticeable in relation to the attempts to regulate marketing. The Commonwealth grant of power covered foreign and inter-state trade and commerce, but left intra-state regulation to the state governments. Moreover, even this grant of power to the Commonwealth was not exclusive, which meant that while the state alone could deal with intra-state trade, both state and Commonwealth, could legislatate with regard to interstate and overseas trade, 'the state law in this sphere being subject to Commonwealth law.'[76] The words trade and commerce have been given a wide meaning by the High Court, since they have been held to include 'all the commercial dealings and all the accessory methods, in fact, adopted by Australians to initiate, continue and effectuate the movement of persons and things from state to state.'[77] Transportation is included, while the power has been used to cover legislation on a number of subjects closely connected with trade and commerce, such as agreements restraining trade, the carriage of goods by sea, and the licensing of waterside workers. But if the construction placed upon the terms in which the Commonwealth grant of power was couched has been wide, the limitations upon that power have been even more remarkable. These, apart from the exclusion of intra-state trade and commerce, have related mainly to section 92, which categorically declares that trade among the states 'shall be absolutely free.'[78]

Attention was earlier drawn to the fact that the desire for fiscal unity and the fear that if it were not achieved colonial tariffs would breed enmity were powerful forces in the achievement of federation. It is in the interplay of these forces that

75. *Studies in the Australian Constitution*, p. 75.
76. K. H. Bailey and L. F. Giblin, "Marketing and the Constitution" (*The Economic Record*, December, 1936, p. 152).
77. 1929 *Report*, Commission on the Constitution, p. 143.
78. Sec. 99 also restricted the Commonwealth's freedom of action.

one may find the genesis of what later became section 92. At the Federal Convention of 1891 Parkes placed before the members a number of resolutions which he believed should be the foundation for any future constitution. One[79] of these referred to freedom of interstate trade, and was subsequently transplanted into the constitution as section 92. In view of the diversity of opinion about the interpretation to be given to the section, it is interesting to note the comment of Bailey and Giblin[80] that many of the lawyers who were members of the conventions were dubious about the wisdom of the section in the form in which it stood. Mr. Isaacs (as he then was) warned that the language 'went much further than it is intended,' while Sir Samuel Griffith believed that it would be wiser to qualify the word 'free' by inserting the words 'from taxes, charges or imposts.'[81] The politicians, however, did not share the disquiet of the lawyers, and the words were left unaltered. The result has been confusion, primarily because of the failure to make explicit just 'what it is that inter-state trade is to be free from.'[82]

The history of the interpretation of this section has been a chequered one. In fact, the varied meanings given to section 92 show once again the disadvantages associated with the interpretation of a written constitution. Little uniformity has been displayed in the opinions expressed by the judges upon the section, while inconsistent decisions have deprived both state and federal legislatures of any certainty as to the legality of their legislation. At first, the injunction was regarded as binding upon the Commonwealth as well as upon the States. In 1916, however, in the case of *Duncan v. the State of Queensland*[83] doubts were thrown upon the validity of that assumption, and four years later in *McArthur's Case*[84] it was overruled by the High Court, who accepted the view that section 92 did not bind the Commonwealth. The argument which now found favour with the court was based upon the belief that if section 92 bound the Commonwealth, then the constitution would be made to contradict itself in the most flagrant way. It was agreed that the words 'absolutely free' were so expansive that they must imply complete freedom from governmental interference. But under section 51

79. The second resolution: "That trade and intercourse between the Federated Colonies, whether by means of land carriage or coastal navigation, shall be absolutely free." Proceedings of the National Australasian Convention, Sydney, March-April, 1891 (*Victorian Parliamentary Papers*, 1891 (4), p. 11).
80. In "Marketing and the Constitution" (*The Economic Record*, December, 1936, p. 153).
81. *Ibid.* 82. *Ibid.*, p. 154. 83. 22 *C.L.R.* 551 (1916).
84. 28 *C.L.R.* 530 (1920), *W. and A. McArthur Ltd. v. Queensland.*

(1) the Commonwealth had been given authority to make laws with respect to trade and commerce among the states. If, therefore, section 92 applied to the Commonwealth a fundamental contradiction would arise, since trade and commerce among the states could hardly be both completely free from Commonwealth governmental interference and subject to Commonwealth legislative control. The only way out of such an impasse, argued the High Court, was to assume that section 92 was intended to bind the states alone.[85] The decision was of the greatest importance, for it meant that the scope of Commonwealth legislation with regard to trade and commerce among the states could be greatly expanded, though the Commonwealth was still forbidden by section 99 to give preference to one state over another. Moreover, in the belief that the case had been rightly decided the federal government embarked upon legislation which was designed, in co-operation with state acts, to provide a comprehensive scheme of marketing.

Unfortunately for the success of this legislation, the judges of the High Court began to waver in their allegiance to the view that section 92 did not concern the Commonwealth. The confusion over the interpretation to be given to the section was most plain in *The King v. Vizzard; ex parte Hill,*[86] where the whole question of the effect of the section upon the Commonwealth and the states was reconsidered. The result of the deliberations of the High Court could hardly be called encouraging, for the Chief Justice was forced to announce that it had been 'impossible to get a distinct ruling by a majority of the Court.'[87] Evatt and McTiernan and Gavan Duffy himself believed that the section did bind the Commonwealth, but as the court was evenly divided the Chief Justice refrained from overthrowing previously accepted decisions by the exercise of his casting vote. The court therefore adhered to its previous ruling in *McArthur's Case,* and allowed the matter to be settled by the Privy Council, when giving its decision in *James v. the Commonwealth.*[88]

---

85. See Bailey and Giblin, *The Economic Record,* December, 1936, p. 162. Knowles, *The Australian Constitution,* pp. 83-4.
86. 50 *C.L.R.* 30 (1933).   87. *Ibid.,* p. 47.
88. 55 *C.L.R.* 1 (1936). It should be remembered that *James v. Commonwealth* in 1935-6 was the first real challenge of a Commonwealth law under Sec. 92. In the first twenty years of federation, there was no challenge of a Commonwealth law under this section. It would, therefore, seem that the great reversal in *McArthur's Case* did not make as much difference to the Commonwealth as is sometimes supposed. The real significance of the decision was only appreciated later, after the State marketing schemes had been found unconstitutional.

The decision of the Privy Council reversed the judgment of the High Court, overruled *McArthur's Case*, and re-established the principle that the Commonwealth was bound by section 92. It did, however, far more than that, for it rendered invalid existing Commonwealth legislation upon marketing, and placed serious obstacles in the way of effective future regulation. Judicial decision has, therefore, been responsible for a considerable curtailment of the Commonwealth grant of power over trade and commerce. The position at the moment is that the Commonwealth has no right to legislate with regard to intra-state trade and commerce, while its authority over interstate trade and commerce has been so limited by the operation of section 92, at least, in so far as marketing is concerned, that little action remains possible under this sub-section. In short, the Commonwealth power is wholly inadequate to the demands which it has to seek to satisfy.

The injunction of complete freedom of trade has had its effects upon the states no less than upon the Commonwealth. Section 92, which, of course, bound the states, has, indeed, been repeatedly responsible for upsetting state legislation of importance, notably, as in the case of the Commonwealth, on the subject of marketing. State acts, designed with the object of securing efficient and profitable marketing for various kinds of produce grown in the state, were overthrown because their operations inevitably entailed certain restrictions upon individual freedom of trade, which could be challenged as an infraction of section 92.

State legislation affected by section 92 has covered a wide range of subjects as may be gathered from the restriction of state activity in the following instances.[89]   Queensland has been prevented from fixing the price at which goods subject to an inter-state contract might be sold in the state, from enforcing the compulsory acquisition for marketing of all peanuts by the Peanut Board,[90] and from disallowing the sale of motor spirits in Queensland without a licence and without the purchase at fixed prices of a prescribed quantity of power alcohol.[91]   South Australia has not been permitted either to tax goods from another state which had 'not yet become mixed with the goods of South Australia' or to fix the quota of dried fruits which might be marketed outside the state.[92] Both New South Wales and Victoria have been subject to the last prohibition, while Victoria has been

89.   See 1929 *Report*, Commission on the Constitution, p. 148.
90.   48 *C.L.R.* 266 (1933), *Peanut Board v. Rockhampton Harbour Board.*
91.   51 *C.L.R.* 108 (1934), *Vacuum Oil Co. Pty. Ltd. v. Queensland.*
92.   40 *C.L.R.* 1 (1927), *James v. South Australia.*

prevented from banning, on the ground that they might spread disease, the importation of Tasmanian potatoes,[93] and New South Wales from excluding from the state persons convicted of crime in some other State.[94]

Though the limitation upon the trade and commerce power imposed by section 92 has invalidated state legislation upon a number of subjects, its greatest importance has lain in its effect upon attempts to carry out marketing schemes. The dried fruits industry provides the most startling example. Since neither the Commonwealth nor the states possessed complete power over the subject of marketing, any attempt to enact a comprehensive scheme had perforce to be by way of co-operation between them. The federal government, therefore, assumed the task of legislating with regard to export from the Commonwealth, while the state governments were to draw up regulations covering the dried fruits industry within the state itself. In 1924 the Commonwealth passed the *Dried Fruits Export Control Act* under which the minister was authorized, by means of a licensing system, to control the export of dried fruits. At the same time, a Dried Fruits Control Board was established, the function of which was to handle the fruits acquired under the licences. Since these regulations related solely to export, complementary legislation was passed by both Victoria and South Australia. It was the South Australian act to which objection was later taken. That act purported to lay down the percentage of dried fruits produced in South Australia which might be marketed outside the state. The validity of the act was challenged by a South Australian producer of dried fruits named James, who proceded to disregard its provisions and sell his dried fruits in other states in greater quantities than the quota allowed. When action was taken against him James sought a declaration from the High Court that the determinations of the board were invalid on the ground that they violated section 92. The judgment in *James v. South Australia,*[95] which was delivered on 22 August 1927, declared that the provisions of section 20 of the South Australian act and the determinations of the board were *ultra vires* as offending against section 92 of the constitution. In this instance an attempt had been made to regulate marketing by prescribing the proportion of dried fruits which might be marketed in Australia. Persons in South Australia could, therefore, only

93.   52 *C.L.R.* 157 (1935), *Tasmania v. Victoria.* This was an instance in which a state invoked section 92 to protect its freedom of interstate trade.
94.   16 *C.L.R.* 99 (1912), *R. v. Smithers; Ex parte Benson.*
95.   40 *C.L.R.* 1.

sell a specified quota in any of the states. Such a scheme was foredoomed to failure under the prevailing constitutional conditions, since it was in obvious conflict with the provisions of section 92. 'If this,' said Lord Atkin, 'leaves inter-state commerce "absolutely free," the constitutional charter might as well be torn up.'[96]

The matter was not to end there, for new attempts were made by the state of South Australia to render the existing marketing schemes constitutional. Once again James disregarded the provisions of the South Australian act, with the result that his dried fruits were seized by the state Minister for Agriculture. James immediately brought an action against Cowan, the minister in question, for seizure of his property. The Minister admitted having done so, but justified his action under sections 28 and 29 of the *Dried Fruits Acts* 1924-27 of South Australia. By a majority decision the High Court determined that seizure had been authorised by the act, and that no infringement of section 92 had taken place.[97] The judgment given was based upon the belief that the case before the court was similar in character to the *Wheat Acquisition Case*,[98] in which the High Court had declared valid a New South Wales act authorising, through notification in the *Government Gazette*, the acquisition of wheat and the conversion of rights in respect to the wheat acquired into a claim for compensation. Isaacs, J., however, dissented from the judgment, and attacked the view that the act in question was similar to the *Wheat Acquisition Act*. It was, he claimed, 'the very antithesis' since the *Dried Fruits Act* made 'the repression of inter-state trade the *causa causans* of the expropriation, which is only the means selected to carry out effectively the attempted control of inter-state trade.'[99] In determining whether section 92 had been violated or not it was essential to look to the purpose of the act. To do so was to see that its intention was unmistakably the limitation of inter-state trade. 'In plain terms,' said the learned Judge, 'it is to prevent inter-state trade in surplus fruit.'

Since the decision of the High Court did not involve any question 'as to the limits *inter se* of the constitutional powers of the Commonwealth and those of any state or states,' the permission of the court did not have to be obtained before an appeal

96.   47 *C.L.R.* p. 393 (1932), Privy Council Appeal, *James v. Cowan.*
97.   43 *C.L.R.* 386 (1930), *James v. Cowan.*
98.   20 *C.L.R.* 54 (1915), *New South Wales v. Commonwealth.*
99.   43 *C.L.R.*, p. 405.

could be made to the Privy Council. Leave to appeal was granted by the Privy Council, which proceeded to reverse the decision of the High Court in *James v. Cowan*, by declaring that the *Dried Fruits Act* 1924-27 (S.A.) did not authorize the compulsory acquisition of dried fruits in South Australia, with the object of forcing surplus dried fruit off the Australian market, since such a provision would not only violate section 92 of the constitution, but would also be contrary to the act itself, which was expressly stated to be subject to that section of the constitution.[1] Their lordships agreed with the argument advanced by Isaacs, J., that the object of the act was to regulate inter-state trade in dried fruits. Statements made by the minister and the board only served to strengthen that opinion. Lord Atkin said:

> To force the surplus fruit off the Australian market appears necessarily to involve two decisions: first, the fixing of a limited amount for Australian consumption (a necessary element in the conception of a 'surplus'); secondly, the prevention of the sale of the balance of the output in Australia.[2]

The reversal by the Privy Council of the High Court's decision in *James v. Cowan*, and the consequent invalidity of the South Australian legislation upon the marketing of dried fruits aimed a severe blow at efforts made or likely to be made by state authorities for the marketing of goods produced within their boundaries. The significance of the decision was by no means limited to the dried fruits industry, for the implication from the interpretation given to section 92 by the Privy Council was that the section would act as a barrier against similar schemes for the regulation of marketing. The correctness of this inference was borne out by the High Court's decision in *Peanut Board v. Rockhampton Harbour Board*, where legislation by the Queensland parliament, which aimed at securing efficient marketing of Queensland grown peanuts, was declared to be in conflict with section 92 and accordingly invalid.

The Queensland parliament had passed an act, known as the *Primary Producers' Organising and Marketing Act* 1926-30, by which the governor-in-council, upon a petition from fifty growers, was empowered to declare any product of the soil of Queensland a commodity under the act, to establish a board, and to endow it with the right of ownership in the commodity concerned. By an order-in-council peanuts were declared to be a commodity within

1. 47 *C.L.R.*, p. 386, Privy Council Appeal, *James v. Cowan*.
2. *Ibid.*, p. 397.

the meaning of the act, and a board was set up whose function it was to market peanuts both in Queensland and elsewhere. In May, 1932, the Peanut Board began an action in the Supreme Court of Queensland against the Rockhampton Harbour Board. It would appear that the Harbour Board refused to hand over some 3000 bags of peanuts which had been deposited upon its wharves by certain persons without the authority of the Peanut Board. The Peanut Board desired a declaration that the peanuts were the property of the board and an order for their surrender. Such were the facts of the case, but the real issue underlying them was whether the board had the right to enforce the compulsory acquisition of peanuts, and thus prohibit an individual grower from marketing his produce when and how he liked.

When the case came before the High Court it decided by a majority that the board did not have the right, and that growers could not be prevented from engaging in inter-state trade in peanuts, since the provisions of the act offended against section 92 and were in consequence invalid.[3] This decision was the direct outcome of the application of the judgment delivered by the Privy Council in *James v. Cowan*, as witness the statements by Rich and Dixon, J.J. 'The reasons,' said Rich, J., 'given in the Privy Council (*James v. Cowan*) . . . make it quite plain that compulsory acquisition may directly operate to interfere with the freedom of inter-state commerce.'[4] 'The protection,' declared Dixon, J., 'conferred by section 92 is not a mere accident of property, but is enjoyed by the individual who may not be deprived of his goods in order to prevent his exercising his freedom of trade among the states (*James v. Cowan*—Privy Council).'[5] Evatt, J., who dissented from the verdict of the majority, took a quite contrary view of the character of the Queensland legislation. It was, he held, neither specifically concerned with nor did it discriminate against inter-state trade. Looking to the object of the act, he argued that, 'the one purpose of the scheme was to secure efficient and advantageous marketing, irrespective of the geographical situation of the market.'[6] If that were so a declaration by the court that such legislation violated section 92 would produce consequences of the utmost gravity. If this act was invalid it was scarcely conceivable that any legislation framed by the states with the object of assisting marketing could be declared constitutional. Mr. Justice Evatt,

3. 48 *C.L.R.* 266 (1933), *Peanut Board v. Rockhampton Harbour Board.*
4. 48 *C.L.R.*, p. 275.   5. 48 *C.L.R.*, p. 287.   6. 48 *C.L.R.*, p. 267.

therefore, issued a warning not to minimize the implications of the case, which was, in his own words, one 'of far-reaching importance, because various schemes of compulsory pooling of the products of an industry are by now thoroughly accepted throughout the Commonwealth.'[7]

The decision in this case had, as Evatt prophesied, serious consequences, for it meant that legislation intending to organize the marketing of primary products could not extend to the control of any part of a commodity if the producer wished to engage in inter-state trade.

In commodities where there is no substantial inter-State competition, the schemes can operate unimpaired. Where, however, there are substantial inter-State dealings, the establishment of a Marketing Board under State legislation is very nearly valueless. Indeed, in many commodities, inter-State dealings can readily be created, even if they did not previously exist, and a determined minority can speedily break down the control of the market by the Board.[8]

Section 92 of the constitution has rendered invalid the majority of attempts at state regulation of marketing. Nevertheless, it would be untrue to say that this section has been interpreted as establishing the rule of complete *laissez-faire* so far as inter-state commercial transactions are concerned. This is made plain by the consideration of a number of cases relating to inter-state transport, in which the High Court declared that no violation of section 92 had taken place. In *Willard v. Rawson*[9] and *The King v. Vizzard; Ex parte Hill*[10] motor trucks which had only been licensed in one state were being employed in inter-state transport. In both cases state authorities in the state in which no licence had been taken out charged the driver with an infringement of the act under which licences were imposed upon vehicles operating in the state. The defendants desired a declaration from the High Court that the additional licences were a violation of section 92, but it was held in each case that the state legislation had not interfered with the freedom of inter-state trade. Again, in *Duncan and Green Star Trading Co. v. Vizzard*,[11] a company possessed a New South Wales licence for a lorry engaged in inter-state transport. This licence purported to impose special conditions with regard to distance of carriage and competition with

7. 48 *C.L.R.*, p. 294.
8. Bailey and Giblin, "Marketing and the Constitution" (*The Economic Record*, Dec., 1936, p. 160).
9. 48 *C.L.R.* 316 (1933).   10. 50 *C.L.R.* 30 (1933).
11. 53 *C.L.R.* 493 (1935).

railways which the company claimed were an interference with inter-state freedom of trade. Once more, however, the High Court decided that the state legislation did not contravene section 92. These decisions appear to have been based upon the view that the acts in question were non-discriminatory and that their intention was not to impose a burden on freedom of trade, but only to regulate transport efficiently within the state. Nevertheless, this standpoint was not adopted by a minority of the court who dissented from the judgment in *The King v. Vizzard*. Starke, J., held that while the New South Wales act did not prohibit transport from one state to another it did penalize 'persons engaging in such transport . . . unless the vehicle is licensed and the person operating it a holder of such licence.'[12] Dixon, J., regarded the act as an infringement of section 92, because 'the essential criterion of the legislation' was its concern with motor vehicles as implements of commerce.[13]

During the hearing of the transport cases the effect of section 92 upon state legislation was discussed, and some attempt was made to clarify the principles of interpretation to be adopted with regard to that section. Perhaps the most striking feature of this attempt was the divergence of opinion which it revealed. It seemed that no clear and unanimous declaration of opinion upon the meaning of the section could be given by the court. On the whole, a tendency towards a more restricted interpretation was apparent. For instance, Evatt, J., expressed the opinion that a state act would only be invalid if it could be shown that the legislation 'pointed directly at the act of entry, in course of commerce, into the second state.'[14] 'This,' he said, 'is the principle laid down by Higgins, J., in *Roughley v. N.S.W.* (1), and, I think, also recognised by Lord Atkin in *James v. Cowan.*' Gavan Duffy, C.J., also favoured an interpretation which interfered as little as possible with state legislation. In his opinion, before an act should be declared invalid under section 92 the court had to determine that the real object of the legislation was interference with freedom of trade.[15] If, however, the transport cases had shown that certain limits were to be placed upon section 92, and that, at least some of the judges were in favour of a more restricted interpretation being given to the section, it yet remained true that these were at best slight compensations. Much important state legislation upon marketing had been declared unconstitutional, and

---

12. 50 *C.L.R.*, p. 54.   13. 50 *C.L.R.*, p. 68.
14. 48 *C.L.R.*, p. 335, *Willard v. Rawson.*
15. 50 *C.L.R.* 47, *The King v. Vizzard; Ex parte Hill.*

it was evident that the states did not possess the power to deal effectively with the subject.

The existence of section 92 is by no means the only reason why state marketing schemes have been largely ineffective. Even though the section were abolished, the state would possess inadequate authority, since marketing, if it is to be efficient, demands uniform regulation throughout the country. Without national regulation standards of grading, for example, will vary to a harmful degree, while competition between states may well become more than a possibility. So much was evident from the discussion which took place upon the marketing of products at the Premiers' Conference of 1929. Mr. Butler, premier of South Australia, testified to the evil effects of non-uniform grading by declaring that one-twelfth of the Australian fruit sent to the Scottish market had been called unsalable. 'So long,' said Mr. Butler, 'as each state has different laws we will never have uniformity.'[16] He, therefore, wanted greater Commonwealth control over the inspection of fruit. Mr. Thorby, New South Wales Minister for Agriculture, in supporting the demand for uniform standards, spoke trenchantly of the ineffectiveness of state efforts at marketing.

The difficulty is that when our State organizes effectively and exports its surplus, thus stabilising its own market, a neighbouring State usually comes in and gluts that State's market, placing it in a worse position. . . . Their system of control is then broken down, because there is no means by which they can force a neighbouring State to respect a controlled market within their own area.[17]

By converting the whole of Australia into a single free-trade area federation was intended to destroy the harmful spirit of state economic nationalism, which found expression in tariff barriers and competitive railway rates. This was to be achieved principally by conferring the power to impose customs duties exclusively on the Commonwealth and by the insertion of section 92. Under the constitution, however, the states still retained wide trade and commerce powers as well as the chief responsibility for developmental policy. The states have undoubtedly fostered economic nationalism. By their actions they have shown that they are intent upon protecting the primary producer both against his

16. *Proceedings*, the Premiers' Conference, May, 1929, p. 42.
   There was, of course, no constitutional barrier to the uniform grading of export fruit. The Commonwealth possessed the necessary authority to take action if it desired to do so. The failure of the state legislation does, however, emphasize the ineffectiveness of state action in this field.
17. *Ibid.*, p. 43.

competitor in other states and at the expense of the consumer.[18]
Their efforts to extend protection against rival producers in other
states have been made in the face of serious difficulties, since most
of the more obvious methods of securing protection for a commodity, such as the imposition of an excise duty or the provision
of a bounty, are denied to the states. As already indicated, section
92 has also imposed severe limitations upon state freedom of
action, so much so, indeed, that despite the employment of devious
means and the exercise of considerable ingenuity most state attempts at economic nationalism have been frustrated by the existence of this section.

Examples of attempts at state protectionism are not far to seek.
Use has been made of the power to compel inspection of goods
passing in or out of the state, and the power to impose charges for
executing such laws. Resort has also been made to quarantine
laws which enable a state to control the entry of diseased plants
and goods. There can be little objection to legislation designed
and administered solely for the purpose of excluding diseased or
unwholesome goods. But such legislation has often been given
a protective colouring, as may be judged from the action of South
Australia, instanced by Bailey and Giblin, in imposing upon tomatoes sold in the state an inspection law which was rigorously enforced against tomatoes from Western Australia, but loosely
applied to the South Australian product. Nor is this an isolated
case.

> It is believed that there is a very considerable amount of
> quarantine legislation on the statute books of the several States
> in Australia which was designed to operate, and does, in fact,
> operate, simply as a measure of State protection.[19]

Nevertheless, the use of inspection and quarantine laws for
protective purposes is an uncertain method of securing this objective, since the Commonwealth has power to annul state inspection
laws, and section 92 impedes excessive distortion of the quarantine power. At the same time, the dangerous use to which such
powers may be put is exemplified by the cattle-tick case,[20] in
which the High Court, on the casting vote of the Chief Justice,
upheld a New South Wales law prohibiting the importation of
stock from a district in Queensland in which disease was thought
to be prevalent, despite the fact that the stock concerned had been
inspected and declared free from the disease. The decision in this

18. Bailey and Giblin, "Marketing and the Constitution" (*The Economic
     Record*, Dec., 1936, p. 156).
19. *Ibid.*
20. 42 *C.L.R.* 209 (1928), *Ex parte Nelson*, No. 1, Knowles, p. 85.

case has been said to define 'the high-water mark of state quarantine power,'[21] and later decisions have tended to cast doubt upon the validity of the judgment in the cattle-tick case.   In 1935, for instance, the High Court found it necessary to declare a proclamation under the Victorian *Vegetation and Vine Disease Act* 1928, prohibiting the importation into Victoria of potatoes from Tasmania on the plea that importation was likely to introduce disease into Victoria, invalid because it so obviously represented an attempt to curtail the freedom of inter-state trade.[22]

Perhaps an even more startling example of state economic nationalism may be found in efforts by Queensland to protect the power alcohol industry.   The means to be employed were ingenious, to say the least   The idea was to make 'the purchase of power alcohol from the producers a necessary incident in, or condition of, the sale of some other, and more necessary, commodity in Queensland.'[23]   Petrol was finally chosen, probably because it was not produced in Queensland.   Petrol could not be sold in the state without a licence, and a licence could only be obtained on the understanding that the holder purchased at a fixed price a stated quantity of power alcohol for every unit of petrol sold. Obviously such legislation was an attempt to defeat one of the key principles upon which the colonies had agreed to federate, namly, that Australia should be allowed to develop as one economic unit.   As Evatt, J., clearly demonstrated, if such legislation was valid the states could divide Australia into artificial economic areas and render freedom of inter-state trade a mockery.

If such a law is valid the State of New South Wales can compel the first seller in New South Wales of Queensland sugar to buy a proportionate quantity of New South Wales flour; the Victorian parliament can compel the first seller in that state of cane sugar to buy a proportionate quantity of beet sugar produced in Victoria, and Tasmania can make a similar law in order to compel the importer of Queensland sugar to purchase Tasmanian fruit.   Instead of inter-State trade in Queensland sugar being absolutely free, it would be subjected to a series of embargoes in the several States.

In my opinion. therefore, the Queensland act substitutes for the free sale in Queensland of a New South Wales commodity a completely inconsistent economic doctrine which directly restricts each and every such sale by requiring the purchase of a proportionate quantity of a Queensland product.[24]

21. Bailey and Giblin, *op. cit.*, p. 157.
22. 52 *C.L.R.* 157 (1935), *Tasmania v. Victoria.*
23. Bailey and Giblin, *op. cit.*, p. 158.
24. 51 *C.L.R.*, p. 138 (1934), *Vacuum Oil Co. Pty. Ltd. v. Queensland.*
     Quoted Bailey and Giblin, *op. cit.*, p. 158.

The whole record of attempts at regulating trade and commerce, particularly with regard to marketing, reveals not only that state control over such matters is ineffective, but also that it may be positively harmful. The authority of a state parliament to regulate trade and commerce within its own state is subject to severe limitation because almost all attempts at regulation lead to some restriction upon inter-state freedom of trade and therefore violate section 92 of the constitution. The state, both by reason of the Commonwealth control over foreign and inter-state trade and commerce, and because of other constitutional, regional and competitive limitations, is an unsuitable authority to legislate with regard to trade and commerce generally and marketing in particular.

Since the states were unable to deal with marketing on their own authority the Commonwealth, acting on the assumption that *McArthur's Case* had been rightly decided, came to their aid, and passed legislation with the object of implementing state schemes. The federal government introduced the Commonwealth *Dried Fruits Act* of 1928, which prescribed the conditions under which dried fruits might be marketed for export. The Commonwealth legislation re-imposed the quota system for dried fruits, and only permitted inter-state trade under licence. Much the same system was later adopted for dairy produce, while in 1935 a similar method was, with modifications, to be applied to the wheat industry. Commonwealth action was intended to permit organization on a national scale, but it is necessary to remember that the Commonwealth was dependent for the successful operation of the schemes on complementary state legislation, since the Commonwealth had no authority over intra-state trade and commerce. The validity of the Dried Fruits Act was not immediately challenged, but the deliberations of the High Court in other cases were disturbing, for they showed that there was considerable doubt as to the exact meaning of section 92, and especially as to whether or not the section affected the Commonwealth.

The decision of the Privy Council for which the High Court had waited, proved disastrous for the Commonwealth power and for the future of marketing regulation in Australia. It reversed the judgment of the High Court in *James v. Commonwealth* 1935, declared section 92 to be binding on the Commonwealth, and, by so doing, invalidated the Commonwealth *Dried Fruits Act* 1928-35.[25] When the case came before the High Court James had alleged first that the Commonwealth had caused the seizure of

25. 55 *C.L.R.* 1 (1936) Privy Council Appeal, *James v. The Commonwealth*; Bailey and Giblin, *op. cit.*, p. 164.

dried fruits belonging to him which were being delivered to
buyers in New South Wales, and, secondly, that the Commonwealth had informed those engaged in the transport industry that
they would be penalized if they carried dried fruits owned by
any person not possessing a licence under the *Dried Fruits Act*.
He complained, further, that the holder of an owner's licence was
compelled to export a fixed proportion of various classes of his
dried fruits, and that the Commonwealth had refused to permit
him to sell his dried fruits in other states unless he took out such
a licence. James asked for a declaration that the act and regulations thereunder were contrary to section 92 and therefore invalid.
The High Court, however, following the decisions in *McArthur's
Case* and *James v. Commonwealth,* held that as the Commonwealth
was not bound by section 92, the legislation was valid. In December, 1935, the Privy Council gave leave to appeal. New South
Wales, Victoria and Queensland intervened in support of the Commonwealth, and it is interesting to note, in view of the grievances
of the 'claimant' states, that Tasmania and Western Australia also
intervened, but in support of James.

The importance of the issues which came up for decision in
this appeal are best illustrated through the arguments submitted by
counsel for the contesting parties. Mr. Menzies, on behalf of
the Commonwealth, repeatedly emphasized the evil effects which
would flow from a decision that section 92 did restrain the Commonwealth. Bound up with the immediate question of the
validity of the Commonwealth *Dried Fruits Act* was the far
greater issue of whether or not 'the whole power of the Commonwealth' was competent to legislate in such a way as to control
marketing throughout Australia.[26] The dried fruits industry
was not the only one affected, for legislation of a similar character
had been passed to cover the marketing of wheat and dairy
products. If the Commonwealth dried fruits legislation proved
invalid marketing schemes dealing with other industries would
become unworkable. It was for this reason that New South Wales
and Queensland had intervened on behalf of the Commonwealth.
The governments of those states wanted 'to protect certain State
legislation . . . regarded by them as vital legislation for the purpose of carrying out not only marketing schemes, but other schemes
and in general for regulating the internal affairs of those States.'[27]
Since all state legislation upon marketing was 'ineffectual' without
Commonwealth support the protection of state legislation demanded

26. Mr. Menzies for the Commonwealth, 55 *C.L.R.*, p. 20.
27. *Ibid.*, p. 30.

the preservation of the Commonwealth power. It followed that without that preservation a zone of anarchy would be created, in which no government would have authority to legislate with respect to trade and commerce. The point could hardly have been put more clearly than it was by Mr. Menzies.

> If the Commonwealth cannot control inter-State trade and commerce to the extent illustrated by the act immediately in question, then it is clear that the States cannot control it. It will, therefore, be clear that nobody can control it. If neither the Commonwealth nor the States can control that element the control of marketing in Australia is impossible. The result would be that the totality of legislative power in Australia will prove to be less than the totality of power in other civilized countries.[28]

The Commonwealth, therefore, urged either that the decision in *McArthur's Case* that section 92 did not bind the Commonwealth be confirmed or alternatively that if the section did apply to the Commonwealth it should be interpreted to mean, as Sir Samuel Griffith had suggested it should mean, freedom 'from taxes, charges or imposts.' The Privy Council, however, refused to accept either of these contentions.[29]

In law, as Sir Stafford Cripps hastened to point out,[30] the question of inconvenience could not be regarded as 'a proper criterion for interpretation,' and, therefore, the arguments of Mr. Menzies upon the repercussions of a declaration unfavourable to the Commonwealth were largely irrelevant. At all events, they did not prevent the Privy Council from reversing the High Court's decision and declaring that the Commonwealth was bound by section 92. The Commonwealth refused to accept this diminution of its authority over trade and commerce without a struggle. Consequently, in March, 1937, the federal government submitted to the electors by referendum proposals for the amendment of the constitution in favour of the conferring upon the Commonwealth freedom from section 92 in respect of marketing laws.[31] Even if a favourable vote had been recorded it would still have been necessary for the Commonwealth and the states to act in close collaboration because of the division of power with regard to trade and commerce. The states would have regulated intra-state transactions, while the Commonwealth dealt with inter-state and overseas commercial activities. The amendment, however, was

28. 55 *C.L.R.*, p. 20.
29. Bailey and Giblin, *op. cit.*, p. 164.
30. For the states of Tasmania and Western Australia intervening.
31. See *Round Table*, xxvii, 651.

heavily defeated, with the result that the federal government remains without adequate authority to legislate for the efficient marketing of Australian products.

While the decision in *James v. Commonwealth*[32] and the interpretation given to section 92 have done much to hamper the organization of marketing by both state and Commonwealth governments they have not meant that no action of any sort could be attempted.   Indeed, in an effort to escape from a situation in which it appeared that no government could effectively legislate the High Court, in recent decisions, has shown a tendency to confine more narrowly the operation of section 92, and to support the validity of Commonwealth legislation which, though intended to regulate marketing, was based not on the Commonwealth's trade and commerce power, but on the use in combination of the excise power and the grants power.

Since the decision in *James v. Commonwealth* state legislation dealing with marketing, though its legality was often open to doubt on constitutional grounds, has not only been enacted, but has been upheld to a surprising extent.   The main Victorian marketing legislation, the *Marketing Primary Products Act,* was passed in 1935, and has operated with reasonable success, though it was found necessary to exempt commodities engaged in interstate trade from the operation of the act.   The decision in *Hartley v. Walsh*[33] supported the legality of the Victorian dried fruits marketing scheme, while that in *Milk Board v. Metropolitan Cream Proprietary Ltd.*[34] upheld New South Wales legislation on the marketing of milk and cream.

The decision in the latter case and the judgments which supported it are of sufficient importance to warrant closer examination.   The *Milk Act* 1931-1936 of New South Wales set up a Milk Board, which was charged with 'the complete regulation and control of milk distribution in Sydney and its suburbs for (a) hygienic purposes, (b) social purposes, (c) economic purposes, that is fixation of prices.'[35]   The act covered all milk intended to be used in the metropolitan area, but only applied to milk produced in another state when the milk reached a district specified in the act.   The Metropolitan Cream Proprietary Ltd., without the consent of the board, had been selling in the milk-distributing district of Sydney 600 gallons of Victorian cream a week.   The board maintained that milk or cream brought from

32. 55 *C.L.R.* 1 (1936).   33. 57 *C.L.R.* 372 (1937).
34. 62 *C.L.R.* 116 (1939).   35. *Ibid.,* p. 118.

Victoria for use in Sydney had become the property of the board under the act.

The main contention for the defendant was that the Milk Act was invalid as an infringement of section 92. The case was notable for a discussion, especially by Latham, C.J., of the interpretation which should be given to this section. The Chief Justice outlined the history of the interpretation of the section, stressing the 'difficulty of the co-existence in the same constitutional document of section 51 (1) (power to legislate with respect to inter-state trade and commerce) and section 92 (such trade and commerce to be absolutely free),[36] a difficulty which had led to the decision in *McArthur's Case*. In presenting his own view of the interpretation which should be given to the section Latham, C.J., began with the assumption that trade and commerce involved 'orderly dealing.' This implied that the words 'absolutely free' could not mean that inter-state trade and commerce was to be 'exempt from all law.' Such trade was specifically stated to be free, but 'free' must be given the meaning of 'governed by law.' But if inter-state trade could be regulated by any law enacted by a parliament section 92 would lose all significance. It was, therefore, necessary to discover some criterion by which laws relating to inter-state trade which did infringe section 92 could be distinguished from those which did not. The Chief Justice declared :

> One proposition which I regard as established is that simple legislation prohibition (Federal or State), as distinct from regulation, of inter-State trade and commerce is invalid. Further, a law which is 'directed against' inter-State trade and commerce is invalid. Such a law does not regulate such trade, it merely prevents it. But a law prescribing rules as to the manner in which trade (including transport) is to be conducted is not a mere prohibition, and may be valid in its application to inter-State trade, nothwithstanding section 92.[37]

The present case, in the view of the Chief Justice, put the issue squarely of whether section 92 made a system of control of production, transport and marketing impossible in Australia, at least in so far as commodities engaged in inter-state trade were concerned.

Perhaps the most significant passage in the judgment was the analysis of the reasoning of the Privy Council in *James v. Commonwealth*,[38] especially with reference to the *Peanut Board*

36. *Ibid.*, p. 124, Latham, C.J.   37. *Ibid.*, p. 127.
38. 55 *C.L.R.* 1 (1936).

Case. The decision in the *Peanut Board Case* had been approved by the Privy Council, but Latham, C.J., argued that approval was due to the fact that the act had been construed as involving 'a compulsory marketing scheme, entirely restrictive of any freedom of action on the part of the producers.'[39] Even so, he admitted that the references in *James v. Commonwealth* to the *Peanut Board Case* would have implied that it was not possible for a state parliament to formulate a compulsory marketing scheme for any commodity in which there was a measure of inter-state trade had the Privy Council not elsewhere in its judgment maintained the view that 'a state parliament is not necessarily and as, of course, prohibited from controlling the sale of any commodity within its borders by the imposition of a collective marketing scheme.'[40]   Such a scheme would only be invalid if it could be shown that it was 'directed wholly or partially against inter-state trade in the goods,'[41] i.e., that the real object of the legislation was to impose restrictions on inter-state trade.   By adopting this interpretation of the view enunciated by the Privy Council the Chief Justice was able to conclude that a state parliament could establish a compulsory marketing scheme provided that it was not 'directed against inter-state trade, and was not merely a prohibition as distinct from a regulation of such trade.'[42]   Moreover, he believed that in the present instance the Milk Act could be sustained under such an interpretation since the real object of the act was not interference with inter-state trade.   The majority of the High Court were in agreement with the arguments of the Chief Justice, and reached the conclusion that the act did not contravene section 92.

It is clear from this decision that a different construction had been placed upon the section to that which had been current previously. The ability, it is true, of a state parliament to enact marketing legislation was still hedged about by constitutional difficulties arising out of the presence of section 92, for such legislation would have to be carefully framed in order to avoid interference with inter-state trade of a character likely to conflict with the meaning now given to section 92 by the High Court.   Nevertheless, as a result of this decision it became possible for a state to attempt regulation of trade, even in commodities in which there were some inter-state traffic, provided that the main object was that of regulation, and not that of interference with inter-state trade.   The advantages to the states of such an interpretation of section 92 are undoubtedly very

39. 62 *C.L.R.*, p. 131, Latham, C.J.
40 *Ibid.*, p. 132.   41. *Ibid.*   42. *Ibid.*

real, though, in view of past experience of the use to which such powers have been put it seems highly likely that any extension of state control over trade and commerce which might result from a restricted interpretation of section 92 will probably lead to a resurgence of state economic nationalism.

This latest shift in the interpretation of section 92 not only underlines the great difficulty which the High Court has experienced in giving any clear meaning to the wording of the section, but also serves to emphasise the uncertainty which has arisen out of attempts to reconcile High Court pronouncements on this subject. The tangled history of the section may be illustrated from the judgment of Latham, C.J., in the *Milk Board Case* itself. Though finding in favour of the legality of the legislation, the Chief Justice confessed:

> Not long ago I should have regarded such a case (i.e., the defendant's) as quite unanswerable on the basis of decisions of this court, and should have thought that nearly every point was well taken, whatever the consequences might have been in limiting the powers of parliaments to give effect to economic policy.[43]

In a later passage 'the difficulties involved in reaching any reasonable interpretation of section 92' were again stressed.

> Since the decision in *McArthur's Case,* and, notwithstanding that decision, other cases showed how difficult it was to obtain any general agreement upon the meaning and application of section 92.[44]

Nothing, however, revealed more clearly the confusion prevailing over the meaning which should be given to the section than the dissenting protest of Starke, J., with its implied warning of the dangers of state protectionism.

> The constitution, we have been told, must not be mocked (*James v. Cowan*), but judicial decisions are rapidly destroying the effectiveness of the guarantee contained in section 92 of the constitution that trade and commerce among the States shall be absolutely free. Transport may be licensed; prices may be controlled; trade in goods among the States may be regulated by laws directed towards procuring standards of quality, condition or grade of articles of commerce, and now we are called upon to declare that the States may compulsorily acquire commodities for like purposes, and thus prevent or hinder all trade in such commodities among the States.[45]

43. *Ibid.*, p. 123.   44. *Ibid.*, p. 124.
45. *Ibid.*, p. 143. Starke, J. There is always the possibility that the confusion may be heightened by a further change in the attitude of the High Court towards the interpretation of section 92.

Just as the scope of section 92 has been restricted to validate certain types of state legislation on marketing, so judicial decision has upheld Commonwealth legislation intended to circumvent the obstacles placed in the way of Commonwealth regulation of trade and commerce by the decision in *James v. Commonwealth*. Thus the wheat industry assistance legislation of 1938 was upheld by the Privy Council, which in *W. R. Moran Pty. Ltd. v. Deputy Federal Commissioner of Taxation (N.S.W.)*[46] affirmed the decision of the High Court. The plan to assist the wheatgrowers showed considerable ingenuity. At a conference between the prime minister of the Commonwealth and the premiers of the states it was decided that the various governments would co-operate in order to carry out a scheme which would ensure to the wheatgrowers a payable price for wheat. The Commonwealth agreed to impose a tax upon flour sold for home consumption in Australia, while the states undertook both to pass legislation fixing prices for flour sold for home consumption and to arrange for the distribution of the tax to wheatgrowers 'in proportion to the quantity of wheat respectively produced by them.'[47] It was thought necessary, however, to make some special arrangement for Tasmania, since Tasmania was the only State to import wheat from other states, mainly because she produced relatively little wheat of her own. It was recognised that if no special treatment were accorded Tasmania the people of the state would have to pay the excise duty on flour without adequate compensation in the form of payments to Tasmanian wheatgrowers.

It was decided that the difficulty should be overcome by providing that, while the tax on flour consumed in Tasmania should be levied at the same rate as on flour consumed in the other states, Tasmania should receive financial aid from the Commonwealth to the extent of an amount not greater than the tax on flour collected in that state. The legislation required for the enforcement of the scheme as a whole was passed by the Commonwealth and the states, but, despite the fact that the acts of the Commonwealth parliament, in accordance with the constitution, imposed uniform taxation, the validity of the Commonwealth legislation was challenged on the ground that the attempt to extend special treatment to Tasmania involved discrimination contrary to section 51 (ii).

The scheme as a whole depended upon the 'exercise in combination of three powers.'[48]   Under section 51 (ii) the Common-

46.   63 *C.L.R.* 338 (1940).
47.   *Ibid.*, p. 343.   Preamble to *Wheat Industry Assistance Act* 1938 quoted.
48.   *Ibid.*, p. 346, Viscount Maugham.

wealth parliament had the right to impose taxation which did not
discriminate between states, and under section 96 the right to
grant financial assistance to any state, while the third power was
that of the Tasmanian parliament to distribute the Commonwealth
grant to those Tasmanians who paid flour tax. In defence of the
scheme it was argued that any discrimination which might exist
would not invalidate the legislation, because it was not 'within the
prohibition on Commonwealth powers contained in section 51
(ii).'[49]

The Privy Council refused to uphold the contention that there
had been discrimination in violation of section 51 (ii), pointing
out that

> Such discrimination as may result between millers or their
> customers in Tasmania and in the other States is a by-product,
> so to speak, of the endeavour to equalize the burden of the
> legislation by diminishing the special burden on Tasmania; and
> it is of the first importance to note that this is brought about
> by an exercise of power under section 96, which does not itself
> prohibit discrimination.'[50]

The Privy Council, therefore, affirmed the decision of the
High Court that the various Commonwealth and state acts, considered together, contained nothing prohibited by the constitution.
It should be noted, however, that while their lordships accepted
as correct the final conclusion of the High Court on what was
substantially a question of fact, they appear to have disagreed
with the principles of law enunciated by the majority of the High
Court and to have accepted rather the principles enunciated by
the dissenting justices. At least, it may be said that the Privy
Council viewed with extreme caution the doctrine that every
case could be justified in which an act imposing a non-discriminatory tax was followed by 'an appropriation act or a tax-assessment
act passed by the Commonwealth parliament authorizing exemp-
tions, abatements or refunds of tax to taxpayers in a particular
state.'[51] Indeed, while reaching the same conclusion as the High
Court the Privy Council issued a warning that in its view the
Commonwealth parliament could not exercise its powers under
section 96 'with a complete disregard of the prohibition contained in section 51 (ii), or so as altogether to nullify that constitutional safeguard.'[52]

So far as the wheat industry itself was concerned it may
be said that a means had been found whereby the Commonwealth

49. *Ibid.*   50. *Ibid.,* p. 349.   51. *Ibid.,* p. 345.
52. *Ibid.,* p. 349.

and the states acting in co-operation could enact marketing legislation which would guarantee to the growers a payable price for wheat by establishing a home consumption price for that commodity.   Moreover, by a combination of Commonwealth powers the obstacles which had invalidated previous marketing legislation had been surmounted, and the vital significance of the existence of section 96 (the grants power) foreshadowed, even though its possibilities were not fully revealed until the *Uniform Tax Case*. Much can, no doubt, be achieved by strategems of this kind, involving the use in combination of powers which would be ineffective if employed singly, but these are devious and unsatisfactory, even if ingenious, methods of taking action.   What is more, they are methods which have been forced upon the Commonwealth and the states by the inadequacy of the Commonwealth power over trade and commerce and by the restricting influence of section 92.

In 1929 the majority report of the Royal Commission on the Constitution opposed the bestowal upon the Commonwealth of unlimited power to legislate with respect to trade and commerce, although the minority report was as emphatically in favour of national regulation.   Since 1929, however, judicial interpretation has whittled away the Commonwealth power and has made plain the difficulties confronting both the Commonwealth and the states in their efforts to control marketing.   Some change is generally recognized to be imperative, and there is little disagreement about the direction which that change should take.   Both constitutional authorities of the eminence of Professor Bailey and Sir Robert Garran, and the political leaders of the United Australia Party,[53] and the federal Labour Party, have alike pronounced in favour of full Commonwealth powers over trade and commerce.   Nor is any other solution practicable, since conditions no longer admit the possibility of arbitrarily dividing trade and commerce into intra-state and inter-state divisions and of assigning control over each to different authorities. Such a division is wholly illogical for trade and commerce is 'one and indivisible.'   It is, moreover, intimately connected with other subject matters of legislation which either are or should be assigned to the Commonwealth.   Control over industry has been shown to be bound up with the regulation of trade and commerce; company law is likewise affected; while transport, which is the life-

---

53. Since the Curtin government put forward its proposals for constitutional reform the leaders of this party have somewhat modified their attitude. See Chapter VI, The Commonwealth at War.

blood of commerce, cannot legitimately be divorced from the trade and commerce power.

The damage which has been wrought by the incorporation of section 92 within the constitution may be said to be threefold. In the first place it canalizes, and therefore distorts, the discussion of inter-state problems relating to trade and commerce by forcing such problems to be represented, as though they were always of the kind envisaged by the section. In this way the question at issue is often prevented from being set forth in a full and realistic manner. Secondly, it places the Commonwealth and the states in a false position, since they have either to twist their legislation to get it covered by the section, or to twist the section to make it cover the legislation. The result of such an approach is that eventually the interpretations placed on the section cannot by any means be said to follow from a 'plain construction' canon of interpretation. Lastly, the unreal presentation of problems arising out of the section gives the public, when asked to decide by referendum, an equally unreal impression of the state of affairs.

The elimination of the existing division of power with regard to trade and commerce, however desirable in itself, would not provide a complete solution to the problem so long as section 92 operates as a check on all legislative power. Even if the Commonwealth parliament were given full authority over trade and commerce its liberty of action would still be severely circumscribed while section 92 remained in force. The position, therefore, with regard to the section is wholly unsatisfactory, for it means that the totality of legislative power in both Commonwealth and states is insufficient to establish whatever form of commercial regulation may be thought desirable.

It is clear, moreover, that the existence of section 92 in the constitution has led to problems of the utmost complexity. The language employed in the section has created its own special problems, so much so that the High Court has experienced the utmost difficulty in endowing the wording with any clear meaning. The declaration that trade and commerce among the states must be absolutely free, while imposing a salutary break upon state economic nationalism has nevertheless thwarted attempts by both the Commonwealth and the states to regulate commercial relations, notably in the sphere of marketing. In view of the obvious defects of the section, some modification of the present position either in the direction of the elimination or the curtailment or the rewording of the section has become imperative.

Section 92 may best be approached through a realisation of the special reasons for its insertion. The incorporation of this particular section within the constitution was due fundamentally to the fact that the union of the several colonies was to be achieved upon a federal basis, or, to put it another way, that it was to be an incomplete form of union under which the states would still exercise very wide powers, especially over economic matters. The desire for fiscal union was one of the most impelling motives for federation, and that desire was in no small measure the outcome of the unhappy experience of colonial economic rivalry, which on more than one occasion had caused bitterness and which if persisted in for any length of time might well have proved fatal to the creation of an Australian Commonwealth. In view of past experience it was felt that the states must be prevented from continuing a policy of protection and commercial rivalry, and it was believed that the best way to achieve this object was to insert a declaration in the constitution guaranteeing absolute freedom of trade among the states.[54]   Of course, the danger of economic rivalry between the states had been automatically lessened by giving the Commonwealth exclusive control over the tariff, but it was recognized that without some constitutional prohibition it might continue to flourish by more devious means.   Events have shown that these fears were by no means baseless, for, despite the existence of section 92, the states have attempted to foster with the means at their disposal a policy of protectionism.   But for the presence of section 92 there is little doubt that the states would have made even more strenuous efforts to engage in large-scale protection of local interests, thus frustrating the broad desire of the founders of the federation that Australia should develop as one economic unit.

In Australia federation marked a stage in the development towards nationhood. At the time when the Commonwealth was formed the feeling of national unity was still incomplete which meant that the only system which could command allegiance was one granting limited powers to the central or national government.   Despite the rapidity with which economic unification took place, further political or constitutional advance could only come about when petty local jealousies had been submerged by a consciousness of national unity.   It would appear that this stage has now been reached, for there is little doubt that to-day the

---

54. No doubt the jealousy of the colonies towards the future Commonwealth and fear of a possible combination of the more powerful states were other motives for the insertion of the section.

major allegiance of the citizens of the Commonwealth is to Australia and not to any individual state. If this be so, the moment has arrived for fundamental constitutional change with the object of concentrating power in the hands of the national parliament. So long as the states retain extensive powers over industrial and commercial life some safeguard of the sort contained in section 92 is necessary against the possible abuse of those powers. But once the states have been relegated to the role of administrative units and the national parliament has assumed full authority the necessity for the section disappears and its retention would only prove hampering to effective Commonwealth regulation of trade and commerce. The future of the section may well depend largely upon the nature of the constitutional edifice under which Australia is to be governed. But whatever the form, it is clear that some modification of the section is desirable. Should the federal system persist, or be modified in the direction of greater authority for the Commonwealth, it should be made plain by insertion of specific language in the constitution that section 92 in no way binds the Commonwealth. If, on the other hand, unification were to take place the section should be eliminated altogether.

V

THE POSITION OF THE STATES WITHIN THE COMMONWEALTH, AND THE WORK OF THE COMMONWEALTH GRANTS COMMISSION

OVER forty years' experience of the working of federalism under the Australian constitution has bred dissatisfaction among all the states, and among the least developed and smallest populated states a sense of disillusionment so profound as to lead to talk of, and in one case an attempt at, secession. The gradual sapping of their authority has engendered in some of the states a feeling of grievance against the Commonwealth, and serious misgivings as to the benefits supposedly accruing from federation. Though this hostility towards the Commonwealth has by no means been equally powerful in all the states, yet all have resented the encroachment of the Commonwealth in fields which they regarded as legitimately their own. All the states can point to the imposition of direct taxation by federal governments and the inclusion of state employees within the jurisdiction of the Commonwealth Arbitration Court. By imposing direct taxation the Commonwealth is felt to have invaded a sphere tacitly understood[1] to have been left to the states, and to have restricted the taxation base of the states to such an extent as to render their financial stability precarious. By the inclusion of state employees within the scope of the federal Arbitration Court, state governments are said to have suffered a diminution of control over their internal affairs, since they have been deprived of authority to deal with their own servants and their own industries. All the states are likewise resentful about a number of specific acts of the Commonwealth which are regarded either as antagonistic to the spirit of federation, or else as a flagrant attempt at evasion of the provisions of the constitution. The imposition of customs duties on goods imported by a state, which was challenged unavailingly by the New South Wales government,[2] has been regarded as an instance of a breach of good faith

1. This claim by the states is, to say the least, dubious. No attempt was made to render such an understanding explicit, and had it been done it would have largely destroyed the financial power of the Commonwealth.
2. 5 *C.L.R.* 818, *A.G. for N.S.W. v. The Collector of Customs.*

by the Commonwealth, and the concealment of the real Commonwealth surplus by the device of payment into trust funds as a deliberate subterfuge to avoid the transference to the states of money to which they were entitled.[3] Again, all states are well aware of the way in which judicial interpretation has led to an extension of Commonwealth authority and a corresponding curtailment of their own. But, above all, the states have been profoundly dissatisfied with the financial relations existing between themselves and the Commonwealth, and not a little aggrieved at the overbearing attitude which the Commonwealth, secure in its financial superiority, has adopted towards them. The conclusion of the financial agreement was not much to their liking, and the invasion of state independence illustrated by the *Financial Agreements Enforcement Act* directed against New South Wales has filled them with alarm. Indeed, the drastic action taken by the Commonwealth on this occasion, when combined with other judicial decisions hostile to the states, has led Western Australia to the conclusion that sections 106 and 107 of the constituion have been abrogated and no longer possess any vital meaning.[4] These sections guarantee the continuance of full powers to the states except upon those subjects which were transferred to the Commonwealth, and read as follows:—

Section 106: The constitution of each State of the Commonwealth shall, subject to this Constitution, continue as at the establishment of this Commonwealth, or at the admission or establishment of the State, as the case may be, until altered in accordance with the Constitution of the State.

Section 107: Every power of the Parliament of a Colony which has become or becomes a State, shall, unless it is by this constitution exclusively vested in the Parliament of the Commonwealth or withdrawn from the Parliament of the State, continue as at the establishment of the Commonwealth, or as at the establishment or admission of the State, as the case may be.

The states are by no means enthusiastic about their financial relations with the Commonwealth. They claim that their resources are inadequate for the fulfilment of the functions en-

---

3. Also challenged by N.S.W., unsuccessfully (7. *C.L.R.* 179, *N.S.W. v. Commonwealth*).
4. *The Case of the People of Western Australia* in support of their desire to withdraw from the Commonwealth of Australia established under the *Commonwealth Constitution Act* (Imperial), and that Western Australia be restored to its former status as a separate self-governing colony in the British Empire, 1934, p. 63.

trusted to them, and that without the possession of adequate sources of revenue there can be no real measure of state independence.

In addition to those grievances which are common to all the states are others which are peculiar to the weaker or 'claimant' states—to South Australia, Tasmania and Western Australia. These states through a combination of factors found themselves in the position of being unable to maintain average Australian standards. They were faced with grave budgetary problems, were unable to provide social services equivalent to those in operation in other states and had to cope with developmental difficulties of exceptional magnitude. The seriousness of their plight made them highly critical of federation and inclined to lay the blame for their misfortunes upon the policies pursued by the Commonwealth.[5] This dissatisfaction among the less populous states was a sufficiently serious source of weakness in the federation to necessitate some attempt at alleviation. Periodical investigations were made by various commissions, but their recommendations either did not touch the roots of the problem or were not acted upon wholeheartedly. At any rate, they did little to remove the sense of grievance. The Commonwealth, however, did recognise that disabilities had been imposed upon some states through federation, and proceeded to allocate special grants to Tasmania and Western Australia.[6] These were not intended to be permanent, but the inability of Tasmania and Western Australia to do without them, together with the increasingly serious financial position in South Australia, meant that a point was reached where the federal system in Australia could only be maintained if regular grants were forthcoming from the Commonwealth.

Dissatisfaction with the results produced by federation has been repeatedly expressed by the political leaders of the weaker states. More recently both grievances and claims for compensation for the disabilities imposed by federation have been tabulated in the Western Australian case in support of secession, and in the evidence presented to the Grants Commission by all three states. It is pertinent to enquire just what position the claimant states believe they occupy within the Commonwealth, and to

5.   e.g., 1933 (First) *Report*, Grants Commission Ch. iii.   The Claims of South Australia, Western Australia and Tasmania.

6.   In 1910 Western Australia was given £250,000 diminishing by £10,000 yearly, and in 1912 Tasmania received £95,000 diminishing by £10,000 over 10 years.   On the termination of these grants fresh payments were found to be necessary.   The total amount paid in grants to Western Australia, Tasmania and South Australia to 1933-34 will be found in a table included in the 1933 *Report*, Grants Commission, p. 26.

examine the grievances which they feel are attributable to federation.

Consider first the case put forward by Western Australia whose dissatisfaction with federation and whose sense of injury at the effects of Commonwealth policy is greater than that of any other state. No doubt where Western Australia is concerned it has to be borne in mind that the state has never been wholly reconciled to the thought of federation. It was with difficulty that she was induced to join the other states in a federal union, and that she did so at all was very largely due to the huge favourable vote recorded by the population of the goldfields which largely consisted of miners recently arrived from the other states.[7] The attitude in 1900 of a great many Western Australians towards federation was set forth in the report of the committee appointed to consider the draft bill to constitute the Commonwealth of Australia.

There is little doubt in the minds of your Committee that, taking into consideration the present flourishing condition of Western Australia, its mineral wealth, its infant industries, its large revenue, and its splendid prospects, it would have been better if federation had come at a time when the colony could have entered the Commonwealth on more equal terms.[8]

Nevertheless, the committee recommended that 'all minor considerations should be waived' in view of the fact that through federation Australia would occupy an enhanced position in the eyes of the world.

Anti-federal feeling did not cease to exist in Western Australia with her entry into the Commonwealth as an original member. Indeed, as early as 1906 the Legislative Assembly passed the following resolution condemning federation:

That the union of Western Australia with the other states in the Commonwealth of Australia, has proved detrimental to the best interests of this state, and that the time has arrived for placing before the people the question of withdrawing from such union.[9]

7. At the referendum on federation, 31 July 1900, the majority in favour for the whole state was 25,109, while the majority in the goldfields electorates was 24,517. *The Case of the People of Western Australia* states that the leaders of Western Australia were "pushed and cajoled" into federation by "two forces of external origin"—the people of the goldfields and Joseph Chamberlain, then Secretary of State for the Colonies. This contention is answered in *The Case for Union, A Reply to the Case for the Secession of the State of Western Australia*, pp. 29-30.

8. *Western Australian Parliamentary Papers*, 1899, Vol. iii. Report of the Joint Select Committee of the Leg. Council and the Leg. Assembly appointed to consider The Draft Bill to Constitute the Commonwealth of Australia.

9. Quoted, *The Case of the People of Western Australia*, p. 377.

Hostility towards the Commonwealth was greatly increased by the practical unification of Australia during the years 1914-18 and immediately after. This was brought about through the liberal interpretation of the Commonwealth defence power which enabled the federal government to interfere in the domestic concerns of the states. In 1924, the Tariff Board issued its 'Report on the Tariff and its Incidence in Western Australia,' which declared that federation had resulted in a feeling of general disillusionment. A year later, following a campaign in favour of secession, came the appointment of the Royal Commission on the finances of Western Australia as affected by federation. The findings of the commission supported Western Australia's contention that grave disabilities had been imposed upon the state by federation. Indeed, such a serious view was taken of the position that the majority report favoured tariff autonomy, while the minority report went so far as to advocate secession. The Commonwealth made no attempt to carry out the recommendations of the commission except with regard to the allocation of a special grant to Western Australia, but staved off dissatisfaction with promises and the appointment in 1927 of the Royal Commission on the Constitution, whose duty it was to furnish a report upon the operation of the federal system in all its aspects. Since the conclusions of the majority of the commission supported the retention of the existing system with only minor changes, their report did little for Western Australia. Meanwhile, the secession movement had been growing in strength.[10] A Dominion League had been formed with the object of fostering secession, and had received the blessing of the premier. Parliament, in the belief that a majority of the people of Western Australia were now in favour of secession, passed a bill submitting the issue to a referendum. The secession campaign was waged in 1933, the issue being considered sufficiently important for a federal delegation, headed by the prime minister, to intervene with the object of securing the defeat of the proposal for secession, and the adoption of the Commonwealth sponsored suggestion for a Constitutional Convention. Despite the efforts of the Commonwealth, the referendum resulted both in a huge majority in favour of secession and in the rejection, though by a smaller margin, of the proposal for a convention to discuss

10. For an account of the growth of the secession movement see *The Case of the People of Western Australia*. It should be pointed out that the material presented in the *Case* is propagandist and needs to be watched critically. *The Case for Union* provides an effective answer to many of the issues raised on behalf of Western Australia.

constitutional reform. The actual figures were: 138,653 for secession, 70,706 against; and 88,275 for a convention, 119,031 against.

In the Western Australian Case it is argued that the 70,000 who voted against secession were not necessarily 'satisfied with the condition of things' but were simply opposed to secession as a solution of their difficulties. No doubt there is a measure of truth in the argument. On the other hand it seems equally probable that a great number of those who voted for secession did not really want secession and did not believe that it was likely to be brought about.[11] What they did want to do was to show their sense of grievance at the consequences of federation to Western Australia, and to record a protest against Commonwealth policy sufficiently emphatic to ensure that the federal government would take some action to pacify opinion within that state. In assessing the importance of the secession vote it has always to be remembered that the vote was taken after a period of severe depression. The economic ills of the state were responsible for transforming secession from a goal favoured by a few extremists into a movement expressive of an almost universal dissatisfaction with existing conditions. With the return of a measure of prosperity secession lost much of its force and the movement receded into the background,[12] where it remains as a potential threat to the unity of the Commonwealth should a new crisis undermine the stability of the Western Australian economic system. The extensive support accorded to the secession campaign in Western Australia should at least have warned the federal government that unless a policy was pursued which would dissipate the sense of grievance among the weaker states those states were likely to become increasingly hostile towards the union in its existing form and might even be tempted to work for its disruption. The most important consequence of the secessionist movement has been its demonstration of the necessity for remedial action in relation to the Australian constitution.

The decision by the British parliament, that it was unable to accede to the request of Western Australia to consider its petition for secession on the ground that such a question had now become one for the Australian people to determine, ensured that there was little likelihood of Western Australia withdrawing

11. This view is reinforced by the fact that up to and including 1919 Western Australia voted in favour of every referendum for increasing Federal powers.
12. *The Australian Quarterly*, March, 1939, p. 5.

from the federation.[13] No Constitutional Convention, such as had been proposed by the federal delegation during the secession campaign, was convoked, so that constitutionally the position of Western Australia after the vote in favour of secession remained exactly the same as it had been before. However, a new factor had appeared in the situation with the appointment in July 1933 of the Commonwealth Grants Commission, whose duty it was to report upon the applications made by South Australia, Western Australia and Tasmania for financial assistance from the Commonwealth under section 96 of the constitution. Special grants by the Commonwealth to a state were in themselves no new phenomenon. Western Australia received such a grant from the Commonwealth as early as 1910, Tasmania obtained help two years later, and in 1929-30 it was found necessary to begin payments to South Australia.[14] In 1925 the Disabilities Commission, which enquired into the finances of Western Australia, had recommended that if tariff autonomy was not to be conceded, the Commonwealth should make a special payment to Western Australia of £450,000 a year commencing from 1 July 1924. Actually, the grant was considerably reduced, since by the time of the appointment of the Grants Commission, i.e., up to 30 June 1933, the state should have received £4,050,000 whereas it received only £2,565,905.[15] Still, the principle of the special grant had been conceded as a result of these payments and others made to Tasmania and South Australia. The establishment of the Grants Commission did not, therefore, imply any new departure in the sense of deciding upon the adoption of a policy of special grants. On the contrary, it was a recognition of a habit which was rapidly becoming an integral part of the Australian federal system. Where the Grants Commission did represent a new departure was in attempting to discover some systematic basis of allocation. Grants were no longer to be given haphazardly, but were to be based 'on definite and sound principles' which were to be discovered by the commission.

Since Western Australia had perforce to remain within the framework of the federation she not unnaturally decided to participate in whatever benefits might be obtained in the way of

13.　For documents relating to the Western Australian petition for secession see *Cross Currents in Australian Finance* 1936. There would be little likelihood of securing secession by any other means than that of legislation by the British Parliament.

14.　1929 *Report*, Commission on the Constitution, p. 192. 1933 *Report*, Grants Commission, p. 26. For special grants to Western Australia see also *The Case for Union*, p. 33.

15.　*The Case of the People of Western Australia*, p. 73.

special grants. 'Western Australia, therefore, in common with Tasmania and South Australia, co-operated with the newly established Grants Commission by placing before it evidence in support of the state's claim for special financial treatment. These cases put before the Grants Commission represent the best expression by the claimant states of their sense of grievance at the position which they have come to occupy within the federation. However, in so far as Western Australia is concerned, "The Case of the People of Western Australia" in support of their desire to withdraw from the Commonwealth of Australia must be regarded as the most complete presentation of that state's grievances and claims. The Western Australian evidence before the Grants Commission will be found to be almost identical with the material gathered together in this report.

The case recites in considerable detail those grievances which are common to all the states. It repeats the story of the expansion of Commonwealth powers through judicial interpretation, protests against specific Commonwealth actions such as the imposition of customs duties upon state imports, and the subterfuge employed to avoid payment of surplus revenue, and expresses the conviction that the superior financial power of the Commonwealth, together with the terms of the Financial Agreement, have placed the continued independence of the states in jeopardy. Thereafter the case proceeds to develop those particular grievances which it holds are either limited to Western Australia or are shared only by Tasmania and South Australia. These are disabilities which Western Australia asserts are traceable directly to 'federal legislative enactment or administrative action pursuing a policy which is framed to suit the conditions prevailing in the states in eastern Australia.'[16] It is said that the problems of Western Australia are either not understood or are ignored, and that legislation is dominated by the interests of Queensland, New South 'Wales and Victoria.

Repeated protests, declares the case, have done little to ameliorate the position of Western Australia. On the administrative side, the state objects to the exercise of control from distant Canberra, and to the duplication and excess costs which federation has introduced by the 'unnecessary establishment of federal departments in 'Western Australia which find their counterpart in others under state control.'[17] Nor, claims the case, has the establishment of the seat of government in Canberra been counterbalanced by effective representation for Western

16. *Ibid.*, p. 176.   17. *Ibid.*, p. 185.

Australia in the Commonwealth parliament. The adoption of
a population basis for representation ensures that the industrialised eastern states will not only retain but probably increase their
preponderance as against a primary producing state like Western
Australia. Yet, because of her isolation, her size and the nature
of her production, Western Australia needs a greater number of
representatives than her population warrants on the present basis
of calculation. 'How,' asks the case, 'can one member adequately
represent the federal electorate of Kalgoorlie which, in the state
Legislative Assembly, is represented by no fewer than seventeen
of the fifty members in the House?[18]   But, it is argued, the real
proof of the inadequacy of the state's representation is to be found
in the fact that her representatives have been utterly unable either
to prevent or to repeal legislation which was inimical to the
best interests of the state.

Two subjects of federal legislation—the reservation of coastal
navigation and the embargo upon the importation of sugar—
were advanced by Western Australia to illustrate her point of
view. The provisions of the Navigation Act had confined trade
between Australian ports to Australian ships, because British and
foreign shipping companies could not carry out the conditions
of the act. The Federal Bill was criticised as an evasion of the
spirit of the Merchant Shipping Act which had been intended to
provide equal facilities for all British ships. Instead, the Navigation Act had deprived Western Australia of the service provided
by British overseas ships, and had left her at the mercy of a
monopoly. The inevitable consequence of monopoly had mani-
fested itself in the shape of increased inter-state freights and
fares, while on the outbreak of shipping disputes the state had
found itself isolated. In addition, overseas freights had been
considerably increased as a direct result of the loss of trade
sustained on the Australian coast. Western Australia therefore
claimed that the legislation had imposed an especially heavy
burden upon the state because of her isolation, her length of coast-
line and her dependence upon exports.[19]

18. This argument is elaborated in some detail in the *Case*, pp. 191-2.
19. For a reply to this contention see *The Case for Union*, Chapter x, Coastal
     Shipping, where it is argued that "no allowance is made for the off-setting
     advantages which accrue to the state through having at command the ser-
     vices of established lines of improving ships, comparable with the best
     of ocean liners in passenger and cargo facilities and running to frequent
     and dependable schedules."   Reference is also made to the findings of
     the 1924 Royal Commission on the Navigation Act and the 1929 Tariff
     Board enquiry, which by no means wholly agree with the Western Aus-
     tralian Case.

The embargo placed upon the importation of sugar is perhaps a clearer instance of how federal legislation, designed to promote the welfare of one of the eastern states, may have a deleterious effect upon the economy of Western Australia. The introduction of sugar into the Commonwealth was prohibited in order to foster the Queensland industry. Queensland, naturally, received by far the greatest benefit but New South Wales and Victoria may also have derived some advantage through an increased sale of their manufactured goods in an expanded Queensland market. Western Australia, on the other hand, experienced the evil effects of the monopoly without any of the compensating benefits. Costs to the consumer and costs of production in industry were alike increased. Indeed, in the case the claim is made that the sugar embargo represented 'a poll tax of £1 per head of population of the state or more than £400,000 annually,' a figure not much below that of the state's exports to all the other states of the Commonwealth, and about twenty times greater than that of exports to Queensland.[20] But the disastrous effects of the embargo have, in the opinion of Western Australia, been far more extensive than might be imagined. They are said to have prevented both the furtherance of land settlement schemes, which were dependent upon the development of the fruit growing and jam making industries, and the opening up of new markets in eastern countries. It is argued that Western Australian primary products —notably flour and meat—could have been sold to Java in exchange for sugar. Since the price of Java sugar was about £7 a ton, whereas Queensland sugar was in the neighbourhood of £30 a ton, the transaction would have represented a very considerable saving to the people of Western Australia and would, at the same time, have provided a stimulus to the pastoral industry. The conclusion of the Western Australian case is, therefore, that in this instance, federal legislation, the object of which was the fostering of Queensland industry, proved hampering to the development of industry in Western Australia.

No doubt opinion in the west would be ready to make some allowance for special treatment for industry in tropical parts of the continent, but the case was emphatic that there could be no excuse for permitting a single company to enjoy a monopoly of sugar distribution throughout the Commonwealth, especially when it was thereby enabled to make enormous profits. Protection to

20. 1932-3. Total value of Western Australian exports of Western Australian origin to all other states equalled £517,630. Exports to Queensland valued £18,670. But see Chapter xi, The Sugar Industry, *The Case for Union*.

tropical industry was one thing, but additional excess costs in the shape of huge profits for the Colonial Sugar Refining Co. Ltd. was quite another. The company, through an agreement with the Commonwealth, had obtained a monopoly over the distribution of Queensland-grown sugar. Its success in building up profits proved little less than phenomenal, and in 1922 drew forth a protest from the Commonwealth Auditor-General:

> There can be no doubt that this company has attained its present prosperous and monopolistic position as a result of the high price which the consumers of Australia have paid and are continuing to pay for sugar.[21]

His opinion was backed by Mr. Fowler, chairman of the 1922 Joint Committee of Public Accounts which investigated the sugar industry. He declared that the committee had reached certain definite conclusions:

> One of these was that the political influence of the wealthy sugar interests was so vast that relief was practically impossible; another, that the key of the whole situation was the extraordinarily rich company, the Colonial Sugar Refining Company, who were able to throw a smoke screen around all their dealings with such effect that the Committee was not able to get at any facts on which to base a recommendation; the third was that this difficulty was deliberately engineered because the company dared not let their huge profits become known.[22]

It was against a system which permitted one company to enjoy a monopoly and impose exactions upon the people of Australia as a whole, and of the west in particular, that the Western Australian case delivered its protest. The conclusions reached by the Committee of Public Accounts are sufficient evidence that the federal system itself has acted as a cloak for the activities of the sugar interests and this opinion is strengthened by the efforts previously made to avoid investigation by a Commonwealth Royal Commission on the ground that the Commonwealth had exceeded its specified grant of power.[23]

21. Commonwealth Auditor-General's report to the Federal Parliament, 19 Feb. 1922. Quoted *The Case of the People of Western Australia*, p. 198.
22. Mr. J. M. Fowler, Chairman of the 1922 Joint Committee of Public Accounts in *The Herald* (Melbourne), 9 Aug. 1930. Quoted *The Case of the People of Western Australia*, p. 199.
23. See 15 *C.L.R.* 182 (1912), *Colonial Sugar Refining Company v. A.G. for the Commonwealth* and 17 *C.L.R.* 644 (1914), Privy Council Appeal. In 1911 the Commonwealth government appointed a Royal Commission to enquire into the sugar industry in Australia. The Commission asked the Colonial Sugar Refining Co. Ltd. to produce documents and give detailed information with regard to the carrying on of their business, whereupon

Fundamentally, however, the [Western Australian case was based upon the belief that all other disabilities paled into insignificance beside those imposed upon the state by the Commonwealth protective tariff and inter-state free trade. Protection it was argued had been 'an all party federal policy.' Indeed, in the words of Professor Hancock it 'had been more than a policy; it had been a faith and a dogma.' It was the submission of Western Australia that increasingly high tariff barriers had placed a far greater burden upon the state than upon any other. Victoria and Queensland were said to receive the greatest benefits; New South Wales occupied a midway position, while the other states, and most notably Western Australia, reaped the disadvantages without the compensating advantages. The burden fell most heavily upon Western Australia because she, more than any other state, was dependent upon primary production. Almost 80 per cent of the total production of the state was primary in character consisting chiefly of wheat, wool and gold. Since the bulk of that production had to be disposed of in the world's markets there was little possibility of passing on the excess costs of the tariff, which therefore fell with particular severity upon the export industries. Gold was quoted as an excellent example since in this industry costs had become so high that it was only saved from destruction by the very substantial rise in the price of gold. In so far as the other export industries were concerned these had found the excess costs of the tariff burdensome in times of prosperity, and were likely to find them ruinous when world prices for primary products were depressed. It is true that protection within Australia had not been confined solely to secondary industries but had been extended to cover certain favoured primary

the Company began an action in the High Court on the ground that the *Royal Commissions Act* 1902-12 was *ultra vires*, and that the Company was not bound to answer any questions or produce any documents. As the High Court was equally divided the case went to the Privy Council, which decided that the Act was void in so far as it purported to give the Commission power to compel answers to questions or to order the production of documents. The judgment given by Isaacs, J., when the case was before the High Court is an illuminating comment upon the way in which effective regulation in matters of national concern may be obstructed under a federal system. "The contention of the objectors," said Isaacs, J., "amounts to this—that the whole combined force of the Sovereign, the two Houses of legislation and the people of the Commonwealth when engaged in the responsible and momentous duty of considering a proposed alteration of the Constitution affecting federation and the states alike, is unavailing to compel any solitary individual in Australia who chooses to defy them, to give the smallest particle of information, however relevant, desirable or necessary that information may be" (15 *C.L.R.* 213).

products.[24]   Western Australian, however, claimed that she derived scant benefit from this form of protection because the majority of the products concerned were not of outstanding importance in her economy. In one other respect Western Australia claimed to have suffered considerably from the policy of protection. Increases in the Australian tariff have naturally led to retaliatory action by those countries against whose goods there was discrimination. Western Australia, by reason of her dependence upon exports, contends that she has been hard hit by these retaliatory measures. The case instances the adverse effect produced by the embargo upon glass, which was prejudicial to Belgian trade and evoked an immediate response from that country. Belgium had been accustomed to buy almost the entire output of the Wyndham Meat [Works for her army, but on the imposition of the embargo the Belgian government announced that it would only continue to buy meat to the value of the glass allowed into the Commonwealth.

In the minds of Western Australians inter-state free trade is closely associated with the evils of protection simply because free trade has nullified whatever advantages might have accrued to the state from a protective policy. High tariff barriers have not fostered the growth of secondary industries in Western Australia since such industries have for the most part been unable to withstand the competition from manufacturers in the eastern states. Heavy capital expenditure would be necessary to establish an industry and the limited market available in the west provides little inducement for such an outlay. Industrial development in Western Australia has, therefore, been slow, her markets have been flooded by manuactured goods from other states while in those instances where local industries were meeting with a measure of success manufacturers in the eastern states were guilty of resorting to such tactics as dumping. This at least is the testimony of the Western Australian case. For these reasons, then, it is argued that the federal tariff when taken in conjunction with the customs union has provided no protection for the local manufacturer, but has aided and abetted his competitors in other states. Should additional proof be needed Western Australia points to her adverse balance of inter-state imports over inter-state exports.[25]

Such are the arguments advanced by the "Case of the People of Western Australia" to justify the contention that the state has

24. e.g., sugar, dried fruits, wine, rice and butter.
25. The "burden" imposed by the tariff on Western Australia is analysed in Chapter viii, The Tariff, *The Case for Union.*

suffered severe disabilities through its membership of the Commonwealth. However, the real significance of the case lies not in its employment of this or that argument in support of some real or fancied grievance, but in the clearly expressed conviction that the people of Western Australia have been disillusioned, even to the point of desiring to withdraw from the Commonwealth, by the consequences of federal union. This discontent is derived from many sources but the basic cause is economic. Moreover, successive governments of Western Australia have found their financial resources inadequate for the fulfilment of the obligations incumbent upon them. The state has had to budget for deficits, and revenue surpluses have occurred in only five of the years since federation.[26]

The arguments and grievances, elaborated with such detail in the Western Australian case, reappear in the evidence submitted to the Grants Commission by that state in support of its claim for financial assistance from the Commonwealth. Indeed, the two cases mirror one another almost exactly. The Western Australian claim affirms the dissatisfaction with the financial relations of the Commonwealth and the states, criticizes the evil effects of federal policy, emphasizes 'the unequal incidence of the tariff' and attributes 'the inability of the state to develop adequately its secondary industries' to inter-state free trade.[27] In addition, considerable importance is attached to the special difficulties which confront the government of the state in its task of developing and administering so huge and isolated an area of the continent. Western Australia contended that in pursuit of a policy of development through land settlement the state had to deal with difficulties which were more onerous than those facing the other states. As evidence, the claim quoted the tremendous size of the state, the scarcity of population, the patchiness of the soil and the difficulties and expense associated with the provision of adequate communications, irrigation works and other facilities. In the course of group settlement losses had been sustained upon schemes which had only been embarked upon after consultation with British and Commonwealth governments. This it was said was work of a national character, and the state deserved some compensation in recognition of that fact. On the administration issue somewhat similar arguments were advanced, with the object of proving that the size and population of the state were factors imposing high administrative costs for

26. i.e., up to the outbreak of war in 1939.
27. 1933 (First) *Report*, Grants Commission, pp. 40-1.

government services. Finally, since the Grants Commission was empowered to take cognisance of the financial position of governments, but not of individuals within the claimant states, the Western Australian claim was defined as the sum total of the effects produced by the aforementioned disabilities upon the finances of the state. The claim concluded by specifying the conditions upon which the state could feel compensated for the disabilities imposed by federation:

> There are two alternatives. (a) A substantial monetary grant agreed on for a term of years. It is claimed that the balance against the Western Australian people (including their government) would not be redressed if any annual grant of less than £1,500,000 were made. (b) The second alternative is tariff autonomy as recommended by the majority report of the 1925 Royal Commission.[28]

The claims made before the Grants Commission by South Australia and Tasmania were based upon almost exactly the same grounds as the case submitted by Western Australia. In fact, the similarity in the attitude adopted by the claimant states is not the least remarkable feature of the evidence placed before the commission, and is in itself a vindication of the view that federalism as a governmental device has failed to protect the interests and independence of at least some of the component parts of the federation. The arguments employed by South Australia and Tasmania in support of their claims can best be judged from the summary given by the Grants Commission in their 1933 report:

South Australia.[29]
> (a) The losses sustained by the state owing to the changes in the methods of adjusting the financial relationships of the Commonwealth and the states.
> (b) The impact of federal policy generally on state policy and finance.
> (c) The unequal incidence of the tariff.
> (d) The burden arising from industrial policy.
> (e) The effects of the Navigation Act.
> (f) The financial difficulties of the state.

Tasmania.[30]
> (a) Suffering from the economic effects of federation and federal policy, e.g., the protective tariff, the Navigation Act and industrial arbitration.
> (b) Financial assistance from the Commonwealth has been inadequate and sometimes embarrassing.

28. *Ibid.*, p. 42.   29. *Ibid.*, p. 34.   30. *Ibid.*, p. 45.

(c) The state has been forced to carry on essential services at a standard much below that of the other states.

(d) The state has been forced to adopt the unfortunate expedient of charging to loan funds expenditure properly chargeable to revenue.

(e) The state has found it impossible to maintain adequately the assets of the state. This has seriously impaired financial stability.

(f) The state has been unable to provide adequate assistance or facilities for the necessary development of the resources of the state.

(g) The cost of development has been relatively high (due largely to the physical features of the state).

(h) Low taxable capacity.

(i) Small population.

(j) The adverse influences of the above on state finances.

In the cases submitted in elaboration of the above arguments those points which most keenly affected either state were naturally singled out for especial emphasis. South Australia placed most stress upon the unsatisfactory financial relations between the Commonwealth and the states. She maintained that there had been 'an implied promise that the weaker states would not be allowed to suffer through federation,' but that this had not prevented a reduction in the amount of revenue returned to the state after the expiration of the Braddon clause. The Financial Agreement had been forced upon the states, and the balance of the constitution upset through the superior position attained by the Commonwealth:

> The relationship of the Federal Parliament towards the states has been one of increasing dominance. It has persistently refused to recognise the need for some definite scheme for ensuring continuous financial adjustments as required from time to time.[31]

A further point raised by South Australia, and one which had not appeared in the evidence presented by Western Australia, was the adverse effect produced by federal arbitration awards. It was contended that the existence of both a federal and state tribunal for the determination of wages and conditions of employment had imposed an unnnecessary burden upon employers, and particularly upon the state as one of the largest employers. Very much the same point was made by Tasmania, though her complaint was that 'due regard had not been paid to the special conditions of

31. 1933 *Report*, Grants Commission, p. 35.

Tasmanian industry' which necessitated different regulations and different rates of pay from those prevailing on the mainland.

Throughout the Tasmanian case considerable emphasis was placed upon disabilities resulting from the state's isolation. It was, for example, her dependence upon sea communications which provoked hostility towards the Navigation Act. Tasmania claimed to have suffered special disadvantages by the act which had led to less frequent services and increased fares and freights. In addition, through the operation of the act, Tasmania had been handicapped in competitive trade, her tourist and other industries had been impeded, and the state isolated in times of maritime disputes because of the ban upon British shipping. In all, the Tasmanian claim estimated the minimum annual costs and losses resulting from the Navigation Act at £420,925.[32]

An examination of the South Australian and Tasmanian claims reveals that fundamentally the basis for the claims is that of fiscal need. In the case of South Australia, evidence was adduced to show that budget equilibrium had rarely been attained since 1913-14 and that years of unbalanced budgets had brought the state to the position where it could not effectively carry out its duties.[33] Fiscal need was also implicit in many of the arguments advanced by Tasmania. Attempts were made to prove that essential services were carried on at a standard much below the normal average for Australia, that dubious methods of finance had become necessary, that the assets of the state could no longer be properly maintained and that inadequate funds were available for needed developmental work. These are all statements calculated to prove the inability of the state to finance even its more important operations. Actually, the Tasmanian case does to some extent recognise that need should be the determinant of any grant in its favour, for it asserts that the measurement of the claim should be based on 'the actualities of the finances of the State to date; and the amount necessary to bring Tasmanian fundamental services to the average of the other five States.'[34]

The cases submitted by the three claimant states in 1933 all show a confusion about the basis upon which claims should be made. In reality, the arguments advanced were a mixture of two possible bases for claims. The first was founded upon the idea that since federation and Commonwealth policy had imposed disabilities upon certain states, compensation should be paid to

---

32. *Ibid.*, p. 46.
33. South Australian revenue deficits; 1928-9, £930,858; 1929-30, £1,625,823; 1930-31, £1,813,857; 1931-32, £1,063,360; 1932-33, £1,008,898.
34. 1933 *Report*, Grants Commission, p. 46.

them by the Commonwealth to an amount equivalent to the injury inflicted. The second was an expression of the belief that no state within a federation should be permitted to sink below the level of performance realised by the other states and that, if it did so, financial aid should be extended in accordance with its needs. The commission later pointed out that these two possible grounds for grants were not carefully distinguished by the claimant states, and went on to add that the states could not expect to have it both ways. If the claims were to be based upon need there was no place for additional claims in respect of disabilities.[35]

In July 1933 the Lyons government appointed the Hon. F. W. Eggleston, Professor L. F. Giblin and J. W. Sandford, Esq., as members of the first Commonwealth Grants Commission to report on applications made by the states of South Australia, Western Australia and Tasmania for financial assistance from the Commonwealth under section 96 of the constitution. The appointment of the commission was an earnest attempt to remove the grievances of the weaker states. Its reports constitute the last of a series of enquiries into the working of the Australian federal system. Other surveys have been made by such bodies as the Commonwealth Tariff Board, the 1925 Royal Commission on the Finances of Western Australia, and the Royal Commission on the Constitution, which reported in 1929. However, no fundamental change was brought about in the system by any of these reports. Hitherto, the most important method of allaying grievances had been the payment of grants by the Commonwealth to states whose finances were depressed. Western Australia and Tasmania were early recipients of such special grants, and at a later stage South Australia was also considerably benefited. The task before the Grants Commission was to discover a systematic body of principles upon which to base their recommendations for financial assistance to the claimant states. Within recent years the commission, though only directly concerned with the allocation of grants, has been performing for Australia a work similar to that recently carried out in Canada by the Royal Commission on Dominion Provincial Relations. In its annual reports the Grants Commission has in fact surveyed many, if not all, aspects of the operation of federalism in Australia, special

---

35. 1935 (2nd) *Report*, Grants Commission, pp. 33-36. It is interesting to note that several of the briefs submitted to the Canadian Royal Commission on Dominion-Provincial Relations have agreed that whatever the nominal ground, the real basis for grants to the provinces in the past has been fiscal need, and have urged that need is the only satisfactory basis to adopt.

attention being paid to the effects of the system upon the claimant states.

The substance of the evidence submitted to the Grants Commission in support of their claims by South Australia, Tasmania
and Western Australia has already been presented. The first
task of the commission was the consideration and evaluation
of this body of evidence. It adopted the attitude that the onus of
proving either that a state was suffering from particular disabilities, or that its government could no longer perform its functions
without financial assistance, rested not with the commission but
with the claimant state.   Nevertheless, the commission felt
obliged to conduct a thorough investigation into all problems
associated with the grievances of the claimant states. It was well
aware of the magnitude of such a task, involving as it did a survey
of the resources of the states, a calculation of the effects of
Commonwealth policies, and some consideration of other external
factors such as the world depression.

Before there could be any estimation of the disabilities imposed by federation, the commission held that it was necessary
to recognise the compensating advantages which had resulted from
the creation of the Commonwealth.[36] Not all of these were
easy to estimate in monetary terms, particularly those of a more
intangible nature such as the increasing sense of nationhood which
had been fostered by federal union. Broadly speaking, however,
the advantages were of two types—those which were common to
all the states and sprang from federal legislation relating to
subjects upon which the desire for unified action had brought
men to federate, and those which more particularly benefited
individual states.   Examples of the former were a common
defence and foreign policy and a common immigration standard.
Advantages of the second type were dealt with at considerable
length by the commission which quoted a number of instances
in which each of the claimant states had derived a particular
benefit from federation. In the case of South Australia the Commonwealth had relieved the state of its debt upon the Northern
Territory and upon the Port Augusta-Oodnadatta Railway. It
had built the Trans-Australian Railway which had facilitated the
marketing of South Australian cattle and led to the erection of
workshops at Port Augusta. It had paid since 1931, either in
the form of bounty or of relief to wheat growers, £1,382,000 to
South Australia which was about three times as much as the
state would have been entitled to on a population basis. There

36. 1933 *Report*, Grants Commission, pp. 48-53.

had been other payments such as the Wine Export Bounty and the Sulphur Bounty where the bulk of the expenditure had been in favour of South Australia. Finally, the Commonwealth had given very considerable financial help to the state in promoting schemes of soldier land settlement and in providing unemployment relief. It was very much the same story with regard to Western Australia and Tasmania. The Commonwealth had benefited the western state by the construction of the Trans-Australian railway. It had made substantial interest concessions over the migration agreement, paid wheat and gold bounties, subsidised civil aviation and given a donation toward unemployment relief. Tasmania had received the federal receipts from lottery taxation, a greater percentage of the money allocated for road grants than was her due, relief to fruit growers and important shipping subsidies. Lastly, it had to be remembered that the three claimant states had been given special grants out of Commonwealth revenue which meant not only that they had been specially favoured but that the more prosperous states had been forced to shoulder the burden. These special grants, in the opinion of the commission, represented 'an automatic compensation for difficulties . . . so substantial that large amounts on the debit side would be necessary to outweigh them.'[37]

Having taken into consideration the advantages conferred by the Commonwealth, the commission proceeded to analyse the more important grievances of the claimant states. Particular counts against the Commonwealth, such as the Navigation Act and the results produced by federal arbitration awards, were dealt with but the main attention of the commission was focussed upon two issues—the losses occasioned by state developmental projects and the influence upon state finances of the policy of protection. The significance attached to the Navigation Act by the Tasmanian government which had estimated the damage at over £420,000 per annum, ensured that it would receive the special attention of the commission. The result of its investigations could hardly be considered favourable to the claims of that state. While admitting that adequate consideration had not been shown for the special needs of Tasmania, the commission held that it was questionable whether the state would have been better off under conditions of free competition. The Tasmanian case had argued that the Navigation Act must be injurious because freights to Tasmanian ports were dearer than those for equivalent distances along the mainland coast. This the commission believed to be

37. *Ibid.*, p. 71.

a false assumption because other factors such as the quantity of traffic had to be taken into consideration.[38] Tasmania, as an island, was more dependent than any other state upon regular and efficient sea transport. This the Navigation Act was designed to ensure, and the commission inclined to the belief that under Australian conditions some measure of protection was necessary to bring it about. Tasmania was not upon the regular route and since the state was insufficiently wealthy to afford her own shipping Commonwealth action had, therefore, been necessary to ensure regular services. In view both of the state's partial exemption from the Act in the interests of the Tasmanian tourist industry, and of the subsidies paid by the Commonwealth for shipping services, the commission did not feel that the Tasmanian claim for such heavy damages had been proven.

The developmental policies pursued by the states were the subject of very extensive enquiry by the commission. It adopted the view that mistakes had been two sided, that if state finances had been adversely affected by disabilities arising from Commonwealth legislation they had also suffered as a result of state policy. Somewhat surprisingly, in view of the nature of the evidence submitted by the states, the commission reached the conclusion that the chief cause of the financial difficulties of the states was to be found in the losses arising from the policies of development which they had pursued. For instance, in the year 1932-3 the deficits of the claimant states had totalled £1,928,000 whereas the losses upon their own undertakings for the year were £5,858,000. In the opinion of the commission, these losses justified the view that the states were themselves primarily responsible for their financial plight. 'If those (losses) had not been incurred,' read the 1933 report, 'the States named would have been able to balance their budgets and to reduce taxation by a very considerable amount.'[39] The matter, however, was not quite

38. 1936 (3rd) *Report*, Grants Commission, p. 69. Compare also Chapter x, *The Case for Union*, where the Navigation Act is discussed.
39. 1933 *Report*, Grants Commission, p. 54. The authors of *The Case for Union* reached very much the same conclusion with regard to Western Australia. Analysing the state's budgetary position, they found that deficits were in the main due to losses on loan services. "The capital of state trading enterprises (shipping, meat works, implement works and other) at 30 June, 1932, amounted to £3,553,000, and ascertained losses were £1,030,000. Of £10,000,000 spent on Group Settlement £7,500,000 on the estimate given by the Chairman of the Agricultural Bank Board at an enquiry, are regarded as irrecoverable." "As a result of unwise spending of borrowed money," said Sir James Mitchell in his Budget Speech (1932-33), "we are burdened with a heavy debt" (*The Case for Union*, p. 36).

so simple as that, as the commission hastened to admit. The claimant states in the development of their territories were faced with difficulties of an exceptionally onerous character since all possessed large infertile areas within their borders. Much of Tasmania was mountainous and, despite its early occupation, a third of the state supported no population at all. Western Australia and South Australia were marginal states possessing great tracts of land where the rainfall was either wholly inadequate or barely sufficient to support cultivation. It was under such difficult conditions that these states had to plan and give effect to schemes for land settlement. With the occupation of the more easily accessible lands the states attempted to develop those upon the margin of cultivation. This was pioneering work which, if successful, might greatly add to the national wealth but, if unsuccessful would involve very heavy capital losses. The work of settlement was extremely costly, involving as it did the construction of railways and roads, the provision of irrigation services and the supply of credit to settlers through agricultural banks and such like institutions. The achievements had been by no means inconsiderable. Experiments in South Australia produced a dry farming technique which aided settlement of Mallee country, not merely in that state and Western Australia but also in New South Wales and Victoria. If, however, much of this settlement was worth while there was also little doubt, in the opinion of the commission, that in many areas the extension of settlement had been carried too far. In South Australia the commission instanced the Murray Mallee country and Eyre's Peninsula where the yield in wheat has proved very low and settlement has been insufficiently concentrated, and in Western Australia the Southern Cross and Esperance Districts. Since the limits of settlement could only be discovered by experiment it was perhaps excusable that some unsuitable land should have been occupied. Where the commission believed the state governments were to blame was in continuing to make advances 'to perpetuate unprofitable production.' Such a policy, it was suggested, showed a lack of 'real insight into the problem of marginal settlement' and could only lead to continual and heavy losses.[40] Nevertheless, it was admitted that the onset of the depression had very considerably increased the losses arising out of state schemes for land settlement. 'At no time,' declared the commis-

40. This opinion is supported by John Andrews, "The Present Situation in the Wheat-Growing Industry in South-Eastern Australia" (*Economic Geography*, April, 1936, pp. 109-135).

sion, 'since the war has the policy been really successful; but a great part of their losses on loan activities is due to the depression.'[41]

The extensive nature of the losses incurred by the claimant states through their developmental policies raised serious problems for the commission. The states were demanding that at least a percentage of their losses should be made good by the Commonwealth and advanced a number of arguments in support of their contention. The more important were that a state had a duty to develop its territory and that those states which were faced with greater difficulties should receive assistance, that much of the work of development was national in character, as witness group and soldier settlement and the opening up of the north-west of Western Australia, and that the Commonwealth by its association with certain developmental schemes had acquired a measure of responsibility. The commission, in discussing these claims and the arguments upon which they were based, refused to accept the view that a state had 'an inherent right' to compensation from the Commonwealth. It had throughout adopted the standpoint that if the financial disabilities of a state were the result of its own mistakes that fact would have to be taken into consideration when estimating the size of the grant. The examination of the various settlement schemes had revealed such grave 'faults in administration and conception'—particularly in the case of Western Australia[42]—that the commission felt obliged on that account to make a deduction from the amounts to be recommended as grants. At the same time, it recognised that some, at least, of the work was national in character and that the Commonwealth had been associated with certain of the projects. For these reasons it was of the opinion that some addition should be made to the size of the grants.

In its second report the Grants Commission, after a further investigation of the evidence presented by the states in support of their claims, reached the conclusion that apart from the possible effects of the protective policy there was no proof that serious disabilities had been imposed either by federation or Commonwealth legislation. The report declared:

The only part of Federal policy which appears to impose serious disabilities on any of the claimant states is the protective policy, whether carried out directly or through other agencies. There is no convincing evidence of serious disabilities on other accounts, and our impression is that the net effects of all the

41. 1933 *Report*, Grants Commission, p. 62.
42. *Ibid.*, p. 80.

rest of federal policy are more likely to be favourable than unfavourable to the claimant states.[43]

If, therefore, some reasonably accurate measurement of the disability imposed by the protective policy could be made the commission believed that this would represent, roughly, the 'net effects of all federal policy.' The first report had included a discussion of the effects of the tariff in which it had been agreed that those states with the greater percentage of unsubsidised export industry would have to shoulder the greater proportion of the costs of the tariff. That report had also stressed the difficulty of making any accurate measurement of the effects of the tariff upon the government finances of the claimant states and had frankly admitted that, as the evidence then stood, the commission could not form any reliable estimate. It did, however, venture the opinion that the net adverse effect of the policy of protection was 'considerable for South Australia, still greater for Western Australia, but doubtful for Tasmania.'[44]

The submission of additional evidence in subsequent years enabled the commission to conduct a much more thorough investigation into the effects of the protective policy. While again emphasizing that its conclusions were provisional, the commission in its second report estimated that the excess costs of the tariff for Western Australia—the state most affected—were in the region of £1,160,000 for the year 1933-34.[45] This figure was compared with the benefits received by the state from the allocation of Commonwealth revenue and was found to be in excess by £394,000. If however, the benefit derived by the State from exchange, which had been estimated at £414,000, was taken into account it would be seen that the excess costs of the tariff and the benefit from Commonwealth distribution of revenue cancelled out. That meant that the special grant was entirely to the good. It meant also that the financial predicament in which the state found itself must be due to causes other than disabilities imposed by federation. Similar results were reached when estimates of excess costs of the tariff and of benefits from Commonwealth revenue were balanced for South Australia and Tasmania.[46] The third report served to strengthen the findings of the second. Even without including any benefit from exchange, the commission was of the opinion that 'benefits and burdens from federation almost balance for South Australia and Western Australia

43. 1935 (2nd) *Report*, Grants Commission, p. 89.
44. 1933 *Report*, Grants Commission, p. 70.
45. 1935 (2nd) *Report*, Grants Commission, p. 92.
46. *Ibid.*

while for Tasmania there is a net benefit of nearly £1 a head.'[47] As a result of their investigations the commission had come to the somewhat surprising conclusion that 'the major cause of the relatively inferior financial position of the claimant states was not to be found in federation or federal policy.'[48]

It is important to understand what such a pronouncement implies. In the first place, the conclusion is limited to the financial position of the claimant states when compared with the non-claimant states. The commission does not say that the financial position of the states as a whole has not suffered from federation, or has not worsened in comparison with that of the Commonwealth. Secondly, the commission's conclusion does not mean that no disabilities have been imposed upon the claimant states. The reports admit such disabilities in at least some instances, but maintain that these have been compensated for by Commonwealth contributions from revenue. Yet even though the burdens and the benefits from federation balance, the states, and particularly the claimant states by reason of their inferior wealth, may stand in need of very much greater financial resources than they at present possess, if they are to discharge their responsibilities adequately. Lastly, it cannot be said that a balance for disabilities has been achieved through Commonwealth contributions in the form of grants until the conditions in which and upon which those grants have been given have been ascertained. State responsibility may be sapped not only by inadequate finances but also by the manner in which money is obtained.

The work of the Grants Commission has by no means been confined to the investigation of grievances alleged to have been imposed upon the claimant states. It believed its task was to discover a systematic body of principles upon which grants might be based, and to apply those principles in calculating the amounts

47. 1936 (3rd) *Report*, Grants Commission, p. 68.
48. *Ibid.*, p. 69. Much the same view is recorded in *The Case for Union*, Chapter xvii, Summary of What the Facts Disclose, e.g., p. 84: (5) From the beginning of Federation, Western Australia, by reason of acknowledged disabilities, has been the subject of special financial consideration. Over and above the regular annual payments to which it was ordinarily entitled as a member state of the Federation, Western Australia has received monetary grants and reliefs amounting in all to £10,000,000. Its budgetary difficulties are mainly due to losses on enterprises financed from loan money—losses that have been accentuated by the depression conditions which have affected all other states in common with Western Australia. (6) The Commonwealth tariff has not had an oppressive incidence to the degree claimed in the case. The general increase in the cost of goods to consumers is much less than assumed, and the direct charges of the tariff on the plant and other working requirements of the primary producer are inconsiderable.

which should be paid to the claimant states. In its first report the commission pointed out that the applications for grants were made by governments and that the commission was 'primarily concerned' with the condition of government finances within the three states. The same report stated that after investigation the conclusion had been reached that the claimant states were:

> In an inferior position in respect to a number of important features—the severity of taxation, the scale of the social services, the maintenance of capital equipment, as well as in their real budgetary position.[49]

In face of depressed government finances the commission had to decide upon some basis for the provision of relief. It refused to agree that a state should be compensated for 'relatively inferior natural resources,' but partially modified this attitude when poverty of natural resources became an important factor in the debility of state finances. Its attitude did, however, imply that the commission might ultimately adopt as its basic principle for the allocation of grants the financial needs of the claimant states. In this first report the commission went so far as to embrace the view that no state which was a member of the federation should be allowed to function at a standard much inferior to that enjoyed by the other states. Recognition of that fact led the commission, somewhat reluctantly, to accept the principle that the amount of the grant should be determined in accordance with the amount of assistance necessary to allow the state to function at a standard reasonably close to that of the other states in the federation.

The second report reaffirmed the commission's adherence to the principle which it had adopted in the first.[50] Re-examination had convinced the commission that the only satisfactory foundation for a system of special grants was the relative financial position of the states. It was explained that this did not imply that the states were to be placed upon an equal footing by the provision of grants, for to do so might destroy the incentive to make a special effort on the part of a less prosperous member. This question of principles was considered in great detail in the second report. It was pointed out by the commission that the transfer of revenue from one authority to another had long been accepted in the Commonwealth, and was indeed an inevitable feature of all federations. Special grants were, therefore, in one sense but an extension of a principle already accepted and acted upon in the federation. But in making their claims the states had

49. 1933 *Report*, Grants Commission, p. 133.
50. 1935 (2nd) *Report*, Grants Commission, p. 31.

emphasized disabilities arising from Commonwealth policy, and had based their cases upon a demand for compensation. Such an attitude seemed to the commission illogical and, while it examined alleged grievances, it was insistent that disabilities did not provide a satisfactory basis for the allocation of grants. Instead, the commission elaborated its own viewpoint that in the interests of the federation as a whole a state must be prevented from functioning at an abnormally low standard.

> It is . . . a fundamental obligation for the Commonwealth (and indeed for the other states) to make it possible for a state government in distress to function at some standard.[51]

It is obvious that by this stage the commission had fully committed itself to the view that fiscal need should be the determinant of any grants made to the states. Indeed, the affirmation of its belief was stated in categorical terms. 'The only ground for this assistance is the inability of the state to carry on without it. Therefore, adverse effects of Federal policy . . . are not in themselves ground for assistance to the government any more than to the people of a state.'[52] According to this view, even though disabilities had been inflicted by federation, if a state could function in spite of them at what had been agreed upon as the minimum standard there could be no ground for a grant in compensation. The feasibility of basing a claim upon disabilities having been rejected, the commission proceeded to repeat the principles upon which it had decided to act. These were enunciated with such clarity that misinterpretation was hardly possible.

> Our thesis here is that the cause is irrelevant to the necessity of a special grant. . . . The fundamental law for all governments is self-preservation. It is on this basic principle which cannot be argued that we put special grants.[53]

Moreover this attitude has been consistently endorsed in all subsequent reports of the commission regardless of the changes in membership. When a new commission, consisting of the Hon. F. W. Eggleston (chairman), Dr. G. L. Wood and Sir George Pearce, was appointed for a term of three years[54] from 1 January 1939 it announced its willingness to re-examine the fundamental principles upon which the work of the commission had been based. Apparently, however, re-examination only confirmed the commis-

---

51. *Ibid.*, p. 36.   52. *Ibid.*, p. 36.   53. *Ibid.*, p. 37.
54. The resignation of Sir Frederic Eggleston was accepted on 4 November 1941, and Professor R. C. Mills was appointed Chairman in his place for a term of three years from 5 November, 1941. Associate Professor G. L. Wood and Sir George Pearce were reappointed for a three-year period from 1 January, 1942.

sion's belief in the validity of the past approach since the Sixth Report emphasised the commission's adherence to the principle of needs. Once again the commission rejected as impracticable the assessment of special grants on the basis of disabilities resulting either from federation or from the effects of Commonwealth policy.

> The reactions of federal policy, notably of the protective tariff policy, are so interwoven with the financial and economic structure of Australia as a whole that it is impossible, in our opinion, to express in monetary terms their full effects on the finances of the individual states.[55]

The commission not only preferred to adhere to the method of assessing grants on the basis of financial needs, which had been elaborated in the Third Report, but stressed the advantage of such a procedure.

> It is adaptable to changing conditions; it tends to produce a stable and more balanced economy; and, save for minor modifications, it recognizes the principle of equality of financial competence for all state governments.[56]

Succeeding reports issued in the years 1940-43 displayed the same devotion to the principle of needs though this basic conception was applied 'with ever increasing refinement.' The repercussions of war and war policy markedly affected the budgetary position of the states and raised special problems for the commission's consideration. Nevertheless the commission believed that its principles and methods were still valid and could be made to operate successfully, if through the exercise of 'informed judgment' they were adapted to meet changed conditions. "In our view, the basic principle which we follow, i.e., the assessment of grants according to financial needs, can be preserved by adapting our method to changing circumstances from year to year."[57]

The adoption of the principle of need led the commission to seek about for methods by which the amount required to enable a state to function at a reasonable standard of efficiency could be discovered. It concluded that grants could best be determined from an elaborate comparison of the financial position of the several states, since such a comparison would indicate the extent to which a claimant state was in a position of inferiority. In addition, it was hoped that the standard at which the claimant state should function could be ascertained. Actually, to do so two standards had to be determined—a 'normal' standard for the

55. 1939 (Sixth) *Report*, Grants Commission, p. 10.
56. *Ibid.*, p. 11.
57. 1943 (Tenth) *Report*, Grants Commission, p. 9.

financial operations of the states and a 'minimum' standard at which a state could be 'expected to function effectively.'[58] The normal standard was to be discovered by an examination of the governmental activities of the three non-claimant states. Since, however, at the time of the first investigation by the Grants Commission, New South Wales was considered to be in a peculiar position, the normal standard was to be 'the simple average in respect to deficits per head, severity of taxation, provision of social services and all other items' for Queensland and Victoria.[59] By the time of the fourth report New South Wales was thought to have returned to normal and was, therefore, included in the calculations.

The assessment of needs may therefore be said to have been based upon a comparison of the budgetary position of the claimant states with a standard derived from an analysis of the budgetary position of the non-claimant states, namely, Queensland, Victoria and New South Wales.

The commission believed that the minimum standard should not be far below the normal because the limits within which a state could either economize or increase its revenue were very narrow. The minimum standard was also interpreted by the commission in terms of the effort to be required by a claimant state. When once this standard had been determined it might be modified in one direction or the other according to the causes which had been responsible for the financial inferiority of the state. If the distress was largely occasioned by the state itself a more severe standard might be expected, but if it was due to external forces the severity of the effort required could be reduced. But in no case did the commission consider that the effort required from a claimant state should exceed ten per cent of normal social services expenditure.

The method employed by the commission to determine its standards was that of budgetary comparison. The commission began with two assumptions: that the budget of a state was a fair reflection of the state's effort 'to provide for the needs of its people' and that it was legitimate 'to compare the finances of one state with those of another.' At the same time it recognised that grave difficulties stood in the way of effective comparison of the budgets of the states. Not only was there no uniformity in methods of accounting but there also existed considerable variation in the financial policies pursued, in the functions con-

58.   1935 (2nd) *Report*, Grants Commission, p. 48.
59.   1937 (4th) *Report*, Grants Commission, p. 72.

trolled, and in the financial relations between state governments and local government and semi-government authorities. In consequence, a measurement of the relative financial position of the states involved the commission in corrections to published budget figures. These related to the following matters:

(a) Allowances for items brought into account in the budgets of some states, but not in those of others;

(b) Adjustments of items of revenue and expenditure so that these items will refer only to the activities of the year under review;

(c) Adjustments to eliminate the effects of windfalls in revenue, of emergency expenditure, and of variations of accounting practice.[60]

The commission believed that once such adjustments had been made a fair comparison of the real budget position of the states could be obtained. The next step was to adjust the financial position of the claimant states to the normal standard, i.e., to the deficit (or surplus) arrived at by taking the mean of the adjusted budget position of New South Wales, Victoria and Queensland. The commission speedily discovered when making budgetary comparisons that adjustments would also have to be made when estimating standards in such items as the maintenance of capital equipment, economy in expenditure and the effort exerted in raising revenue. The calculations of the commission in relation to these matters proved complicated in the extreme and necessitated enquiries into such questions as the costs of administration, the scale of the social services, the severity of taxation and the charges made for services.

There was, it seems, less objection to the principles outlined by the commission than to the methods which the commission employed in measuring the relative financial position of the states. Western Australia, for example, criticized the approach to the question of severity of taxation on the grounds that it was 'complicated and not entirely convincing,' argued that too great a sum had been deducted from her grant because of over lavish expenditure upon social services, and declared that an 'inadequate allowance' had been made 'in respect to losses charged to loan funds which should have been charged to revenue.'[61] Tasmania and South Australia adopted a similarly critical attitude upon

60. 1940 (Seventh) *Report*, Grants Commission, p. 83. An example from the year 1938-9 will illustrate the Commission's method. Queensland used £100,000 from loan repayments to pay sinking fund contributions. Since other states met these charges from revenue the Commission decided to reduce the Queensland surplus by £100,000.

61. 1935 (2nd) *Report*, Grants Commission, p. 17.

many points where they conceived either that the calculations
of the commission were inaccurate, or that deductions were
excessive or allowances insufficiently liberal. Apart from such
criticisms of detail, the states do not in the early years of the
commission's life appear to have raised grave objections to the
principles of the commission. Tasmania declared herself to be in
wholehearted agreement and South Australia accepted, with the
reservation that the state should be entitled to base its claim on
some other ground were another body established to assess grants.
Western Australia, on the other hand, persisted in her claim for
a grant on the ground of disabilities.[62] Apparently, however,
Western Australia, though disapproving, decided to co-operate
on the basis of the principles adopted, for the new commission
in its first report[63] declared that no state had either brought forward evidence with the object of proving claims based on disabilities, or requested the commission to change its main principles
or seriously revise its methods.[64]

Despite the valuable work achieved by the commission and the
ingenuity which it has displayed, it is doubtful whether the
commission has been able to overcome all the obstacles in the
path of the successful application of its principles and methods.
The adoption of the principle of fiscal need entailed a thorough
examination of governmental finances in all states and involved
the assumption that it was 'valid to compare the finances of one
state as an organic whole with those of another.'[65] More than
one critic has questioned whether such an assumption was justi-
fiable in view of the obvious differences between the states in
population, resources, area and stage of economic development.
'The very fact that some states are claimant is in itself not quite
consistent with the assumption of homogeneity in governmental
finance.'[66] Moreover, even if it be conceded that comparison is
legitimate grave practical difficulties have to be faced in making
the comparison since no uniformity exists in the allocation of
functions to governmental bodies within a state.

The commission itself has certainly not been unaware of the
difficulties which its methods involved and has on a number of
occasions stressed the almost insuperable obstacles in the way of
effective comparison of governmental expenditure. Two
examples, quoted by the commission, will suffice—the measure-

---

62. 1937 (4th) *Report*, Grants Commission, p. 12.
63. The first report by the new commission, but the fourth in all.
64. 1937 (4th) *Report*, Grants Commission, p. 12.
65. 1936 (3rd) *Report*, Grants Commission, p. 96.
66. J. A. Maxwell, "Problems of the Commonwealth Grants Commission" (*The Economic Record*, Dec., 1938, p. 179).

ment of administrative costs and the comparison of unemployment expenditure. The commission testified that each year since its establishment considerable attention had been paid to the administrative costs of the different states in an effort to discover some standard by which relative costs could be gauged. But despite this concentration of effort the commission had to acknowledge its inability to solve the problem satisfactorily. 'Investigation . . . reveals wide differences in the nature and magnitude of the functions controlled by the various state governments, and in the financial policies connected therewith.'[67] The commission furnished examples. The Mines Department of a state with scanty mineral resources, e.g., South Australia, should cost less than the department of a state with important resources, e.g., Western Australia. The costs of Lands Departments varied according to the amount of Crown lands unalienated and according to the settlement policies pursued by the states. Departments which were similar in name could not be compared with one another satisfactorily because their function varied from state to state. 'In view of these circumstances the commission is satisfied that no convincing statistical basis can be evolved for inter-state comparisons of administrative costs.'[68] All that could be done was to 'observe significant trends in administrative expenditure in each state,' which meant that emphasis had to be placed not so much upon statistical calculations as upon broad judgment.

The Ninth Report provided similar testimony, this time to the difficulty of comparing unemployment expenditure in the several states. The obstacles preventing effective comparison were listed as:

(1) Unemployment varies between states because of the unequal effects of general economic changes and the special effects of local circumstances;

(2) There is no consistent practice followed by state governments in allocating unemployment expenditure to revenue or to loan funds;

(3) Some states debit specific unemployment relief accounts with expenditure on services such as roads, water supplies, irrigation, and harbours, while others do not;

(4) The relative financial responsibilities assumed by state and local authorities in respect to unemployment relief differ considerably among the states;

(5) Statistics relating to unemployment and to unemployment expenditure in the various states are defective.[69]

67. 1939 (Sixth) *Report* Grants Commission, p. 73.
68. *Ibid.*
69. 1942 (Ninth) *Report* Grants Commission, p. 33.

The commission then confessed that in view of the circumstances it would, so far as the treatment of relative unemployment expenditure was concerned, have to rely upon the exercise of broad judgment based upon consideration of such variable factors as changes in financial policies and in economic conditions and 'the relative effects on the finances of the states of war expenditure, loan allocations, and financial assistance given to the states by the Commonwealth.'[70]

One of the most serious handicaps the commission has had to face in making its comparisons has been the marked lack of uniformity in the compilation of state statistics. Indeed, at the time of the establishment of the commission the situation was so bad that no two states drew up their accounts in the same way. 'Items are handled differently from state to state because of historical reasons, because of accounting technique, and because Treasurers sometimes wish to make the financial position look better or worse than it really is.'[71] The commission in its reports has repeatedly drawn attention to the difficulties arising both from a want of reliable statistics and from the failure to achieve uniformity in accounts. In its First Report great stress was placed upon the necessity of achieving a greater uniformity in the presentation of public accounts and statistics.

In the absence of such uniformity the task of any body investigating the problems of Australian finance is unnecessarily complex and its decisions cannot have the certainty, and therefore the authority, they should.[72]

The commission's advice has not received the attention which it warranted with the result that the commission has been handicapped in its measurement of the relative financial position of the states. Some improvement has no doubt been achieved. One of the claims advanced on behalf of the commission has been that the form of budget and other financial statements has vastly improved because of the representations of the commission. This contention is supported by Maxwell in so far as it refers to the public accounts of the claimant states, but he denies that the accounts of the non-claimant states have been similarly influenced and points out that these are vitally important because they furnish the 'standard' by which fiscal need is computed.[73]

But the most telling testimony to failure on the statistical front

70. *Ibid.*
71. J. A. Maxwell, "Problems of the Commonwealth Grants Commission," *The Economic Record*, Dec. 1938, p. 180.
72. 1933 (First) *Report* Grants Commission, p. 136.
73. *The Economic Record*, Dec. 1938, p. 181.

is provided by the commission itself. Despite repeated references in earlier reports to the difficulties resulting from a want of reliable statistics, the commission found it necessary in its Sixth Report to return to this matter and stress its views under the headings "Necessity for Better Statistics and Uniformity of Accounts." The commission acknowledged that improvements had been made but went on to add:

> The value of uniformity of public accounts cannot be stressed too strongly, and we hope that Treasury officers, Auditors-General and Statisticians will continue to use their influence to secure greater uniformity, not only in the presentation of accounts, but also in the financial principles followed in allocating expenditure to revenue and loan funds.[74]

The commission has attempted to overcome the defects of its material by making adjustments which are intended to render the financial positions of the states comparable. But the commission's methods would be less open to criticism if its researches produced less debatable results and if the state accounts were rendered more easily comparable in the future.[75] Some progress has undoubtedly been achieved, while the commission in making its corrections and assessments has displayed an acumen and an objectivity which has contributed to its prestige. Nevertheless it should be noted both that the commission is condemned to much repetition in its enquiries, because the conditions under which it works do not afford a thoroughly satisfactory basis for comparison, and that the claimant states continually criticize the commission's calculations and adjustments. Indeed, the claimant states have contested the results obtained by the commission at almost every stage of the process of comparison and have in addition opposed many of the principles by which its actions have been guided including the special effort required of a claimant state and the imposition of the penalties imposed for unsound policy. Given the principles and methods espoused by the commission it was of course inevitable that this would happen. Since it was to the interest of the claimant states to receive as large grants as possible those states naturally attacked any calculations of the commission which would have the effect of reducing the size of the grant. The reports afford ample evidence of criticism of specific calculations, notably on the grounds that the method employed produced a result which was unduly harsh from the claimant state's point of view or that insufficient weight had been

74. 1939 (Sixth) *Report* Grants Commission, pp. 86-7.
75. *The Economic Record*, Dec., 1938, p. 180.

allowed for the special difficulties under which the claimant states laboured. Without entering into the technical discussion which such criticisms almost invariably involved, it is possible to illustrate the type of objection raised by the claimant states. Examples could be drawn from all the reports. In the Seventh Report, for instance, reference is made both to Tasmania's submission that the special allowance granted to her because of greater difficulties in providing essential slocial services was inadequate,[76] and to South Australia's contention that the commission's method of introducing local government taxation into its calculations was 'arbitrary' and produced results 'which vary too much from year to year and which are not in accord with the facts.'[77] Turning to the Ninth Report, one finds both Tasmania and South Australia repeating the above criticisms and furnishing additional evidence in support of their viewpoint. Another example from the same report will serve to show the kind of criticism directed against the work of the commission. South Australia submitted that:

(a) Unless the commission is prepared to take into account movements in 'unadjusted expenditure' the specific adjustments which it makes will not be adequate to preserve fair relativity among the states.

(b) The restricted field of expenditure actually compared by the commission in its calculations has not in the past given an adequate measure of comparative economy and frugality, and at the present time is likely to be even less adequate.[78]

Undoubtedly the most persistent objections raised by the claimant states have related to the 'effort' required of them by the commission. Once the principle of needs had been adopted the commission felt that a state seeking assistance should be expected to make a somewhat greater effort because of its claimancy. The commission concluded that what it regarded as a 'reasonable effort' could be expressed 'as a percentage of the social services expenditure per head of the non-claimant states,' and that the penalty should not exceed ten per cent. of normal social services expenditure. But the commission also took the view that it would be unreasonable to expect the commonwealth to shoulder the full responsibility for the financial difficulties of the claimant states where these were due to past mistakes and extravagance. In order to foster a sense of responsibility the commission decided, when such mistakes could be shown to have occurred, to

75. 1940 (Seventh) *Report* Grants Commission, p. 50.
77. *Ibid.*, p. 74.
78. 1942 (Ninth) *Report* Grants Commission, p. 32.

impose an additional penalty not exceeding ten per cent. of normal severity of taxation.

As a matter of statistical convenience, the maximum effort required of a claimant state was expressed as a percentage of social services expenditure, i.e., the commission believed that expenditure on the social services provided the best criterion for measurement, because here 'the data for comparison were most satisfactory.' This did not imply, as the commission repeatedly insisted, that the effort required would entail a reduction in the standard of the social services within the claimant states.

> The State is left free to express its effort in greater economy of administration than the average, in less generous provision of social services, in greater severity of taxation, in higher railway freights and fares, or in any combination of these and other methods of adjusting the budget. It may keep its social services equal to or above the average, provided that it makes a correspondingly greater effort in some other direction.[79]

Nevertheless, the claimant states have on more than one occasion asserted that the commission's methods impose a reduction in social services expenditure. Admittedly, such criticism is wide of the mark in view of the oft-reiterated statements of the commission that the effort is required, because of claimancy, and that the estimate is made upon social services expenditure simply as a matter of statistical convenience. At the same time the objections of South Australia, in particular, are not wholly without weight for, as Maxwell has pointed out,[80] if a state is relatively economical in its expenditure on the social services it is able to reduce its penalty, despite extravagance elsewhere. The effect would in this instance be to augment the grant, since the penalty would not only be diminished because of low social services expenditure, but the state's deficit would be greater because of extravagance in other directions.

In Maxwell's view the penalty on social service expenditure is subject to the disadvantage that the technique adopted by the commission 'creates the impression that the penalty is *on* this expenditure.' He believes, moreover, that the method employed has misled the commission itself, and that this confusion was responsible for the adoption in the Fourth Report of a modified penalty on the ground that the cost of providing social services varied from state to state. In the belief that 'the cost per head of social services is in some sort of inverse ratio to the density

79. 1939 (Sixth) *Report* Grants Commission, p. 12.
80 *The Economic Record*, Dec. 1938, p. 184.

of population in the social service area' the commission decided, after calculating the area and population density of each state, to permit additions to the standard expenditure of three per cent for South Australia and Tasmania and seven per cent for Western Australia.   But since the commission has repeatedly emphasized that the penalty is calculated upon social services expenditure solely for purposes of statistical convenience it can hardly argue with any validity that the unequal cost of social services warrants a modification of the penalty unless it assumes that the relative cost of the social services provides an effective guide to the relative cost of all governmental expenditure.[81]

The criticisms of the claimant states and their repeated assertion that the commission's methods compelled them to lower the standard of their social services finally induced the commission to change its 'method of expressing the effort required.'   The character of the change was indicated in the Tenth Report:—

> The degree of effort will now be shown as a separate item in our summary of the relative financial position of the States. We shall, however, continue to use social service expenditure as a basis for our estimate of the degree of effort required, because that field of expenditure is large and the figures are comparable.[82]

It is obvious that the attempt to determine the 'reasonable effort' which might be expected from a claimant state and the decision to assess penalties when financial embarrassment was due to 'the state's own past mistakes,' would necessitate the commission undertaking a survey of the past policy and administration of all states seeking financial aid.   This has been the avowed intention of the commission, and there is striking evidence of the extent to which the commission has probed into and passed judgment upon the claimant states' conduct of their affairs.   The commission has investigated, among other things, railway policy, industrial legislation, land settlement and development, loan expenditure, local government establishment and public works.

Just how far the commission has gone may be illustrated by its comments on railway management in the claimant states.   With reference to Tasmania it was pointed out that the railway deficit (the total loss for 1937-8 being over £500,000) placed a crushing burden on the state's finances.   The commission did not, however, content itself with drawing attention to the effects of the

81. *Ibid.*, p. 185.
82. 1943 (Tenth) *Report* Grants Commission, p. 53.

deficit on the budgetary position of Tasmania, but proceeded
not only to criticize managerial policy by asserting that the increase
in staff in recent years was unjustified, but also to impose a
penalty on that account.[83] Similarly, with regard to South Australia, the commission, after an analysis of transport management,
declared that the government had 'not dealt adequately with the
control of motor transport,' and that the situation demanded 'a
more effective policy.' 'We feel that the non-control of the
activities of ancillary vehicles on the one hand, and the long
list of 'exempted' goods on the other, have seriously undermined
transport regulation in that state.'[84]

Much the same procedure was adopted in relation to other
matters. South Australia was admonished[85] for not having
made a sufficiently resolute attempt to recover outstanding debts
due to the Crown, and a nominal penalty was imposed to stimulate her to greater effort. Tasmania was censured[86] for her large
expenditure on roads and bridges; the wisdom of raising further
loans for roads was questioned, and it was suggested that a percentage of motor taxation revenue should be used to defray a
part of the considerable annual debt charges on loan moneys
spent on roads. Western Australia was warned in connection
with the Harvey irrigation scheme that the commission was 'concerned about the annual charges on the budget in respect to
projects of this kind,' and informed that the time had arrived
'when unproductive expenditure should be reduced as far as
possible.'[87] Further examples could be selected at will from
all the reports.

The commission, in its dealings with the claimant states, has
been confronted with a real dilemma on the issue of responsibility. It has recognised—rightly—that a state cannot expect
that all deficits will automatically be made good irrespective of
the reasons which have produced its losses. If such a position
were conceded there need be no limits to state extravagance, and
no responsibility could be sheeted home to those in control of the
state machinery. But the logic of the commission's attitude is
such that the commission is compelled to investigate and pass
judgment upon all state policy, since the budgetary position of
the state is in its view simply the financial reflection of the character of a state's policy. The commission has assumed that its
principles will permit the unimpaired operation of a genuine

83. 1939 (Sixth) *Report* Grants Commission, pp. 53-4.
84. 1941 (Eighth) *Report* Grants Commission, p. 41.
85. 1940 (Seventh) *Report* Grants Commission, pp. 53-4.
86. *Ibid.*, p. 66.   87. *Ibid.*, pp. 63-4.

federal system in Australia, but there is every indication, as the examples cited above show, that political responsibility—independent action in those fields reserved to the states—may be undermined if such a body as the commission assumes the right to sit in judgment upon the policies of the states and determine the amount of financial assistance it will grant in accordance with its own view of the correctness or otherwise of the actions of the governments in the claimant states. It is at least possible that the commission, in seeking to enforce safeguards against financial irresponsibility, is opening the way for a serious curtailment of responsibility in the claimant states in those matters which have been entrusted to them under the constitution.

The claimant states have persistently opposed the commission's attitude that an effort should be required of them above that of the standard states, and have urged that the deductions made on this account should either be reduced or abandoned altogether. Their objections to the system, listed in several reports, are as follows:—

(1) That losses on loan expenditure in the past were due, in part, to Commonwealth policy;

(2) That the imposition of penalties tended to aggravate the concentration of industrial development in Victoria and New South Wales, thus causing loss of capital and population, higher taxation, and lower standards of social services in the claimant states.

(3) Grants shall be assessed on the basis of equality of taxation and social services all over Australia.

(4) To the extent that grants are to be determined by economic considerations, the commission should adopt an interpretation of financial needs based on the concept of an optimum location of the means of production. Given that other objectives of policy are not thereby obstructed, grants should be made consistent with the principle of maximizing economic welfare—of securing the optimum distribution of productive resources and labour between different industries and different regions.[88]

More recently new arguments in favour of some relaxation of the effort demanded of the claimant states have been advanced, based in the main on the contention that the introduction of the uniform income tax has meant that the states no longer possess the same opportunity for making an additional effort, since they are unable to increase the severity of their taxation. Tasmania, for instance, pressed the point that having 'lost control of their

88. 1941 (Eighth) *Report* Grants Commission, pp. 32-3.

most flexible source of revenue . . . the additional effort should be reduced from ten per cent. to five per cent., representing a more reasonable measure of economy on the expenditure side.'[89] The degree of effort required with regard to past loan losses was also attacked by South Australia and Western Australia as inequitable.[90]

One other argument in favour of some modification of the standard of effort has received considerable stress. The claimant states have been fearful that war conditions might further upset the balance of the federal system, and suspicious that Commonwealth war policy might prove prejudicial to the less industrialized states. They have therefore urged the commission to reconsider its policy with regard to both the standard of economy in expenditure and the penalties imposed for past mistakes:—

Without abandoning the principles involved, the commission might admit more liberal standards in these matters in wartime, as a method of correcting in part the adverse effects of the war on the federal system.[91]

The Commonwealth Treasury strongly opposed this viewpoint, and in its submission urged that no relaxation of the standard of effort should be made with a view to offsetting the adverse effects of the war on the claimant states. It pointed out that if the budgetary position of a claimant state deteriorated as the result of war conditions or war policy, the grant would be varied accordingly by the commission, and that there was therefore no justification for additional concessions. Moreover, the financial

---

89. 1943 (Tenth) *Report* Grants Commission, p. 51.
90. South Australia urged that the adjustment for loan losses should be eliminated for two reasons—(I) In South Australia these losses have been greatly reduced. While this was due in part to the increased revenues of public utilities arising from the effects of war, it was also due partly "to the energy, initiative, foresight and economy of the Government and the people of the State". (II) "With the removal of income tax from the control of the State, and the reduction of the scale of expenditure already to a minimum, the only effect of such a penalty will be to force the State finances into deficit."
Western Australia stated its views in these terms—The degree of effort required in respect of past loan losses is inequitable in its incidence, since it "is not related to the financial embarrassment of the State, but is related to its taxable capacity. In other words, the penalty varies with the fluctuations in the State's prosperity." It was suggested, therefore, "that the degree of effort might be expressed as a percentage of the figure representing loan losses, and provided the claimant State involved did not increase its loan expenditure on such undertakings, even though a loan loss might increase due to adverse economic conditions, the degree of effort might be steadily reduced until it was removed." 1943 (Tenth) *Report* Grants Commission, pp. 50-1.
91. 1942 (Ninth) *Report* Grants Commission, p. 43.

burden imposed upon the Commonwealth by the war was so great
that every effort should be made to prevent unnecessary and
avoidable increases in grants to the states:

> . . . the claimant States should not expect to enjoy, by
> means of larger grants, amelioration of their conditions at a
> time when the maximum efforts, financial and otherwise, of
> the nation are required for the preservation of the national
> life. The most efficient diversion of resources to war, designed
> as it is for the continuance of the federation as an independent
> entity, is in the direct interests of all members of the federation.
> We take the view, therefore, that the special grants will be
> such as will impede as little as possible the most efficient trans-
> fer of resources to war production.[92]

In this instance, the commission agreed with the Treasury, asserting that it did not believe that it was its function to recommend grants which were intended to compensate a state for any
adverse effects resulting from the war policy of the Commonwealth :

> We hold the view that our methods of assessing special
> grants take into account the effects of federal policy in so far
> as they are shown in the finances of the states. The stimulus
> of war expenditure is reflected unequally in the budgets of
> the states, e.g., in taxation revenue and in railway revenue, and
> under our methods of assessing special grants based on needs
> these factors are not ignored.[93]

To the plea of the claimant states that the standard of effort
should be relaxed or abandoned the commission replied that the
special grants which it recommended were intended to place the
claimant states on about the same financial footing as the other
states, and that in view of the grants which had been paid in
the past it did not believe that the claimant states could demonstrate that they had been 'in any way handicapped.'[94] The commission refused to abandon its stand that the welfare of the
federation as a whole demanded the retention of reasonable safeguards, so long as grants were assessed on the basis of needs,
and went on to assert that it was necessary to maintain the
principle of a special standard of effort in order to keep alive
a sense of responsibility.

The arguments advanced for modification of the effort required
because of past financial policy, notably the Western Australian
submission that the degree of effort should be expressed 'as a

92. 1943 (Tenth) *Report* Grants Commission, p. 52.
93. 1942 (Ninth) *Report* Grants Commission, p. 44.
94. 1941 (Eighth) *Report* Grants Commission, p. 33.

percentage of the figure representing loan losses,'[95] were countered by a more detailed exposition and defence of the position adopted by the commission.   It was pointed out that the degree of effort imposed upon a claimant state because of losses from loan policies was arrived at as the result of 'a survey of all the circumstances connected with those policies,' including both their past financial history and their future prospects.   The main determinants were the responsibility of the state for loan losses and the ability of the state to maintain the effort proposed.   According to the tenth report:

> The effort we impose is not to be judged merely by a comparison of the loan losses per head in each state, but by all the causes which gave rise to these losses.[96]

Implicit in this attitude was the belief that, though losses per head might be greater in one state than another, the discrepancy might well result from conditions which made the provision of services more difficult and more costly.   Similarly, it was possible that a reduction in loan losses might be achieved for which the state could hardly take the principal credit.   The commission believed that, with increasing prosperity, the standard of effort demanded of a state should rise, and that the establishment of any definite figure for effort would be open to the objection that under improved conditions it might well represent a reduced effort.   The contention of Western Australia that effort should be tabled as a percentage of total loan losses from year to year was therefore rejected.   Instead, the commission reaffirmed its own principles, merely conceding that the effort required should be reviewed each year in accordance with changing circumstances.

> Some of the present financial burdens of the claimant states are due to their own policies, and we think it is reasonable that they should bear at least a part of them from their own resources.   In our view a denial of this principle would be detrimental to the interests of the federation as a whole.[97]

Dissatisfaction with the commission's methods has led to the submission of alternative proposals, notably for the adoption of a mechanical formula and for a greater reliance upon what is called broad judgment.   The procedure evolved by the commission has inevitably entailed 'a time-lag,' since the grants recommended are based on the financial position of the states in the year previous to that in which the commission's investigation is conducted, e.g., the grants recommended for 1941-42 were based

95. 1943 (Tenth) *Report* Grants Commission. p. 51.
96. *Ibid.*, p. 53.   97. *Ibid.*, p. 54.

on the budgetary position of the states in 1939-40. The commission was not unaware of the problems posed by the existence of a time-lag, and itself pointed out that if conditions were altering with any rapidity the grant proposed might not be suitable to the particular requirements of a state. Its policy was, however, defended on two grounds: any error which might result was not cumulative, and there was no satisfactory alternative to the prevailing procedure.

While general economic conditions are deteriorating, the grant on these lines will be too small. When conditions are improving it will be too great. The differences will balance out over a term of years. When a state, on account of worsening conditions, is receiving too little, a temporary increase in the deficit must be recognised as legitimate. When conditions are improving, it may be hoped that any excess grant on this account will be used by a state to improve its future position. . . .[98]

One possible method whereby the time-lag could be eliminated was by the application of a mechanical formula, which would permit special grants to be fixed automatically for a period of years. But the commission resolutely rejected proposals for an automatic formula on the ground that no formula could be devised capable of taking into account the relative consequences resulting from changes in prices and wages, trade fluctuations, unemployment, population movements, droughts, floods and bushfires and the external influences affecting the national economy.

Our conclusion is that the relative financial positions of the states fluctuate so considerably from year to year that any constitutional change or the use of a fixed formula may speedily become inapplicable and unjust.[99]

In the Tenth Report the commission was still of the same opinion, though it emphasized that the commission's method would have to be adapted to meet changing circumstances if the principle of financial needs remained the basis for the assessment of grants.

South Australia, in particular, has within recent years displayed an increasingly critical attitude towards the basis of assessment adopted by the commission. The Ninth Report, for instance, referred to the South Australian contention that the existing system of budgetary comparison was no longer satisfactory, since the commission had not taken into account in any adequate way the increasing discrepancy between expenditure on certain services in South Australia and in the non-claimant states. In the following year South Australia adopted an even more antagonistic attitude.

98. 1941 (Eighth) *Report* Grants Commission, p. 83.
99. 1939 (Sixth) *Report* Grants Commission, p. 14.

Not only did this state contend that the basis of comparative budget results was no longer valid, since 'the methods of calculation of grants previously adopted by the commission can no longer be applied because of vital changes in Australian public finance,'[1] but the South Australian Grants Committee, with the consent of the premier, formally notified the commission that 'it withdrew its acceptance, in principle, of the method previously employed by the commission in assessing special grants.'[2]

South Australia objected that it would be quite unrealistic to base grants payable in 1943-44 upon state budgets of 1941-42, since budgets of that year could not be considered 'as at all representative of the prospective situation in 1943-44, because of the radically changed and rapidly changing conditions.'[3] This state therefore proposed that the commission should altogether abandon its accepted methods, and instead should base its recommendations 'upon the latest information available.' The commission was not slow to point out that this meant that its recommendations would be based upon an assessment of 'current trends of revenue and expenditure within each state,' in short upon estimates. It professed no faith in the validity of such a procedure, pointed to the notorious discrepancies which frequently existed between estimates and actual budget results, and gave concrete illustration by reference to the figures for 1941-42. In that year it was estimated that the total deficit for the six states would be £301,000, but, in fact, the figures showed a total surplus of £3,024,000.[4] The commission therefore rejected the South Australian suggestion, and decided to adhere to its accustomed methods. At the same time it did display a willingness to place increasing reliance upon broad judgment in the interpretation of statistics.

For a number of years the commission has been pressed to rely less on statistical data and more upon the exercise of broad judgment. In the Ninth Report the issue was discussed at some length, and the arguments in favour of the use of broad judgment were tabulated in the following way:

(a) Published budgetary results are not a true reflection of the relative financial position of the states;

(b) State budgets do not fully reflect the unequal effects of federal policy;

1. The changes were related to the uniform taxation legislation and wartime finance generally.
2. 1943 (Tenth) *Report* Grants Commission, p. 40.
3. The state had lost control over income tax and did not believe that it could increase its revenue sufficiently to meet rising expenditure resulting from increases in wages, salaries and prices.
4. 1943 (Tenth) *Report* Grants Commission, p. 41.

   (c) The time-lag in the special grants recommended may lead
to grants which are not in accordance with current financial needs;

   (d) The commission does not make adequate allowance for
'unadjusted expenditure';

   (e) The commission's treatment of local government finance
does not make adequate allowance for the lower standards
of local government services in the claimant states;

   (f) The specific adjustments made in respect of extravagance
and mistakes in loan policy are too severe and should be
modified or abolished.[5]

The Commonwealth Treasury also looked with favour on the
placing of greater reliance upon the exercise of broad judgment,
notably in the consideration of the repercussions of war conditions on public finance.   In particular, the Treasury stressed
its view that if a budgetary position was achieved by the non-
claimant states which 'was stronger than was required for financial stability' there was no justification in war-time for the payment of higher grants to the claimant states, with the object
of placing them on an equivalent footing with the non-claimant
states.   Moreover, if the survey conducted by the commission
revealed major improvements in the financial position of the
non-claimant states, the Treasury believed that the commission
should impose a greater degree of effort on the claimant states.
Implicit in this argument were two assumptions: (a) that it
was not essential for the budgetary position of the claimant states
to improve to the same extent as the standard states; and (b)
the demands made by the war on Commonwealth resources were
so great that there could be no justification of a grant by the
Commonwealth which would place the claimant states in a
stronger financial position than was necessary for stability.[6]

While the commission has refused to abandon the statistical
technique which it has evolved and has reaffirmed its intention of
using statistical data as the foundation for the grants which it
recommends, it has at the same time displayed no marked hostility to the plea that in the interpretation of statistics considerable
reliance should be placed on the commission's broad judgment of
the situation as a whole.   Repeatedly the commission has emphasized that its technique is designed simply to provide a basis
for its calculations, and that it is not compelled to recommend as
grants the sums suggested by the crude figures.   Indeed, from
time to time the commission has not hesitated to ignore the

5. 1942 (Ninth) *Report* Grants Commission, p. 45.
6. 1943 (Tenth) *Report* Grants Commission, p. 52.

results produced by its statistical calculations when other considerations seemed to warrant such a departure. For instance, the commission did so[7] when it made advances to Western Australia in order to overcome special difficulties resulting from prolonged drought, and again when additions were made to the Tasmanian grant in 1934-35, 'because of known abnormalities in the finances of the state.' It may be said, therefore, that the commission has conceded that there are certain types of problems which do not admit of solution by purely statistical methods. The attitude which it has finally adopted is to describe its methods as a 'combination of research and judgment,' and there is good reason to believe that an increasing emphasis is being placed upon judgment. 'The basic figures which we use are a guide only to our judgment, and are not the sole determinant of the grants which we recommend.'[8]

A combination of research and judgment is no doubt superior to guesses made entirely in the dark. At the same time, the suspicion remains that the elaborate mechanism which has been constructed has partially concealed from the commission the extent to which its results are dependent upon arbitrary assessment. The commission itself concedes that judgment rather than statistics determines the ultimate result, but what it is perhaps less ready to admit is that 'almost every figure which enters into the final calculations is more or less dependent upon that judgment.'[9] Just how arbitrary the commission's methods may become has been tellingly illustrated by the examples cited by Butlin from the Fifth Report. He points out that while the commission abandoned its attempt to measure administrative costs it decided to bestow a bonus of £20,000 under that head on each of the claimant states. Even more significant was the adjustment for tax severity. The commission discovered that there had been a marked rise in the estimated taxable capacity of Tasmania, which had the effect of lowering the tax severity for the state, and so of diminishing the grant. It was decided that the difficulty had arisen over the sum estimated for assessments in respect of Tasmania on central office companies. The amount in question, £74,500, was regarded as excessive. Arguments were advanced in support of this belief, but these failed to indicate how much in excess the figure might be. Despite this omission,

7. 1941 (Eighth) *Report* Grants Commission, p. 46.
8. 1942 (Ninth) *Report* Grants Commission, p. 46.
9. S. J. Butlin, "The Commonwealth Grants Commission" (*The Economic Record*, Dec. 1938), p. 260.

it was decided to cut down the amount to £50,000 and recalculate tax severity.

The effect of this apparently innocent change was to reduce Tasmania's penalty for low taxation by £111,000, and thus to raise its grant by this figure. The consequential changes for other States meant that Western Australia, which would have attained the required tax standard, lost £29,000 by falling below it, while South Australia's penalty increased from £67,000 to £101,000. The net increase in total grants was £58,000.[10]

Increasing use of broad judgment has also been made by the commission in an endeavour to overcome the difficulties associated with the time-lag. As already indicated, the commission is aware that its procedure is subject to the disadvantage that in a period of rapid change the grant recommended may not accord accurately with the financial needs of a state. The commission has evolved a method whereby it hopes to overcome this difficulty. Whenever the evidence seems to indicate a large disparity between current financial needs and the grant arrived at by the commission's methods, the commission has decided to recommend either that payment of a portion of the calculated grant be deferred or that an advance payment be made which could be adjusted in a subsequent year. The commission's procedure may be indicated from the recommendations of the Ninth Report.

The commission is of opinion . . . that the grant based on the year 1940-41, viz., £1,220,000, which is payable in 1942-3, is in excess of South Australia's current needs, and we recommend that payment of £670,000 of that amount be deferred until 1943-44. Our reasons for this recommendation are based upon an examination of the main factors which contributed to South Australia's surplus of £1,287,000 in 1941-42, and upon other considerations relative to South Australia's financial outlook in 1942-3.[11]

It is clear that when recommending deferred or advance payments the commission, for its assessment of current needs, is forced to rely largely upon budget estimates, which are notoriously unreliable, and upon its evaluation of economic trends. In short, for this purpose the commission is leaning heavily upon broad judgment. The commission, however, claims that by retaining its existing method of statistical comparison and adding to it the principle of deferred and advance payments based largely on its judgment of current needs, it is able to

10. *Ibid.*, p. 260.
11. 1942 (Ninth) *Report* Grants Commission, p. 60.

overcome some of the difficulties associated with the time-lag without the dangers attendant upon the abandonment of its elaborate system of assessment in favour of a system of grants based wholly on judgment of current needs. For if errors of judgment occur in the recommendations of deferred or advance payments the commission argues these should be reflected in the state budgets and would be subsequently taken into account. 'Such an error is not cumulative, and the application of our method should preserve relativity in the grants recommended from year to year.'[12]

The commission is obviously bent on having the best of both worlds. It intends to retain its elaborate mechanism for statistical comparison, in the belief that final budget figures are superior to budget estimates, and at the same time to import the principle of broad judgment into its assessment of current needs in the hope of overcoming the difficulties of the time-lag which its own procedure creates.

The war has affected the work of the commission and has created special problems which either did not exist before or were present in a less acute form. The commission's principles of assessment have forced it to take into account changes in Commonwealth-state financial relations and to assess the effects of the repercussions of war policy and war finance on state budgets. Reference was made in the Tenth Report to the far-reaching changes which have undoubtedly occurred in financial relations as the result of exclusive Commonwealth control of income tax and entertainments tax, Commonwealth payment of child endowment and widow's pensions and the unequal incidence of war expenditure.[13] War policy, motivated by strategic considera-ations and by the desire for effective mobilisation of economic resources, has affected the states unequally and has therefore produced special problems with which the commission has had to deal when assessing special grants.

One of the most important problems created by war conditions was whether the commission 'should take a surplus standard or a balanced budget standard as the level to which the adjusted deficits of the claimant states should be raised.' Until the year 1940-41 the budget results of the three 'standard' states as modified by the commission, had produced an average deficit. The commission therefore aimed at adjusting the deficit per head of each of the claimant states to the deficit per head of the

12. 1943 (Tenth) *Report* Grants Commission, p. 82.
13. *Ibid.*, p. 8.

standard states. But in 1940-41 the comparable budget results of the standard states yielded an average surplus per head, which meant that the commission was forced to decide whether to adopt a surplus standard or a balanced budget standard.[14] In the ·Ninth Report the commission, after concluding that the average budget surplus was largely the result of war expenditure and war policy, agreed to accept a balanced budget standard.

In the Tenth Report evidence is included which shows that the decision to adopt a balanced budget standard was challenged by Tasmania and, to some extent, by South Australia. The Tasmanian case was based on the following contentions:·

(a) Special grants were assessed upon the relative financial position of the states and the reasons responsible for a surplus in a standard state were irrelevant;

(b) The amount of a surplus was likewise irrelevant. The commission should adhere to the results indicated by its statistics;

(c) The decision to adopt a balanced budget standard meant a significant and unwarranted change in the commission's principles and methods;

(d) The Commonwealth's war obligations provided no justification for an alteration in the commission's method. Responsibility for payment or non-payment of the grant arrived at by the commission's methods lay with the federal parliament.[15]

South Australia in turn argued that if a balanced budget standard were now adopted, the state would be denied the measure of financial assistance which it regarded as essential.

The Commonwealth Treasury, on the other hand, vigorously opposed the Tasmanian submission and supported the decision of the commission to adopt a balanced budget standard. In its view, the primary task of the commission was to see to it that the claimant states could achieve a measure of financial stability

14. The Commission explained just what it meant by a balanced budget standard. "As a grant is paid to a claimant State in a financial year two years later than the year of review, such a grant is not calculated to produce budget balance in the year of payment. Its relation to budget balance has reference only to the year of review. If, for example, a deficit standard were selected by the Commission, then, provided that a claimant State conformed to the standards which we adopt, the grant finally assessed should enable the State to have in the year of review no more than the average per head deficit of the standard States. Similarly, if the Commission adopted a balanced budget standard or a surplus standard, a claimant State, subject to like conditions, should have a balanced budget in the year of review or a surplus no smaller than the average per head surplus of the standard States." 1943 (Tenth) *Report* Grants Commission, p. 44.

15   1943 (Tenth) *Report* Grants Commission, pp. 42-3.

which would be adequate to ensure the well-being of the federation as a whole. It believed that the adoption of a balanced budget standard would achieve this end, and that to provide more generous assistance was not only unwarranted but might well create awkward problems with the standard states.

We support this action of the commission and submit that the upward limit of assistance must be that which will enable a claimant state to balance its budget. Beyond that the commission is not required to go. Indeed, to go further than that limit might raise difficult questions with the standard states.[16]

The Treasury envisaged with dismay two possibilities if the commission assessed grants on a surplus standard—first, that a standard state with a balanced budget, or a surplus smaller than that of the standard agreed upon for grants to the claimant states, might apply to the Commonwealth for a grant to raise its position to that of the claimant states; and, secondly, that a claimant state with a balanced budget would be in a position to apply for a grant to enable it to achieve a surplus equal to the surplus standard.

In addition to the backing afforded by the Commonwealth Treasury the commission also derived some support from the claimant states. Thus Western Australia agreed,[17] in view of the Commonwealth's commitments, that in war-time the claimant states could not expect to achieve surpluses through grants simply because the standard states happened to possess them, while even the South Australian representative[18] conceded that the commission was within its rights in examining the causes of surpluses and admitted that, if a standard state had obtained a war-time surplus as the result of special war expenditure in that state, there was no reason why South Australia should benefit. Nevertheless, though willing to compromise in the emergency of war, the claimant states made it plain that their acceptance of a balanced budget standard was only a temporary concession to exceptional circumstances, and that in more normal times they would expect to be placed on a comparable financial basis with the standard states. Mr. Reid, representing Western Australia, declared:

In peace times I should say that the principle already laid down by the commission that the claimant States should be put on a comparable financial basis with the non-claimant states should apply, and if the non-claimant States have surpluses, so the claimant States are entitled to enjoy surpluses also.[19]

16. *Ibid.*, p. 44.   17. *Ibid.*, p. 43.
18 Mr. Wainwright, Chairman of the South Australian Grants Committee.
19. 1943 (Tenth) *Report* Grants Commission, p. 43.

The commission had no hesitation in rejecting the Tasmanian objections to a balanced budget standard. It insisted that there was nothing automatic about the adoption of a standard, whether surplus or deficit. That was a question to be determined by the commission, and did not depend so much upon the existence of an average surplus or an average deficit in the standard states as upon the causes which had produced either surplus or deficit. 'We consider the proper conclusion to be drawn is . . . the determination of a standard after all the causes of the combined budget results of the standard states have been examined.[20]

As the recommendations of the Tenth Report were based upon the budget position in 1941-42 and the average surplus for the standard states for that year was held to be in the main due to war conditions, the commission reached the conclusion that it would be unreasonable to adopt a surplus budget standard. It therefore adhered to its decision of the previous year to take as its standard a balanced budget. For the future the commission enunciated the broad lines of the procedure which it would follow when determining a standard.

We shall first examine the causes of a deficit budget standard or of a surplus budget standard. If the standard, deficit or surplus, is small, we shall accept that as our starting point, provided that there are no serious abnormalities in the budget figures. On the other hand, if the standard, deficit or surplus, is large, we shall carefully examine the causes contributing to it and arrive at a standard which we consider just in all the circumstances.[21]

Since the issuing of the Tenth Report the question of the justice of adopting a balanced budget rather than a surplus standard has become a matter of political discussion. Dame Enid Lyons, when moving the adjournment of the House of Representatives to discuss the allocation of grants to the states, attacked the existing system of assessment and argued that no really satisfactory solution of the difficulties inherent in making grants could be reached until a federal convention met to overhaul the constitution. Despite the work of the Grants Commission, in Dame Enid's view 'the disabilities suffered by the less populous states had not decreased' and she envisaged the possibility that adoption of a balanced budget standard for the payment of grants would mean that at a time when the standard states were building up large surpluses the claimant states would remain impoverished and so 'fall behind in post-war reconstruction.'[22] The result of the commission's

20. *Ibid.*, p. 46.   21. *Ibid.*, pp. 46-7.
22. *Sydney Morning Herald*, 23 Nov. 1944, report of proceedings in the House of Representatives.

decision would therefore be the development of 'an irretrievable degree of financial inequality' between the states.

Mr. Chifley, Commonwealth Treasurer, replying to Dame Enid's allegation, denied that the government had sanctioned any injustice to the claimant states. He pointed out that the commission had been established by a government headed by Mr. Lyons, had no affiliations with the present government party and was an impartial body. He did, however, defend the commission's decision to adopt a balanced budget rather than a surplus budget standard.

> Some time ago all the non-claimant states had achieved surpluses. If the commission had worked on the old principle it would have had to provide the claimant states with grants based on the surpluses achieved by the non-claimant states. The government believed that payments by the commonwealth should be for the absolute needs of the claimant states.[23]

Since its appointment in July 1933 the Grants Commission has established an enviable record of achievement. Just prior to its appointment the federal structure had been subjected to considerable strain, and dissatisfaction with the results achieved under the federal system was being openly voiced by the less populous states, an attitude of mind perhaps best illustrated by the secession movement in Western Australia. Special grants by the Commonwealth to states in financial need had been made on a number of occasions before the establishment of the commission, but these had not been accompanied by any thorough and scientific investigation of the real financial requirements of the states concerned. Such grants were the minimum necessity if the federation were to remain intact and able to function with even moderate effectiveness. But they savoured of a dole grudgingly paid by the Commonwealth Treasury and certainly did little to dissipate the feeling of discontent which existed among the poorer states. Dissatisfaction with previous methods of providing Commonwealth assistance to the states in financial need was voiced in the speech to the House in which Mr. Lyons sponsored the creation of the Grants Commission.

> Unfortunately it has not been found possible, hitherto, to formulate any definite principle or basis upon which the Commonwealth parliament and government could be guided in the making of such grants. This has meant that, in the end, the amount of the grants has been determined in a more or less arbitrary manner.

In order to remedy such a haphazard method of assistance Mr. Lyons declared in favour of an independent investigating body

23. *Ibid.*

whose recommendations would be likely to be accepted by all parties. 'The. government now desires that a comprehensive investigation shall be made by an impartial body which does not owe allegiance to either the Commonwealth or the States.'

In assessing its work it has to be remembered that the commission was faced not only with the legacy of hostility between the states and the Commonwealth but also with considerable suspicion as to the part which it, as a newly created umpire, would be called upon to play. In addition, the commission was confronted with the task of establishing definite principles upon which grants could be based, and when that had beeen done with those difficulties of investigation which have been previously emphasized. Nor was it easy to win acceptance either from the Commonweath or the claimant states for its principles and methods once these had been determined. The Commonwealth Treasury, in particular, has always maintained that special grants should be a form of compensation for disabilities arising from federation and from Commonwealth policy, and has only reluctantly acquiesced in the principle of needs adopted by the commission. Finally, the commission could not expect much guidance from experiments conducted within the commonwealth or abroad since the question of financial relations between central and state authorities has proved a thorny and largely unsolved problem in most federations.

Despite handicaps, the commission can lay claim to considerable success in achieving its main objectives. Its investigations have been notable for their thoroughness, and the outcome has been a more scientific approach to the problem of special grants. What is of almost equal importance, the commission has done much to overcome the suspicions of the claimant states and, while they have by no means always agreed with the commission's approach and have indeed repeatedly criticized the commission's principles and findings, they have displayed a spirit of co-operation which has greatly aided the commission in its work. Indeed, it has been claimed on the commission's behalf that the states receiving grants are reasonably satisfied, because they know that their claims now receive fair consideration by an impartial body, because the grants recommended have been adequate to ensure financial stability, and because they are now in a position to plan ahead, fortified by the knowledge that adequate assistance will be extended provided they make a reasonable effort.

While such claims may be unduly exaggerated, it can be said that the commission, by its impartiality and careful investigation of the case of the claimant states, has enabled the federation to function with less friction than would otherwise have been possible. The contentions and objections of the claimant states have been thoroughly investigated and answered to the satisfaction of the commission, if not invariably to the satisfaction of the claimant states. Indeed, the surprisingly few occasions on which the commission found it possible to compromise with the views and criticisms propounded by the states' representatives leaves the impression not only that the commission is 'well satisfied with its work' but that it is over-anxious to defend its findings. Nevertheless, from the financial point of view its success is attested both by the invariable acceptance of its recommendations and by the ability of the claimant states to achieve reasonable stability. The commission claims that the elaborate mechanism which it has created for the determination of grants is responsible for this result. On the other hand a considerable measure of the commission's success is no doubt due to the fact that the grants which it has recommended have fallen within limits which the Commonwealth government was willing to meet and the states to accept.[24]

One feature of the commission's work may well prove to be of lasting importance to the federation. The commission was appointed as a non-partisan body to investigate a highly contentious aspect of Commonwealth-state relations. Its prestige has grown from year to year, and the impartiality which it has displayed in discharging a difficult task has done much to remove the issue of special grants from the arena of party politics. Commonwealth governments, whatever their political complexion, have implemented the recommendations of the commission without question. It may well be that the experience afforded by the work of the commission will lead to the creation of other bodies, similarly constituted, whose prestige and independence will be sufficient to guarantee an impartial and scientific investigation of complex administrative and governmental problems.

The importance of the work carried out by the Grants Commission should certainly not be under-estimated. Since its appointment in 1933 it has conducted continuous investigations into the working of the federal governmental machinery within Australia. It has raised and discussed problems of vital importance in any federation, as well as others which are confined solely to the Commonwealth. The commission has, therefore, accomplished much by way of throwing into relief the major problems associ-

24. *The Economic Record*, Dec. 1938, p. 260.

ated with federalism under the Australian constitution.   But though the surveys of the commission have been thorough, and often revealing, many of the conclusions which have been deduced from these investigations do not seem wholly justified by the evidence of the past forty odd years. In particular, the analysis made by the commission of the existing status of federalism in a chapter devoted to the underlying causes of inequalities between the states is open to serious objection, and not least because it conflicts with the commission's own findings.[25]   Here the commission devoted considerable attention to proving that economic integration has taken place in the Commonwealth. But having argued that economic integration is an accomplished fact, that industry is organised upon a national and not a local basis and that the economic structure of the states shows a marked similarity, the commission then proceeded to pronounce in favour of a political division of power between the states and the Commonwealth which would cut across the single economic unit. It is difficult to discover the logic behind a proposal to regulate an economically integrated unit by means of a political division of power among a number of authorities. In view of the importance of economic factors there seems little likelihood of control in the economic sphere being effective if economic unification has taken place and political unification has not.

The commission summed up its conclusions by saying that there were only two real alternatives, grants of assistance or unification, and that in its opinion the problems created by the federal system should be solved not by unification but by voluntary co-operation between the members of the federation.[26] There are, however, a number of objections, some of considerable weight, to the commission's judgment in favour of the retention of federalism and the continuance of grants of assistance. In the first place, the commission has itself emphatically asserted that it is 'quite contrary to a healthy development of the constitution for states to become chronically dependent on grants to keep them from bankruptcy.[27] Of greater importance is the fact that the claimant states have rejected grants as a permanent solution of their problems. Tasmania and South Australia have asserted that equitable financial relations between the Commonwealth and the states cannot be established by a system of special grants, and Western Australia that special grants cannot remove her disabilities.

25   1935 (Second) *Report* Grants Commission.   Chapter iv—The Underlying Causes.
26.   1935 (Second) *Report* Grants Commission, p. 47.
27.   1933 *Report* Grants Commission, p. 81.

A further objection is that the allocation of special grants itself raises problems not easy of solution. The difficulties of estimation, and particularly the complexity of the methods which must be employed in the measurement of the relative financial position of the states, are so great as to be in themselves a strong argument in favour of unification of finances. Nor are the standards at which a state is to be permitted to function easily determined. Indeed, it seems more than doubtful whether it is possible to fix such a standard with any rigidity. The needs of a state government will depend very largely upon the character of its programme, and the use of a standard formula for the measurement of grants for governments with radically different objectives or widely differing social and political philosophies can have but slight validity. Again, the object with which grants are conferred is the preservation of the states as independently functioning units. Though it is true that a redistribution of revenue is not necessarily a vicious principle, at the same time the conditions which are attached to grants may well prove destructive of state independence. The Grants Commission believes that state independence can be safeguarded by not prescribing the way in which special grants shall be spent. But much the same effect is produced, because the Grants Commission in its estimation of the amounts for grants not only takes into consideration the policies pursued by state governments but actually penalizes the states for aspects of their administration of which it disapproves. 'The recipient states,' said the commission, 'will be able to formulate the policy for the expenditure of the grant and this will be taken into account in next year's recommendations.'[28] It can hardly be maintained that the control of the state over its policy is complete when the commission in the assessment of subsequent grants regards the way in which the previous grant was spent as one of the factors to be considered. Finally, and perhaps most important, is the persistence of a sense of grievance among the claimant states. This is not likely to be eradicated by the allocation of special grants, for the disease is psychological as well as financial. A state which believes itself to be suffering from disabilities not experienced by other states, or a state which is perpetually reminded of its inferiority to other states, must remain discontented with its position in the Commonwealth. It is difficult, therefore, to accept the implication in the judgment of the Grants Commission that federation will be satisfactory when once a little financial patching has been done.

28. 1933 *Report* Grants Commission, p. 127.

VI

THE COMMONWEALTH AT WAR

THE years immediately preceding the outbreak of war in September 1939 were marked by an increasing dissatisfaction with the operation of the federal system, a dissatisfaction which found expression in the insistent demands made from time to time for an alteration of the constitution. Of these, perhaps the most important was that put forward on 18 November 1938 by Mr. Scullin who, in an eloquent plea to the House of Representatives, stressed the urgency of reform. After enumerating the 'outstanding problems confronting Australia,' he went on to declare, 'the bulk of them cannot be as effectively handled under the present system as under a unified system of government. After thirty-eight years' experience of the federal system, I doubt whether there is one thinking man who is satisfied with the results.'[1]

His speech created a favourable reaction, and the then Attorney-General, the Rt. Hon. R. G. Menzies, listed and discussed what he called eight anomalies, eight instances in which the national parliament lacked power to deal with questions of national importance. On the same occasion he intimated that it was his government's conviction that wider powers should be bestowed upon the Commonwealth, and announced that early in the following year parliament would be given an opportunity to discuss 'both the objectives at which we ought to aim, and the means we ought to adopt to achieve them.'[2]

This promise was reiterated by Mr. Menzies, who in the meantime had become Prime Minister, on 3 May 1939, in a statement to the House of Representatives that time would be made available during the same session for discussion of proposals for alteration of the constitution. However, no discussion took place, and on 2 June Mr. Menzies declared that it had not been found practicable to hold a constitutional session during the sittings which were just concluding, but that such a session would probably be held when parliament reassembled. This statement was shortly followed by important pronouncements in favour of constitutional

1. For Mr. Scullin's full speech see *Commonwealth Parliamentary Debates,* clviii, pp. 1728-34.
2. *Ibid.,* pp. 1815-1821, for full text.

reform by both Mr. Curtin, then leader of the Federal Opposition, and Mr. Hughes, then Federal Attorney-General. 'Several of the major sides of national life,' declared Mr. Curtin, 'are now partly or completely vested in the States, although in these matters the interests of all Australia are uniform and indissolubly inter-connected. The control and regulation of these should most certainly be the function of the National Parliament.' He went on to specify the aspects of national life which in his view should come under Commonwealth jurisdiction. These included 'the great body of laws regulating the relations of employer and employee, of interstate and intrastate trade and commerce, of company law, banking, standards of commodities, carrying of goods and the like.'[3]

Mr. Hughes confirmed Mr. Curtin's assessment of the position. 'The Commonwealth parliament should have not the mere shadow of power that it possesses now, but reality of power . . . the Commonwealth lacked power in laws relating to companies and corporations, trade and commerce and industrial matters.'[4]

The stage was thus set for a new attempt to secure an alteration of the constitution in the direction of enlarged Commonwealth powers when Australia became involved in war. No doubt, there were groups in the country, some of them powerful, wedded to localist interests and hostile to revision, but it yet remained true that Commonwealth political leaders, irrespective of party, had endorsed the view that the constitution was seriously outmoded and had committed themselves to attempt its modernisation. Speaking of the strain to which the constitution had been subjected the *Sydney Morning Herald* commented on the widespread recognition that the constitution stood in need of radical revision. 'In recent months this need has been recognised by such widely separated critics as Sir Robert Garran, Mr. Stevens, Mr. Hughes and Mr. Curtin. It has long been evident, in fact, that a constitution framed during the nineteenth century is inadequate to meet the new demands of the twentieth.'[5]

On the outbreak of war the proposal of the Menzies government to hold a constitutional session to debate suggested amendments had to be abandoned for matters of more pressing urgency. Nevertheless, it was noteworthy that discussion of constitutional matters—especially the necessity of reforming the constitution in the direction of greater Commonwealth powers—continued to occupy a prominent place in public affairs in the months immedi-

3. *Sydney Morning Herald*, 10 July 1939.
4. *Ibid.*, 11 July 1939.
5. Leading article, "Constitutional Reform," *Ibid.*, 27 July 1939.

ately after the declaration of war.[6] Symptomatic of the prevailing public interest and concern was the introduction into the Legislative Assembly of New South Wales of a resolution favouring the abolition of State parliaments and the substitution of bodies resembling county councils, which would be under the control of the federal parliament. Much the same outlook was reflected in statements made during October by a number of federal ministers, notably Mr. Spender, Mr. Harrison and Sir Frederick Stewart, all of whom advocated[7] in one form or another a considerable expansion of Commonwealth authority. However, most significant of all, especially in view of later developments at the 1942 Constitutional Convention, was Mr. Curtin's comment[8] on the proposals to abolish state parliaments. Without opposing abolition as a principle, he emphasised that while at war the Commonwealth was in a position to exercise enormously increased powers. The Commonwealth parliament had, as it were, by an accident been afforded a unique opportunity of demonstrating its capacity to use expanded powers for the benefit of all parts of Australia. Nor can there be much doubt that Curtin was correctly interpreting the attitude of the majority of the Australian people when he implied that the use the Commonwealth made of its expanded authority in the war years would be viewed as an experiment by which the desirability of conferring wider powers on the national parliament would be decided. It would be a testing time during which the Commonwealth government would either vindicate or invalidate its claim to be capable of exercising virtually complete governmental powers for the whole of Australia. Curtin put it this way: 'You have the power; you can ignore the State parliaments. Demonstrate to us that the powers you have are to be used ably and effectively. This is a challenge to you.'[9]

The course of the war, and particularly the disasters which befell the Allied Nations, inevitably distracted attention from questions of constitutional reform. These became of small consequence in comparison with the major issue of survival, and not least because defeat would have rendered discussion of constitutional matters meaningless. However, as the war progressed and the allied position strengthened, interest somewhat revived. Even as complete defeat might well have entailed the destruction of

6. e.g. the articles contributed to the *Age* on 2, 4, and 5 December 1939 by Sir Isaac Isaacs. For extracts see *Post-war Reconstruction: A Case for Greater Commonwealth Powers*. Prepared for the Constitutional Convention at Canberra, November 1942, pp. 128-31.
7. As reported in the *Sydney Morning Herald*, 19 October 1939.
8. *Ibid.*, 20 October 1939.
9. *Ibid.*

the constitution so victory might provide the allied Nations with an opportunity for a new social and economic advance. Many Australians therefore began to ask themselves whether the constitution under which Australia was governed was a suitable instrument for the realisation of their hopes. If not, was it capable of adaptation in such a way as to satisfy the demands likely to be made upon it in the post-war world? One result of this new confidence in victory was a revival of the earlier discussion upon the alteration of the constitution. The argument may be said to have continued intermittently until Dr. Evatt introduced his bill for the revision of the constitution in the House of Representatives on 1 October 1942.

Shortly after the commencement of the war, the Commonwealth parliament, following the example of the United Kingdom parliament, passed emergency legislation conferring exceedingly wide powers upon the executive. In particular, two laws of outstanding importance were passed—the *Trading with the Enemy Act* and the *National Security Act,* which was the modern version of the *War Precautions Act*[10] of 1914. So tremendous were the powers possessed by the executive under the National Security Act that government could virtually be carried on by regulation. For instance, with some exceptions, other acts of parliament could be amended or rendered inoperative by means of regulations[11] under the National Security Act. The habit of substituting emergency legislation by regulation for parliamentary legislation meant that parliament found one of its principal functions, that of enacting legislation, seriously curtailed. Parliament, therefore, suffered a further loss of prestige as its place was to some extent usurped by the administration. This, of course, has been a trend characteristic of modern government, but more than one commentator has felt that the Commonwealth parliament might well have displayed a greater activity in discussing and criticising the conduct of the administration.

Under the authority of the National Security Act successive Commonwealth governments have issued emergency legislation of the most far-reaching kind. The grant of power has been sufficiently comprehensive to embrace such various matters as the control of alien internees, price-fixing, manpower, debtor's relief, control of commodities which were difficult to obtain or of special significance for war, relations between landlords and tenants, wine

10. See Knowles, *The Australian Constitution*, pp. xxiii, 27.
11. K. H. Bailey, "The War Emergency Legislation of the Commonwealth" (*Public Administration*, Journal of the Australian Regional Group of the Institute of Public Administration, March 1942), p. 12.

marketing and a host of other questions,[12] many of which lay beyond the limits of Commonwealth peace-time authority.

It is clear, then, that under the compulsion of total war the Commonwealth has attempted to mobilise and direct the resources of the country on a national scale and that this has implied Commonwealth intervention in many matters which ordinarily fall within the province of the states. In view of the widespread ramifications of Commonwealth war-time activity, it is pertinent to examine the constitutional foundations upon which this assumption of authority rests. Is the position, in fact, such that in time of war the federal system as established by the constitution gives place for all practical purposes to a unitary state? That, at any rate, would appear to have been the view of the Royal Commission on the Constitution of 1929, which said:—

> In time of war the Commonwealth Parliament may pass any law or may give the executive authority to make any regulation which it considers necessary for the safety of the country. The Commonwealth in time of war was for practical purposes a unified government.[13]

This view was, of course, based on experience during the Great War and in particular upon the interpretation given to the defence power by the High Court. That interpretation amounted to a vindication of the right of the Commonwealth parliament in war-time to deal with any matters which 'may conceivably in such circumstances even incidentally aid the effectuation of the power of defence.' Giving judgment in the vital Bread Case in 1916, which determined that a Commonwealth regulation fixing the war-time price of bread in special areas was valid, Mr. Justice Isaacs agreed that where such a connection could be established

> the Court must hold its hand and leave the rest to the judgment and wisdom and discretion of the parliament and the executive it controls—for they alone have the information, the knowledge and the experience, and also, by the constitution, the authority to judge of the situation and lead the nation to the desired end.[14]

During the present war one may say that the principles of constitutional interpretation adopted in 1914-18 in relation to the scope of the defence power have been accepted and extended though certain modifications, to be noticed subsequently, have been introduced. Moreover, the decline in the prestige and power of the states, which was observable as a peace-time trend, has been accelerated by war conditions. The overwhelming supremacy of

12. *Ibid.*, p. 13 for additional examples.
13. *Report*, Royal Commission on the Constitution, 1929, p. 120.
14. 21 *C.L.R.*, pp. 455-6, *Farey v. Burvett*.

the Commonwealth, when taken in conjunction with the absorption of the national energy in the task of prosecuting the war, has meant that state activities have either been completely overshadowed or else have simply formed a subordinate part of the Commonwealth's war-time organisation. In either case, the states have appeared as objects of secondary importance, and this has been reflected in the diminished public interest in both state elections and the programmes of the state governments. The task of organising Australia for war has in many ways been a co-operative effort, but it is equally true that the Commonwealth has been in a dominant position. Writing of the war organisation of Australia, the Post-war Reconstruction Pamphlet declares:

> The net result is this: gradually the States and local authorities are becoming geared together in a total war effort for the performance of the supreme national task. The Commonwealth has the final responsibility for the successful prosecution of the war, which includes the defence of the States, as well as the nation. The Commonwealth has the general supervision of our whole war effort.[15]

Since the Commonwealth is responsible for the organisation of the national war effort, and it is to-day a commonplace that total war involves the marshalling of all the resources of the nation, what powers does the Commonwealth possess in time of war for the performance of its task? Without doubt the so-called 'defence power' (section 51 (vi) of the constitution) has proved the most important. This has been the foundation upon which the Commonwealth has erected its edifice of war-time organisation. Nevertheless, as pointed out by Professor Bailey, the Commonwealth has other reservoirs of power available to it. It retains, for instance, all the normal powers bestowed by the constitution, and many of these bear a direct relationship to defence. In addition, there is the King's war prerogative, some of which would appear to be exercisable in Australia by the Governor-General.[16] While these additional powers exist, and are important, it is upon the defence power that the Commonwealth has depended most heavily for its war-time organisation. The construction given to the defence power by the High Court, both in the last war and this, has been broad and liberal, though more recent judgments have indicated that there are limits[17] to what may be done by the Commonwealth under its authority. During the Great War, despite challenges in

---

15. *Post-War Reconstruction Pamphlet* (A Case for Greater Commonwealth Powers), p. 15.
16. *Public Administration*, March 1942, pp. 14-15.
17. See e.g. 66 *C.L.R.*, pp. 488-534, *Victoria v. The Commonwealth*; 67 *C.L.R.*, pp. 95-115. *The King v. University of Sydney; ex Parte Drummond.*

the courts, there was no occasion on which Commonwealth legislation or regulations was held to be beyond the scope of the defence power. This war has produced a spate of regulations, stemming from the *National Security Act,* which prescribe minutely the action which the individual concerned must take. Yet, despite the number and varied character of the regulations dependent upon the defence power, comparatively few have been invalidated. In order to issue a successful challenge it has been necessary to show clearly that the Commonwealth legislation was not a relevant factor in the defence of the country.

Apart from the *Uniform Tax Case,* the most important constitutional case to come before the High Court during the present war has been that of *Andrews v. Howell.*[18] Here the decision represented a triumph for the Commonwealth. The principles of interpretation established in 1914-18, especially in *Farey v. Burvett,* were again unhesitatingly affirmed and additional evidence afforded of the amazing breadth of the defence power in time of war. The scheme which gave rise to litigation was the Commonwealth plan for the acquisition of apples and pears. The Australian apple and pear industry was dependent to a considerable extent on overseas markets, which meant not only that shipping was required, but also refrigeration. When war came the Commonwealth government had to consider whether shipping space, previously devoted to the transport of apples and pears, might not have to be diverted for other war purposes. After enquiry, the conclusion was reached that it would not be possible to export the usual quantity of apples and pears. The Commonwealth government, therefore, had, in the words of Sir Owen Dixon, to 'weigh the consequences of the course proposed, and in arriving at a decision . . . consider what alternatives are open for alleviating the consequences of a diversion of shipping.'[19]

A scheme designed to prevent the swamping of the home market and to guarantee an adequate price to the grower was ultimately evolved, whereby the Commonwealth should acquire the crop, pay compensation and market the fruit. Regulations[20] under the *National Security Act* were issued, and these set out both the objects of the scheme and its relation to defence. The disclosed aim was 'to minimise the disorganisation in the marketing of apples and pears because of the effects upon shipping of the present war.'[21]

18. 65 *C.L.R.* (1941), p. 255.
19. *Ibid.,* p. 278.
20. *National Security (Apple and Pear Acquisition) Regulations.*
21. *Ibid.,* Reg. 2. See 65 *C.L.R.* (1941), p. 256.

The litigation before the High Court arose out of the successful prosecution of Andrews for a breach of the *National Security (Apple and Pear Acquisition) Regulations*. Andrews, in defiance of the regulations, had moved[22] twenty-seven cases of apples acquired by the Commonwealth, but still held in his possession. He appealed to the High Court and the Court, by a majority decision[23], upheld the regulations as a valid exercise of the defence power of the Commonwealth. The case against the validity of the regulations rested on four main objections, each of which was specifically answered by Acting Chief Justice Rich. The first contention was that 'the entire plan was foreign to the defence power (section 51 (vi))'. This was easily disposed of, since the defence power was being interpreted along lines laid down in previous cases. 'After *Farey v. Burvett*', said Rich, A. C. J., 'and the decisions during the last war which followed that case I should have thought the argument was a hopeless one.'[24] He proceeded to quote with approval passages from the judgment of Isaacs, J. in the Bread Case, in which he had argued that in wartime the widest possible construction should be placed upon the defence power.

It is the *ultima ratio* of the nation. The defence power then has gone beyond the stage of preparation; and passing into action becomes the pivot of the Constitution, because it is the bulwark of the State. Its limits then are bounded only by the requirements of self-preservation.[25]

Secondly, the appellant attempted to prove that the 'plan as a marketing scheme violated section 92 of the constitution,' i.e., was an infringement of the absolute freedom of inter-state trade prescribed by the section. Here, the Court, following its customary procedure of looking to the real object of the legislation, reached the conclusion that it was designed to aid defence rather than regulate trade. Previous discussions, notably *Milk Board (N.S.W.) v. Metropolitan Cream Pty. Ltd.*,[26] had determined that legislation primarily directed towards purposes other than the regulation of inter-state trade could be valid, even though it might incidentally affect inter-state commerce.

The third objection to the regulations was that they 'transcended

22. *Ibid.*, Reg. 15. 'Except as provided in these regulations, and with the consent of the board, no person shall (a) part with the possession of or move any apples or pears acquired by the Commonwealth which are in his possession; (b) take into his possession any apples or pears which are the property of the Commonwealth; or (c) purport to sell or offer for sale or purport to buy or offer to buy any apples or pears which are the property of the Commonwealth' (65 *C.L.R.* 1941, p. 256).
23. Rich A.C.J., Dixon and McTiernan JJ. (Starke J. dissenting.)
24. 65 *C.L.R.*, p. 263.   25. 21 *C.L.R.* (1916), p. 453.
26. 62 *C.L.R.* (1939-40).

the limitations of section 51 (xxxi) of the constitution and attempted to acquire property in apples and pears on terms that were not just.[27]   In the opinion of Rich, A. C. J., this argument was based upon the obscure way in which the provisions dealing with compensation to growers had been drafted, but, despite such faults in expression, he believed that it was still obvious that growers did receive just compensation.

The last contention was that 'it was an unnecessary and extravagant use of the power to prohibit the custodian of apples and pears from moving them, and that this particular provision was unreasonably wide.'[28]   If interpreted literally, this section of the regulations would, as pointed out by Dixon, J., have prevented the owner of a storing shed from moving a case of fruit from one part of his store to another.   There was, however, general agreement that there was no need to interpret the word 'move' in such literal fashion.   Obviously the movement it was intended to prohibit was that from one locality to another, and, construed in this way, the provision was judged to be valid.

The real significance of *Andrews v. Howell* is apparent from two passages appearing in judgments given respectively by the Acting Chief Justice Rich, and Mr. Justice Dixon.   'I cannot see,' said Rich, A. C. J., 'how in a totalitarian war a court could say that an organisation to deal with a not unimportant primary industry is outside the scope of the defence power.'[29]

'. . . The course of the war,' declared Dixon, J., 'has made it clear enough that it is impossible to treat the internal condition of a combatant country as a thing which can have at best only an indirect bearing upon the prosecution of the war.'[30]

It should be emphasised that the regulations were not designed to implement a plan intimately connected with military operations, but were concerned purely with the protection of the home producer against the consequences of the disorganisation in marketing resulting from the war conditions.[31]   The decision that such a scheme came within the ambit of the defence power therefore amounted to a vindication of the Commonwealth's right to organise the nation for total war.   It represented a reaffirmation, in the strongest terms, of the principles governing the interpretation of the defence power as adopted during the Great War.

The liberal construction placed upon the defence power does not mean either that in time of war there are no limits to what the Commonwealth may do, or that the country functions simply as a

27. 65 *C.L.R.*, p. 264.   28. *Ibid.*   29. *Ibid.*, p. 263.   30. *Ibid.*, p. 279.
31. K. H. Bailey, "Federation Under Fire," *The Austral-Asiatic Bulletin*, p. 14.

unitary state. The defence power conferred on the Commonwealth is itself 'subject to the constitution,' and must be read in conjunction with the other sections. This would imply that the Commonwealth can only take such action under the defence power as is not expressly forbidden by the constitution. Despite this limitation, the defence power remains of enormous importance, because it may be used, broadly speaking, to make good deficiencies in the other powers conferred by the constitution on the Commonwealth. Professor Bailey declares that:

> In time of war the defence power will enable Parliament to supplement the other powers to whatever extent is necessary for the public safety. The mere fact that under the other powers these matters must be left to the States will not prevent the defence power from including them if Parliament thinks it advisable. In effect, the Commonwealth swallows up for the time being all the so-called 'reserve powers' of the States.[32]

It is generally recognised that the constitution should, if possible, be interpreted in such a way as to avoid contradiction. But in time of war this may not be easy to achieve, because of the existence within the constitution of a number of express prohibitions which it may prove difficult to reconcile with the enlarged defence power. The question for decision is therefore 'what are the limitations imposed on the operation of the defence power by these prohibitions?' Examples of such prohibitions may be found in section 92, which states that trade, commerce and intercourse between the states shall be 'absolutely free'; in section 114, which declares that 'the Commonwealth shall not impose any tax on property of any kind belonging to a State'; in section 116, which asserts that 'the Commonwealth shall not make any law for establishing any religion, or for imposing any religious observance, or for prohibiting the free exercise of any religion'; in section 99, which prescribes that 'the Commonwealth shall not, by any law or regulation of trade, commerce, or revenue, give preference to one state or any part thereof over another state or any part thereof'; and in section 51 (ii), which confers on the Commonwealth the power to legislate with respect to taxation, but only in such a way as 'not to discriminate between the States or Parts of States.'[33]

The extent to which such prohibitions have limited the effectiveness of the Commonwealth's efforts to organise the nation for war may be judged from an examination of the decisions of the High Court. So far, section 92 has not operated to invalidate Common-

32. *Public Administration*, March 1942, p. 16.
33. For the interpretation given to these sections, *see* Knowles, *The Australian Constitution*.

wealth legislation, since the Court has taken the view that where legislation did affect commercial activity it was designed not with the specific object of regulating trade, but for the more adequate defence of the country. In the Apple and Pear Case, for instance, the contention that the regulations were contrary to section 92 was not upheld.

Section 114 would appear to be quite explicit. The Commonwealth could hardly tax property belonging to a state under the authority conferred by the defence power.

Section 116 opens up more interesting possibilities. The *National Security (Subversive Associations) Regulations* gave the Attorney-General power to declare unlawful any body, the existence of which seemed to him prejudicial to the defence of the Commonwealth or to the efficient prosecution of the war. It also became an offence to disseminate in print any doctrines held by such a body or for two or more people to meet with the object of propagating such doctrines. Acting under the authority of the regulations, the body known as Jehovah's Witnesses was declared unlawful. Members of the society regard, according to the submission made on their behalf, all organised political bodies, including the British Empire, as 'organs of Satan.' Holding these views, they refused to swear allegiance to the King. Accordingly, the sect was declared an unlawful association and on 17 January 1941 a Commonwealth officer took possession of buildings in Sturt Street, Adelaide, styled Kingdom Hall.

It was decided to test the validity of the Attorney-General's actions in the hope that section 116 would be thought to limit the operation of the defence power. The case[34] came before the full High Court, which returned a majority verdict (Rich, Starke and Williams, J. J.) that the *National Security (Subversive Associations) Regulations* were invalid in their entirety. It was also held to be impossible to sever one regulation from the other. The minority view (Sir John Latham, C. J., and McTiernan, J.) was that the dissolution of Jehovah's Witnesses was valid, but that the regulation authorising a Commonwealth official to take possession of property was invalid.

As anticipated, the main attack on the regulations was as an infringement of section 116, but the interesting point about the case is that although the verdict favoured Jehovah's Witnesses, the regulations were not held to be a violation of section 116. The main contention, therefore, failed, and the regulations were de-

34. 67 *C.L.R.* (1943), pp. 116-168. *Adelaide Company of Jehovah's Witnesses Inc.* v. *The Commonwealth.*

clared invalid on quite different grounds. What those grounds were was set forth plainly in the majority judgments. The real objection was to be found in the consequences which followed from the regulations which, though of a temporary nature, purported to dissolve the body permanently. The definition given to 'unlawful doctrines' was held to be too wide for substantiation since it could include any doctrine or principle advocated by a declared body. This meant that 'the doctrines of a declared body, whether they be religious, political, economic or social, innocent or injurious, are all prohibited, whether they be or be not prejudicial to the defence of the Commonwealth or the effective prosecution of the war.'[35] The regulations were described by Mr. Justice Starke as 'arbitrary, capricious and oppressive'[36] since bodies could be dissolved and divested of their rights and property simply by the declaration of the executive government. He also expressed the opinion not only that the regulations exceeded the authority conferred upon the Governor-General-in-Council by the *National Security Act*, but that the parliament itself did not possess the requisite authority under the constitution to enact legislation of this sort. Mr. Justice Williams, in support of the majority's viewpoint, also pointed out that property could only be forfeited permanently under section 51 (xxxi) of the constitution which declared that 'the acquisition of property by the Commonwealth must be on just terms.'[37]

On examination of the history of section 116 it may be said that so far the section has not operated in such a way as to curtail the scope of the defence power. At the same time, the Jehovah's Witnesses' case has made it plain that, even in war time, the defence power can only successfully bridge gaps in the Commonwealth's ordinary powers when it can be proved that the legislation concerned bears a direct relationship to the defence needs of the country. In this case the Commonwealth's plea that the legislation was necessary to the conduct of the war did not carry conviction;

> . . . the vice of these Regulations is that the consequences to a body, to those interested in the property of a body as shareholders and creditors, and to third persons which flow from the declarations are so drastic and permanent in their nature that

---

35. 67 *C.L.R.*, p. 153, Starke J.   36 *Ibid.*, p. 154.
37. 'The mere fact that the corporation or individual or body is carrying on some activity which in the opinion of Parliament or of some Ministers is prejudicial to the defence of the Commonwealth, cannot, in my opinion, conceivably require that the Commonwealth should enact that the property of such corporation or individual or body should be forfeited to the Crown, and the rights of all corporators and creditors in that property under State laws completely destroyed' (67 *C.L.R.*, 1943, p. 163).

they exceed anything which could conceivably be required in order to aid, even incidentally, in the defence of the Commonwealth.[38]

No further proof is needed that the Commonwealth in war time, as in peace, must have regard to constitutional limitations imposed upon its power by the existence of a written federal constitution.

With regard to section 51 (ii), the constitution gives the Commonwealth the right to raise any form of taxation, provided the tax does not involve discrimination between states. The states, too, may levy any form of taxation apart from customs and excise. Ever since the entry of the Commonwealth into the income tax field during the last war, the position has been that all states and the Commonwealth have levied their own income tax. So far as the states are concerned, there has been a lack of uniformity which has led in turn to considerable divergence between the income tax rates imposed by the various state governments. Such differences may not have been of fundamental importance during peace, but they speedily became so as war expenditure mounted and the Commonwealth was faced with the necessity of exploiting to the full the taxable capacity of the nation. The Commonwealth therefore felt that in view of its numerous commitments it could no longer condone a system which entailed a substantial loss of revenue in some states, notably in Victoria.[39]

The chief difficulty confronting the Commonwealth Treasurer arose out of the provisions of the constitution, since section 51 (ii) prevented discrimination in taxation between states. The Commonwealth tax, therefore, had to be uniform, which implied that when taken in conjunction with prevailing state income tax rates the burden on high incomes in some states and low incomes in others would be unduly severe.

A solution of the problem was finally attempted when the Commonwealth, despite the refusal of the states to co-operate, decided in 1942 to implement the recommendations of a special committee which the federal government had established to enquire into the question of 'the Commonwealth being the sole taxing authority in the field of income tax for the duration of the war.'[40]   Four separate acts were passed, which embodied the suggestions of the committee: the *Income Tax Act* 1942; the *Income Tax (Assessment) Act* 1942; the *States Grants (Income Tax Reimbursement) Act* 1942; and the *Income Tax (War-Time Arrangements) Act*

---

38. Williams J., 67 *C.L.R.* (1943), p. 166.
39. For a more detailed account see K. H. Bailey, "The Uniform Income Tax Plan (1942)" (*The Economic Record*, Dec. 1944), pp. 170-188.
40. *Report* of the Committee on Uniform Taxation March 1942, p. 1.

1942. Of these, the *Income Tax Act* 1942 imposed a progressive income tax, which operated on a uniform basis throughout Australia and took no account of state boundaries. The *Assessment Act,* while it altered the basis of assessment, derived its chief importance from a provision requiring the taxpayer to discharge his obligations to the Commonwealth before paying any income tax imposed by a state Act.[41] The *Grants Act* authorised the Commonwealth to pay to any state which refrained from imposing an income tax a specified amount set out in the schedule to the Act.[42] Finally, the *War-time Arrangements Act* permitted the Commonwealth to transfer compulsorily for the duration of the war state public servants engaged in the assessment and collection of taxation and 'any office accommodation, furniture and equipment specified in the notice.'

Since the Commonwealth legislation had been put through in the face of the opposition of the states, it was not surprising that the governments in a number of states (South Australia, Victoria, Queensland and Western Australia) decided to test its validity in the High Court.[43] Counsel for the states contended that the four acts had to be considered together, since they embodied a single legislative scheme. The object of such a contention was to secure the consideration of the legislation as a whole since the states had little desire to see the *Grants Act* and the *War-time Arrangements Act* declared invalid if the *Income Tax Act* and the *Assessment Act* were upheld and remained in force.[44] 'The four Statutes under consideration must be construed together; their essential subject matter is state taxation in various aspects.'[45]

Arguing on this assumption it was urged on behalf of the states that the Commonwealth was not legitimately exercising its taxation power, (that power being confined to taxation 'by the Commonwealth for Commonwealth purposes'), since the real object of the legislation was to interfere with the power of the states to collect taxation for their own purposes. The Commonwealth was deliberately using its taxation power to destroy the constitutions of the states and was thus upsetting the whole balance of the federal constitution. Neither the Commonwealth nor the states, it was asserted, had the right to exercise their legislative powers in such a

---

41. For the duration of the war and one year thereafter.
42. If this amount proved insufficient a state had the right to appeal for an additional grant through the Commonwealth Grants Commission.
43. 65 *C.L.R.* (1942), pp. 373-472. *South Australia v. The Commonwealth* (Uniform Tax Case).
44. *The Economic Record,* Dec. 1944, p. 183.
45. 65 *C.L.R.* (1942), p. 386. *South Australia v. The Commonwealth.*
46. *Ibid.,* p. 387.

way as to interfere with the capacity or functions of the other.[47]
By an improper use of the power to confer grants under section 96
the Commonwealth was attempting to do 'indirectly what it is forbidden to do directly.'[48]   Its action really amounted to an attempt
'to introduce a unitary system without amending the Constitution.'[49]   Nor could the legislative plan embodied in the four acts
be justified by the defence power, widely as that power might be
construed.   Not only was the defence power to be interpreted 'subject to the Constitution,' but in this instance there could be no justification for legislation on the ground of necessity, because the Commonwealth possessed quite adequate financial powers, and these
could be used for the defence of the country.

Such was the gist of the main argument advanced against the
legislation, but the states also voiced the objection that the acts involved 'discrimination contrary to section 51 (ii) of the Constitution.'[50]   The contention that the Uniform Tax Legislation must
fail as a violation of section 51 (ii) depended upon the view that
the *Tax Act* and the *States Grants Act* should be read together,
which would mean that, in combination, they represented a law
with respect to taxation, and, therefore, came within the operation
of the section.   Likewise, the *States Grants Act* as a law appro-
riating revenue was subject to section 99.   Thus it was argued
that the *Tax Act,* although nominally imposing a uniform tax,
when joined with the *Grants Act* discriminated between the states
in a number of ways.   Discrimination could take place when money
was taken from one state and given to another.   It would arise
from 'the pronounced difference between the income tax rates of
the various states, the difference in population, and the difference in
the income of the citizens of each state.'[51]

The High Court unanimously decided that the *Tax Act* and the
priority clause (section 31 of the *Assessment Act*) were within the
powers of the Commonwealth parliament to make laws with respect
to taxation, while the *Grants Act,* despite the conditions of
abstinence from imposing income tax attached to the grant (Starke,
J., dissenting) was held to be a valid exercise of the Commonwealth's right to grant financial assistance to any state.   Neither

---

47.   The Engineers' case created difficulties for anyone propounding a doc-
      trine of mutual non-interference but an attempt was made to argue
      that while the Court "denied the principle as laid down in the wide
      terms of *D'Emden v. Pedder*" it did not "deny the principle that neither
      the Commonwealth nor the States can purposely direct its or their
      legislation towards destroying or weakening the functions or capacities
      of the other" 68 *C.L.R.,* p. 389.
48.   65 *C.L.R.,* p. 387.   49.   *Ibid.,* p. 389.
50.   *Ibid.,* p. 406.   51.   *Ibid.,* p. 393.

the *Tax Act* nor the *Grants Act* could be considered invalid on the
grounds of interference with the constitutional functions and capa-
cities of the states, or on the plea of discrimination contrary to
section 51 (ii) or of preference contrary to section 99.   The
War-time Arrangements Act, which authorized the Commonwealth to take over from the states such officers, premises and
equipment as had been used for the assessment and collection of
income tax, was by majority decision also declared a valid exercise
of the Commonwealth's defence power.

The reasons which induced the High Court to declare the legislation valid may be summarised from the penetrating analysis of
the case presented by the states, which was contained in the
judgment given by the Chief Justice.   Turning first to the *Tax
Act,* Latham, C. J., dealt with the following arguments:

(a) *The object of the Tax Act is to accomplish indirectly what
the Commonwealth parliament cannot do directly.*   The assertion
that the object of the Act was not simply to collect revenue and
to make grants to the states, but rather to prevent the states
imposing taxation upon incomes could be granted.   'But the
validity of legislation is not to be determined by the motives or the
"ultimate end" of a statute.'[52]   Once a grant of legislative power
had been made, neither the indirect consequences of its exercise
nor the motives of the legislature should be considered when
judging the validity of its exercise in a particular case.   The *Tax
Act* was a law with respect to taxation, and since its provisions
dealt with no other matter the argument employed in *Barger's
Case* that the Act was not in reality a *Tax Act* did not apply.   The
Commonwealth power to legislate was subject to a number of limitations contained in the constitution, but the *Tax Act* had not
infringed these provisions.

(b) *The Tax Act really raises money for state purposes and
not for Commonwealth purposes:* The inference here was that the
raising of money by the Commonwealth for payment to the states
was forbidden, but such a condition could hardly be sustained, in
view of the fact that several sections of the constitution (sections
87, 89, 93, 94, 96, 105, 105A) specifically authorise such action.[53]

(c) *The Commonwealth Parliament itself creates the need for
assistance.*   The argument was that the *Tax Act,* by excluding the
states from essential sources of revenue, had created the need
which the Commonwealth was to relieve by financial grants.

---

52. *Ibid.,* p. 412.   Compare the principles of interpretation adopted in
    Andrews v. Howell 65 *C.L.R.,* 1941.   On this point see pp. 220-22 of this
    chapter.
53. *Ibid.,* p. 413.

Grants of this kind, it was alleged, were not covered by section 96 of the constitution. In answer, the Chief Justice pointed out that the need for financial assistance to states was frequently the result of the operation of Commonwealth policy, and that the fact that such a need had been created by a Commonwealth law did not preclude the Commonwealth parliament from alleviating the financial need of a state by a grant under section 96.[54]

(d) *One object of the Tax Act is to raise money for payment under the Grants Act.* This argument assumed that the *Grants Act* was invalid and implied that since the *Tax Act* was intended to raise money for an unconstitutional purpose it must itself be invalid. But, as the Chief Justice emphasised, the money raised by the *Tax Act* was as a matter of fact not earmarked in any way. Neither Act contained any provision that money obtained under the *Tax Act* should be used to make payments under the *Grants Act*. In actuality, the appropriation made by the *Grants Act* was made out of the Consolidated Revenue Fund.[55]

Turning to a consideration of the validity of the *Grants Act* the Chief Justice examined the character of the Act under several heads.[56]

(a) The *Grants Act* does not purport to repeal state income tax legislation. Obviously the Commonwealth parliament could not repeal an act which it had no authority to enact.

(b) The *Grants Act* does not require, in order that a state should qualify for a grant, that the state parliament should abdicate its power to impose taxes upon incomes. All that it does require before payment is made is that the Commonwealth Treasurer should be satisfied that in fact a state has not imposed a tax upon incomes in any particular year.

(c) The act does not purport to deprive the state parliament of the power to impose an income tax. The Commonwealth has no authority to deprive any state of its power in this respect. The *Grants Act* could not affect the validity of any income tax imposed by a state, though the passage of such legislation would mean that the state would not receive a grant under the act.

(d) The *Grants Act* offers an inducement to the state parliaments not to exercise a power, the continued existence of which is recognised—the power to impose income tax.

It was agreed that the Commonwealth might legitimately induce a state to exercise its powers through the offer of a grant. The Chief Justice held that the converse was also true, that the Commonwealth might induce a state by money grant to abstain from

54. *Ibid.*   55. *Ibid.*, p. 414.   56. *Ibid.*, pp. 416-19.

exercising its powers. But it had been argued that the proposition was radically altered when the inducement was virtually equivalent to coercion—when the state for political or economic reasons was in no position to refuse the Commonwealth grant. Such a contention was emphatically rejected by Sir John Latham. 'This identification of a very attractive inducement with legal compulsion is not convincing.'[57] The fact was that the *Grants Act* 'did not compel the states to abandon their legislative power to impose a tax upon incomes.' The states could lawfully refuse to abstain from imposing an income tax if they so desired. No attempt had been made to order them not to impose such a tax.

A survey of the judgments in the *Uniform Tax Case* makes it plain that the financial provisions of the constitution place the Commonwealth in a position of unquestioned superiority and leave the states almost wholly dependent upon the goodwill of the Commonwealth. While it is true that section 51 (ii) would prevent the Commonwealth from adopting the more direct procedure of imposing taxation which discriminated between the states, it is equally apparent that the Commonwealth, by an ingenious combination of its existing constitutional powers—the taxation power, the grants power and the defence power—has been able to circumvent the prohibitions contained in section 51 (ii) and achieve its avowed objective of preventing the states, at any rate during the war time, from imposing an income tax. The High Court was decisive in its judgment that the existence of the discrimination clause in section 51 (ii) could not act as a bar to legislation of the type enacted by the Commonwealth.

In view of the High Court's decision, which represented an overwhelming victory for the Commonwealth against the states, a victory the full significance of which has yet to be determined, it might be thought that the Commonwealth's march to unassailable supremacy was unlikely to be retarded, at least during the war period, by judicial decision. It has to be remembered that the bulk of the legislation reviewed in the *Uniform Tax Case* was upheld without reference to the defence power, though the *War-time Arrangements Act* was directly dependent upon it for its validity. Nevertheless, it became obvious during the hearing of the case, that the High Court, despite its decision, did not accept the view that in war-time any measure passed by the Commonwealth could be justified through the existence of the defence power. Indeed, the court would almost certainly have regarded a direct order to the states not to impose income tax during the war as unjustified by the defence power. The court undoubtedly favoured a wide in-

57. *Ibid.*, p. 417.

terpretation of the defence power, the Chief Justice himself quoting with approval from judgments in earlier cases in which a broad interpretation had been accepted. However, it did not follow that in war-time no limits should be set to its operation. The test for the validity of legislation under the defence power was that it must bear some relation to the defence of the country.

Unless there is to be no definition whatever of defence, so that the defence power is absolutely unlimited, there could be no wider definition or description than in the passages quoted. But the Commonwealth can support legislation under the power only if it can satisfy a court that there is some connection between the legislation in question and the defence of the country.[58]

Subsequent decisions have confirmed the view that, important and wide as the defence power is in time of war, it is still not capable of filling all the gaps in the Commonwealth's constitutional armour. Undeniably, the scope of the Commonwealth's authority is enormously expanded, while the states become for the time being very junior members in the partnership, yet regard still has to be paid to constitutional niceties and it would be an over-simplification to assert that in wartime the country functions as a unitary state. A part at least of the elaborate structure of war-time controls, erected by the Commonwealth government in the belief that the defence power would justify any measure which it chose to regard as necessary to war-time administration, has been condemned by High Court decisions invalidating specific Commonwealth regulations.

The High Court, for instance, declared that Regulation 4 of the *National Security (Contracts Adjustment) Regulations* was invalid on the ground that there was no power in the *National Security Act* to invest state courts with federal jurisdiction. More pertinent, perhaps, was the decision[59] that statutory rules made under the *National Security Regulations* prescribing additional pay for Victorian Public Servants who had worked on certain holidays were invalid.[60] In this instance the Commonwealth had attempted by regulation to set aside the provisions of the Victorian Public Service Act and substitute conditions differing from those in the state statutes.[61] The case provided a clear-cut example

58. Latham C.J., *ibid.*, p. 432.
59. 66 *C.L.R.*, pp. 488-534, *Victoria v. The Commonwealth.*
60. "Sub-regulations, 8, 9 and 10 of regulation 29 of the *National Security (Supplementary) Regulations*, in so far as they purport to control the holidays and remuneration of members of the public service of the State of Victoria who are not engaged in work associated with the prosecution of the war, are not within the ambit of the defence power of the Commonwealth" (66 *C.L.R.*, p. 488).
61. The Victorian legislation prescribed that such public servants could take their holiday at a different time.

of the limitations of the defence power since the Commonwealth regulations purported to deal with state servants irrespective of whether or not they were engaged in war work. As the Chief Justice pointed out, the Commonwealth parliament might well possess authority, under the defence power, to prescribe conditions of employment for state servants engaged in war work for the Commonwealth, but it had no power to legislate generally with respect to the public service of a state. The defence power could not be construed to mean that all governmental authority had passed into the hands of the Commonwealth. If such an interpretation was sustained and the Commonwealth could validly regulate the pay, hours and duty of all state public servants, then it would control the machinery of governmental administration throughout Australia. 'The Parliament would become a Parliament not with limited powers, but with unlimited powers. Such a result is simply a contradiction of the Constitution.'[62] In such circumstances the federal system would have ceased to exist in all but name.

The limitations of the defence power were even more strikingly emphasised when the High Court, by majority decision (Rich, Starke and Williams J.J.) invalidated the National Security Regulation providing quotas for university students,[63] since in this instance the regulations appeared to fulfill the test, previously prescribed in High Court judgments, that the defence power would suffice to support legislation provided it could be shown that 'some connection existed between the legislation in question and the defence of the country.' Moreover, in the view of the minority of the Court (Latham C.J., McTiernan J.) the connection between the regulations and the defence of the Commonwealth was 'obvious and direct' because the object of the regulation was a more efficient organisation of manpower for the conduct of the war. Nevertheless, the majority of the court was of the opinion that the regulations could not be sustained under the defence power. Mr. Justice Rich held that it was not within the power of the Commonwealth parliament to exercise a general control over education in the schools and universities,[64] while Mr. Justice Starke believed that the regulations were defective because those who were excluded from quotas were 'not diverted to the armed forces or to any purpose of defence or used for the security

---

62. Latham C.J., 66 *C.L.R.*, p. 509. Dealing with the interpretation to be given to the defence power the Chief Justice said: "If the alleged connection between a particular power of legislation and the subject of defence is either non-existent or so attenuated as to be practically non-existent, the legislation cannot be supported under that power."
63. 67 *C.L.R.*, pp. 95-115, *The King v. University of Sydney; ex parte Drummond.*
64. *Ibid.*, p. 105.

of the Commonwealth.'[65]   There was agreement among the majority that the existing provisions of the Defence Act and Manpower Regulations were adequate to ensure the effective organisation of manpower for the prosecution of the war and that there could therefore be no justification for the view that the University Commission regulations were essential to the defence or safety of the Commonwealth.

The examples cited above are by no means the only cases in which Commonwealth regulations have been declared invalid[66] by the High Court but they suffice to show that the Commonwealth cannot lightly assume that the authority which it wields in war-time is equivalent to that possessed by the government of a unitary state.   Moreover, the very fact that a number of regulations, which the Commonwealth Government believed could be justified by its defence power, have been declared invalid breeds uncertainty by casting doubt on a good deal of other Commonwealth legislation which so far has not been challenged in the courts.   The Commonwealth, therefore, even in war-time, has to consider the constitutional limitations imposed upon its authority by the existence of a federal constitution.   In short, the Commonwealth government cannot proceed solely on the basis of taking action in accordance with the demands of the situation, but must also watch warily the constitutional validity of its procedure.   As Mr. Menzies pointedly remarked in his speech[67] to the House of Representatives on constitutional reform, '. . . the first problem is: "What ought we to do?"   Then we invariably have to turn to a second problem.   We have to say to ourselves, "Now that we have made up our minds what we ought to do, can we do it? Let us bring the lawyers in, lest we find ourselves in the High Court, or other appropriate tribunals.   Let us determine whether we have the power to do what we believe ought to be done." '

Some indication has been given of the extent—and the limitations—of the Commonwealth's war-time authority, but it is also pertinent to enquire what use the Commonwealth has made of its war-time powers.   The objectives of the Commonwealth may be summed up succinctly as the total organisation of

65. *Ibid.,* p. 108.
66. See *e.g.,* 67 *C.L.R., Silk Bros. Pty. Ltd. v. State Electricity Commission of Victoria* (Regs. 15 and 16 of the *National Security (Landlord and Tenant) Regulations* declared invalid); 67 *C.L.R., Peacock v. Newtown, Marrickville and General Co-operative Building Society No. 4 Ltd.* (The *National Security (Contracts Adjustment) Regulations* invalid); 67 *C.L.R., Johnston Fear and Kingham and The Offset Printing Co. Pty. Ltd. v. The Commonwealth* (The *National Security (Supply of Goods) Regulations* (S.R. 1939 No. 129 and 1942 No. 164) invalid).
67. *Commonwealth Parliamentary Debates,* clviii, pp. 1815-21.

the resources of the nation for war, though such a statement does not of course imply that Commonwealth governments have been invariably successful in the implementation of the plans which they have devised for this purpose.

The present war, as compared with that of 1914-18, has necessitated a much more intensive regulation of the nation's life and a correspondingly greater intervention by the Commonwealth in matters which normally would fall within the jurisdiction of the states. The reasons which have compelled an expansion of Commonwealth activity, leading to the establishment of a highly intricate system of Commonwealth controls which penetrate into almost every phase of the life of the community, are obvious enough. The threat to Australia's security has been more direct than in 1914-18 and the demands made upon the Australian economy by the Allied nations more exacting. Then again, the development, whether in terms of population growth, exploitation of natural resources, or industrial progress, which has taken place since 1918 has greatly altered, and complicated, the social and economic pattern of Australian society. This has meant in turn that the Commonwealth, when confronted by a crisis threatening its very survival, has had to devise an intricate national organisation, suited to the needs of a more complex society, which would enable it to harness the total resources of the nation for war.

This organisation, which has been brought into being by legislation, regulation and administrative orders, finds its legal basis in the war-time powers possessed by the Commonwealth. The Commonwealth, of course, can utilise all the powers entrusted to it under the constitution, but these would be far from adequate were it not for the liberal construction placed upon the defence power in war-time. Since much of the war legislation sponsored by the Commonwealth would undoubtedly be declared invalid in peace time it is no exaggeration to assert that the defence power is the key-stone supporting the Commonwealth's war-time edifice.

Naturally enough, the first objective in the Commonwealth's task of war organisation[68] was the development, in the narrow sense, of an effective military machine i.e. the recruitment, maintenance and supply of the Australian Navy, Army and Air Force. This in itself was a formidable task in view of the military unpreparedness of the country and the consequent necessity of

68. For an excellent analysis see K. H. Bailey, "The War Emergency Legislation of the Commonwealth" (*Public Administration*, March 1942). Additional material may be found in the *Post-War Reconstruction Pamphlet*: *A Case for Greater Commonwealth Powers*, Chapter 1—War Organisation of Australia.

enormously expanding all branches of the services. Closely allied to this primary objective was what has been called 'the home-base or civilian aspect of military security.'[69] In this connection the Commonwealth has issued regulations under the *National Security Act* to deal with such matters as espionage, control of aliens, censorship, acquisition of property for military purposes, trade with the enemy and a host of other subjects.

The second stage of the Commonwealth's war planning was simply the recognition of what has long been a commonplace, that to maintain an effective military effort it was essential to remodel the life of the nation along lines which would ensure the most thorough exploitation of national resources, whether human or material. On the human side, the Commonwealth has established machinery to organise manpower, control employment and regulate industrial conditions. This aspect of Commonwealth war activity is of particular interest because the Commonwealth was here entering fields from which it is constitutionally excluded in time of peace. The Commonwealth has not hesitated to lay down conditions governing wages, hours and conditions of employment. To facilitate efficiency—and so aid the war effort—it has embarked on what amounted to factory legislation by establishing uniform working conditions throughout the country in relation to such matters as lighting, ventilation and first aid equipment, while a good deal of attention has also been paid to the provision of welfare services of various kinds.[70]

The ramifications of Commonwealth intervention in industry have been so widespread that few compartments have escaped regulation of one sort or another. New federal authorities have been created with far more extensive powers than would normally be sanctioned by the Constitution. For instance, the Commonwealth has ignored the fact that its powers of conciliation and arbitration in industrial matters are confined to 'disputes extending beyond the limits of any one State' and has assumed that, under the defence power, it has the right to establish special authorities with power to intervene in non-inter-state disputes with the object of minimising the consequences to the war effort of industrial unrest.

Under these new arrangements industrial unrest is reported at an early date. Commonwealth authorities are enabled to intervene in a dispute on their own initiative, and without reference by the parties. The appointment of further Conciliation Commissioners is authorized in order to investigate

69. Bailey, *op. cit.*, p. 14.
70. *A Case for Greater Commonwealth Powers*, p. 10.

industrial matters at any time and in any place. All industrial disputes, whether of an inter-state character or not, may be prevented and settled, and an award or determination made effective throughout any trade or industry. Owing to constitutional limits these necessary arrangements are impossible in time of peace.[71]

Problems arising from the attempt to control manpower to the greatest advantage have also been responsible for the entry of the Commonwealth into the sphere of education, long a closely-guarded state preserve. When, for example, manpower shortages were revealed in the skilled trades, the Commonwealth arranged for special courses in technical training and also sponsored dilution agreements permitting the introduction of semi-skilled workmen under specified conditions.[72] The establishment of the Universities Commission provides a further illustration of Commonwealth activity in relation to education.

On the material side, the Commonwealth, after a survey of existing and potential resources, sought to curtail the production of non-essential goods and services and to utilise the surplus for war purposes. This diversion of resources to war has entailed a wide variety of controls intimately affecting the individual's liberty of action in the conduct of his business, in his pursuit of relaxation and in his capacity as a consumer. Exports and imports have been controlled, as have foreign exchange and investment. Building has been strictly limited, expansion of plant and equipment regulated and transport facilities controlled. Moreover, goods in short supply, or those which possess a special significance for war, have been either frozen or rationed by governmental agencies.

Total war has aroused, even among politicians, an interest in social psychology. It has come to be recognised that morale is an important war-winning weapon and that the morale of a nation is to no small extent dependent on the belief that sacrifices, which are recognized to be inevitable in war, are being spread with reasonable equity. In order to satisfy this demand for equality of sacrifice, and at the same time maintain a satisfactory financial equilibrium, the Commonwealth has established a number of controls basically designed to maintain the country's economic stability.[73] Rationing of goods in short supply and price control in its various forms, notably the pegging of rents at equitable rates, are obvious examples of attempted safeguards against the

---

71. *Ibid.*   72. *Ibid.*, p. 11.
73. *Ibid.*, pp. 11-13; *Public Administration*, March 1942, p. 21.

development of privileged groups or the exploitation of the community by war profiteers.

One of the more outstanding aspects of Commonwealth wartime organisation has been the devising of plans for the production and marketing of primary products. The motives behind the decision to control these commodities have varied, being dependent on whether there was a glut or a shortage of a particular product. In some instances, action has been necessary because Australia was unable to produce a given article in sufficient quantity to meet her own requirements. In others, control was required because shortages have been due to the demands made upon Australian stocks by the Allied countries, while in others again the reason has been the inability, during war-time, to export in quantity commodities which normally find their market overseas. To take one instance, it was to safeguard the producer against unnecessary hardship that the Commonwealth devised its apple and pear marketing scheme. The customary method has been for the Commonwealth to acquire the entire output of a particular commodity and then arrange for its marketing 'through a central board or committee assisted by the states and the organised producers.'[74] In this way the Commonwealth through its war-time powers has developed agencies with the object of achieving a stable market in the interest of both producers and consumers.

Sufficient has been said about the Commonwealth war-time organisation to indicate the nature and extent of the Commonwealth's war powers and the motives which have prompted the Commonwealth to take action. The increase of such powers does not in itself indicate that the Commonwealth has been invariably successful in achieving its objectives, or even that the mechanism which it has devised has functioned with a completely satisfying smoothness. Like other states, whether unitary or federal, the Commonwealth has found the organisation of a nation for purposes of war a stupendous task and, like governments elsewhere, the Commonwealth authorities have made mistakes. What however is clear is that only a central government is competent to meet the shock of war and organise not only the military defence of the country but the national effort required for survival. But this applies with equal force to the aftermath of war, for war almost invariably dislocates the existing structure of society, ushers in periods of change and creates the problems of the ensuing peace. Since these problems may well be comparable in gravity to those involved in organisation for war it is not

74. *A Case for Greater Commonwealth Powers*, p. 13.

unreasonable to infer that a national government will alone be capable of grappling with their solution.

Those who think either that the retention of a federal system is desirable, or inevitable, tend to believe that much may be done to overcome the difficulties inherent in a federal system by the development of co-operatoin between state and central authorities. During the war years there have been attempts at such co-operation and the experience gained when combined with that of peacetime, should afford some criterion by which the potentialities of co-operation may be judged.

Certainly in attempting the task of organising the nation for war Commonwealth governments have depended not only on their own administrative agencies, but on a system of co-operation which has enabled the Commonwealth to utilise the experience and machinery possessed by the states. War organisation has therefore had a direct effect on relations between the Commonwealth and the states, and has provided further valuable experience of co-operation in action in a federal system.

As Commonwealth powers are sufficiently expansive in time of war to permit almost all forms of national planning which are essential to the war effort, it follows that the states will inevitably find their sphere of activity curtailed. Action has perforce to be taken on a national basis because so many of the controls which are essential in war-time would be wholly ineffective if confined by state boundaries. In such matters as the control of manpower and the maintenance of economic stability uniformity is the first prerequisite. In order to administer and enforce the plans for social and economic organisation the Commonwealth has greatly expanded its own agencies and instrumentalities—so much so indeed that the states have complained that there has been unnecessary duplication. At the same time the Commonwealth has invited the co-operation of the states and has made considerable use of state agencies where it believed that it was practicable to do so. On the administrative side, therefore, there has been a good deal of co-operative action, while contact between governments has been maintained through the Premiers' Conference and through meetings between state and Commonwealth ministers. Consultation has been fairly regular at both the political and administrative level.

Broadly speaking, the system has operated in the following way. The Commonwealth has been responsible for formulating the general plan and for indicating the principles which it wished to apply, while the states have been called upon to administer the detailed operation of particular schemes. Actually, the nature of this co-operation has varied a good deal, though the basic result has been to achieve a measure of administrative decentralisation. In some cases the states act by virtue of their own powers, while in others powers are conferred upon them by the Commonwealth and the limits within which they may operate are specifically defined. When this occurs, the states may for all practical purposes be said to be 'acting as a Commonwealth instrumentality.'[75]

Some examples will illustrate the diverse character of war-time co-operation. Wide-ranging powers have been delegated by the Commonwealth to the premiers of the states. In this way authority is conferred for war-time purposes to permit a premier to take action for the protection of the civil population in an emergency and to dispense with the provisions of state law in such matters as sporting fixtures, sale of liquor and proceedings of friendly societies. The states have also been given authority to administer, and modify, Commonwealth controls imposed, for example, by the *Fair Rents Regulations,* the *Landlord and Tenant Regulations* and the *Wheat Industry Stabilisation Scheme*. The Fair Rents and Landlord and Tenant Regulations may be taken to illustrate the way in which this co-operation works.[76] The regulations were designed to prevent hardship and profiteering, and dealt with the termination of tenancies, the obtaining of possession, the ejection of tenants and the establishment of a fair rent. But the Fair Rents Boards, which the regulations envisaged, were to be set up by the states, which were also given powers to exempt from the operation of the regulations certain areas and certain types of premises.

An even more instructive example of the interlocking character of war-time administration is afforded by the *Emergency Supplies Regulations.*[77] These aimed at ensuring an adequate quantity of essential supplies throughout the country as a whole in the event of any dislocation of normal communications. The plan was dependent upon the establishment of a number of regions which were to consist of the various states and territories. However, it was provided that the Commonwealth Minister for Commerce, with the approval of the Governor in Council of a state, might enlarge a region by adding a territory of the Commonwealth to a state. The state was given the responsibility for creating the administrative authority for its area, while the Commonwealth retained the right both to name the commodities which were to

75. See *Public Administration*, March 1942, p. 25.
76. These illustrations have been drawn from K. H. Bailey, *op. cit.*
77. *Ibid.*, pp. 24-5.

be conserved for an emergency and to place orders for the delivery of these goods to the responsible administrative body. Thereafter the state authorities were in control and could make such regulations as they thought fit for controlling the emergency stocks, though the Commonwealth retained the power to disallow regulations of which it disapproved.

The illustrations cited above show how the administrative side of war-time organisation has been facilitated through the assistance of the states in the administration of schemes planned by the Commonwealth. But the burden of organisation has also been lightened through the initiative of the states, notably in the form of state offers to place at the disposal of the Commonwealth the machinery which they had built up for their own administrative purposes. The nature of the co-operation extended by the states may be gauged from the evidence furnished by Mr. Mair, of the way in which New South Wales has assisted the Commonwealth during the war. His list includes:

The carrying out from state funds of a number of works of defence of strategic value, e.g., road works, aerodromes.

The making available of the technical and labour resources of state departments to carry out at cost certain defence works —roads, railway sidings, water and drainage works, clearing and levelling of aerodrome sites, and provision of hutments.

The loan of public buildings (schools, etc.) in connection with recruiting and compulsory training call-up.

Encouragement of enlistment and the keeping down to the lowest possible minimum requests for exemption from training, etc.

The conduct of certain administrative functions as the agent of the Commonwealth government, e.g., in respect of the control of prices. In this instance the state bears the major portion of the cost and provides most of the staff.

The adaptation of technical training instruction and adjustment of classes to meet military needs.

The extension of material assistance by the state police to the military authorities, particularly in the direction of the registration of aliens, numerous general inquiries on behalf of the military authorities, and generally in connection with preparatory measures prior to the outbreak of war.

General assistance by various state departments, e.g., in preparation of maps, securing of sites, etc., drafting work, the purchase of material and provision of facilities by the Health Department.[78]

78. A. Mair, "Role of the States. Co-operation in War." *Sydney Morning Herald* 20 May 1940.

In view of the numerous examples cited, it was all the more significant that Mr. Mair should add that much more could be done and that co-operation had by no means been fully worked out.[79]

Despite the extensive nature of war-time co-operation, it is doubtful if co-operation provides a sound basis for optimism in a post-war period, which will see a reversion to more normal constitutional relations.   Certainly its limitations are clear.   The states have remained dissatisfied with the comparatively minor role allotted to them in the war period.   Thus, Mr. Mair, when pressing for the revival of the National Council, was in effect arguing that the states should share with the Commonwealth as more equal partners in war organisation.   He considered, in particular, that 'the long and intimate experience of measures relating to industrial administration,' possessed by the states had not been fully utilised and that a greater blending of state and Commonwealth officials in the new administrative agencies would have produced more satisfactory results.   Above all, he believed that the economic controls established by the federal government had made scant provision for effective collaboration.

In many new administrations embracing investment control (with its far-reaching effects throughout industry,commerce and government), exchange control, transport control, export licensing, regulation of supply, rationing, etc., there is scarcely a vestige of provision for collaboration with the states.   The sole exception is in relation to price control.[80]

The attitude adopted by representatives of the states towards the Uniform Tax legislation, the 1942 constitutional convention and the reference of powers to the Commonwealth indicates, beyond reasonable doubt, that the states are jealous of their status and have no intention of willingly accepting a largely administrative role in the governmental structure.   The resolutions passed by the parliaments of Victoria, South Australia and Western Australia prior to the meeting of the 1942 convention make it plain that many state politicians are uncompromisingly opposed to any alteration in the balance of the federal system which is likely to diminish their prestige and curtail their power.

1. That this House is opposed to the *Constitution Alteration (War Aims and Reconstruction) Bill* 1942 or any alterations which destroy the federal character of the Constitution.

79. This however was at a comparatively early stage of the war and new avenues of co-operation were subsequently developed.
80. *Sydney Morning Herald*, 22 May 1940.

2. That the federal Constitution is essential for the welfare, progress and development of Australia, particularly of the outlying parts . . . (South Australia).[81]

. . . that if, after the holding of the forthcoming convention, amendments to the Constitution are considered necessary, they be limited to specific additional legislative powers required for post-war reconstruction proposals for a limited period of years only (Western Australia).[82]

Nothing, it would seem, is more likely to impede effective co-operation in the post-war period than this suspicion of Commonwealth intentions and this jealous preservation of state rights. Indeed, such an outlook has been evidenced even in war-time when the Commonwealth's authority is far less open to challenge. Mr. Curtin, at the Premiers' Conference of August, 1942, not only felt it necessary to rebuke the premiers for their antagonism to the Commonwealth, but complained that they appeared to regard the Commonwealth almost in the light of some alien aggressor bent on overriding state laws. He pointed out that the complexity of war organisation necessitated a co-operative attitude on the part of the states, yet the states, while incapable of adopting a united approach to problems, complained of Commonwealth intervention. 'We find every state has a different method of dealing with these matters. Complaints come back to the Commonwealth, yet when we bring the matters to the Premiers' Conference we are told we are invading state rights.'[83]

It can hardly be denied that much may be achieved by co-operation between governments if the will to co-operate genuinely exists and if political obstacles are not insuperable. Indeed, it is the only method whereby a federal system at the Australian stage of development can be converted into a tolerably efficient instrument of government. There is, however, scant evidence, either from the last war, or this, or from peace-time experiments, to suggest that co-operation is likely to provide a solution for the difficulties inherent in federalism. What the experience of the recent war years has shown is that co-operation is likely to be much more effective when the Commonwealth is in a virtually unassailable position and the states act largely as administrative agencies. This may in itself prove a valuable lesson, for should the Commonwealth in the future be entrusted with vastly expanded powers it will need to employ some system of decentralised

81. *Record of Proceedings*, Canberra Convention on proposed alteration of the Commonwealth Constitution, p. 63. Quoted by Mr. Playford (S.A.).
82. *Ibid.*, p. 71. Quoted by Mr. Willcock (W.A.).
83. *Sydney Morning Herald*, 13 August 1942.

administration. It could then make use of the agencies developed by the states and draw upon the deposit of experience which they now possess. But if a federal system be retained, with rigid constitutional limits set to Commonwealth authority and major legislative powers left to the states, so-called co-operation will become a matter of bargaining, with a jealous regard for prestige at a premium, and the rights of the states will be placed above concern for the national good.

The relations between the Commonwealth and the states have by no means been unaffected by the war years, and the shift in their relative power and in the prestige which they enjoy within the community has been sufficient to modify significantly the place of each within the Australian governmental structure. In wartime the Commonwealth has naturally enjoyed a dominant position. It has occupied the centre of the stage in a period of national crisis during which the old habit of looking to the states has largely been supplanted by that of looking to the Commonwealth. The waning interest in state politics during the war, as evidenced at the elections, is in itself an indication of the extent of the ground which the states have lost. It may be that interest will revive, and with it the prestige of the states, once more normal conditions have returned, but it should not be forgotten that a new habit of Commonwealth leadership has been engendered which makes it at least doubtful whether the states will ever regain their former importance. The sense of nationhood has become more fully developed, and the Australian's primary allegiance may in the future well go to his national rather than to his state government. Moreover, the Commonwealth has tasted power and will be reluctant to accept a role of diminished significance.

The changing character of Commonwealth-state relations and the further deterioration of state power could hardly be better illustrated than by the war-time struggle over the Uniform Income Tax plan. Though proposals for the creation of a single income tax authority had been made in the pre-war period it was essentially the demands of war finance[84] which led the Commonwealth government first to insist upon the necessity of such an arrangement, and then finally to put it into operation in opposition to the wishes of the states. The main objective was to eliminate competition between Commonwealth and state governments in the

---

84. "The position has become so serious that strong and definite action must be taken by the Commonwealth to cut the gordian knot, if any simplification of Commonwealth-state taxes is to be achieved in the interests of the war effort." Mr. Chifley, Commonwealth Treasurer, 15 May 1942. *Commonwealth Parliamentary Debates*, clxx, p. 1286.

income-tax field. It had become imperative to mobilise the taxable capacity of the nation to the full, yet the existing system of multiple income-taxes made this almost impossible. As Mr. Chifley asserted, every Commonwealth Treasurer could testify that the different rates of Commonwealth and state taxations formed 'a maddening maze of figures, which must be studied whenever the preparation of a budget calls for additional Commonwealth revenue'[85]—a statement fully approved by Mr. Fadden among others.

With the outbreak of war interest in the establishment of a single income tax revived and projects were evolved for submission to the states. Early in 1941 Mr. Fadden, who was then treasurer, put forward a number of suggestions to the states with the object of securing a greater degree of uniformity in taxation. These proposals came to nothing mainly because the states were unwilling to make the sacrifice which they believed would be entailed. By June, Mr. Fadden, now convinced that the urgency of the situation demanded immediate action, suggested[86] to the states that they should vacate the income-tax field for the duration of the war and obtain their income instead through grants from the Commonwealth. Since such a suggestion had scant appeal for the state representatives no agreement was reached, with the result that Mr. Fadden substituted his scheme for 'post-war credits' as an alternative method of overcoming his budgetary problem.

When Labour became the government, Mr. Chifley, as treasurer, was confronted by the same problem of the hampering effect upon the Commonwealth 'of six states imposing eleven taxes on income at widely differing rates.'[87] The first step in the search for a solution was the appointment, in February, 1942, of a committee consisting of Professor R. C. Mills, Mr. J. H. Scullin and Mr. E. S. Spooner 'to consider the question of the Commonwealth being the sole taxing authority in the field of income tax for the duration of the war, and of payment of compensation to the states by way of grants.'[88] The committee in its report recommended the introduction of such a plan for the duration of the war, and for one year afterwards, and worked out the details necessary for its application. In particular, it suggested, after the consideration of various proposals, that the basis for compensation to the states

85. *Ibid.*
86. See K. H. Bailey, "The Uniform Income Tax Plan (1942)", *The Economic Record*, Dec. 1944, p. 171.
87. *Report* of the Committee on Uniform Taxation, p. 1.
88. *Ibid.*

should be 'the average of state collections from taxes on income in the two war-time financial years 1939-1940 and 1940-1941.'[89]

The government decided to implement its committee's recommendations in their entirety, but it soon discovered that it would have to do so in the teeth of the hostility of the states. The government's proposals, like those previously submitted by Mr. Fadden, were roundly rejected by the premiers. What was more, no serious counter-proposals were advanced by the state representatives, or at least none which the Commonwealth was prepared to regard as offering a genuine solution to the problem. Despite the opposition encountered, the Commonwealth government was by this time determined to proceed with its plan, and that determination was reinforced when it sensed that public opinion was favourable to the scheme and antagonistic to the stand being taken by the states. Indeed, to most Australians state representatives appeared as living in an unreal world, as men incapable of adopting a national outlook and dangerously divorced from the state of public feeling.[90] Mr. Curtin was therefore in a position to remain adamant and to insist that the government would proceed with its legislation. 'If you accept the principle of one taxing authority, we will discuss with you how it should work. If you cannot accept the principle, I shall refer the matter to the Commonwealth Parliament.'[91]

The case for the Commonwealth, as presented by Mr. Curtin and Mr. Chifley, was based upon war necessity. To a large extent it mirrored the findings of the Uniform Tax committee. It was argued that only[92] by some such measure could the Commonwealth government control the taxable capacity of the nation and mobilise the country's resources in the most advantageous and equitable way. Or as Mr. Curtin said:

This is a war measure arising from the necessities of war. In no way, other than that provided in this legislation, can this Parliament obtain command over the resources of the nation

89. *Ibid.*, p. 3.
90. Compare leading article, *Sydney Morning Herald*, 21 May 1942: "There can be no doubt that the overwhelming majority of the Australian people approve of the uniform taxation plan in principle if not in all its details . . . It is hard to avoid the conclusion that the opposition of state political bodies to the plan is prompted not by consideration for the people they represent but by anxiety over their own political power."
91. *Sydney Morning Herald*, 23 April 1942.
92. "Nothing short of complete control by the Commonwealth during the war will meet the huge demands that have to be faced. National rights must take precedence over state rights. The rights of the sovereign people are paramount to the sovereign rights of the States." Mr. Chifley, *Commonwealth Parliamentary Debates*, clxx, 1286.

in order to mobilise them for the purpose of war. It must have the right to declare, without equivocation or hindrance, the rate of contribution, which it considers proper that every citizen should make to the nation.[93]

Under the existing system Commonwealth revenue was declining and state revenue increasing. What the Commonwealth wished to do was to peg state revenue at a figure based on the revenue obtained by the states during the two preceding years. If the states were compensated on this basis they would have no ground for complaint.

Yet in fact the states did complain, and complain bitterly, and the majority of the state governments subsequently contested the legislation before the High Court. What were the grounds of this objection? As put forward by spokesmen for the states at the Premiers' Conference in April, 1942, these centred about three main issues. Easily most important was the surrender of state sovereignty, which the plan was said to entail. This objection was voiced by all the premiers, but perhaps most emphatically by Mr. McKell (N.S.W.), who maintained that to take away from the states their power to tax was to take away their power to govern. Nor was his opposition lessened by the fact that the Commonwealth proposed to grant money compensation, since this did not affect the main issue, that there would be no compensation for the loss of fundamental rights. 'If the compensation were double, it would not in the least affect my attitude.'[94] The second objection might be classed as financial. Here the states disputed the Commonwealth's main argument, that the plan was imperative for the effective prosecution of the war, by contending that the Commonwealth had not hitherto been hampered in its war effort by lack of money, but rather by physical difficulties. The third criticism related to the way in which the scheme had been put to the states. It was argued that the states had not been consulted about the plan—despite the fact that the proposals were revolutionary and would alter fundamentally the financial relations between the states and the Commonwealth—and that other schemes might well be devised which would be less objectionable to the states and yet give the Commonwealth financial satisfaction. It was pointed out by Mr. Dunstan (Victoria) that the Commonwealth committee had been set up without consultation with the states and that the states had no representation upon it.[95] The attitude of the Commonwealth was one of 'stand and deliver,'

93. *Ibid.*, clxxi.
94. *Sydney Morning Herald*, 23 April 1942.
95. *Ibid.*

and it was his belief that such proposals, if adopted, would lead ultimately to unification. Mr. Forgan Smith (Queensland) challenged the plan on slightly different grounds. At least one of his objections to it was that the maintenance of the scheme in the form suggested would depend entirely on the attitude of the Commonwealth. There was no contract between Commonwealth and states, and therefore no safeguard against alterations, e.g., in the amount of compensation, and this might prove disadvantageous to the states.[96]

The Commonwealth government was not deterred by the refusal of the states to co-operate in carrying out its plan, and submitted its proposals to the Commonwealth parliament which put them into effect. In view of the hostility expressed by the states it was not surprising when Victoria, Queensland, South Australia and Western Australia challenged the validity of the legislation in the High Court. The actions were, however, dismissed.

A number of not unimportant conclusions may be drawn from the struggle over the introduction of the Uniform Income-Tax plan. There is overwhelming evidence that, in a time of national crisis, over an issue of major importance the method of co-operation proved a total failure. Despite repeated approaches to the states, no common ground could be discovered and the alternative schemes propounded by the states were only too clearly produced when it was discovered that the Commonwealth intended to proceed with its legislation. It is difficult to escape the conclusion that the scheme finally adopted was forced on the Commonwealth by the unwillingness of the states to co-operate in any plan which would eradicate the obstacles preventing the Commonwealth from obtaining the maximum revenue required for war purposes. The opposition displayed by the premiers was alleged to be due to their concern for state rights, but if this were so, state rights must be narrowly interpreted, since hostility appeared to spring not so much from a tender concern for the interests of the people they represented as from fear that their own political power, and with it their prestige, might be endangered.

The premiers would appear to have voiced their objections on behalf of themselves and the political machines which they represented. Within the various states there were few signs of political differences being sunk in favour of an all party line up in defence of state rights. Thus the state Labour parties in both Western Australia and Victoria adhered to the view that nothing must be done to embarrass the federal Labour Party and dissociated them-

96. *Ibid.*

selves from the action taken by the state premiers in contesting the legislation before the High Court.[97] In New South Wales the McKell cabinet, having committed the indiscretion of announcing its intention to join in the challenge without awaiting the decision of the Labour Conference, speedily discovered that its attitude was so unpopular with Conference that it recanted and announced the abandonment of its challenge.[98] In the federal House of Representatives, in the voting on the uniform tax measures—41 to 11 in favour,—few members showed any inclination to place their allegiance to their state above either their party interest or the national interest as they conceived it. Queensland members at one stage appeared likely to espouse the view enunciated by Mr. Forgan Smith but their opposition melted away and they ended by supporting the government's plan. Opposition members from Victoria and South Australia voted against the legislation, but members of the Victorian state A.L.P. supported it. Most significantly of all, representatives from Tasmania, who may perhaps more easily judge trends in public opinion because of the smallness of their electorates, voted unanimously in favour of the plan.

Despite the fact that the uniform income-tax plan in the form in which it has been adopted is a temporary measure it may well determine the future character of the federal-state financial relationship. There would appear to be no[99] constitutional barrier to the continuance of the plan in peace time if the Commonwealth government believes that it would be politically expedient to do so. Apart from the *Wartime Arrangements Act,* which was a purely machinery measure, the legislation which was essential to the implementation of the plan was upheld without reference to the defence power. The High Court unanimously upheld the validity of the *Tax Act* and the Priority clause and, even without the *Grants Act,* these measures might ensure the success of the scheme since if the Commonwealth Tax rates were high it would be difficult, and perhaps impossible, from a financial and political point of view for a state to superimpose its own income tax.[1]

97. Western Australia State A.L.P. Executive decided unanimously that with regard to the uniform tax plan Western Australian Labour members in the federal parliament were to be bound solely by the decisions of the federal caucus, i.e. the State Executive refused to support the request made by the Western Australian Legislative Assembly to Western Australian federal members to oppose the uniform tax proposals. *Sydney Morning Herald*, 23 May, 1942.
98. *Sydney Morning Herald*, 17 June, 1942.
99. *The Economic Record*, Dec. 1944, p. 187.
 1. *Ibid.*, p. 187.

Moreover, in the opinion of many who are competent to judge, the *Grants Act* too does not depend for its validity on the war-time powers of the Commonwealth.[2] If this be so, there is certainly no constitutional reason why the Commonwealth cannot enact similar legislation in peace time. Indeed, there are already signs that the Commonwealth contemplates maintaining uniform taxation as a permanent measure. At the Premiers' Conference at Canberra in August 1945 when the Victorian Premier, Mr. Dunstan, attacked uniform taxation and sought its repeal, the Prime Minister, Mr. Chifley, replied that it was his belief that uniform taxation should remain the form of tax for all time and added that he considered the general public would be of the same opinion.[3]

As the result of the *Uniform Income-Tax* case there is also a new appreciation of the significance of section 96 of the constitution —'the Parliament may grant financial assistance to any state on such terms and conditions as the Parliament thinks fit.'[4] The Commonwealth it is true, had previously made considerable use of this section to persuade states receiving grants for specific purposes to implement a policy of which it approved. This could be done because the language of the section was sufficiently broad to permit the Commonwealth to impose the conditions on which it would agree to pay a grant to the states. Thus through the technique of the grant in aid the Commonwealth has been able to influence policy in a number of matters upon which the Commonwealth under the constitution could not legislate.[5] In addition to the payments recommended by the Commonwealth Grants Commission, which operates under section 96, the Commonwealth has made grants on conditions for such things as road construction, housing and assistance to wheat farmers. The difference between the earlier legislation and the *State Grants (Income Tax Reimbursement) Act* 1942 was in the nature of the conditions laid down by the Commonwealth. In the latter instance the Commonwealth provided that a state which wished to qualify for a grant under the Act must not exercise its power to impose an income tax. Though Starke J. maintained that section 96 did not authorise the Commonwealth to lay down

2. This view is held by Professor K. H. Bailey.
3. *Sydney Morning Herald*, 24 August 1945.
4. Knowles, *op. cit.*, p. 90.
5. *Victoria v. The Commonwealth* (1926), 38 *C.L.R.*, 399. The High Court held that the *Federal Aid Roads Act* 1926 was a valid exercise of the power conferred on the Commonwealth parliament by section 96 to grant financial assistance to any state on such terms and conditions as the parliament thinks fit.

conditions of this nature the majority of the Court held that the Commonwealth had not exceeded its authority.[6] The implication of this decision is clear. The Commonwealth by the use of section 96 in combination with other powers may do many things indirectly which it cannot validly do directly. As Professor Bailey has remarked, 'a constitution that contains a section 96 contains within itself the mechanism of Commonwealth supremacy, to be used as and when the people of Australia desire it.'[7]

The importance of the procedure adopted over the imposition of a uniform income tax is accentuated by the fact that there is no reason why a similar technique should not be applied to other kinds of taxation.[8] If the Commonwealth chose to impose its own tax in every one of the existing fields, and then legislated under section 96 to reimburse the states for their loss of revenue on condition that they refrained from imposing similar state taxation, the legislation could not be invalidated and the states would be confronted with the same difficulties as they recently faced over income tax. Indeed, during war time the Commonwealth has already made some move in this direction, for despite the reluctance of the states it has adopted the same procedure with regard to the entertainment tax.[9]

The implications which the uniform income-tax plan holds for the future of the Commonwealth-state financial relations have nowhere been demonstrated more clearly than in the judgment of the Chief Justice.

It is perhaps not out of place to point out that the scheme which the Commonwealth has applied to income tax of imposing rates so high as practically to exclude state taxation could be applied to other taxes so as to make the States almost completely dependent, financially and therefore generally, upon the Commonwealth. If the Commonwealth Parliament, in a Grants Act, simply provided for the payment of moneys to states, without attaching any condition whatever, none of the legislation could be challenged by any of the arguments submitted to the Court in these cases. The amount of the grants could be determined in fact by the satisfaction of the Commonwealth with the policies, legislative or other, of the respective States, no reference being made to such matters in any Commonwealth

6. It seems clear, however, that the Commonwealth parliament could not have directly prohibited a state parliament from imposing an income tax. 65 *C.L.R.* (1942), pp. 416-17: Latham C.J., *South Australia v. The Commonwealth.*
7 *The Economic Record,* Dec. 1944, p. 185.
8. *Ibid.,* p. 176.
9. *Sydney Morning Herald,* 12 Aug. 1942. Mr. Dunstan described the proposal as "one more nail in the coffin of the states."

statute. Thus if the Commonwealth Parliament were prepared to pass such legislation, all state powers would be controlled by the Commonwealth—a result which would mean the end of the political independence of the States. Such a result cannot be prevented by any legal decision. The determination of the propriety of any such policy must rest with the Commonwealth Parliament and ultimately with the people. The remedy for alleged abuse of power or for the use of power to promote what are thought to be improper objects is to be found in the political arena and not in the courts.[10]

The protests voiced by the premiers at the 1942 Premiers' Conference were based on the conviction that power to govern was meaningless without the power to tax. Legally no doubt the power to impose income tax remained, but the Commonwealth legislation made it politically almost impossible to exercise that power. The states at least see clearly that if they lose control over taxation they lose much more as well, since in large measure the extent of their independence rests upon their liberty of action in the financial sphere. If the implications of the uniform tax legislation as underlined by the Chief Justice have any validity— and there is little doubt that they have—it is not too much to say that the relationship of the states to the Commonwealth, and indeed their status in the Australian governmental system, are likely to be profoundly modified by war-time developments in finance culminating in the uniform income-tax case.

As the threat to Australia diminished and prospects of ultimate victory steadily improved the federal Labour government became increasingly concerned with problems of peace-time re-organisation. It was uneasily aware that the national war structure depended to a large extent upon the Commonwealth's defence powers and that with peace these would be so shrunken that national reconstruction could not be made to depend upon them. Holding the view that peace problems would be no less urgent than those of war, and that they could only be effectively solved by a national approach, the government, after examining its normal constitutional powers, reached the conclusion that an attempt would have to be made to amend the Constitution by granting vastly increased powers to the Commonwealth. The government, instigated by Dr. Evatt, therefore announced the proposed amendments which it considered essential in the post-war period.

The government's case for the alteration of the constitution, though amplified in parliament and further expounded during

10. Latham C.J., 65 *C.L.R.* (1942), p. 429: *South Australia v. The Commonwealth.*

the referendum campaign, through the press, radio and public speeches, was presented in its essentials in the Post-War Reconstruction pamphlet[11] prepared for the Constitutional Convention which met at Canberra in November 1942. Here may be found a clear presentation of the grounds on which the government based its claims for wider powers. Fundamentally, no doubt, the desire for amendment was the result of experience of the weaknesses revealed in the past working of the Australian federal system combined with the realisation that the constitution in its existing form was no longer a satisfactory instrument of government in view of the radical social, economic and other changes which had occurred since federation. This argument was the corner-stone in the case as presented by Dr. Evatt for constitutional reform.

In short, events have proved that the Constitution which the Australian people adopted in 1900 is flexible enough for the needs of war. But it is equally true that it is not flexible enough to serve Australia in the great task of post-war reorganisation which the declared war aims of the United Nations will involve.

. . . the peace-time powers of the Commonwealth though numerous and detailed are hedged round with severe limitations. Although they were written down in the 1890's, many of the words and phrases were simply transcribed from the American constitution of 1787. The general approach belongs to the horse-and-buggy age of social organisation. This is especially true of the economic powers that are so vital an element in a modern industrial community. For instance, 'trade and commerce' is so divided between the Commonwealth and the state authority that neither can deal effectively with it. Such topics as production, employment, investment, industrial conditions, are either not committed to the national Government at all or are granted in jealous, limited, qualified or indirect terms. The Constitution of 1900 is outmoded.[12]

This was the broad approach determining the government's attitude. But other, more specific, arguments for alteration were also advanced. Basically the government's appeal was a plea for a planned economy. The war-time powers of the Commonwealth had permitted the war crisis to be met by organisation on a national scale, but the restoration of peace would so greatly contract Commonwealth power that it would be insufficient to deal with the no less urgent peace crisis.

11. *Post-war Reconstruction: A Case for Greater Commonwealth Powers.* Prepared for the Constitutional Convention at Canberra, November 1942.
12. For full text see *Commonwealth Parliamentary Debates*, clxxii, 1338-41.

In the fires of war we have fashioned a new machinery of government diverse yet unified, with its roots in the people and yet with effective central direction; we have, too, fashioned a system of economic regulation by which we have built and maintained a gigantic war machine and at the same time protected our people from want and insecurity. We profoundly believe that this machinery of government and this system of control and organisation are necessary and well adjusted to handle the equally difficult and urgent problems of the post-war period. Are we to plan for peace as we have planned for victory in war? Or are we to revert to the divided responsibility, the insecurity, the waste, the unemployment, which characterised so much of Australia's pre-war period?

This is the broad issue—plan or no plan? Plan or chaos?[13]

The conviction that immediate and extensive alteration was necessary was reinforced, so the authors of the Case for Greater Commonwealth Powers believed, by experience after the war of 1914-18. Faced by demands for the abolition of restrictions and informed by expert advisers that the defence power could not safely be used in peace to deal with the economic repercussions of the war, the Government repealed the *Commonwealth Prices Regulations* in January 1919, and the *War Precautions Act* and most other war regulations in December 1920. For a time boom conditions prevailed and by the end of June 1920, to take but one example, the Comptroller of Repatriation was in a position to declare that all but 6,049 discharged and fit members of the Expeditionary Forces in Australia had been re-established in civilian occupations. But prosperity was short-lived.

Prices, which had rocketed up, dived down again during the sixteen months ending in December 1921. Business contracted. Farm incomes fell. The percentage of trade unionists recorded as unemployed was doubled between the third quarter of 1920 and the second quarter of 1921. Not till the present war did recorded unemployment ever fall again to the 1913 level.[14]

The slump was not of course confined to Australia but it was contended that its effects could have been cushioned by national planning if the constitution had made this possible. This, at any rate, was the view of the then Prime Minister, Mr. Hughes, who sponsored alterations to the constitution designed to clothe the Commonwealth with additional powers to deal with the problems of peace.

The problems of reconstruction are great and pressing; they need the assistance of strong and effective government. In

13. *A Case for Greater Commonwealth Powers*, pp. 6-7.
14. *Ibid.*, p. 31.

Australia it is, and must be, to the Commonwealth that the people look during the period of reconstruction for the establishment of the social and industrial conditions which alone can enable us to reap a harvest of blessing from the horrid tillage of war. . . .

The cure must be drastic, and the programme of reform must be comprehensive. It must deal with the whole intricate web of causes. Profiteering must be put down with a strong hand, but that alone is not enough. If we are to stimulate production, it is necessary to have full control of production, which involves control of both labour and capital, the elements of production. It is necessary to have full control of trade and commerce, by which the results of production are distributed and brought to the consumer. Trade is controlled by corporations; it is captured by monopolies; it too, is affected by organisations of capital and labour. All these must be controlled, and the government which is to control them must be able to do so fully and effectively, to deal with the problem as a whole, not only with a bit here and a bit there. Unless it can so deal, government is futile.[14a]

In essence, the case presented by the Curtin government in 1942 was the same as that fathered by Mr. Hughes in 1919. The Curtin government, however, hoped to profit by avoiding the errors which it believed had proved fatal to the Hughes government's amendments.

It remarked that proposals for amendment of the constitution had not been made until after the war and deduced from this that they had been put forward too late. Arguing from the assumption that preparations for national planning of the post-war order were 'an essential war-time task and an aid to the war effort,' and believing that on this occasion the urgency was greater because the problems of reconstruction were more complex, the government concluded that it would be folly to delay its plans until the war terminated. But since the very nature of its plans depended upon the extent of the constitutional power possessed by the Commonwealth, the government believed it had no alternative but to submit for approval the alterations which it regarded as essential for securing an orderly transition from war to peace. This decision to sponsor amendments amounted also to a rejection of the possible alternative procedure of co-operation. Past experience, both of the difficulty of attaining agreement between the states for the reference of powers to the Commonwealth and of the failure of the states to take common action once agreement

14a. *Commonwealth Parliamentary Debates*, lxxxix-xc, pp. 12841 sq.

had been reached, left the Commonwealth with little faith in the virtues of reference as an alternative to a grant of power by amendment.

The government's plea for additional powers, as presented in the Post-War Reconstruction pamphlet, was also buttressed by reference to the inadequacy of its existing authority in relation to such basic matters as employment, arbitration, price control, marketing and primary production. It was pointed out that the Commonwealth's industrial powers are limited, being confined in the main to section 51 (xxxv) (conciliation and arbitration for the prevention and settlement of industrial disputes extending beyond the limits of any one state) and to section 51 (i) (trade and commerce with other countries and among the states). The Commonwealth's war-time industrial regulation was therefore dependent almost entirely upon its war powers and it was recognised that in time of peace it would have no authority to prescribe general standards of hours or conditions. Lacking power to deal with the general regulation of industries it would have to rely to a large extent upon the states for the maintenance of employment when depression threatened. Its policy of training and placement would be jeopardised and the Commonwealth would face serious difficulties in fulfilling its war-time commitments in relation to such matters as 'the reinstatement of employees either voluntarily enlisted in or called up for the armed forces, and the resumption of apprenticeship agreements interrupted by war conditions.'[15]

Similarly, with regard to price control it was contended that in peace time no satisfactory scheme could be operated under the powers possessed by the Commonwealth.[16] War-time price control had also depended for its validity largely upon the defence power. In peace the Commonwealth would still be able, if it wished, to retain a system of import licensing, and might be able to make limited use of its trade and commerce power. But the authority conferred under this power is not only confined to overseas and inter-state trade but is also restricted by the operation of section 92 which asserts that 'trade commerce and intercourse among the states shall be absolutely free.' Moreover, experience has shown that if price control is to operate with reasonable equity it must rest upon national powers. Since the Commonwealth in peace time does not possess the requisite authority no successful

15. *A Case for Greater Commonwealth Powers*, p. 20.
16. *Ibid.*, pp. 21-24.

scheme can be implemented. The states cannot effectively fill the breach for they suffer from similar disabilities since their area of control is limited and they, too, are subject to the provisions of section 92. Yet contrasted with this absence of power was the evident need to control prices in the immediate post-war period if the community was to be protected against inflationary tendencies and profiteering. As the government saw the position 'the alternative to Commonwealth powers is inflation of prices, profiteering, ruination of many merchants and the old tragic story of alternate boom and slump.'[17]

Considerable stress was also laid on the inadequacy of Commonwealth power in relation to the marketing and stabilisation of primary products. War-time powers had enabled such schemes to operate but with their curtailment primary producers would discover that the methods of control which they themselves had advocated[18] would be based on a precarious constitutional foundation. Though it was admitted that some measure of control might be possible through a combination of the taxing power and the grants power, as for instance had been done in the wheat scheme of 1938, it was pointed out that such plans were dependent to a large extent on effective co-operation from all the states and were simply cumbersome expedients designed to overcome constitutional obstacles in the way of a national scheme. 'They are precarious and complicated at the best, and are always liable to be held up to the pace of the slowest partner to the agreement. They will plainly be unequal to the many exigencies and changes of the post-war world.'[19] The obvious step, therefore, seemed to be to clothe the Commonwealth with adequate powers in the field of primary production.

An attempt was also made by government spokesmen, dictated no doubt to some extent by strategic considerations as to its propaganda value, to link the issue of constitutional amendment with the war aims and objectives of the United Nations. It was argued that the character of international obligations was changing and that far more emphasis was being placed upon social and economic matters. Australia had entered into solemn international commit-

17. *Ibid.*, p. 24.
18. *Ibid.*, p. 26 e.g. the decision reached at the 1942 conference of the Wool Executive of the Primary Producers' Association of Western Australia to request the Commonwealth government to secure an amendment of the constitution which would enable the stabilisation and marketing schemes for primary producers to be continued.
19. *Ibid.*, p. 26.

ments which could only be fully honoured through domestic action on the part of the national parliament.[20]   As evidence, it was possible to point to the articles of the Atlantic Charter, notably Article 5, 'They desire to bring about the fullest collaboration between all nations in the economic field, with the object of securing for all improved labour standards, economic advancement and social security;' to the 'four freedoms' especially the third, freedom from want; and to the pronouncements by statesmen of the Allied nations that from the sacrifice of war must come an improvement in the lot of the ordinary man.   To these objectives of social security and internal economic stability the Australian government had subscribed.   But it found that on many issues, intimately connected with social and economic security, action by the national government was either prevented or hampered by constitutional barriers.   The comparison was, therefore, made between a new world capable of construction by boldly conceived action and a constitution which had outlived its usefulness but which remained as an obstacle to further advance.

The government believed that the nature of the powers required by the Commonwealth could be ascertained through a consideration of the essential tasks confronting the nation.   A fair indication of the role which the Commonwealth government wished to play may be discovered from the list of objectives provided by the authors of the *Case for Greater Commonwealth Powers*:

It will be necessary—

(1) to find employment for, and place in suitable occupations, the members of the fighting and associated services;

(2) to transfer from war work those no longer required in war production;

(3) to provide continuous worth-while employment under decent conditions;

(4) to restore civil industry, which has been stripped and depleted for the task of war, in accordance with a plan for regional development of industry in the less industrialized states and in rural areas;

(5) to co-ordinate production, in kind and quantity, to meet the most urgent needs of Australia and of a war-shattered and impoverished world; to rebuild markets, at home and abroad; . . .

(6) to control prices and profits, to prevent the evils of chaotic prices and unscrupulous profiteers;

20. The dilatoriness or failure of Australia to ratify International Labour Conventions has been in no small measure due to the existence of a federal system.

(7) to develop the physical resources of Australia in order to help support a larger and more prosperous population; . . .

(8) to encourage the growth and settlement of population, and in its distribution to avoid the evils of congested and over-crowded cities;

(9) to use and adapt for peace purposes much of the organisation that has been set up for the war effort;

(10) to fulfill and share with other peace-loving peoples the duty of the peace so dearly bought.[21]

Fundamentally, the government's case for greater Commonwealth powers rested on the belief that these objectives were unattainable without a considerable measure of government planning and control. Economic confusion was seen as the alternative to a planned economy. National standards were regarded as essential for all Australians.

The tasks of reconstruction will be as difficult and complex as those of war. They will require the same mobilisation of our economic, industrial and intellectual resources. Only by such action can our promises be fulfilled.[22]

The Curtin government finally decided to sponsor specific proposals for amendment of the constitution in the direction of vastly increased Commonwealth powers and on 1 October 1942 the Attorney-General, Dr. Evatt, brought his *Constitution Alteration (War Aims and Reconstruction)* 1942 bill before the House of Representatives. The title was itself an indication of the government's motive in pressing for amendment, while Dr. Evatt's speech embodied the arguments which were later expounded in the Post-War Reconstruction handbook prepared for the Canberra Constitutional Convention. In his speech Dr. Evatt stressed the contraction of Commonwealth power which would take place with the return of peace and the inadequacy of Commonwealth authority in the face of the perplexing problems inevitably asso-

---

21. *Ibid.*, p. 86.
22. *Ibid.*, p. 87. Compare the views of the Parliamentary Joint Committee on social security. "It has been pointed out that Australian social services have tended to develop in a piecemeal fashion, that we have suffered from the lack of a general plan, that certain services have expanded in some states more than others, and that some states have spent much more per head than others. This is unjust, because all Australians should be able to obtain similar treatment wherever they live. The Committee is of opinion that the time has arrived for the working out of a comprehensive plan of social development, so that all future social services can be introduced as part of a pre-determined plan which will cater for the most urgent needs first." First Report, *Commonwealth Parliamentary Papers*, 1940-1, No. 48 (Group H). Quoted, *Ibid.*, pp. 150-1.

ciated with a transition from war to peace. The constitution was out-dated and would be found an inadequate instrument for the solution of contemporary social and economic issues. Moreover, the Commonwealth had given specific pledges both international and domestic, which could only be honoured if Commonwealth powers were expanded.

The method of alteration adopted in the bill was not to add to or alter the powers contained in sections 51 and 52 since this it was thought would be confusing. Instead it was proposed to insert in Chapter 1, after Part V., a new part—Part VI.—War Aims and Post-War Reconstruction—which would enumerate the additional powers to be conferred on the Commonwealth. Attention was drawn by Dr. Evatt to certain special features of the proposed amendments.[23]   Of these, the most significant were the incorporation into the constitution of authority to implement the war aims and objects of the United Nations, the provision that none of the limitations contained in the rest of the constitution should apply to the powers contained in the new section 60 (A) and the proposal to prevent the High Court from pronouncing legislation under the new powers invalid by conferring on parliament the right to make any law 'which in the declared opinion of the Parliament will tend to achieve economic security and social justice.'

The special powers enumerated in Part VI., 60 A (2) were as follows:

(a) The reinstatement and advancement of those who have been members of the fighting services of the Commonwealth during the war and of the dependents of such members who have died or been disabled as a consequence of the war;

(b) employment, including the transfer of workers from war-time industries;

(c) the development of the country and the expansion of production and markets;

(d) the production and manufacture of goods and the supply of goods and services, and the establishment and development of industries;

(e) prices of goods and services, including their regulation and control;

(f) profiteering;

(g) the encouragement of population;

(h) carrying into effect the guarantee of the four freedoms, that is to say—

(i) freedom of speech and expression;

(ii) religious freedom;

23. *Commonwealth Parliamentary Debates,* clxxii, 1338-1341.

(iii) freedom from want; and

(iv) freedom from fear;

(i) national works and services, including water conservation and irrigation, afforestation and the protection of the soil;

(j) the improvement of living standards in both rural and urban areas;

(k) transport, including air transport;

(l) national health and fitness;

(m) the housing of the people; and

(n) child welfare.[24]

Dr. Evatt asserted that the proposals were not looked upon by the government as a party measure, that their present form was not regarded as final and that criticisms and suggestions would be invited from the states, the federal opposition parties and other interested citizens. There was certainly no lack of response to this invitation. Criticism in the main centred about the vague and indefinable nature of the terminology in which the Commonwealth's proposed powers were couched, and was fed by the suspicion that the language was so broad as to give the Commonwealth virtually unrestricted power—that these proposals in effect meant the end of the federal era in Australia. By attempting to write 'the war aims and objectives of Australia as one of the United Nations' into the constitution Dr. Evatt had laid himself open to the kind of criticism voiced by Mr. Menzies at the Constitutional Convention when referring to the first (subsequently abandoned) bill.

Every one sitting here will at once agree, whatever his views on our war aims may be, that that is an expression incapable of definition, the meaning of which is utterly impossible of ascertainment. Who is to say what our war aims are? They range from the blunt, forthright view of the man who says, 'My aim is to win and wipe out the Germans,' to the remote view of the man who says, 'My aim is a special Utopia of which I can provide the plans and specifications at a moment's notice.' Between those two extremes you can get hundreds of accounts of what the war aims of Australia as one of the United Nations must be.[25]

Persistent objection was also raised both against the proposal to release the powers in the new section 60 (A) from the limitations contained in the rest of the constitution and against the suggestion to exempt legislation which parliament had declared

24. Bill introduced by the Right Honourable H. V. Evatt, the Attorney-General, and read a first time in the House of Representatives, 1 October 1942.

25. *Record of Proceedings*, Canberra Convention 1942, pp. 21-2.

would facilitate the achievement of economic security and social justice from the interpretation of a High Court which in Mr. Menzies' words would be 'not abolished, but out of work.'

Amid the clamour of criticism, voices were also raised favouring constructive amendments. Of these the best supported was the demand for a more effective guarantee of both religious freedom and freedom of speech and expression—a demand which was met by the insertion of constitutional guarantees in the bill[26] presented by Dr. Evatt to the constitutional convention.

Haunted by the memory of repeated Commonwealth failures to secure amendments in the past, the sponsors of the 1942 proposals made a determined bid to win as widespread support as possible for increased Commonwealth powers from both the states and rival political parties. Above all, it was desired to avoid converting a constitutional issue into either a political fight or a struggle between the states on the one hand and the Commonwealth on the other. These considerations probably induced the government to decide upon the calling of a constitutional convention to discuss suggested alterations. From the government's standpoint, such a move had much to commend it. In view of the enormous difficulty of securing amendment under Australian conditions, it would obviously be of great advantage if the government could present to the electors proposals which had the approval of a convention attended by delegates from both the states and the Commonwealth. The summoning of a convention could also be represented as a return to the method which had been successfully used to bring about federation.   .

If the attempt to imitate past procedure was seriously intended it can only be said that those responsible for the summoning of the Canberra convention would have been wise to pay more attention to a study of the process whereby federation was achieved. The 1942 Convention was a gathering of 'professional politicians' summoned on the invitation of the Commonwealth government. The Convention consisted of delegates representing on the one hand the federal government and the opposition in the federal parliament and on the other the premiers and opposition leaders in the various states. It was not a body elected by the people for the purposes of constitutional amendment and it could not claim to be genuinely representative. Whatever may be thought of the attitude adopted by Mr. Fadden at the convention, he was undoubtedly on solid ground when he claimed that there was small similarity between the conventions which had met to frame

26. *Ibid.*, pp. 11-2.

a constitution for Australia and that which now sat to deliberate upon its amendment.

It would be consistent with the history and the spirit of the Australian Constitution if a specially elected Constitution Convention were to be assembled to make recommendations to the people concerning the extra powers which should be granted to the Commonwealth Parliament.[27]

Not only would an elected convention have possessed the authority denied to a nominated body but an opportunity would have been afforded for the people to elect as their representatives men who were not necessarily professional politicians yet were eminently fitted to deliberate on constitutional issues. Few would deny that the stature of the convention would have been increased by the inclusion of such men as Sir Isaac Isaacs, Sir Robert Garran and Professor K. H. Bailey—to name only some of the distinguished constitutional experts who might have been persuaded to stand for election.

Dr. Evatt, when seeking an explanation of the fate of past referendums, reached the conclusion that defeats had been due to a failure to educate public opinion to the necessity for amendment. 'The fifteen proposals for the amendment of the Commonwealth Constitution were rejected because the people could not be reasonably sure how the powers would be exercised. What is needed is to tell people more about the objects to be achieved.'[28] Yet Dr. Evatt was heedless of his own advice. The various conventions held before federation were important instruments in the education of public opinion. A notable advance both in public interest and in the understanding of the issues involved is observable in the years between the holding of the first and last convention. An elected convention with candidates informing the people about the problems to be faced and their own attitude towards them might in 1942 well have produced fruitful results.

The time factor was also important. In the 'nineties the issues were discussed over several years. An opportunity was also provided for unofficial bodies such as the Australian Natives Association and various leagues advocating federation to educate the people to acceptance of a wider allegiance. At Canberra the convention met for little more than a week and had to discuss not the bill which had been previously circulated but a new measure altogether.

This in itself was a serious handicap to the deliberations of

27. *Ibid.*, p. 17.
28. *Commonwealth Parliamentary Debates*, clxxii, 1340.

the convention and more than one delegate echoed Mr. Hughes' astonishment at the procedure adopted by the government.

We were invited here to consider a bill which was submitted to the legislatures of the various states. They at least had a nodding acquaintance with it, and their representatives came here in the firm belief that that was what they had to consider, but, before a shot was fired, the Attorney-General discarded it, and pulled out from his sleeve an entirely new measure—a fifth ace.[29]

The Attorney-General in his explanation[30] to the convention dealt with the reasons which had prompted the substitution of a new measure and with the differences between the new and the old bill. Dominated by the desire to secure increased powers for the Commonwealth the government believed that it was sound strategy to attempt to meet the major criticisms directed against its original proposals. It also hoped by the incorporation of other suggestions to endow the amendments with greater popular appeal. The more important modifications of the original bill related to those points against which criticism had been loudest. First, the authority of the High Court to interpret the Commonwealth's grant of power was to apply to proposed post-war powers as well as to those already in existence. Secondly, the sub-section (60A (3)) stating that the new Commonwealth powers 'might be exercised notwithstanding anything contained elsewhere in this Constitution or in the Constitution of any State' was modified. This sub-section had been inserted mainly in order to circumvent the difficulties occasioned by the existence of section 92, but it also released the Commonwealth from other limitations incorporated in the constitution. In the new bill the sub-section was limited to the exemption of marketing and price-fixation legislation from the operation of section 92. Thirdly, the terms in which the main grant of power to the Commonwealth were stated were considerably altered. The original proposal which had conferred power on the Commonwealth parliament to legislate 'for the purpose of carrying into effect the war aims and objects of Australia as one of the United Nations' had been attacked on the ground that the language employed was far too indefinite. With the object of rendering the grant of powers more specific 'for the purposes of post-war reconstruction' was substituted in place of 'the war aims and objects of Australia as one of the United Nations.' But since post-war reconstruction itself required some definition, or at least illustration, it was provided

29. *Record of Proceedings*, Canberra Convention 1942, p. 34.
30. *Ibid.*, pp. 7-10.

that, without limiting the generality of the expression, parliament should have authority to legislate upon twelve specific subject matters.[31]

Two other modifications of some significance were also introduced. Constitutional guarantees of religious freedom and freedom of speech and of the press were inserted in the new bill, while co-operation between the Commonwealth and the states was to be facilitated by the incorporation of a new sub-section empowering the Commonwealth parliament to

make laws authorizing any State or any Minister, officer or instrumentality of a State, or any local authority constituted under a law of a State, to assist in the execution of any power conferred on the Parliament by the section.[32]

Confronted by the government's proposals it was obvious from the start that there was little unanimity of outlook among the delegates to the convention. The majority were unable to adopt a national outlook and the fact that they were gathered together at a constitutional convention to consider alterations to the Australian governmental structure did not mean that they were able to shed their traditional outlook or politics. While agreeing that additional powers were required by the Commonwealth the representatives of the federal opposition betrayed a deep-seated suspicion of the government's designs. Both Mr. Fadden and Mr. Menzies protested against the consideration of fundamental changes in the constitution during war-time and considered that the proposed grant of power to the Commonwealth in the new bill was still too vast and too vaguely worded.

31. (a) The reinstatement and advancement of those who have been members of the fighting services of the Commonwealth during the war and of the dependents of such members who have died or been disabled as a consequence of the war;
(b) employment and unemployment, security of employment, the improvement of standards of living and the relations between employer and employee;
(c) trade, commerce and industry (including the production, manufacture and supply of goods and the supply of services);
(d) companies:
(e) investment;
(f) profiteering and prices;
(g) the marketing of goods;
(h) transport;
(i) national works;
(j) social services and social welfare;
(k) health and housing; and
(l) the protection of the aboriginal natives of Australia.
32. *Constitution Alteration (Post-war Reconstruction)* 1942 Bill. Proposed insertion Part VI 60A (3).

What is being submitted to the people (said Mr. Menzies) is a vague proposition, couched in ornate phrases, about post-war reconstruction, social justice and the like, concerning which the people are being told that if they do not give the Commonwealth parliament power they will never enjoy them. I submit that the issues are being put before the people in an entirely false light. The real issue, in fact, is whether the Commonwealth parliament shall be given an unrestricted, unconfined and uncontrolled power, and whether it shall be substantially freed from the operations of section 92, except in relation to 'intercourse.'[33]

Mr. Fadden, discerning cunningly camouflaged political designs beneath the proposals, did not hesitate to say so and labelled the draft bill 'a party document.'

The inclusion of the particular subjects enumerated in subsection 2 is nothing more or less than an attempt to embody in the Constitution, and as a paramount part of it, the political programme of the Australian Labour Party . . . and there is no doubt that under the amendment to the Constitution complete socialisation could be introduced in the guise of 'post war reconstruction.'[34]

Mr. Hughes, who throughout his career had consistently favoured an expansion of Commonwealth powers, was more co-operative, but he too condemned the old and the new bills as a violation of the basic principles of the federal pact. If unification were desired the government should have put forward proposals for the abolition of state parliaments and the assumption of full power by the Commonwealth. That at least would have been a straightforward proposal capable of being understood by the people. But instead, Dr. Evatt, said Mr. Hughes, 'adopts the strategy of the Trojan horse. The members of the Government come into the citadel and propose, upon the pretence of some innocent and beneficent purpose, to disembowel, to eviscerate, to emasculate the constitution, and to do all this while still posing as federalists.'[35]

The hostility displayed by the representatives of the federal opposition parties towards suggestions for constitutional amendment in the immediate future was sufficiently striking to invite comment by other delegates to the convention. Astonishment was expressed at what Mr. Cosgrove called the 'yes-but' attitude of members of this group, by which he meant that while the group admitted that the Commonwealth needed wider powers it was

33. *Record of Proceedings*, Canberra Convention 1942, p. 25.
34. *Ibid.*, p. 14.　　　　　　35. *Ibid.*, p. 34.

using all its ingenuity to discover reasons why no action should be taken. He believed that the motive for this opposition could be discovered in the unwillingness of the federal opposition to approve constitutional alterations which might pave the way for fundamental changes in the post-war period.

Underlying the speeches of the opponents of the Government's proposals is the desire to get back to the old order. Those who would retain the old order do not want to organize for post-war reconstruction, because they do not believe in it.[36]

Similar criticism of the obstructionist tactics employed by this group was voiced by Mr. Cooper, who argued that Messrs. Fadden, Menzies and Hughes, while professing to criticize what they regarded as objectionable features in the proposals were, in fact, intent on preventing amendment of any sort. 'Behind their efforts,' declared Mr. Cooper, 'to discredit the amendments, one felt that there was something deeper, something which the shallow thinker might not fathom. It was evident that their real purpose was to delay the taking of any effective action, and so they supported Mr. Fadden's proposal.'[37]

The attitude of the state representatives towards the proposals was to a large extent determined by their political convictions. Broadly, Labour premiers and Labour opposition leaders were in favour of some amendment conferring wider powers on the Commonwealth parliament, though all state delegates were emphatic that there was need, and opportunity, for much closer co-operation between the Commonwealth and the states. For instance, Mr. McKell, while supporting the bill, came out strongly in favour of closer collaboration between all governments and their departments.

The results have been so beneficial that the co-operation found necessary in time of war should be continued when peace returns. With their existing organisations, there are many things that the States can do to assist the Commonwealth authorities. In that way, much can be done to avoid the centralisation which is so frequently associated with the concentration of powers in a central authority.[38]

The inveterate state-righters, notably Mr. Dunstan and Mr. Playford, were uncompromising in their hostility to the proposals. Both believed that the amendments would amount to a grant of plenary legislative power for the Commonwealth parliament and would sound the death knell of the states as important partners in the Australian governmental system. The Victorian premier

36. *Ibid*, p. 50.   37. *Ibid*., p. 44.   38. *Ibid*., p. 41.

also argued, with some vehemence, that the parliaments of the states would hardly be 'less efficient than would the Commonwealth Parliament in dealing with the problems of the future,'[39] and stressed that one pre-requisite of constitutional amendment was that the powers and functions of the states should be both 'clearly defined and properly safeguarded.'

Mr. Playford not only concurred in these views but also voiced his suspicions that the motive behind the proposals was political, that the Commonwealth government was seeking to achieve what amounted to unification with the object of 'forcing a system of state socialism upon the unsuspecting people of Australia.'[40]

At the conclusion of his initial speech to the convention Mr. Fadden moved the following resolution which, if carried, would have had the effect of postponing consideration of constitutional amendment until after the war:—

That, while this convention recognizes the need to confer increased powers upon the Commonwealth, it is of the opinion that the war pre-occupation of many hundreds of thousands of Australians (including those in the fighting services and prisoners of war) who have a vital interest in improved post-war conditions and a right to an informed vote, renders it impracticable to secure a deliberate judgment on the complex problem of such a fundamental change in the whole system of government in Australia as is proposed. Accordingly it expresses the view that:

(a) the war powers of the Commonwealth being very extensive, advantage should be taken of the opportunity during the war of securing practical experience in co-operative Commonwealth and state action in relation to social and economic questions; so that in due course specific constitutional changes may be made with the greatest possible knowledge;

(b) the consideration of what changes should be made in the Commonwealth Constitution to meet new circumstances should, at an appropriate date, be referred to an elective convention representative of the people.[41]

The essence of Mr. Fadden's proposal was, as Mr. Curtin pointed out, that no convention should be held during war-time, that the Commonwealth parliament should not submit proposals for amendment to the people while the war continued and that no steps should be taken prior to victory to provide the requisite constitutional machinery for coping with the problems of transition from war to peace.

Mr. Fadden's motion proposes that when the war ends, there shall be a hiatus before the people can be given an opportunity

39. *Ibid.*, p. 57.   40. *Ibid.*, p. 67.   41. *Ibid.*, p. 18.

to decide what power shall be given to the Commonwealth parliament. From the day the war ends until demobilisation commences we are to revert to a condition of affairs which has been described as impossible, namely, the pre-war limitations of Commonwealth powers.[42]

Once Mr. Fadden had moved his resolution it appeared as though the convention might suffer early shipwreck, especially as support for his proposal was forthcoming from subsequent speakers, e.g. Mr. Menzies and Mr. Hughes. But a way out was found by the suggestion that instead of a war-time referendum there should be a reference of powers by the states. This suggestion was first placed before the convention by Mr. Hughes. The former war-time Prime Minister, though supporting Mr. Fadden's view that a referendum was inadvisable at the moment and, in a typically Hughesian speech, trenchantly criticising the government's approach to the question of constitutional alteration, went on to express the hope that 'some satisfactory via media' might be found which would enable specific powers required for purposes of post-war reconstruction to be conferred on the Commonwealth. He suggested that a solution of the difficulty might be discovered if the states should prove willing to refer powers to the Commonwealth and urged the convention to give serious consideration to this method of procedure.

Mr. Hughes' proposal was taken up by the Tasmanian premier, Mr. Cosgrove, who, while hostile to the idea of a referendum in war-time, was convinced that the Commonwealth would require considerably expanded powers to enable it to cope satisfactorily with the highly complex problems of the immediate post-war years. Mr. Cosgrove's strategy was to discover middle ground, to take up a position which would meet the major objections of the critics of the government's proposals yet at the same time would permit some action to be taken by the convention. Mr. Cosgrove, therefore, moved the following amendment to Mr. Fadden's motion:

That all words after 'that' be deleted with a view to inserting the following words:—

This Convention is of opinion that—

(a) Adequate powers to make laws in relation to post-war reconstruction should be conferred on the Parliament of the Commonwealth;

(b) It is undesirable that permanent alterations of the Constitution should be effected at this critical stage in Australia's history;

42. *Ibid.*, p. 18.

(c) For this reason, legislative powers with respect to suitable additional matters in relation to post-war reconstruction should be referred to the Parliament of the Commonwealth by the Parliaments of the States under section 51 (xxxvii) of the Constitution;

(d) Such reference should be for a period of seven years from the cessation of hostilities and should not be revoked during that period;

(e) At the end of such period of seven years, or at an earlier date, a referendum should be held to secure the approval of the electors to the alteration of the Constitution on a permanent basis.[43]

Mr. Cosgrove's amendment was astutely framed. It affirmed, what even the critics of the government's proposals had conceded, that greater powers were required by the Commonwealth. At the same time, by avoidance of a war referendum it met one of the chief objections voiced at the convention. Those who feared that the proposed amendments would entail unification were mollified by the procedure of reference and even more by the time limit which was to be placed on the operation of the powers. Yet hope was not denied to those who wished for permanent alteration to the constitution, since after a period of experiment in the use of the expanded powers the people were to pass judgment by referendum.

It would be idle to assert that the federal government's representatives were enthusiastic about the procedure of reference by the states under section 51 (xxxvii) of the constitution, or that they would not have preferred the endorsement of the proposals which Dr. Evatt had placed before the convention. For one thing, they were only too well aware that in the past such attempts had almost invariably proved unsatisfactory. As Mr. Forde pointed out:

One was tried in 1915 when the States agreed to refer certain powers to the Commonwealth until after the war. It came to nothing. The undertakings given by the Premiers at the conference were not upheld by their Parliaments. Again, in 1920, the States agreed to transfer powers relating to air navigation. Only one State fully honoured the agreement; the rest did nothing at all or did less than they had promised. The whole proposal ended chaotically.[44]

He believed that there were two serious weaknesses in procedure by reference, one being that no state would 'readily surrender real power and authority' and the other that guarantees

43. *Ibid.*, p. 53.   44. *Ibid.*, p. 97.

given by one government were not necessarily binding on subsequent governments.

Nevertheless government supporters, and notably the Prime Minister himself, realised that it was preferable to take what one could get rather than jeopardise agreement by adhering too rigidly to the government's proposals. Mr. Curtin was sensible of the advantage of putting before the people changes which had the sanction of the unanimous approval of the convention. Indeed, without detracting from the important preparatory work performed by Dr. Evatt, it is clear that what success the convention did achieve was largely due to patient and skilful handling by Mr. Curtin, who, throughout its sessions, sought to maintain the debate on a national and non-partisan level. When tempers grew hot and the main issues tended to become blurred, Mr. Curtin repeatedly intervened in order to keep before the convention the serious task for which it had been assembled. He invariably sought to discover what measure of general agreement could be reached, and showed a willingness to adopt whatever procedure seemed likely to yield the most worthwhile results. When, for instance, the government proposals encountered heavy weather and it was not unlikely that the deliberations of the convention would prove abortive, Mr. Curtin by intervening displayed his readiness to abandon the government's proposals rather than see the convention conclude without accomplishing its purpose:

If it likes the Convention can scrap the whole draft bill and, starting with a plain sheet of paper, settle down to the business of deciding what readjustment of Commonwealth and State powers is necessary to meet changing conditions in the world.[45]

The same determination to discover the extent of possible agreement is reflected in Mr. Curtin's summary of the real issues before the convention:

1. (a) Is the Convention in favour of increased Commonwealth powers for post-war reconstruction?
   (b) If the answer be 'yes', what powers should be granted?
2. To give effect to the foregoing, what measures should be adopted, viz:
   (a) Referendum involving Commonwealth legislation.
   (b) Reference, involving State legislation.
      or
   (c) Postponement.[46]

Once it had become apparent that there was considerable support for conferring increased powers on the Commonwealth by way of reference from the states, Mr. Curtin announced the government's

45. *Ibid.*, p. 68.   46. *Ibid.*, p. 136.

willingness to accept Mr. Cosgrove's amendment both because it had the support of the convention and because it made immediate action possible.   Since, however, procedure by reference had been unsuccessful in the past Mr. Curtin declared that he would only be willing to adopt the proposal if certain conditions were observed.   These were that the powers granted should be adequate to cope with the problems of the post-war reconstruction period; that the period of the grant should be sufficiently long; that provision should be made to prevent any revocation of the grant without the approval of the electors in any state; that the present convention should recommend the powers to be granted and should frame a draft bill; that the premiers and opposition leaders in the states should agree to support the passage of the draft bill into law; and that the draft bill should become law within a comparatively short period.

In view of past experience such conditions appear eminently reasonable and they won the whole-hearted support of Mr. Hughes, among others.

I am glad that Mr. Curtin has adopted the principles which are set out in Mr. Cosgrove's amendment, but I think he is right to attach to it the conditions which he mentioned. . . . I say that it is proper that the Commonwealth should know what are its powers, and that if it agrees to accept a reference of powers, it must have some assurance that the grant will be adequate, and that it must not be revocable at will and in so short a time as to defeat the purpose for which it was made.[47]

After the announcement by Mr. Curtin of the government's acceptance of the Cosgrove amendment, events moved rapidly. The convention unanimously resolved to adopt the Cosgrove formula with the modification that the period of reference should be 'not less than five years and not more than seven years from the cessation of hostilities.'   Mr. Curtin expressed the view that it was the duty of the convention to determine the specific powers which should be referred to the Commonwealth by the states, and suggested that the convention should appoint a drafting committee to consider just what powers would be adequate to the Commonwealth's needs.   His proposal was adopted and the convention appointed a committee of eight, consisting of the premier of each state and Dr. Evatt and Mr. Hughes as Commonwealth representatives.

After deliberations extending over two days, the drafting committee reported that its recommendations were unanimous, and submitted for the convention's consideration a draft bill which,

47. *Ibid.*, p. 138.

when enacted, would be given the title of the *Commonwealth Powers Act* 1942. Its more important features were stressed in speeches by Dr. Evatt and Mr. Hughes, who respectively moved and seconded a motion that the convention give its approval to the draft bill. The committee had agreed that fourteen matters should be referred by the states and that any dispute as to the interpretation to be given to each head of power should be determined by the High Court. In order to meet the demand, voiced at earlier sessions of the convention, that there should be in the post-war years close co-operation between Commonwealth and state authorities, a declaration was inserted in the preamble of the draft bill enjoining the Commonwealth to enlist the assistance of state governments and their instrumentalities in the administration of legislation passed by the Commonwealth under any of the referred powers.

The period during which the powers would operate was fixed at five years from the termination of hostilities. This was a shorter period than originally suggested by Mr. Cosgrove but the contraction was to some extent offset by the provision that the grant of power should commence as soon as the bills had been passed by the state legislatures. Safeguards were also inserted to prevent, as far as possible, any revocation of the grant of power during the agreed period by providing that the bill should not be amended or repealed unless the electors in the state concerned had first given their approval. Finally, Dr. Evatt announced that the state premiers had promised to exert every effort to secure the passage of the bill through their respective parliaments.[48]

48. The fourteen subject matters to be referred to the Commonwealth parliament were these:
   (a) The reinstatement and advancement of those who have been members of the fighting services of the Commonwealth during the war and the advancement of the dependents of those members who have died or been disabled as a consequence of the war;
   (b) employment and unemployment;
   (c) organised marketing of commodities;
   (d) uniform company legislation;
   (e) trusts, combines and monopolies;
   (f) profiteering and prices (but not including prices or rates charged by State or semi-governmental or local governing bodies for goods or services);
   (g) the production (other than primary production) and distribution of goods, and, with the consent of the Governor-in-Council, primary production, but so that no law made under this paragraph shall discriminate between States or parts of States;
   (h) the control of overseas exchange and overseas investment; and the regulation of the raising of money in accordance with such plans as

When the motion recommending approval of the draft bill was placed before the convention, it at once became apparent that a good deal of dissatisfaction about the procedure being adopted was felt by members of the convention who had not been included on the drafting committee. This was especially pronounced in the case of the leaders of the opposition parties in the various states who protested that the convention as a whole was not being given any opportunity 'for serious and detailed consideration'[49] of the draft bill. They objected to Dr. Evatt's omission to deliver an explanatory speech setting out the reasons which had induced the committee not only to include specific powers but also to frame them in the language adopted in the bill. As Mr. Nicklin demonstrated, it was essential that state opposition leaders should possess full information about the reasons which had prompted unanimous acceptance of the selected powers if they were to assist in the passage of legislation through the state parliaments. It was this same failure to provide for adequate discussion which provoked Mr. Baker to say, 'I suggest that the Convention is proceeding in the right way to wreck any hope of success.'[50]

At this stage Mr. Curtin intervened once again and succeeded in dissipating the dissatisfaction of those who had not participated in the discussions of the drafting committee. After indicating how necessary it was that the convention should specify what it regarded as adequate powers if the state parliaments were to pass bills 'in identical terms', Mr. Curtin suggested that objections about inadequacy of debate could be removed if the convention adopted the report of the committee, suggesting approval of the draft bill, and then considered the bill clause by clause. This procedure was accepted with the result that, after debate and enquiries upon the implications of specific powers, approval was given to the committee's recommendation that the fourteen matters which it had listed should be referred to the parliament of the Commonwealth.

The convention, which at one stage seemed likely to end in

are approved by a majority of members of the Australian Loan Council;
(i) air transport;
(j) uniformity of railway gauges;
(k) national works, but so that the consent of the Governor-in-Council shall be obtained in each case before the work is undertaken and that the work shall be carried out in co-operation with the State;
(l) national health in co-operation with the States;
(m) family allowances; and
(n) the people of the aboriginal race.
49. *Ibid.*, p. 158.　　　　50. *Ibid.*, p. 158.

complete failure, therefore, concluded with the members in agreement not only upon the necessity of conferring wider powers on the Commonwealth but also upon the procedure which should be adopted to bring this about. The government's proposals had been jettisoned and a decision reached to avert a war-time referendum by adoption of the alternative procedure of reference of powers to the Commonwealth by the states. Even more important was the fact that the convention had achieved agreement on the nature of the powers to be referred and was able to make a unanimous recommendation on the subject matters for reference. Finally, a promise had been given by state members at the convention that they would support the necessary legislation in their respective state parliaments.

The results at first sight appeared impressive, as did the unanimity finally achieved. A feeling of optimism, even of elation and self-congratulation, engendered no doubt by the attainment of unanimous agreement where for long no agreement seemed possible, was reflected in the speeches during the concluding stages of the convention, especially in Mr. Curtin's:

That there should emerge from the drafting committee a unanimous submission to this convention is a great and splendid demonstration of Australia's capacity to deal with high political problems. It is, moreover, a tribute to the good sense of Australian leaders that since the submission of the committee's draft bill the debate has been directed towards making that instrument more constructive.[51]

"I think," said Mr. Fadden, "the bill that we have just passed can be accepted as a monument of co-operation, and as evidence of unselfishness and compromise on the part of every one, particularly those who have represented the States here."[52]

Despite such utterances, it might be argued that the appearance of unanimity was deceptive. The government's representatives, it is true, had finally accepted the suggestion of procedure by reference, but only when it had become apparent that its own proposals were unlikely to win the approval of the convention. Moreover, doubts as to the likelihood of obtaining satisfactory results through the method of reference cannot have been totally dispelled. Past failures clearly intimated that the attainment of enlarged Commonwealth powers through co-operative action among the states would not be easily achieved. The conditions, laid down by Mr. Curtin, upon which the government would be willing to give approval to Mr. Cosgrove's suggestion indicate that the government was aware of the dangers of procedure by reference.

51. *Ibid.*, p. 180.   52. *Ibid.*, p. 181.

Indeed, the final condition that 'the draft bill should be passed into law within a reasonably short period' reveals that the government did not intend to blind itself to the possibility of failure, since the implication underlying this condition was that if identical legislation was not passed by the states the government would be free to take alternative action.

The strategy of the government's representatives at the convention was, it seems, to accept what they could get rather than jeopardise the success of the convention by adhering too rigidly either to the government-sponsored proposals or to the procedure of amendment by referendum. There was, however, one important proviso to this attitude, namely, that the powers to be bestowed upon the Commonwealth, by whatever means, should be adequate to the Commonwealth's post-war needs. The government's policy was also based on the hope that, if specific proposals for enlarged Commonwealth powers could obtain the sanction of a convention representative of the main political parties in both the states and the Commonwealth, the convention's recommendations would carry sufficient prestige with the electorate to avoid any possibility that the issue might become either the subject of party struggle or a contest between the states and the Commonwealth. In short, the government's willingness to scrap its own proposals in favour of a compromise agreement was an expression of its desire to avoid conflict and ensure the passage of legislation which would have the approval of all political groups represented at the convention.

The unanimous support ultimately forthcoming from state representatives for the proposal to refer expanded powers to the Commonwealth was even more deceptive. It is at least open to doubt whether those state representatives, who had expressed such patent hostility to the government's proposals and such fervent championship of the rights and capacity of the states, were really converts to the wisdom of conferring, even if only temporarily, such wide powers on the Commonwealth. Their final readiness to support such a procedure was probably the result of the state of public opinion at the time. It is clear that in 1942 the tide was running strongly against the states and that the majority of people were in no mood to countenance obstruction on the part of state politicians. The attitude of state representatives at the convention was almost certainly tempered by the knowledge that a too uncompromising stand might well mean the immediate submission of proposals to abolish the states, with every prospect that they would be approved. Such considerations must be taken into account when evaluating the apparent solidarity of outlook achieved by the convention. Whether genuine or not at the time, it was a unanimity which had no lasting quality, for it failed to endure once a fluctuating public opinion made it politically practicable to adopt an antagonistic attitude to the plea for expanded Commonwealth powers.

The *Convention Bill* was submitted to the various state parliaments, but any hopes the Commonwealth government may have entertained that all the states would pass uniform legislation were soon dispelled. Some state houses showed a marked reluctance to transfer, even for a limited period, the fourteen powers which the convention had concluded that the Commonwealth would require in the immediate post-war years. At best, they were willing to support an emasculated bill with certain powers eliminated and others amended. The outcome was that New South Wales and Queensland both passed the *Powers Bill* in the terms agreed upon by the convention, while South Australia and Western Australia sanctioned amended legislation. Tasmania rejected the bill, and Victoria adopted the strategy of passing the bill with the proviso that it should not take effect until all other states had passed uniform legislation on the subject. Dr. Evatt, in particular, made repeated pleas that those states which had amended the list of powers, or failed to pass the necessary legislation, should reconsider their decision. A deaf ear was turned to his requests which made it plain that there was little likelihood of any transfer by the states of identical powers to the Commonwealth.

In order to end the prevailing confusion, the federal government decided to seek approval for expanded powers from the electors through a referendum. A bill to amend the constitution was, therefore, submitted by Dr. Evatt and ultimately passed by both houses. In so far as the specified powers were concerned it adhered closely to the draft Canberra Powers Bill, differences being confined simply to verbal changes 'rendered absolutely necessary in order to turn a bill for a State Act into a Commonwealth Bill for formal Constitutional alteration.'[53] Indeed, the government made it clear that its intention was to adopt not only the substance of the convention's recommendations but also, if possible, their precise form. The new bill, therefore, included provisions ensuring co-operation with the states, as well as a number of safeguards for state rights such as the reservation that

53. Dr. Evatt in the House of Representatives, 11 February 1944 (*Sydney Morning Herald*, 12 Feb. 1944).

proposed powers over primary production could only be exercised in any state with that state's consent. The grant of power to the Commonwealth was to be limited to a five year period.

In addition, however, to the fourteen powers drafted at the convention the bill contained guarantees for the maintenance of the fundamental freedoms of speech and religion and also certain safeguards designed to prevent bureaucratic excesses.[54]

Even after the bill had been approved by both houses, Dr. Evatt pointed out that the door was 'not irrevocably closed to action by the State Legislatures in accordance with the Canberra decision' and that it would still be possible to avoid a war-time referendum if all States passed uniform legislation. However, the states concerned chose to ignore this final appeal and the proposed alterations were submitted to the electors on 19 August 1944. The result of the poll was a heavy defeat of the amendments, majorities being secured in only two states.

	Yes	No
Queensland	216,262	375,862
New South Wales ..	759,211	911,680
Victoria	597,848	614,487
Tasmania	53,386	83,769
South Australia	196,294	191,317
Western Australia ..	140,399	128,303
	1,963,400	2,305,418

What can account for the heavy defeat at the referendum in 1944 of proposals sponsored by a Labour party which had won a striking victory in the elections of the previous year? Certainly no simple explanation, such as the machinations of the opposition, or the unwillingness of the electorate to confer wider powers on the Commonwealth, carries conviction. The causes responsible for defeat were complex and, though varying in importance, they interacted in such a way as to produce a mental atmosphere of distrust which was unfavourable to the government's plea that wider Commonwealth powers were essential for the achievement of post-war stability.

The time factor was of vital importance because events demonstrated, beyond reasonable doubt, that the government had committed a grave error of strategy in not submitting amendments by referendum in 1942. In that year not only were the stocks

54. For the full provisions of the Constitution Alteration (Post-war Reconstruction and Democratic Rights) 1944 Bill see Appendix at end of chapter.

of the Commonwealth high but the prestige enjoyed by the states was lower than ever before—a position due in large measure, though not wholly, to war conditions and the gravity of the crisis confronting the country. In the face of threatened invasion, Australians were welded together as a nation and experienced a feeling of solidarity not customary under more normal conditions. Attention was focussed upon the Commonwealth and it was to the federal government that Australians everywhere looked for leadership. There was an almost total lack of interest in state activities, apart from a display of cynicism on those occasions when state politicians attempted to emphasise local as against national interests. State elections were followed by the electors with apathy and there is no doubt that the stand taken by the states over the question of uniform taxation was generally unpopular. This disinterest is partially explained by the subordinate position occupied by the states in the governmental structure during war-time, though the poor calibre of most state politicians and the growing belief that the day of the states was over also played their part. In the long run what may prove more important is the unlikelihood of the states recovering their pre-war prestige with a return to normal peacetime constitutional relations.

The Commonwealth missed its opportunity by not submitting alterations when its own prestige was high and that of the states low. The explanation of the government's failure to act must be found in its belief that the dismal record of past referendum defeats had convinced the government of the necessity of securing the sanction of all important political parties, whether state or federal, before placing proposals before the people. This endeavour to avoid controversy by securing prior agreement was responsible for the summoning of the Canberra convention, the decision to reject a referendum in favour of procedure by reference and the further delay involved in attempting to persuade the state legislatures to pass identical legislation. In an attempt to placate all possible opposition—a forlorn prospect at best—the Commonwealth government was forced into a policy of delay which proved fatal to its project.

Delay operated against the recording of a 'yes' vote in a variety of ways. In the first place, the gravity of the danger to the country diminished, and as it did so the sense of national unity declined. Vested interests of all kinds became increasingly vocal in their own defence, while particularist and localist tendencies regained much of their old vitality. Secondly, time was permitted for the organisation of a wide-spread and ably conducted campaign in opposition to the proposals. This began early, especially in the press of the less populous states, and continued with increasing vehemence up to the date of the referendum. Thirdly, between 1942 and 1944 anti-government and anti-Commonwealth feeling grew in volume as the public became increasingly restive under war-time restrictions.

If reliance can be placed on the results obtained by Australian Public Opinion Polls, there is little doubt that the submission of a referendum late in 1942 on the issue of the abolition of state parliaments, would have been successful. In November 1942, interviewers asked cross-sections of people in all states the question "Should State Governments be abolished—or continued?" with the result that of each 100 men and women interviewed,

  60 said 'Abolish State Governments';
  22 said 'Don't abolish them';
  11 were undecided; and
  7 (chiefly women) did not answer.

'Neither the age,' read the report, 'occupation, nor political affiliation of the people interviewed had a significant influence on their opinion, but sex and locality (State) did.

Among men the "Abolish" vote reached 71 per cent. compared with 50 per cent. for women, of whom 28 per cent were either undecided or unable to give an answer. The "Don't Abolish States" vote was 22 per cent for both men and women.

In New South Wales the "Abolish" vote was six to one, and in Queensland, Victoria and South Australia it exceeded two to one. In both Tasmania and Western Australia, however, half of those interviewed were against abolishing State Governments; about a quarter favoured abolition, and the rest were undecided.'[55]

Of great importance for the negative vote was the fact that the referendum followed several years in which war-time restrictions had been in operation. The government's stringent controls were felt to be increasingly irksome by the people, especially as the war showed a more favourable aspect. Not only were Australians unaccustomed to such regulation but they were aware, through personal experience, that the controls were not always administered with sympathy and efficiency. This, indeed, was almost inevitable, since the pre-war Commonwealth civil service was inadequate in numbers and in training to cope with the task of organising the nation for total war. Not only was it necessary to improvise and learn through mistakes, but the service itself

55. *The Sun* (Sydney), 26 November 1942.

had to be enormously and rapidly expanded. Under such circumstances, errors in administration were unavoidable, but they left a legacy of bitterness which was reflected in the size of the negative vote.

Viewed in this light a section of the 'No' vote can be regarded as a protest both against the government and against governmental regulation and administration. It was not so much a question of whether people believed the controls to be justified or unjustified, it was simply that the referendum provided an opportunity for expressing their irritation—often an irrational irritation, but none the less felt on that account. It was an opportunity for getting one back on the government and had little relation to the constitutional issues involved.

The government's tactics were again seriously at fault in so far as the method of submission to the electors was concerned.[56] By adopting an all or nothing attitude, by insisting that the electorate approve or reject all the fourteen points, the government was following a policy which made it reasonably certain that the referendum would fail. It is true that the powers submitted to referendum mirrored fairly exactly those which had been approved for reference by the convention and true also that there was much substance in the government's contention that the more important powers were so interconnected that the government's post-war plans would be jeopardised if one or more were sanctioned and others were not. At the same time, if it was necessary to submit a list of powers—and alternative methods had much to commend them—it would, from a practical point of view, have been wiser to submit each for separate approval. The procedure adopted must have placed many electors in a dilemma. Mr. Jones might well have favoured, say, points six and eight, but found himself opposed to the remainder, while Mr. Smith might have been in the position of approving nearly all the points but of objecting vehemently to one or two. In such cases the balance of probability is that both Mr. Jones and Mr. Smith would vote against the proposals as a whole rather than sanction the Commonwealth acquisition of powers of which they disapproved. It is not unreasonable to suppose that if the government had submitted its points for separate approval it would have secured the passage of a number of vital powers even if one or two fell by the wayside. Indeed, there is some ground for believing that it was the insertion of point (ii), employment and

56. This point is ably expounded by Ian Milner, "Referendum Retrospect" (*The Australian Quarterly*, December 1944).

unemployment, in a list which had to be approved or rejected as a whole that was basically responsible for the defeat of the proposals. At best it might be said that its insertion was responsible for much of the negative vote among soldiers. Having been subjected to army discipline for several years, many soldiers had no intention of conferring on the Commonwealth government a power which seemed to imply a right of direction in employment after their discharge.

The referendum and its outcome also posed in an acute form two interrelated questions of profound importance. Is it possible in a modern industrialised and capitalist society to examine proposals envisaging important constitutional changes in a non-controversial way? Is a referendum a satisfactory method of dealing with proposed constitutional amendments?

It is often contended that it should be possible to examine proposed changes in the constitution on their merits, and form a judgment in the light of the experience of the working of the existing system with its revelation of the adequacy or otherwise of the powers possessed by the central authority. If the lack of power is evident and the need for increased authority obvious, one would expect that this would be recognised by all sections of the community and by all organised political groups. On this view, constitutional questions should not be closely related to the question of the political use which may be made of the powers by the particular party which becomes the government. It is argued, with much force, that the question of the use to be made of any powers entrusted to the Commonwealth is a purely political issue which can be decided at the polls. If the electors dislike socialisation, or disapprove of private enterprise as the basis of the economy, they have their opportunity to express this disapprobation by voting against the party espousing views to which they object.

On this thesis, once general agreement has been reached that the powers possessed by the central government are inadequate to its needs it should be possible to remedy constitutional defects without the distraction of argument about the use which any political party may make of the Commonwealth's expanded authority. The direction of policy can be left as a purely political issue for decision at the elections. But one difficulty about such a view is that experience has shown that amendment by referendum does not lend itself to an easy divorce between constitutional and political issues. In the case of the 1944 referendum the government had specifically sought to ensure that the question would be discussed in a non-political way. It had moreover at least some grounds for believing that its efforts would be successful. All Commonwealth party leaders had at different times expressed their belief in the necessity for greater Commonwealth powers, while at the convention all the state premiers and opposition leaders had not only agreed that wider powers were required but had also affirmed their support for a specific list of subject matters on which Commonwealth authority was inadequate. Nevertheless, when the time came to submit proposals for popular approval, it was clearly demonstrated that the anti-Labour political leaders and their parties were not willing to regard constitutional questions as non political. Instead they insisted that the proposals sponsored by the Labour government were designed, not so much to clothe the Commonwealth with authority to meet the needs of the post-war period as to free the Labour Party from constitutional obstacles standing in the way of the implementation of its party programme. In short, the opponents of the referendum directed their heaviest artillery not so much against the proposed powers themselves as against the use which might be made of them by a Labour government.

Supporters of a 'No' vote were in this respect much more astute in their understanding of the psychology of the electorate than their opponents. The campaign demonstrated that the majority of people were not greatly concerned about the weaknesses in the constitution, as revealed by its operation, but that they were vitally interested in the practical question of what programme the government intended to carry out if it were given the powers requested. Opponents of the proposals, aware of this attitude of mind, exploited their opportunity to the full by playing upon the fears of many in the community that a 'Yes' vote would mean a curtailment of individual freedom, regulation by government departments and full-blooded socialisation. The 'Yes' advocates, despite the fact that they should have had weapons ready to their hands in the shape of detailed plans the implementation of which depended on the passage of the referendum, inexplicably failed to counter their opponents' charges with any effectiveness. Government spokesmen neglected to reveal, except in broad and rather vague terms, what their programme for reconstruction would entail. In short, they failed[57] signally to inform the people on the vital question of what use would be made of the powers, and, by neglecting to do so, they created a climate favourable to the growth of the suspicions engendered by those seeking a negative

57. *Ibid.*, p. 45.

result. In addition, government spokesmen, as the campaign developed, instead of concentrating upon an exposition of the practical use to which the powers would be put, themselves stooped to misrepresentation by implying that the loss of the referendum would endanger Commonwealth social benefits such as the payment of Child Endowment. Such tactics were on the whole easy to refute and simply provided additional points of attack for the opposition.

The character of the campaign conducted by opponents of the proposals was also an important reason for an adverse decision. Much has been made of the inconsistency displayed by members of the federal opposition parties, because, though vocal in their past utterances on the need for greater national powers, they ultimately decided to urge the defeat of the Government's proposals. Similar charges of inconsistency have been levelled against those state premiers who fought campaigns on behalf of a negative vote after agreeing at the convention that wider powers for the Commonwealth were essential. Certainly their inconsistency, in both cases, was sufficiently striking to invite comment. Mr. Menzies and Mr. Dunstan provide outstanding instances. Mr. Menzies had repeatedly pronounced himself in favour of greater Commonwealth powers. When Attorney-General he delivered a striking speech in the House of Representatives on 22 November 1938 in which he listed as 'grievous anomalies' eight instances which showed clearly that the distribution of power under the Constitution was defective and that greater authority was 'required from the nation for this National Parliament.' In view of his subsequent stand during the 1944 referendum it is instructive to note that on the same occasion Mr. Menzies also delivered an eloquent plea that constitutional problems should be considered in a non-controversial spirit. 'If we are to deal with these problems of national power, we must shut our eyes and minds completely to all idea of which party is putting forward, or of what such and such a party will do if such and such powers are granted.'[58] Mr. Dunstan's inconsistency lay perhaps more in his support for the proposals agreed upon at the convention than in his subsequent hostility to the referendum, since his whole political career had demonstrated that he was a fervent champion of the rights of the states. Nevertheless, Mr. Dunstan had been a member of the drafting committee which unanimously submitted subject matters, upon which it was believed Commonwealth power was inadequate, for approval by the convention and ultimately for

58. *Commonwealth Parliamentary Debates*, clviii, 1821.

reference by the states. His change of front during the campaign, when he argued that the success of the referendum would mean the virtual destruction of the states, was in itself sufficiently remarkable.

Though such inconsistency undeniably existed, it is doubtful if it should have occasioned the surprise it evidently did in some quarters. Experience should have informed those seeking a 'Yes' vote that little else could be expected. As Mr. Hughes pointed out at the convention, 'every proposal to amend the Constitution put forward by the Government has been strongly resisted by the Opposition parties. In 1919 the Labour Party opposed the amendments they had advocated in 1911, 1913 and 1915. And the attitude of the non-Labour parties was not less inconsistent.'[59] Again, referring to the attitude adopted by the opposition toward the Scullin government's 1930 proposed amendments, Mr. Hughes, speaking in the House of Representatives, declared:' . . . I have heard from this side of the chamber the most amazing confessions of inconsistency from those whose voices had been raised trumpet-tongued in favour of constitutional amendment. They were still in favour of amending the constitution, but they were against the amendments because the government had introduced them.'[60] It is apparent that whichever party happens to be in opposition has believed, even when confronted with constitutional problems, that its function was to oppose.

In the absence of adequate government explanation of the programme which it intended to apply if the referendum succeeded, the opponents of a 'Yes' vote were able to concentrate upon the possible ways in which a Labour government might abuse increased federal powers. Through press,[61] radio, and the public platform, the opposition imputed ulterior motives to those sponsoring the referendum and implied that, under the cloak of a plea for powers for post-war reconstruction, a gigantic conspiracy was being engineered to rob the nation of its freedom. It can hardly be denied that the character of the opposition campaign was prejudicial to any impartial consideration of the government's proposals. So far from adopting the approach advocated by Mr. Menzies in 1938, when he said, 'we must shut our eyes and minds completely to all idea of which party is putting them (amendments)

59. *Record of Proceedings*, Canberra Convention, 1942, p. 33.
60. Quoted by Mr. Hughes at the convention (*ibid.*)
61. The vast majority of Australian papers came out in opposition to the proposals and though past election results have shown that the power of the press to influence public opinion can be exaggerated this newspaper opposition presumably swelled the size of the negative vote.

forward, or of what such and such a party will do if such and
such powers are granted,' the advocates of a 'No' vote dissemi-
nated highly coloured political and emotional propaganda which
rendered any reasonably objective approach to the proposals impossible.[62]   The 'No' case was presented in such a way that the
real issues were distorted beyond recognition.   Electors were told
that their choice lay between regimentation by bureaucrats reluctant to shed their war-time authority and the (largely undefined)
freedom of the individual to follow his own legitimate interests in
an economy in which there would be ample rewards for industry
and initiative.   Freedom, with all its emotional appeal, was inscribed on the opposition banner by those who, because of their
antagonism to a planned economy, now acquired a new devotion
to the cause of individual liberty.   The Commonwealth government was hailed as a tyrant bent on depriving the individual of
his traditional freedoms by constructing a society in which industrial conscription, manpower direction and curtailment of choice
of livelihood would have full play.   Nor was the mischief undone
when government spokesmen said in reply that freedom interpreted in terms of absence of restriction was all too often meaningless.   Both Mr. Curtin and Dr. Evatt attempted, by way of
defence, to show that if freedom were to have a positive content
it could only be enjoyed in a society in which adequate economic
opportunity existed for at least the majority of its members.   'If,'
said Mr. Curtin, 'freedom meant positive opportunity, opportunity
for the many, not merely for the few; opportunity to work at a
job that was reasonably paid and secure; opportunity to enjoy
the improving standards of living which the rising productivity
of labour made possible; opportunity to share in the adventure
and achievement of building Australia, then to vote "Yes" was to
vote for freedom.'[63]

The 'No' campaign was also in part inspired and financed by
organised bodies, which had a vested interest in the retention of
the federal system.   Both the United States and Canada have provided evidence that those who control powerful financial and business institutions believe that their activities are more likely to
escape effective governmental supervision under a political system
in which the authority of all governments is limited.   For this
reason they have been active in their efforts to prevent the aboli-

62. Compare the divergent views expressed on the nature of the opposition
     campaign and on financial backing for the campaign by Ian Milner,
     Australian Quarterly, Dec. 1944, and J. L. Paton, *Australian Quarterly*,
     March 1945.
63. Quoted Milner, *Australian Quarterly*, Dec. 1944.

tion or modification of the prevailing federal systems. The referendum furnished confirmation of the existence of the same attitude
in Australia. The Chamber of Commerce, the Associated Chamber of Manufacturers, the Constitutional League and important
organised pastoral bodies all[64] came out strongly in opposition to
the proposals and worked consistently for their defeat.

While the organisers of the 'No' campaign did undoubtedly stoop
to misrepresentation of the most flagrant sort—and this playing
upon the fears of the electors was one of the reasons for the
referendum defeat—it would be inaccurate to infer, as Milner
appears to do, at least by implication, that all opposition to the
amendments was due to interested motives of the kind which
inspired the hostility of those who felt their economic position to
be jeopardised. Account must also be taken of the fact that a
not insignificant percentage of those advocating a 'No' vote did
so from the genuinely held conviction that to sanction the demands of the Commonwealth government for increased powers
would not be to the advantage of the country as a whole. Here
again the reasons for opposition were varied. Some, who sincerely
believed that the retention of a federal system was desirable for a
country as vast as Australia, were afraid that the success of the
referendum would mean an important step in the direction of unification; others held the view that, despite governmental denials, an
increase in Commonwealth authority would entail centralisation of
administration; while yet others were sincere in their belief that
in a planned society it would be even more difficult to defend the
rights of the individual against the mammoth power of the state.
It is, of course, impossible to determine what percentage of the
electorate was swayed towards a negative vote by such considerations, but it would seem reasonable to infer that amongst the 'No'
voters were many who felt that principles which they cherished
would be endangered if the referendum were not rejected.

The task of those opposing the proposals was made much easier
by the government's decision to submit for approval no less than
fourteen points, all of which had either to be granted or refused.
Opposition campaigners took full advantage of the opportunity
presented to them. Realising that defeat was assured if a sufficient number of electors could be persuaded that any one of the
points was thoroughly obnoxious, they refused to commit the
error of condemning every point as objectionable. Their attitude
was rather that it was unreasonable that electors should be asked
to swallow the entire fourteen points simply because the Common-

64. *Ibid.*, pp. 40-2.

wealth stood in need of expanded powers in relation to three or four matters. With considerable astuteness the organisers of the 'No' vote urged that some of the proposed powers were satisfactory, others were unnecessary, and yet others were not merely objectionable in principle, but dangerous to the people's liberties and had been inserted merely to enable the Labour party to implement its political programme.

This two-fold technique of seizing upon individual points as objectionable, while admitting that others might be desirable, and of attacking the principle of wholesale acceptance or rejection, was eminently successful in its objective of securing the rejection of the proposals. But it did more than that. It revealed that the very method of submission adopted by the government, i.e., the submission of numerous subject matters upon which the Commonwealth sought expanded power, was vulnerable to attack and also confirmed the view that where constitutional amendment is to be attempted by referendum simplicity is the first essential. For this if for no other reason, the Commonwealth government might have been better advised, if, instead of proposing fourteen additional points, it had followed Mr. Hughes' suggestion at the convention 'to ask the people to repose in the Commonwealth Parliament all the reserve power, and authorise it to delegate to the states certain enumerated powers.'[65] Or, alternatively, it might have requested the abolition of the states and the conferring of all authority on the Commonwealth. Such straightforward proposals, having the merit of simplicity, would have presented to the electors an issue which they could understand and upon which they could vote intelligently. Moreover, though such proposals might have the appearance of asking for even more than was rejected at the referendum, it is possible that either would have met a better reception. It is not without significance in this connection that an Australian Public Opinion Poll, held as late as December, 1943, and released in January, 1944, revealed that there was far more support for proposals savouring of unification than there was for amendment in the direction of increased Commonwealth powers.[66] The alternatives submitted and the results obtained were these:

1. The present federal system with the Commonwealth having no more power than before the war.
2. The present federal system, but with certain powers transferred from the states to the Commonwealth; and

65. *Record of Proceedings*, Canberra Convention, 1942, p. 34.
66. *Sunday Sun* (Sydney), 16 January 1944.

3. The Commonwealth the only government with all powers, some of which would be delegated to provincial or state councils.

Results favoured unification:—

	Men (p.c.)	Women (p.c.)
No. 1 (no change)	17	20
No. 2 (increased federal powers) ...	16	14
No. 3 (unification)	61	41
No opinion	6	25
	100	100

A final cause contributing to defeat was the disunity [67] prevailing within the Labour movement, notably in New South Wales and Queensland. Some federal members of the official Labour party displayed no great enthusiasm for the 'Yes' campaign and left more than a fair share of the burden of advocacy to Dr. Evatt. This might to some extent have been offset by the personal prestige of the Prime Minister if he had found it possible to conduct an intensive nation wide campaign. Mr. Curtin, however, did not feel able to visit all states and his absence must have lost many votes for the 'Yes' cause in those states in which he did not make a personal appearance. More important, however, was the opposition displayed by Mr. Lang in New South Wales and the criticisms voiced by Mr. Fallon in Queensland. As the state director of the Labour Party's campaign, Mr. Fallon chose a singularly inauspicious moment from the point of view of the success of the referendum to deliver an attack against his own party's government. This must have led many hesitant voters in Queensland and elsewhere to play safe and vote in the negative. Mr. Lang's violent campaign, conducted through his paper the *Century,* in which he accused the federal government of departing from traditional labour principles and of aiming at industrial conscription, did even more damage. Its extent is no doubt incalculable, but the vehement opposition of Lang's supporters was certainly responsible for swelling considerably the size of the negative vote in New South Wales.

In assessing the reasons for the defeat of the referendum one thing does emerge with reasonable certainty. Whatever the causes of rejection, the proposals were not defeated because a majority of the electorate was enthusiastic in its allegiance to the states, or because it retained any real belief in the capacity of the states to handle the complex problems of the post-war period. The prestige

67. *Australian Quarterly,* Dec. 1944, p. 44.

of the states has remained low, and it is dubious if they will ever regain their former stature. An explanation must therefore be sought elsewhere than in the desire of a majority of the electorate to defend the position of the states in the governmental structure. No one can pronounce with certainty on the reasons for rejection, but the evidence available would appear to indicate that greatest weight must be attached to (a) the defective strategy of the government, which allowed the favourable moment for submission to pass and permitted time for the organisation of an astute and well-financed defence of the existing order; (b) irritation at war controls which became increasingly evident as the gravity of the danger to Australia diminished; (c) the fears excited by 'No' propaganda over the use to which the powers might be put, combined with the government's failure to elaborate the plans which it proposed to implement if authority was conferred; (d) the decision to submit amendments in the form of fourteen points which had to be accepted or rejected as a whole; (e) the inclusion of point (ii), employment and unemployment, without some guarantee against industrial conscription; (f) the disunity existing in the Labour movement; and (g) the unsatisfactory nature of the referendum itself as an instrument for achieving constitutional amendment.

APPENDIX A

A proposed law to alter the Constitution for a limited period by empowering the Parliament to make Laws in relation to Post-war Reconstruction, and by including Provisions to safeguard Freedom of Speech and Expression and Freedom of Religion.

Preamble

BE it enacted by the King's Most Excellent Majesty, the Senate, and the House of Representatives of the Commonwealth of Australia, with the approval of the electors, as required by the Constitution, as follows:—

Short title

1. This Act may be cited as *Constitution Alteration (Post-war Reconstruction and Democratic Rights)* 1944.

2. The Constitution is altered by inserting, after Chapter I, the following Chapter and section:—

Additional legislative powers and guarantees

"CHAPTER IA.—TEMPORARY PROVISIONS

"60A.—(1.) The Parliament shall, subject to this Constitution, have power to make laws for the peace, order and good government of the Commonwealth with respect to—

(i) the reinstatement and advancement of those who have been members of the fighting services of the Commonwealth during any war, and the advancement of the dependants of those members who have died or been disabled as a consequence of any war;

(ii) employment and unemployment;

(iii) organised marketing of commodities;

(iv) companies, but so that any such law shall be uniform throughout the Commonwealth;

(v) trusts, combines and monopolies;

(vi) profiteering and prices (but not including prices or rates charged by State or semi-governmental or local governing bodies for goods or services);

(vii) the production and distribution of goods, but so that—

(a) no law made under this paragraph with respect to primary production shall have effect in a State until approved by the Governor in Council of that State; and

(b) no law made under this paragraph shall discriminate between States or parts of States;

(viii) the control of overseas exchange and overseas investment; and the regulation of the raising of money in accordance with such plans as are approved by a majority of members of the Australian Loan Council;

(ix) air transport;

(x) uniformity of railway gauges;

(xi) national works, but so that, before any such work is undertaken in a State, the consent of the Governor in Council of that State shall be obtained and so that any such work so undertaken shall be carried out in co-operation with the State;

(xii) national health in co-operation with the States or any of them;

(xiii) family allowances; and

(xiv) the people of the aboriginal race.

"(2.) Neither the Commonwealth nor a State may make any law for abridging the freedom of speech or of expression.

"(3.) Section one hundred and sixteen of this Constitution shall apply to and in relation to every State in like manner as it applies to and in relation to the Commonwealth.

"(4.) A regulation of a legislative character under the authority of any law made by the Parliament in the exercise of any power conferred by sub-section (1.) of this section—

(a) shall, subject to this section, take effect on the expiration of the fourteenth day after its contents have been notified in the manner provided by the Parliament to each senator and each member of the House of Representatives or on such later date as is specified in the regulation;

(b) shall not take effect if, within fourteen days after its contents have been so notified, either House of the Parliament passes a resolution disapproving of the regulation; and

(c) shall take effect on the date of its making or on such later date as is specified in the regulation, if the Governor-General in Council declares on specified grounds that the making of the regulation is urgently required.

"(5.) This section shall continue in force until the expiration of a period of five years from the date upon which Australia ceases to be engaged in hostilities in the present war, and shall then cease to have effect, and no law made by the Parliament with respect to any matter specified in sub-section (1.) of this section shall continue to have any force or effect by virtue of this section after this section has ceased to have effect.".

NOTE.—Section 116 of the Constitution, to which clause (3) of the proposed law relates, is as follows:—

"The Commonwealth shall not make any law for establishing any religion, or for imposing any religious observance, or for prohibiting the free exercise of any religion, and no religious test shall be required as a qualification for any office or public trust under the Commonwealth."

VII

THE FUTURE OF FEDERALISM WITHIN AUSTRALIA

THE defeat of the powers referendum has forced the Commonwealth government to jettison many of the plans for the postwar period which had been prepared in the belief that its plea for wider powers was likely to be successful. Instead of possessing full authority on all matters pertaining to reconstruction the Commonwealth now finds that its grant of power is limited and that the onus for action rests with the states on many issues of vital importance. Constitutional limitations, and the urgency and magnitude of the problems awaiting solution, are therefore compelling all the Australian governments to pool their resources and experience in an effort to achieve effective action through the technique of co-operation. Despite the spur of necessity, united action will not easily be attained, and evidence is already accumulating that a good deal of hard bargaining is taking place between the states and the Commonwealth.

At first sight, the decision at the referendum might be interpreted as a triumph for the states, since they now retain many powers which otherwise would have been surrendered or seriously curtailed. The states, then, have secured a reprieve, and in view of the important powers remaining to them there will no doubt be a resurgence of interest in state politics and particularly in those aspects of state governmental policy connected with rehabilitation. It should not, however, be forgotten that the referendum decision was itself fraught with danger to the states. The constitution, which experience has shown to be badly in need of an overhaul, has to be operated unamended under conditions in which the strain placed upon it is likely to be enormously increased. Since the states retain many basic powers it is upon the states that much of the burden of reconstruction will fall. Yet the states are handicapped by restricted financial resources, by the confines of state boundaries, by competition with one another and by constitutional limitations. Nor does the past record of the states suggest their abiltiy to deal successfully with the immense problems now confronting them. Should the states, as is by no means improbable, demonstrate their incapacity to exercise the important powers entrusted to them, the main result of the failure to modify the constitution by expanding the authority of the national parliament will be to enforce unification at a much earlier date than could otherwise have been expected.

The verdict at the referendum does not imply that all prospects of constitutional revision have vanished.   Mr. Curtin, in comment on the result of the poll, pointed out that political leaders associated with the 'No' campaign had acknowledged that some form of alteration was desirable, and announced his government's readiness to 'give careful and sympathetic consideration to any positive proposals they advance.'[1]   Mr. Menzies, as spokesman for the federal opposition, asserted that he did not interpret the verdict as a vote against constitutional revision and expressed the opinion that after the war the whole question of constitutional alteration should be fully explored.   'For this purpose the Opposition considers that there should be a meeting of a representative convention as soon as possible after the ending of hostilities and the return of our armed forces.'[2]

There have also been signs that neither the federal government nor organised bodies, especially on the Labour side, favouring an extension of commonwealth powers are content to regard the referendum defeat as more than a temporary setback.   For a time it seemed as though Australian pressure for the insertion of a full employment pledge in the United Nations Charter was prompted in part by the hope that it might be possible to utilise the Commonwealth power over external affairs to enact legislation which otherwise would be beyond the scope of the Commonwealth's authority.   Whether or not the government did seriously consider this idea it was finally abandoned as impracticable, and Dr. Evatt on his return from San Francisco categorically denied that the government would employ such tactics to circumvent the decision at the referendum.[3]   Suggestions have also been forthcoming from a number of labour bodies, including the N.S.W. State Annual Conference of the Australian Labour Party, that the Commonwealth government should prepare plans for the holding of a new referendum to amend the constitution in the direction of conferring greater powers upon the Commonwealth.   The government has not specifically committed itself to such a course, but official statements imply that consideration is being given to the advisability of a new appeal to the people.

In the meantime, the Commonwealth is attempting to co-operate with the states through the machinery of the Premiers' Conference.

1. *Sydney Morning Herald*, 21 August 1944.
2   *Ibid*.   3. *Ibid*., 24 July 1945.

The proceedings of the conference, held at Canberra in August of this year, indicate that the Commonwealth representatives feel a certain undisguised pleasure in handing back to the states control of a number of troublesome matters over which Commonwealth authority is defective. To take two outstanding instances, responsibility will in the future lie with the states for the regulation of the coal industry and for the allocation of building materials within the states. In the case of building materials, however, control of imports will remain with the federal government while materials not produced in all states will be allocated to the states by joint decision of the Commonwealth and the states.[4] On some issues the Commonwealth is not content to abdicate its war-time power and has made strong demands for an extension of its authority. In particular, Mr. Chifley stressed that the continuance of price control by the Commonwealth was urgently necessary if inflationary tendencies were to be held in check. He therefore asked the state premiers to make an attempt to get all states to refer powers over price control to the Commonwealth. The premiers agreed[5] that legislation should be introduced authorising a reference of powers over price control for a three-year period, and their willingness to do so in itself testified that the state leaders were aware of the inability of the states to establish effective control and were appalled by the magnitude of the problems with which they would have to grapple.

Both state and Commonwealth delegates realised that the Commonwealth was in a dominant financial position and that this placed a potent weapon in the hands of its representatives. Some state premiers, apparently hoping to regain the liberty of action which had been lost with the introduction of uniform taxation, sought the repeal of the legislation, but the Commonwealth attitude to this request was uncompromising. Mr. Chifley not only refused to entertain repeal before the expiry date, but also expressed his personal view that uniform taxation should be permanently retained.[6] It is quite obvious that the Commonwealth intends to employ its financial superiority to ensure that the states implement policies which broadly meet with its approval. In all probability the Commonwealth will make an increasing use of the device of the grant-in-aid. For the moment state finances are in an unusually healthy position, but with increasing demands on the states their surpluses will dwindle, and the Commonwealth will be in a position to relieve their financial embarrassment through grants under section 96, but these grants will undoubtedly be made

`4 *Ibid.*, 22 August 1945.   5. *Ibid.*   6. *Ibid.*, 24 August 1945.

only in accordance with conditions laid down by the Commonwealth.

The present constitutional position is that, despite the loss of the referendum, plans for revision of the constitution are still contemplated, and, if the states prove unable to discharge their functions efficiently, these proposals for amendment are likely to be far-reaching.

There is, therefore, an insistence upon the necessity of change, and few whose opinions carry weight advocate the retention of the federal system in its present form.

While, however, there is agreement upon the urgent need for constitutional reform there is far less unanimity about the direction it should take, and the extent to which it should go. The alternatives which present themselves range from the dissolution of the federation through the secession of discontented states on the one hand, to the adoption of a completely unified system on the other. Secession cannot be seriously considered as a solution for the governmental problems which face Australia. The tendency, irresistible in the dictatorial states and powerful in the democratic, throughout the world in recent years, has been all in the opposite direction of unification. Secession has, moreover, been rejected as a practicable possibility by the refusal of the Imperial Parliament to act upon the Western Australian petition. The force of the movement, which at one time seemed likely to spread beyond Western Australia, is, at least momentarily, spent. It has lost impetus partly because of the return of a measure of prosperity, and partly because of the payments made to the claimant states by the Commonwealth on the recommendation of the Grants Commission. Nor is it likely that secession would be beneficial to any state which succeeded in withdrawing from the Commonwealth for, as the Grants Commission pointed out, the bounds within which small independent states can exercise their freedom in the modern world are not very large. Western Australia especially would find attempts to develop secondary industries costly, and her lot would be the unhappy one of a small state experiencing all the disadvantages of independence without the assistance which should be obtainable from other members of the Commonwealth. Federation represents a stage of development in the attainment of unity, and to the extent to which a measure of unity is preferable to none at all federation is superior to isolation.

Standing midway between those who advocate secession and those who favour unification is a group whose views were re-

flected in the Majority Report of the 1929 Commission on the
Constitution, which maintained that fundamentally federalism was
a satisfactory system of government for Australian conditions, and
that, with minor reforms, it could be made to operate successfully.
To this group may be added another section of opinion whose
adherents, though not as convinced of the excellence of the system, believe that there is little possibility of securing vital alteration and are therefore content to operate the system as best they
can. Those who hold either of these two viewpoints have been
immensely strengthened in their attitude by the emergence of a
doctrine which preaches that the problems raised by the divisions
of the federal system are capable of solution through the technique of co-operation.

This body of thought has received its most coherent expression
in the United States, where in recent years attempts at co-operation between state and state and between state and federal
authorities have been far-reaching and have taken a number of distinct forms. The outstanding exponent of the possibilities inherent
in the co-operative principle has been Felix Frankfurter. Basing
his case on the assumption of the continued survival of federalism
in the United States, he attempted to maintain that the full potentialities of a combination of state and federal powers had as yet
hardly been explored. 'The combined legislative powers of Congress and of the several states permit a wide range of permuta-
tions and combinations for governmental action.'[7] The United
States constitution enables a state to 'enter into any agreement or
compact with another state' with 'the consent of Congress.' It
was this compact clause which was particularly singled out and
hailed as promising hope for the future. It was thought to provide
a middle way between national action and no action at all, upon a
host of subjects over which neither the central nor the state
authority possessed adequate jurisdiction.[8] It was pronounced to
be a method by which federalism could solve its problems and
yet retain its essential characteristics. Professor Frankfurter
said :—

> The compact idea adds to the resources available to statesmen
> in the solution of problems presented by the growing inter-
> dependence, social and economic, of groups of states forming
> distinct regions.[9]

7. Felix Frankfurter and James M. Landis, "The Compact Clause of the
   Constitution," *Yale Law Journal*, May 1925, p. 688.
8. In Australia this view has been forcibly expressed by Sir Earle Page
   e.g. Federal State Conflict. Co-operation Needed for Effective Government. *Sydney Morning Herald*, 20 February 1945.
9. *Ibid.*, p. 727.

Co-operation is a term which when used in relation to federalism may cover a very wide range of activities. It may mean little more than the expression of a vague desire to work in harmony with other governments within the federation or, on the other hand, it may refer to precise agreements between governments for the carrying out of specific commitments. Between these two extremes lies a whole field in which governments may operate in association with one another in varying degrees of intimacy. In Australia, no less than the United States, attempts to overcome the impediments to action involved in the federal system by means of the technique of co-operation have been current almost from the inception of federation. In Australia, therefore, co-operation may be said to have had fair trial, and an examination of its record should reveal whether or not co-operation can make any valid claim to have bridged the gap of divided control, or to have achieved speedy and concerted action upon questions of national importance.

Co-operation has been attempted in many, if not all, the spheres in which it is possible. It has taken the shape of formal and informal agreement, of exchange of personnel, of the adoption of common departmental methods, of conferences between heads of governments and of the device of the grant-in-aid. The agreements which have been made have been widely different in character and have been concerned with diverse types of subjects. In two instances, the Surplus Revenue Act 1910 and the Financial Agreement Validation Act 1929, the Commonwealth Parliament has legislated on the understanding that the laws would cease to operate after an agreed period. Agreements between several states and the Commonwealth, for example, over the River Murray,[10] and between a state and the Commonwealth, for example, the embargo upon foreign sugar in the interests of Queensland industry, have been implemented by federal legislation.[11] Other types of agreement concluded between the Commonwealth and the states have covered the institution of a Loan Council, at first without and later with statutory authority, the repatriation of soldiers and the supervision of immigration. Co-operation between the departments and officers of the various governments has taken

10. In 1913 an agreement was concluded between the Prime Minister of the Commonwealth and the Premiers of the three states concerned for the conservation of the Murray waters. This agreement was ratified by the River Murray Waters Acts of 1915 passed by the Commonwealth and Victoria, New South Wales and South Australia. In 1917 a permanent River Murray Commission was established.
11. See 1929 *Report* Commission on the Constitution, p. 176,

place when officers have been engaged upon the same type of work. There have been conferences between Health Officers, Railway Commissioners, Taxation Officials and others, while Commonwealth and state departments have worked as one in the collection of income tax. Yet another instance of Commonwealth and state departmental co-operation is provided by the compilation of statistics. More important than any of these instances of co-operation are the Premiers' Conferences, which have been held almost annually since federation, and the conferences which have taken place between Commonwealth and state ministers. Lastly, there is the work done on the financial side by means of the Financial Agreement, the Grants Commission and the grant-in-aid.

Superficially, therefore, the record of co-operation in Australia seems to be an imposing one. However, a deeper probing reveals that actually it is far otherwise because, while there has been co-operation between governments in the sense of continual communication and discussion of vital problems, the results which have flowed from these contacts have been meagre and unusually disappointing. The test by which the principle of co-operation must stand or fall is the speed and efficiency with which it secures action upon problems of major significance. Measured by such a standard the record of co-operation is seen to be dilatory and ineffective. Consider, for instance, the co-operative attempts made in the field of health regulation, which is not by any means an unfavourable example to those who advocate co-operation as a solution of federal problems since it has been quoted as illustrating the merits of co-operative action. The Commonwealth parliament had been given no specific grant of power with regard to health and could only exercise an indirect control through its authority over such subjects as trade and commerce between states, quarantine and imports and exports. It could not deal with industrial hygiene except through an award of the Commonwealth Arbitration Court. In view of the lack of Commonwealth power, efforts were made to secure uniform action through conferences both among the states and between the states and the Commonwealth.[12] The 1913 conference, which followed a smallpox epidemic in New South Wales, was more than usually important because it laid down the circumstances under which the Commonwealth might intervene to declare any district a quarantine area. Federal intervention was regarded as necessary if a state requested

12. e.g. the 1904 Conference, held at the invitation of the Prime Minister, which passed a resolution in favour of Commonwealth control of interstate quarantine; the 1909 conference, which met to discuss the effects of the Commonwealth *Quarantine Act* 1908.

it, if there was danger to other states as a result of neglect by the state in which the epidemic had occurred, or if the infected state did not adopt the advice of the Director of Quarantine.[13]   It is obvious that the degree of co-operation outlined in these resolutions falls far short of national regulation, which permits the imposition of uniform standards where necessary.   Not only did the Commonwealth power remain constitutionally circumscribed, but intervention by the Commonwealth could only take place at the request of a state or after the failure or neglect of a state to cope with an outbreak of disease.   In addition to all the evils associated with divided control went a very dangerous element of delay before national action could be secured.   The character of this co-operation foreshadowed the likelihood of trouble.   It came in 1918 with the outbreak of the influenza epidemic.   A conference, which met in November of that year, passed a number of resolutions which were later embodied in an agreement prescribing the methods which should be employed to co-ordinate state and federal action.   The outcome of this attempt was the complete breakdown of the agreement, as is made plain by the telegram despatched to the state premiers on 3 February, 1919, by the Acting Prime Minister.

In consequence of violation of control of influenza epidemic agreement of 27 November 1918, by states of New South Wales, Queensland, Western Australia and Tasmania, Government of Commonwealth is unable to carry out arrangements voluntarily entered into by Commonwealth and states and gives formal and urgent notice that unless states which have broken the agreement indicate by noon on Wednesday, fifth instant, their intention to abide by it and assist quarantine authorities of Commonwealth to operate it Commonwealth government will renounce agreement and revert to constitutional position it occupied before agreement was drawn.[14]

The failure of co-operation in this instance simply served to confirm the fact that health is a question of national importance and should be in the hands of the national authorities.   The states possess inadequate financial resources to take effective preventive measures, and where one state does act with efficiency its efforts may well be nullified by neglect on the part of another.   Disease knows no state boundary lines, and experience has shown that co-operation is at once too cumbersome and too slow a method to be really successful.

13. For the resolutions of the 1913 conference see *Report*, Commission on the Constitution, p. 168.
14. *Ibid.*, p. 169.

Conferences, which have been held regularly between the states themselves and between the Commonwealth and the states, have provided the most important piece of machinery for the working of the co-operative experiment. An examination of the decisions reached at any Premiers' Conference will show that the possibility of securing united action upon matters of importance through Conference machinery is at best slight, primarily because the governments represented almost invariably follow the lines of party cleavage. With some exceptions, the only instances in which the governments reach a uniform decision are either upon matters of minor importance, such as the dates for public holidays,[15] or upon matters in which the interests of the states are obviously opposed to those of the Commonwealth. In the latter case, when the co-operative process moves to the plane of Commonwealth-state relations, there can be little prospect of achieving united action. The major weakness of the co-operative principle has appeared very plainly in the work attempted by these conferences of governments. Agreement upon the policy to be pursued has been difficult enough to secure but, even when obtained, there is no guarantee that action will follow since the resolutions of the conferences are purely recommendations and can only be carried out if separate legislation is passed by the states and the Commonwealth. In the face of party criticism and a possible change of government in one of the states or the Commonwealth, it is but rarely that a measure is enacted into legislation by every one of the parties to the agreement. Consequently, the same items make their appearance upon the agendas of the conferences with wearying regularity.

Co-operation as a technique for securing uniform action upon urgent but highly contentious social, economic and governmental problems has been shown by Australian experience to be lethargic, complicated and for the most part ineffective. Even in cases where success has ultimately been achieved, as for example in the provision of common electoral rolls, what strikes one most keenly is the difficulties and delays which attended the process. One instance, and that not one upon which agreement would have been thought difficult, will suffice to illustrate the slow-moving character of the co-operative method. The 'Marking of Australian Made Goods' had been the subject of a resolution at the May 1920 Premiers' Conference in favour of the introduction of uniform

15. e.g. The Premiers' Conference, Oct.-Nov. 1921, agreed that Anzac Day should be observed on 25 April and that the holiday should be uniform throughout the states.

legislation by all the states on the basis of the Victorian law.[16] New South Wales thereupon drafted a bill which it submitted to the other states. Alterations were suggested by Tasmania which necessitated its resubmission to the states. Victoria pronounced the bill to be substantially the same as its own, South Australia said the measure was acceptable, and Tasmania introduced legislation which was rejected. As for the other states, Western Australia declared that no opportunity had presented itself for the introduction of a bill and that it would delay action until the matter had been reconsidered at the next Premiers' Conference, while Queensland suggested amendments incorporating certain features of the Imperial Bill.

In 1923, after the return of the New South Wales premier from London, a lengthy correspondence took place between Queensland and New South Wales with the object of elucidating just what amendments Queensland did desire. In January 1925, Mr. Theodore explained that Queensland had no definite suggestions to make, but desired that a measure which was semi-international in character should conform as nearly as possible to the Imperial legislation on the subject. New South Wales replied that further consideration would be given to the Imperial legislation prior to redrafting the proposed Australian bill, but that there would be a delay of some months. There the matter rested and apparently nothing further was done for the 1929 report of the Premiers' Conference announced, 'Up to the present the final draft of the Bill has not been settled.'[17]

The dilatoriness displayed over this question of enacting uniform legislation upon the Marking of Australian Made Goods after adherence to a resolution in favour of uniformity seems well-nigh incomprehensible, yet the same waste of effort and lack of result can be duplicated by many another subject considered at the conferences. Indeed, in Australia the co-operative system is remarkable rather for the things which it has left undone and which it ought to have done, than for its achievements in the direction of uniformity. Nor has the system been able to command a sufficient belief in its own efficacy or its own principles to secure the reference to the Commonwealth parliament by the states of subjects of legislation upon which uniformity was desirable.

The record of co-operation, in so far as it concerns reference

16. Proceedings, Premiers' Conference, May 1929, Appendix A. Marking of Australian Made Goods.
17. *Ibid.*

of powers by the states to the Commonwealth under section 51 (xxxvii), is one of abject failure. In 1915, at a Premiers' Conference in Melbourne, the premiers suggested to the Commonwealth Government that in order to avoid a war-time referendum it should agree to the alternative procedure of reference of powers by the states.[18] The proposal was that the premiers should introduce legislation in their respective state parliaments to refer to the Commonwealth, for the duration of the war and one year after the declaration of peace, the powers which the Commonwealth was seeking to acquire through an alteration of the constitution.[19] This suggestion was accepted by the Commonwealth, but little success attended the efforts of the premiers to secure the passage of the legislation. Though bills were introduced into all state parliaments, the Commonwealth acquired no additional powers. The New South Wales parliament passed the bill but it was not to be proclaimed until similar legislation had been adopted by the other states. In Victoria the bill lapsed, in Queensland it was shelved, in South Australia it was rejected by the Legislative Council and in Western Australia and Tasmania it was simply not proceeded with. The result therefore was the total failure of the experiment.

In 1920 the Commonwealth once more approached the states at a premiers' conference in an effort to reinforce its authority through the co-operation of the states, but again the attempt was unsuccessful. The conference did, however, agree that legislation should be introduced in the state parliaments to refer to the Commonwealth the power of air navigation, though with certain limitations. The fate of the measures is a sorry commentary on the capacity of the states to achieve united action even upon so uncontroversial an issue. New South Wales and Western Australia took no action to enforce the agreement; South Australia and Victoria passed Acts which referred to the Commonwealth powers hardly greater, if at all, than those which it already possessed; Queensland[20] and Tasmania alone passed satisfactory legislation.

18   For full details see Knowles, *op. cit.*, p. 149. Also, *A Case For Greater Commonwealth Powers*, pp. 99-100.
19. The agreement of the Premiers was subject to certain modifications: (a) Railways, the property of a State, to be exempt from the Commonwealth power so far as regards the control or management of such railways, and rates and fares on such railways. (b) In lieu of proposal No. 3 "Industrial matters", substitute the following:—(a) Employment and unemployment; (b) Strikes and lock-outs; (c) The maintenance of industrial peace; (d) The settlement of industrial disputes (Knowles, *op. cit.*, p. 149).
20. The Queensland Act is given in Knowles, *op. cit.*, pp. 156-7. On this question see also, *A Case for Greater Commonwealth Powers*, p. 100.

It is true that in 1937 an agreement to endow the Commonwealth with control of air navigation was reached between the states and was subsequently implemented but it took seventeen years from the time of the original proposal to effect the desired result—hardly testimony to the speed and smooth-working character of the co-operative technique.

The substantial failure of co-operation—for it is nothing less—to deal successfully with the problems with which it has been confronted is evidenced by American experience. Professor Clark, after a recent and thorough investigation into the working of co-operation in the United States, has reached the conclusion that the machinery of co-operation can provide no solution for the difficulties arising from a federal system of government. 'It cannot,' she writes, 'be denied that federal-state co-operation has proceeded with halting and ineffectual steps, and that the devices of co-operation, like the federalism of which they are a part, are frequently complex, cumbersome and unwieldy.'[21]   As in America so in Australia, the record of co-operation is not such as to inspire confidence in its ability to act as the saviour of an obsolescent federalism. That is not to argue either that co-operation has achieved no successes, or that it has not made the federal system more workable than it could otherwise have been, but rather that it is inadequate to the problems with which it has to deal. When considered from the point of view of the magnitude of the problem involved the impression made upon it by co-operation is not convincing. Moreover, the problem is one which can only be judged rightly when placed in the setting of time. Under Australian conditions a high degree of mobility in political action is essential, yet by the method of co-operation uniform standards in matters where uniformity is vitally necessary are not likely to be secured with any rapidity.

The rejection of co-operation as a possible solution leaves amendment in the direction of strengthening the powers of the central government as the only remaining alternative. This may, and in the case of many protagonists does, stop short of complete unification, but among those who advocate conferring wider powers upon the central government the change which is desired is a substantial one. Such an attitude implies a recognition of the fact that the stage at which federalism was a useful governmental technique for Australian conditions has passed away. Federalism may well represent a necessary phase in the evolution of a state from an economy in which the outstanding factors are its agrarian

21. J. P. Clark, *The Rise of a New Federalism*, p. 294.

character and the existence of an expanding frontier, to one in which industrialisation has become of vital importance. Australia has now reached this second stage of development, and federalism is no longer a suitable form of government for dealing with the economic and social problems which industrialization brings with it. In short, a system which continues the present division of powers is incapable of meeting the needs of the Australian people.

To-day the main arguments in favour of federalism have lost their validity because the conditions postulating federalism have altered or altogether disappeared. Defences of the federal system have been based upon its ability to safeguard the independence of the states, yet both in America and Australia perhaps the outstanding feature of the existing governmental structures is the submergence of the states. In the United States, the position occupied by many of the States can be described as little short of ignominious while, in Australia, all the states have declined in power and prestige and the claimant states have reached such a pass that they can no longer discharge their functions without constant Commonwealth assistance. Under the Australian federal constitution, therefore, invasion of state spheres of activity goes on apace and the independence which the states enjoy has become largely fictitious. But if in Australia the power of the states has declined that of the Commonwealth remains circumscribed by constitutional restrictions which are to-day anachronistic because the purposes for which independence was maintained can no longer be fulfilled. Autonomy was intended to confer the right to conduct experiments for purposes peculiar to any one state in what Mr. Justice Holmes described as 'the insulated chambers afforded by the several States.' However, in the face of economic forces and improved communications, the insulation has proved less effective than was supposed, and the justification for individual experiment has disappeared as the conditions prevailing within the states have become common and not particular. The result has been a contradiction in terms between the goal, the attainment of which the division of powers was thought to make possible, and the facts which the system attempted to divide. The demand for the small constitutionally protected unit was based upon the assumption that there are problems peculiar to the small unit. There are, but they are not those which the present division seeks to solve.

The position of the small unit is not a very happy one in the world of to-day. The force which it can command in support of government regulation is ineffective when pitted against that of large scale industry. The objection to the big unit, therefore, loses much of its strength when it is recognised that a government, to cope with its problems, must have access to powers which are equal to the situation with which it has to deal. Since, under the federal system, neither the states nor the Commonwealth can possess the requisite amount of power, the constitution must be altered in such a way as to secure full authority for the central government. Nor are the arguments based upon the size and diversity of Australia of great weight. The Grants Commission has shown that there is a remarkable resemblance between the economic structures of the various states, while the improvement in communications has gone far to destroy the isolation which was at the root of the demand for local autonomy. What is far more true is that the federal system imposes too heavy a strain upon the resources available in Australia for the work of government. Owing to her small population, the calibre of the governing personnel must of necessity be inferior to the demands made upon it by a system which establishes thirteen houses to govern a nation of slightly more than seven million people.

What is required in Australia to-day is that the central government should possess complete power to determine national standards, in so far as such subjects as education, health and conditions of employment are concerned, and complete power to take action with regard to any aspect of the economic life of the nation when it conceives it necessary to do so. It is obvious that, under the existing division of powers, the authority of the central government in almost every important sphere of social and economic activity is so restricted as to be incapable of dealing with the tasks with which it is confronted. A first essential of any reform must, therefore, be that when a redistribution of powers takes place the power of amendment must lie solely with the national parliament. Only in that way can the stumbling block of constitutionally guaranteed state powers be avoided, and only in that way can revision of the distribution of powers between central and local authorities be easily accomplished when necessitated by changed conditions. This is not to argue in favour of centralised administration, for an undue degree of centralisation would carry with it very real dangers, but to maintain that the states are at present entrusted with the regulation of a number of subjects for which they are unfitted. National standards cannot be imposed while the states possess jurisdiction over such subjects as health, education, industry and unemployment, nor could they be effective if Commonwealth action rested upon the consent of the state, since in that case the state would possess the power to aid or prevent the enforcement of a national minimum standard of observance as it saw fit. For that reason the amending power must be placed in the hands of the Commonwealth parliament.

Constitutional guarantees, such as are provided by a federal system, cannot therefore be extended to safeguard local powers of government. Nevertheless those powers will be considerable, for in Australia conditions are such as to necessitate a very extensive provincial structure. The possession of full legislative authority by the Commonwealth parliament would not imply centralised administration. Instead, there would be a wide measure of devolution; but decentralisation as distinct from federalism would involve the delegation of powers by the Commonwealth government to local authorities. Nor is there any reason to suppose that such a system would be unwelcome either to local governing bodies or to unofficial organised groups. In this connection it is necessary to remember that state governments have rarely displayed a genuine interest in local government bodies and have done little to encourage a healthy participation in the affairs of the local community. Instead, they have been the strongest agents in the establishment of a highly centralised system of administration within their own boundaries. There is, in fact, far more likelihood of rapid and progressive expansion of local self government under a system in which the Commonwealth possesses full power and responsibility for general planning and regional and municipal bodies receive adequate financial assistance for developmental projects within their local area. If it be contended that such a system would furnish no protection for local rights of self government the answer must surely be that in any state safeguards are rather a question of convention than of law. Moreover, protection is provided by the fact that every central government must observe 'certain necessary uniformities of treatment.' If it fails to do so, the local unit is not wholly without means of redress since it can, to take one instance, show its displeasure at the elections.

Concentration of political power in the hands of the central parliament has become essential in Australia because unification of economic life has already taken place. The difficulty at the moment is the obvious one that economic unification exists alongside political divisions of power which make effective economic regulation impossible. There is a political lag due to the retention of artificial limitations upon the powers of the Commonwealth. The states are prohibited from taking effective action in the economic sphere by constitutional, geographical and competitive disqualifications and, therefore, become barriers behind which vested interests may entrench themselves and continue to operate unimpeded. The unity achieved by capitalism in an age of large scale capitalistic enterprise demands an equivalent unity in political power if regulation in the economic sphere is to become in any way effective. Unification of political power has become essential to good government in Australia, but the objection is often made that it cannot be achieved because of the hostility of the less populous states which are jealous of their independence and already suspicious of Commonwealth power. The difficulty is not an insuperable one because discontent in the weaker states arises out of a sense of economic injustice. It is clear from the Western Australian Case in favour of secession, and from the evidence submitted by the claimant states, that dissatisfaction is primarily a question of financial distress. If the feeling of injury aroused by that distress could be removed by Commonwealth action there is no reason why the 'claimant' states should not be willing to co-operate in securing a still greater degree of Australian unity. These states do not command adequate financial resources for the development of their territories or for the provision of expanding social services. The Commonwealth, by guaranteeing the satisfaction of such needs could remove much of their antagonism towards unification. If faced with a choice between poor standards with state autonomy, and high standards with unification, there can be little doubt that any one of these states would be willing to sink its identity in that of the wider unit. In this regard the entry of Western Australia into the Commonwealth is not without its significance since the doubts of that state were partially overcome by the promise to construct a railway linking the east with the west. Unification is not likely to be attained except at a price, and it is highly probable that concessions, in the form of heavy capital expenditure upon developmental projects within the claimant states, will be necessary to bring it about. Nor would the price be an excessively high one to pay for the attainment of adequate Commonwealth powers and the destruction of discontent among the present claimant states.

The minimum requirement demanded by conditions in Australia for any constitutional reform is the bestowal upon the central Government of a measure of power sufficient to regulate the economic life of the nation. Without the possession of such authority by the Commonwealth there can be neither national standards of performance nor an adequate supervision of national development, whether in the field of primary or secondary industry. In Australia, therefore, the reform of the federal system would require a grant to the Commonwealth of full powers over trade and commerce, industrial matters, land settlement and development, transport, health and education. It would necessitate also the removal of constitutional prohibitions, such as section 92, imposing limitations upon Commonwealth liberty of action in relation to any question with which the Commonwealth was competent to deal. There is, however, no reason why this should apply to constitutional guarantees of the fundamental freedoms if their insertion in a written constitution were contemplated.

Such a reform is so substantial as to leave few powers of importance to the states, which could not therefore be expected to command the services of men of first rate political calibre. Moreover, since subject matters of legislation are so interconnected the transference of any important power to the central government would later force the transference of others. Consequently, it would be preferable, after the surrender of powers to the Commonwealth, not to retain the untidy remnants of the federal system but to bestow complete control upon the central parliament and allow it to delegate its powers to local authorities. Such a solution would recognise that a constitutionally rigid division of powers between national and provincial authorities is no longer consistent with effective regulation of industry, or the maintenance of a national standard of performance. Autonomy in the modern world can only be justified in a purely cultural sense, and then it is open to discussion how far it should extend its control. What is certain is that in the modern state the amount of autonomy permissible should lie within the discretion of the national authority. Otherwise, the danger remains that constitutionally guaranteed local rights may conflict with the future needs of the nation and act as an impediment to the effectiveness of the national effort. The vital consideration in any reform must be to secure for the central government a grant of power sufficiently extensive to be wholly adequate to the social, economic and other problems which it must seek to solve.

BIBLIOGRAPHY

OFFICIAL DOCUMENTS

CANADA

Report of the Royal Commission on Dominion-Provincial Relations. (Rowell-Sirois Report.)

Submissions to the Royal Commission on Dominion-Provincial Relations.

British Columbia in the Canadian Confederation, 1938.

Canadian Federation of Mayors and Municipalities.

Canadian Manufacturers Association Inc.

Central Committee of the Communist Party.

Cities of Alberta.

Edmonton Chamber of Commerce, Alberta.

Final Report of the National Employment Commission, January 1938.

Manitoba's Case.

Nova Scotia.

Union of Nova Scotia Municipalities.

AUSTRALIA

The Case of the People of Western Australia in support of their desire to withdraw from the Commonwealth of Australia established under the Commonwealth of Australia Constitution Act (Imp.), and that Western Australia be restored to its former status as a separate self-governing colony in the British Empire. 1934.

The Case for Union. Commonwealth of Australia. A reply to the Case for the Secession of the State of Western Australia. Canberra.

Committee on Uniform Taxation, *Report,* 1942.

Commonwealth of Australia. *Parliamentary Debates.*

Commonwealth Grants Commission. Reports on the Applications made by the States of South Australia, Western Australia and Tasmania for Financial Assistance from the Commonwealth under Section 96 of the Constitution. *First Report,* 1933 and annually thereafter.

Commonwealth Law Reports, Vol. 1 to date.

Convention of Representatives of the Commonwealth and State Parliaments on Proposed Alteration of the Commonwealth Constitution, Canberra—Nov.-Dec. 1942. *Record of Proceedings.*

New South Wales *Parliamentary Papers* 1934-5, Vol. iii. New States. Report of the Royal Commission of Inquiry.

Post-War Reconstruction. A Case for Greater Commonwealth Powers. Prepared for the Constitutional Convention at Canberra. Nov. 1942.

Premiers Conferences, *Reports of Proceedings,* but especially—
Premiers Conference, Melbourne, June 1926, held to consider the financial relations between the States and the Commonwealth.
Premiers Conference, Sydney, June 1928.
Premiers Conference, Sydney, May 1929.
Conference between Commonwealth and State Ministers, Melbourne and Sydney, June-July, 1927.
Royal Commission on the Constitution of the Commonwealth, *Report of proceedings and minutes of evidence,* 21 Nov. 1929. Canberra.
The *Australian Tariff. An Economic Enquiry.* Melbourne 1929. Report of an Informal Committee set up by the Rt. Hon. S. M. Bruce, Prime Minister of Australia, in the spring of 1927.
Victorian *Parliamentary Papers,* 1890 (2). Official Record of the Proceedings and Debates of the Australasian Federation Conference 1890, Melbourne.
V.P.Ps. 1891(4). Proceedings of the National Australasian Convention, Sydney, March-April, 1891.
V.P.Ps. 1897(2). Official Record of the Debates of the National Australasian Convention, Adelaide, March-May, 1897.
V.P.Ps. 1897(2). Proceedings of the Australasian Federation Convention, Sydney, September 1897.
V.P.Ps. 1898 (3). Proceedings of the Australasian Federation Convention, Melbourne, January-March 1898.
V.P.Ps. 1900(3). Papers relating to the Federation of the Australian Colonies.
Western Australian *Parliamentary Papers* 1899. Vol. iii. Report of the Joint Select Committee of the Legislative Council and the Legislative Assembly appointed to consider the draft of a bill to constitute the Commonwealth of Australia.
W.A.P.Ps. 1899(3). Reports of Discussions of the Joint Select Committee of both Houses of Parliament appointed to consider the draft of a bill to constitute the Commonwealth of Australia.

PERIODICAL LITERATURE

The student of federalism will find the articles in periodicals of great value. The following selected list should give some guidance:—

Adarkar, B. P. Federal Finance in Australia (*The Economic Record,* vol. xii, June, 1936).
Andrews, J. The Present Situation in the Wheat Growing Industry in South Eastern Australia. (*Economic Geography,* vol. xii, No. 2, April 1936).
'Audax.' The Function of the States (*The Australian Quarterly,* vol. xiii, No. 1, March 1941).
Bailey, K. H. The Report of the Royal Commission on the

Constitution of the Commonwealth (*The Economic Record,* vol. v, No. 9, Nov. 1929).

Bailey, K. H., and Giblin, L. F.   Marketing and the Constitution (*The Economic Record,* vol. xii, Dec. 1936).

Bailey, K. H.   Reform of the Commonwealth Constitution (*The Australian Quarterly,* vol. xi, No. 1, March 1939).

Bailey, K. H.   Federalism Under Fire (*The Austral-Asiatic Bulletin,* vol. v, No. 3, Aug.-Sept. 1941).

Bailey, K. H.   The War Emergency Legislation of the Commonwealth (*Journal,* Institute of Public Administration (Australia), vol. iv, No. 1 (New Series), March 1942).

Bailey, K. H.   The Uniform Income Tax Plan (1942).   (*The Economic Record,* vol. xx, No. 39, Dec. 1944).

Beasley, F. R.   The Secession Movement in Western Australia (*The Australian Quarterly,* No. 29, March 1936).

Bland, F. A.   Inventing Constitutional Machinery (*The Australian Quarterly,* No. 28, Dec. 1935).

Bland, F. A.   Post-War Constitutional Reconstruction (*Journal,* Institute of Public Administration (Australia), vol. ii, No. 3 (New Series), Sept.-Dec. 1940).

Bland, F. A.   Towards Regionalism (*Journal,* Institute of Public Administration (Australia), vol. iv, No. 8 (New Series), Dec. 1943).

Brigden, J. B.   Grants to the States; The Report of the Commonwealth Grants Commission and some of its Implications (*The Economic Record,* vol. x, No. 19, Dec. 1934).

Colebatch, Sir H.   Undermining the Constitution (*The Australian Quarterly,* No. 5, March 1930).

Copland, D. B.   The Economic Situation in Australia, 1918-23 (*The Economic Journal,* vol. xxxiv, 1924).

Cowper, N.   The First Financial Agreement.   (*The Economic Record,* vol. viii, No. 15, Dec. 1932).

Drummond, D. H.   The New States Movement (*The Australian Quarterly,* No. 10, June 1931).

Eggleston, F. W.   The Commonwealth Constitution and the Referendum (*The Australian Quarterly,* No. 6, June 1930).

Ellis, U.   Federal Reconstruction (*The Australian National Review,* vol. v, No. 28, April 1939).

Fenner, C.   The Murray River Basin (*Geographical Review,* vol. xxiv, No. 1, Jan. 1934).

Fisher, A. G. B.   Federal Grants (*The Economic Record,* vol. xii, Dec. 1936).

Frankfurter, F., and Landis, J. M.   The Compact Clause of the Constitution—A Study in Inter-state Adjustments (*Yale Law Journal,* vol. xxxiv, May 1925).

Garland, J. M.   The Commonwealth Grants Commission (*The Economic Record,* vol. xiii, No. 25, Dec. 1937).

Garran, Sir R. The Making and Working of the Constitution (Part I: *The Australian Quarterly,* No. 14, June 1932; part II: *ibid.,* No. 15, Sept. 1932).

Giblin, L. F. Federation and Finance (*The Economic Record,* vol. ii, No. 3, Nov. 1926).

Graves, W. Brooke. The Future of the American States (*American Political Science Review,* Feb. 1936).

Gregory, H. Why Western Australia Should Secede (*The Australian Quarterly,* No. 18, June 1933).

Higgins, H. B. The Australian Federation Act (*Contemporary Review,* vol. lxxvii, April 1900).

Hutchin, A. W. The Smaller States (*The Australian Quarterly,* No. 17, March 1933).

Hytten, T. The Difficulties of the Small States (*The Australian Quarterly,* No. 7, Sept. 1930).

Hytten, T. The Small States and the Commonwealth Grants Commission (*The Australian Quarterly,* No. 29, March 1936).

Kable, V. G. Regionalism Linked with Greater Local Government (*Journal,* Institute of Public Administration, vol. v, No. 3 (New Series), Sept. 1944).

Laffer, K. Taxation Reform in Australia (*The Economic Record,* vol. xviii, Dec. 1942).

Laski, H. J. The Constitution Under Strain (*The Political Quarterly,* vol. viii, No. 4, Oct.-Dec. 1937).

Laski, H. J. The Obsolescence of Federalism (*The New Republic,* 3 May 1939).

Louat, F. The Unconventional Convention (*The Australian Quarterly,* vol. xv, No. 1, March 1943).

Louat, F. The Problem of One Governing System (*The Australian Quarterly,* vol. xv, No. 4, Dec. 1943).

Macmillan, J. W. Interprovincial or Inter-State Co-operation in Labour Laws (*American Labour Legislation Review,* vol. xv, 1925).

Maxwell, J. A. The Basis for Grants to the States (*The Economic Record,* vol. xiii, No. 24, June 1937).

Maxwell, J. A. The Basis for Grants to the States (*The Economic Record,* vol. xiv, No. 27, Dec. 1938).

McCorkle, T. A. Our New Line of Federalism (*The South Western Political and Social Science Quarterly,* Sept. 1935).

Mills, R. C. Financial Relations of the Commonwealth and the States (*The Economic Record,* vol. iv, No. 6, May 1928).

Milner, I. F. G. Referendum Retrospect (*The Australian Quarterly,* vol. xvi, No. 4, Dec. 1944).

Moore, Sir W. H. Constitutional Development in Australia (*The Australian Quarterly,* No. 10, June 1931).

The New Statesman, especially contributions by F.W.E., S.C.L. and W.K.H.

The New Statesman and Nation, passim.

Osborne, R. G., and Walker, E. R.   Federalism in Canada (*The Economic Record*, vol. xvi, Dec. 1940).

Pate, J. E.   Federal-State Relations in Planning (*Social Forces*, Dec. 1936).

Paton, J. L.   Further Referendum Retrospect (*The Australian Quarterly*, vol. xvii, No. 1, March 1945).

Price, A. G.   State and Provincial Disabilities in the Australian and North American Federations (*The Australian Quarterly*, No. 23, Sept. 1934).

Public Administration, *Journal* of the Institute of Public Administration (Australia), vol. v, No. 2 (New Series), June 1944. The Constitutional Referendum Issue by a number of contributors.

The Quarterly Review, Finance and Politics in Australia, vol. 257, No. 509, Article 13, July 1931 (unsigned).

Reddaway, W. B.   The Economic Consequences of Mr. James (*The Australian Quarterly*, No. 32, Dec. 1936).

Reichenbach, G. S.   Federalism and the New Deal (*The Australian Quarterly*, No. 28, Dec. 1935).

Roberts, S. H.   The Constitutional Dilemma (*The Australian Quarterly*, No. 4, 1929).

Roberts, S. H.   The Crisis in Australia (*Pacific Affairs*, vol. v, No. 4, April 1932).

Rogers, N. McL.   The Genesis of Provincial Rights (*Canadian Historical Review*, vol. xiv, 1933).

The Round Table.   The contributions in each number under the headings: Canada; Australia.   The following articles are of special importance:—

Vol. xxv, No. 98, March 1935, The Working of Federalism in Australia.

Vol xxvi, No. 101, Dec. 1935, Federalism and Economic Control.

Vol. xxvi, No. 102, March 1936, The Commonwealth Grants Commission.

Vol. xxvi, No. 104, Sept. 1936, Dominion-Provincial Financial Relations.

Vol. xxvii, No. 105, Dec. 1936, The Privy Council and Marketing.

Vol. xxvii, No. 107, June 1937, The Referendum.

Vol. xxxiii, No. 129, Dec. 1942, Commonwealth and State Taxation.

Vol. xxxiii, No. 130, March 1943, Constitutional Questions.

Scullin, J. H.   Case for Revision of the Constitution (*The Australian National Review*, vol. v, No. 26, Feb. 1939).

Sherrard, K.   What Western Australia Might Gain from Federation (*The Australian Quarterly*, No. 25, March 1935).

Staricoff, J.   Australia and the Constitution of the I.L.O. (*International Labour Review,* vol. xxxii, Nov. 1935).

Taylor, Griffith.   The Inner Arid Limits of Economic Settlement in Australia (*The Scottish Geographical Magazine,* vol. 48, No. 2, March 1932).

Taylor, Griffith.   Australia as a Field for Settlement (*Foreign Affairs,* July 1927).

Uhl, R.   Sovereignty and the Fifth Article (*South Western Political and Social Science Quarterly,* March 1936).

Warner, K. O.   Australian Federalism at the Crossroads (*Pacific Affairs,* vol. iv, No. 2, Feb. 1931).

Wilson, C. H.   The Separation of Powers Under Democracy and Fascism (*Political Science Quarterly,* vol. iii., No. 4, Dec. 1937).

Wilson, F. G.   International Labour Relations of Federal Governments (*South Western Political and Social Science Quarterly,* vol. x, Sept. 1929).

Windeyer, W. J. V.   New States—A Review of the Report of the Royal Commission (*The Australian Quarterly,* No. 26, June 1935).

Wood, G. L.   The Economic Position of Australia (*Pacific Affairs,* vol. iv, No. 9, Sept. 1931).

Woolsey, L. H.   A Comparative Study of the South African Constitution (*The American Journal of International Law,* vol. iv, 1910).

BOOKS

Bland, F. A.   *Government in Australia* (Selected Readings). Second edition, Sydney, 1944.

Brennan, T. C.   *Interpreting the Constitution.* Melbourne, 1935.

Cambridge History of the British Empire, vol. vii, Part 1, Australia.   Cambridge, 1933.

Canaway, A. P.   *The Failure of Federalism in Australia.* London, 1930.

Clark, J. P.   *The Rise of a New Federalism.*

Cockburn, Sir J. A.   *Australian Federation.* 1901.

Copland, D. B., and Janes, C. V.   *Cross Currents of Australian Finance.* Sydney, 1936.

Cramp, K. R.   *State and Federal Constitutions of Australia.* Second edition, Sydney, 1914.

Deakin, A.   *The Federal Story.* Melbourne, 1945.

Dicey, A. V.   *Introduction to the Study of the Law of the Constitution.* Eighth edition, London, 1915.

Drummond, D. H.   *Australia's Changing Constitution.* Sydney, 1943.

Duncan, W. G. K. ed.   *Trends in Australian Politics.* Sydney, 1935.

Fitzpatrick, B.   *The British Empire in Australia.* Melbourne 1941.

Foenander, Orwell de R. *Solving Labour Problems in Australia.* Melbourne, 1941.

Foenander, Orwell de R. *Wartime Labour Developments in Australia.* Melbourne, 1943.

Hall, H. L. *Victoria's Part in the Australian Federation Movement,* 1849-1900. 1931.

Holman, W. A. *Three Lectures on the Australian Constitution.* John Murtagh Macrossan Lectures, 1928. Brisbane.

Hunt, E. M. *American Precedents in Australian Federation.* New York, 1930.

Jennings, W. I. *The Law and the Constitution.* Second edition, London, 1942.

Knowles, G. S. *The Commonwealth of Australia Constitution Act* (as altered to 1 July 1936). Canberra, 1937.

Laski, H. J. *The Problem of Administrative Areas.* 1918.

Laski, H. J. *Capitalism in Crisis.* Forum Series (1933-34), No. 1. (The Roosevelt Experiment).

Laski, H. J. *Parliamentary Government in England.* London, 1938.

Maclaurin, W. R. *Economic Planning in Australia,* 1929-1936. London, 1937.

Maughan, D., and others. *Constitutional Revision in Australia.* Sydney, 1944.

Moore, Sir W. H. *The Constitution of the Commonwealth of Australia.* Second edition, Melbourne, 1910.

Portus, G. V. *Studies in the Australian Constitution.* Sydney, 1933.

Quick, Sir J. *The Legislative Powers of the Commonwealth and the States of Australia.* Melbourne, 1919.

Quick, J., and Garran, R. R. *The Annotated Constitution of the Australian Commonwealth.* Sydney, 1901.

Seeley, Sir J. R. *Introduction to Political Science.* London, 1901.

Shann, E. O. G. *An Economic History of Australia.* Cambridge, 1930.

Shann, E. O. G., and Copland, D B. *The Crisis in Australian Finance,* 1929-1931. Sydney, 1931.

Shann, E. O. G., and Copland, D. B. *The Battle of the Plans.* Sydney, 1931

Sweetman, E.. *Australian Constitutional Development.* Melbourne, 1925.

Tocqueville, D. *Democracy in America,* Vol. 1 (Henry Reeve's translation). London, 1875.

Warner, K. O. *An Introduction to Some Problems of Australian Federalism.* Washington, Seattle, 1933.

Wood, F. L. W. *The Constitutional Development of Australia.* Sydney, 1933.

Wynes, W. Anstey. *Legislative and Executive Powers in Australia.* 1936.

Agencies, governmental, 15, 16.
Air navigation, 303-4.
Alberta, 18.
Amendment: difficult to effect, 1-2,
  100, 103-5, 130, 263, 279, 282,
  285; machinery, 39, 47; present
  position, 294; provision for, 16,
  33, 39, 100; results, 101-3, 130,
  278; 1942 bill, 217, 252-3, 257-
  61; 1942 Convention proposals,
  272-3; 1944 result, 278-290.
Appropriation, 74-5.
Arbitration: 17, 113-132. Commonwealth power, 48-9, 65-6, 68,
  112-13, 118; complexity, 123-4,
  128; duplication, 108, 173-4;
  national regulation, 128-31;
  State protests, 54, 108, 125-7,
  173-4; State regulation, 128-9,
  131.
Atkin, Rt. Hon. J. R., Baron, 13,
  137-8, 141.
Australian Public Opinion Polls,
  280, 288-9.
Bailey, K. H., 6, 20, 61-2, 121, 122,
  133, 143, 154, 219, 223, 251, 263.
Baker Hon. H. S., 274.
Baker, Sir Richard, 37-8.
Bankruptcy Act, 123.
Barton, Sir Edmund, 32, 41, 44, 64.
Bavin, Sir Thomas, 127-8.
Beeby, Judge, 115.
Bills of Exchange Act, 123.
Bird, Hon. B. S., 24, 45.
Braddon Clause, 45, 72-4, 76, 173.
Bruce, Rt. Hon. S. M., 78-9, 127-8.
Bryce, James, Viscount, 2-3.
Butler, Hon. R. L., 75, 142.
Butlin, S. J., 203.
Canada: Federal system, 2, 11, 15;
  grants in aid, 18; influence of,
  32; marketing, 13-14; national
  regulation, 12-13; provincial
  grievances, 17.
Canaway, A. P., 107.
Carruthers, Sir Joseph, 42.
Centralisation, 306-7.
Chifley, Rt. Hon. J. B., 209, 245-6,
  250, 295-6.
Chinese, entry of, 29.
Claimant States: burden of protection, 180-2; developmental policies, 178-80; effort required,
  183, 192-4, 196-9, 202; financial need, 184-6, 188; grievances, 160-3, 165, 177-8; policies
  criticised, 194-5; position of,
  182-3, 308; responsibility in,
  195-6, 198, 213; seek grants,
  164.
Clark, J. P., 304.
Cockburn, Sir John A., 24-5, 39, 43,
  47.
Colonial Sugar Refining Co. Ltd.,
  168.
Commissions: Jones Commission
  (Canada), 52; Royal Commission on the Constitution 1929,
  53, 83, 114, 124, 128-9, 130,
  154, 162, 175, 218, 297; Royal
  Commission on Dominion-Provincial Relations (Canada), 14,
  175; Royal Commission on the
  Finances of Western Australia,
  162, 175.
Committee on Uniform Taxation,
  245-6.
Commonwealth: encroachment: 53-5,
  65, 71, 158; external affairs
  power, 294; Financial Agreement and N.S.W., 91-6; financial supremacy, 72-3, 78-9, 80,
  84, 96-8, 173, 250-2, 295; greater
  powers required, 214-6, 238-9,
  258-9, 264-5, 272-3, 275, 284,
  306-9; industrial control, 100,
  112-13, 116-18, 120, 123-5, 128-9,
  130-1, 159, 256-7; lack of
  power, 73, 81, 98, 100, 105, 107,
  112-13, 117, 120, 124, 147-8,
  154-5, 233-4, 253-4, 256-60, 293,
  300, 305; marketing schemes,
  145-8, 152-4; powers, 54, 72,
  106-7, 299; war organisation,
  217-20, 222, 226, 234-252.
Commonwealth Bank, 88-91.
Commonwealth Bank Board, 88-90.
Commonwealth Legislation: Bank
  Board Amendment Bill, 89;
  Conciliation and Arbitration
  Act, 118, 122-5; Constitution
  Alteration (State Debts) Act,
  81; Dried Fruits Export Control Act, 136, 145-6; Estate
  Duties Act, 77; Income Tax
  Act, 77; Inscribed Stock Act,
  66; National Security Act, 217,
  220-1, 224-5, 232-3, 236, 240;

Salaries Act, 69; Trading with the Enemy Act, 217; War Precautions Act, 217.

Competition, inter-state, 11-12, 24, 30, 41, 128.

Constitution of Commonwealth of Australia: need for revision, 105-6, 306; rigidity, 39-40, 47; Section 51, 101; S.51(i), 133-4, 256; S.51(ii), 152-3, 223, 226, 228-9, 231; S.51(iv), 66; S.51 (vi), 53, 219; S.51(xxxi), 222, 225, S.51(xxxv), 256; S.51 (xxxvii), 270, 303; S.74, 58; S.81, 74; S.87, 73, 229; S.89, 229; S.92, 67, 104, 132-151, 155-7, 223-4, 256-7, 264, 266, 309; S.93, 229; S.94, 229; S.96, 73, 153-4, 164, 228-30, 250-1, 295; S.99, 134, 223, 229; S.105, 229; S.105A, 52, 81-6, 90-3, 95, 102, 229; S.106, 159; S.107, 159; S.109, 69-70; S.114, 223-4; S.116, 223-5.

Constitution Alteration (War Aims & Reconstruction) 1942 Bill, 259, 260, 264-5.

Constitutional guarantees, 262, 265, 307, 309.

Conventions: 1883, 28; 1890, 25-6; 1891, 24, 26, 33-4, 133; 1897, 45; 1898, 48; 1942, 216, 242, 253, 261-277.

Cooper, Hon. F. A., 267.

Co-operation: advocated, 212, 239, 265, 273, 277, 297; defined, 298, difficult to achieve, 108, 277; essential, 293; financial relations, 96; in immigration, 109; in wartime, 239-249; limitations of, 242-4, 246-9, 255-7, 270-2, 277, 299-304; post-war, 295; pre-federation, 30-1; record in Australia, 298-304; success, 267.

Cosgrove, Hon. R., 266, 269-70, 272, 275.

Cowper, N., 87, 90-1.

Cripps, Sir Stafford, 147.

Curtin, Rt. Hon. J., 215-16, 243, 246, 255, 268, 271-2, 274-5, 286, 289, 294.

Customs revenue, 44-5, 72-3, 75, 108.

Deakin, Rt. Hon. A., 28-9, 34, 36, 37, 57-8, 98.

Decentralisation, 22, 307.

Defence, 25-6, 33, 42, 76.

Defence power, 53, 98, 162, 218-226, 229, 231-7, 252, 254.

Derby, Earl of, 28.

Dethridge, Chief Judge, 125.

Developmental policies, 108-112.

Dibbs, Sir George, 43.

Dicey, A. V., 1, 2, 4, 8, 19, 20, 100.

Division of powers: 4-7, 106-157; basis of, 36-7, 47, 106-7; conflict from, 108, 110, 112, 124-7, 129, 132; effects of, 12, 15, 19, 99-100, 105, 107, 112, 124-7, 129, 132; in Australia, 9, 106-7; new division, 131.

Dixon, Mr. Justice, 70, 91-2, 117, 139, 141, 220, 222.

Donaldson, Hon. J., 41.

Downer, Sir John, 49.

Dried Fruits Acts 1924-7 (S.A.), 136-8.

Dunstan, Hon. A. A., 247, 250, 267-8, 284.

Economic integration, 9, 11.

Edwards, Major-General, 26.

Eggleston, Sir Frederic, 175-184.

Estates Duties Act, 77.

Evatt, Rt. Hon. H. V., 91, 93-4, 123, 134, 139-41, 144, 217, 252-3, 259-264, 266, 270-4, 277-8, 286, 289, 294.

Fadden, Rt. Hon. A. W., 245-6, 262, 265-9, 275.

Fallon, C. G., 289.

Federalism: criticisms of, 1; dangers in, 37-9, 99; enquiry into, 37-9; financial relations, 71-3; flexibility, 2-3, 8, 10, 22, 99, 106; nature, 2-4, 7-8, 15, 37; prestige, 1, 35; protection of local units, 15-19, 52-5, 98; weakness, 9-10, 12, 19, 21-2, 99.

Federation: advantages in Australia, 30, 176-7; basis of, 32-6, 40, 51; causes, 31; disabilities imposed by, 165-7, 184; disadvantages of, 40, 51-2, 83, 96, 98-9, 107, 142, 160, 214-15, 284, 286, 306-7; expectations from, 33, 37; fails to protect States, 52, 55, 57, 92, 94-6, 98, 159, 172, 305; interests threatened by, 40-7; national standards, 142, 259, 300, 306; reform demanded, 130-1, 154-5, 214-16, 253-7, 260-1, 283, 294, 296, 304, 306; success of, 51.

Federal Council, 26, 30-31.

Financial Agreement, 78, 80-4, 86-7, 90-2, 96-7, 100, 102, 173, 298-9.
Financial Agreements Enforcement Act, 91-4, 159.
Financial Agreements (Commonwealth Liability) Act, 91.
Financial relations, 17, 54, 57, 71-98, 159-160, 173, 244, 252, 295-6.
Fiscal union, 23-5, 34, 43.
Fisher, Rt. Hon. A., 101.
Fitzgerald, Hon. N., 36.
Forde, Rt. Hon. F. M., 270.
Forgan Smith, Hon. W., 84, 248-9.
Forrest, Sir John, 40.
Forty-four Hours Week Act 1925 (N.S.W.), 121.
Fowler, J. M., 168.
France, 6., 25, 27, 104.
Frankfurter, Mr. Justice, 297.
Free trade, 24-5, 41, 43, 170.
Freer, Mrs., 103.
Garran, Sir Robert, 154, 215, 263.
Gavan Duffy, Sir Frank, Chief Justice, 29, 91, 121, 134, 141.
Gavan Duffy, C., 92.
Germany, 25, 27, 104.
Giblin, L. F., 133, 143, 175.
Gibson, Sir Robert, 87-9.
Gillies, Hon. D., 46.
Glynn, Hon. P. M., 41.
Gordon, Hon. J. H., 25, 47.
Grants to the States, 18, 76, 160, 164, 175.
Grants Commission, Commonwealth: 9, 74, 76, 84, 109-10, 112, 165, 171-2, 296, 299, 306; appointment, 164, 175, 209-10; basis for grants, 174-5, 180, 183-4, 200; broad judgment, 199, 201-2-5; conclusions, 182; criticisms of, 187-8, 191-4, 196, 198, 201-3, 206, 208, 211-13; difficulties of, 188-96, 203-6, 213; examines protection, 180-2; functions of, 182-3; importance of, 175, 209-11; investigates claims, 176-9; mechanical formula, 199-200; methods of, 185-208, 213; principles adopted by, 183-6, 188, 190, 193, 195, 198-208; South Australian claim, 172-4; success of, 188, 209-12; Tasmanian claim, 172-4; Western Australian claim, 171-2.
Great Britain, 4, 6, 8, 21-2.
Griffith, Sir Samuel, 26, 34, 38, 62-3, 133, 147.

Hall, H. L., 31.
Hancock, W. K., 169.
Harrison, Hon. E. J., 216.
Health Regulation, 299-300.
Hentze, M., 31.
Higgins, Mr. Justice, 37, 48, 118-9, 122, 141.
High Court, 5, 58-9, 60-1, 65, 106, 260, 262, 264.
Holman, Hon. W. A., 120.
Holmes, Mr. Justice, 305.
Hughes, Rt. Hon. W. M., 101, 215, 254-5, 264, 266-7, 269, 272-3, 285, 288.
Hunt, E. M., 32.
Immigration, 29, 31, 109.
Immigration Restriction Bill, 29.
Immunity of instrumentalities, 62-4, 67, 69, 117.
Inconsistency of laws, 121-3.
Industrial disputes, 48-9.
Influenza epidemic, 300.
Intercolonial conferences, 23, 28.
International obligations, 257-8, 260.
Inter-State Commission, 42.
Isaacs, Sir Isaac, 61, 115-16, 119-20, 133, 137-8, 218, 221, 263.
James, F. A., 136-7, 145-6.
Jehovah's witnesses, 224-5.
Jones Commission (Canada), 52.
Judges, appointment of, 20.
Judicial decisions: Australia: Appropriation, 75; arbitration, 65-6, 114, 122, 158; customs, 67, 158; defence power, 218-26, 229-34; marketing, 14, 133-140, 144-153, 220-2; mutual non-interference, 61-4; privy council decisions, 59, 61, 153; Section 92, 133, 141, 144-152; Section 116, 224-5; supremacy of Commonwealth, 68-71; surplus revenue, 67, 159; taxation, 66-7, 226-231, 249-252.
Canada: 13, 59.
United States: 12, 20, 59.
Judicial interpretation, 16, 53, 58-71, 114-122, 133-141, 151, 154, 159, 220-5.
Judiciary Act, 58-9.
Kingston, Rt. Hon. C. C., 24, 48.
Knowles, Sir George S., 14.
Knox, Rt. Hon. Sir Adrian, Chief Justice, 121.
Lang, J. T., 90, 94, 289.
Land Tax, 77.
Laski, H. J., 6, 20, 31, 104.

Latham, Rt. Hon. Sir John, Chief Justice, 69-70, 149-151, 229-231, 251-2.
Legalism, 1, 7, 20, 59.
Loan Council, 81-2, 84-91, 96, 298.
Local government, 6-8.
Lyons, Dame Enid, 208-9.
Lyons, Rt. Hon. J. A., 79, 85, 88, 175, 209.
Mair, Hon. A., 241-2.
Marginal settlement, 111-12, 179.
Marketing, Australia: 14-15, 102-4, 132, 134-142, 145-155, 220-2, 238, 257, 264.
    Canada: 13-14.
Marketing Primary Products Act (V.), 148.
Marriott, Sir John, 2-3.
Marshall, Chief Justice, 37, 63.
Maxwell, J. A., 190, 193.
McCormack, Hon. W., 128.
Macrossan, Hon. J. M., 46.
McIlwraith, Sir Thomas, 43.
McKell, Hon. W. J., 247, 249, 267.
McMillan, Sir William, 44-5, 50.
McTiernan, Mr. Justice, 91, 134.
Menzies, Rt. Hon. R. G., 123, 132, 146-7, 214, 234, 261-2, 265-7, 269, 284-5, 294.
Mills, R. C., 78, 245.
Milner, I., 287.
Montesquieu, Baron de, 5, 38.
Munro, Hon. J., 26, 46.
Murray River agreement, 298.
Nationhood, sense of, 156-7, 244.
Natural Products Marketing Act (Canada), 13.
Navigation Act, 17-18, 55, 68, 166, 174, 177-8.
New Caledonia, 27.
New Guinea, 27-8.
New Hebrides, 27-8.
New South Wales: defaults on overseas interest, 91; financial agreement, 91-5; free trade policy, 23-4, 35; marketing, 146, 148-9; protection, 143-4.
New York, state of, 11.
Nicholls, Sir Herbert, 95.
Nicklin, G. F. R., 274.
North Carolina, 12.
Nova Scotia, 14.
Old age pensions, 76.
Old Age Pensions Appropriation Act, 75.
Pacific policy, 27-9, 34.
Page, Sir Earle, 79.

Parkes, Sir Henry, 24, 26, 28, 30, 33, 44, 133.
Party government, 46, 50, 56.
Pearce, Sir George, 184.
Pennsylvania, 11.
Per capita payments, 75-80, 82.
Playford, Hon. T., 38, 49.
Playford, Hon. T. (grandson of above), 267-8.
Pond, W., 68-70.
Premiers' Conferences: as machinery for co-operation, 301-3; Nov. 1915, 303; May 1920, 301; May 1923, 126; June 1926, 78; May 1929, 127, 142, 302; June 1933, 84; Feb. 1934, 83-4; April 1942, 247, 252; Aug. 1942, 243; Aug. 1945, 250, 295.
Premiers' Plan, 87, 90.
Price control, 254, 256-7, 264, 295.
Primary Producers' Organising and Marketing Act (Q.), 138.
Privy Council, 58-9, 61, 65.
Protection policy, 17, 19, 23, 43, 108-11, 169-170, 180-2.
Quarantine, 143-4, 299-300.
Queensland: marketing legislation, 135, 138-140, 146; and New Guinea, 27; protection, 144; sugar industry, 167-8.
Railways, 30, 34, 36, 38, 40-2, 108, 118, 194-5.
Redistribution of revenue, 73-80.
Reference of powers, 255-6, 269-73, 275-8, 295, 303.
Referendum: Arbitration, 102, 130; aviation, 102; essential services, 102; industrial regulation, 100-102, 126, 130; machinery, 47; marketing, 14, 102-4, 147-8; per capita payments, 101; secession, 162-3; Section 105A, 52; senate elections, 100; State debts, 100; success of, 100; unsatisfactory character, 104, 282-3, 288; 1944 proposals, 277-290, 293.
Reforms required, 306-9.
Representatives, House of, 46, 55.
Responsible government, 32, 38-9, 50.
Rich, Mr. Justice, 91-2, 139, 221-233.
Roosevelt, F. D., 10.
Samoa, 28.
Sandford, J. W., 175.
Saskatchewan, 18.

Scullin, Rt. Hon. J. H., 214, 245.
Secession, 39, 162-4, 296.
Section 92: genesis of, 133, 156; effects of, 133, 142-4, 155-7; interpretation, 133-141, 224; and marketing, 136-140, 145-152.
Seeley, Sir J. R., 6.
Senate, 37, 45-46, 55-56, 87.
Separation of powers, 4-5, 58.
Service, Hon. J., 27, 30.
South Australia: Claim to Grants Commission, 172-4; Commonwealth assistance to, 176-7; criticises Grants Commission, 187-8, 192-3, 196-7, 200-1, 206, 212; financial instability, 174, 178-180; grievances of, 84, 110-11; land development, 178 180; marketing schemes, 14, 103, 135; opposes unification, 242-3; protection by, 143; special grants to, 164; tariff burden, 4, 110-11, 181.
Sovereignty, 7-8, 10, 12, 21.
Spender, Hon. P., 216.
Spooner, Hon. E. S., 245.
Starke, Mr. Justice, 91, 141, 151, 225, 233, 250.
State rights, 15, 33, 36-7, 39-40, 43-48, 52, 54, 242-3, 248-9, 276-7, 284.
States: abolition of, 280, 288; autonomy, 62, 73-4, 83, 96, 98-9, 127, 305; decline of, 16, 18, 52, 57-8, 68, 71-2, 94-5, 96-9, 218-19; developmental policies, 108-12, 142; economic nationalism, 132-3, 142-4, 151, 156; economic structure, 111; experimentation by, 305; federalism, no protection to, 52, 57, 71, 75, 81, 92, 94-97, 158-9, 305; financial plight, 74, 77-81, 84, 160; gains from federation, 176-7; grievances of, 17, 54-5, 57, 67, 75, 77-9, 84, 95, 97, 109, 125, 127, 158-9, 165; instrumentalities, 125-8; marketing schemes, 135-141; oppose Uniform Income Tax, 227, 245-9; powers of, 49, 72, 99, 106-7, 113; prestige of, 35, 244, 276, 279; protection for, 38-9, 44-7, 73; revenue sources, 44, 72-7, 97; weaknesses of, 10-11, 15, 99, 141-2, 145, 244, 279, 293, 305.
States Grants Act, 75, 78, 80.

Stewart, Sir Frederick, 216.
Sugar embargo, 167-8, 298.
Supreme Court of United States, 5, 12, 20.
Surplus revenue, 45, 49, 54, 67, 74-5, 77, 298.
Symon, J. H., 49.
Tariff Board, 162, 175.
Tariff Committee 1929, 109.
Tariff policy, 19, 24, 55, 108-11, 169-170.
Tasmania: Claim to Grants Commission, 172 4; Commonwealth assistance to, 177-8; criticises Grants Commission, 187-8, 192, 196-7, 206, 208; disabilities, 172-4, 177-8; financial instability, 174, 178-180; land development, 179; marketing schemes, 103; special grants to, 76, 164; tariff burden, 111, 181.
Taxation, 17-18, 66-7, 69, 71-2, 77, 96-7, 158, 226-231.
Theodore, Hon. E. G., 85, 89-90, 302.
Thorby, Hon. H. V., 142.
Tocqueville, A. de, 1, 9, 22.
Trade and Commerce powers, 132-157; Commonwealth powers, 132, 134-5, 152-5; State powers, 132, 140-1, 145, 148-150; marketing schemes, 136-140, 145-155.
Turner, Sir George, 39.
Unification, 8-9, 218, 266, 287, 294, 308.
Uniform Income Tax, 71, 97-8, 226, 231, 242, 244-252, 295.
Unitary government, 2, 4-8, 18, 21-2.
United States: amendment of constitution, 39; constitution, 9, 21; constitutional practice, 62-3; co-operative techniques, 297, 304; cotton and tobacco controls, 12; federal system, 1-2, 5, 11, 15, 20, 106, 287, 305; grant in aid, 18; influence of, 31-3.
Universities Commission, 234, 237.
Vegetation & Vine Disease Act 1928 (V.), 144.
Victoria: protective policy, 23-24, 35, 43, 144; Section 92 and State legislation, 136, 148.
Virginia: 12.
War-time Arrangements Act, 98.
War-time controls, 236-7, 254-7, 280-1.

Washington, state of, 11.
Western Australia: attitude to federation, 57, 161, 171; case of, 110, 160-1, 163, 165, 170; Commonwealth assistance to, 177, 181; criticises Grants Commission, 187, 196-9, 212; customs revenue, 73; disabilities, 162, 165-171; evidence to Grants Commission, 165, 171-2; financial instability, 171, 178-80; grievances of, 56, 110, 159, 161, 163, 165-171; industrial development of, 170; land development, 171, 178-180; marketing schemes, 103; secession, 162-4; special grants to, 76, 164; tariff burden, 110-11, 169-170, 181; and unification, 242-3, 308.
Willard, M., 31.
Williams, Mr. Justice, 225.
Wilson, C. H., 5.
Wise, Hon. B. R., 49.
Wood, G. L., 184.

INDEX TO CASES

Adelaide Company of Jehovah's Witnesses Inc. v. The Commonwealth, 224-5.
Amalgamated Society of Engineers v. The Adelaide Steamship Co. Ltd. and others, 61, 64, 65-6, 68-71, 118-119.
Andrews v. Howell, 220-222.
Attorney-General for New South Wales v. Collector of Customs for New South Wales, 61, 63, 67.
Australian Boot Trade Employees' Federation v. Whybrow and Co., 120-121.
Australian Workers' Union v. Adelaide Milling Co. Ltd., 118-119.
Barger's Case (R. v. Barger), 229.
Baxter v. Commissioners of Taxation (N.S.W.), 69.
Burkard v. Oakley, 53.
Caledonian Collieries Ltd. v. Australasian Coal and Shale Employees' Federation (No. 1) and (No. 2), 114-117.
Chaplin v. Commissioner of Taxes for South Australia, 69.
Clyde Engineering Co. Ltd. v. Cowburn (Cowburn's Case), 66, 68, 120-1.
Colonial Sugar Refining Company v. Attorney-General of the Commonwealth, 168-9.
Commissioners of Taxation (N.S.W.) v. Baxter, f.n. 59.
Commonwealth v. State of Queensland, 66.
Deakin v. Webb, 69.

D'Emden v. Pedder, 60-2, 64, 70.
Duncan v. Queensland, 133.
Duncan and Green Star Trading Co. v. Vizzard, 140.
Engineers' Case (Amalgamated Society of Engineers v. The Adelaide Steamship Co. Ltd. and Others), 61, 64-6, 68-71, 118-119.
Farey v. Burvett (Bread Case), 53, 218, 220-1.
Federated Amalgamated Government Railway and Tramway Service Association v. New South Wales Rail Traffic Employees' Association, 61, 63, 65, 118.
Ferrando v. Pearce, 53.
Forty-four Hours Case (Cylde Engineering Co. Ltd. v. Cowburn), 66, 68.
Hartley v. Walsh, 148.
James v. Commonwealth, 134, 145-6, 148-150, 152.
James v. Cowan, 14, 138-9, 141, 151.
James v. South Australia, 136.
Lawson v. Interior Tree and Vegetable Committee of Direction (Canada), 13.
McArthur (W. & A.), Ltd. v. Queensland, 133-5, 145-7, 149, 151.
McCulloch v. Maryland (United States), 63.
McLean; ex parte, 122.
Milk Board v. Metropolitan Cream Pty. Ltd., 148-151, 221.

E2